CAXTON
ITALIAN
DICTIONARY

CAXTON EDITIONS

First published in Great Britain by
CAXTON EDITIONS
an imprint of
the Caxton Book Company Ltd
16 Connaught Street
Marble Arch
London W2 2AF

This edition copyright
© 1999 CAXTON EDITIONS

Prepared and designed
for Caxton Editions by
Superlaunch Limited
PO Box 207
Abingdon
Oxfordshire OX13 6TA

Consultant editor Paola Pesavento

ISBN 1 84067 068 1

A copy of the CIP data for this book is available from
the British Library upon request

Printed and bound in India

ITALIANO INGLESE
ITALIAN ENGLISH

Abbreviations

abbr	abbreviation
adj	adjective
adv	adverb
art	article
aux	auxiliary
conj	conjunction
def	definite
dem	demonstrative
etc	et cetera
f	feminine
fam	familiar
fig	figurative
fpl	feminine plural
gr	grammar
indef	indefinite
inv	invariable
m	masculine
mpl	masculine plural
n	noun
npl	noun, plural
num	number
pej	pejorative
pl	plural
poss	possessive
prep	preposition
pron	pronoun
sl	slang
vi	intransitive verb
vr	reflexive verb
vt	transitive verb
vulg	vulgar

A

a *prep* to; in; at; on; by; with; for.

abate *m* abbot.

abbagliante *adj* dazzling: — fari abbaglianti dazzling beams.

abbagliare *vt* to dazzle, to blind (with).

abbaiare *vi* to bark.

abbaino *m* garret.

abbandonare *vt* to abandon; to leave; to forsake; to desert.

abbassare *vt* to dim; to turn down; * *vi* to sink; * ~rsi *vr* to bend down; to abase oneself.

abbastanza *adv* enough; reasonably; relatively.

abbattere *vt* to cull; to fell; to dash (hopes).

abbattimento *m* despondency, dejection.

abbazia *f* abbey.

abbellire *vt* to embellish.

abbiente *adj* well-to-do; wealthy.

abbigliamento *m* clothing; dress.

abbindolare *vt* to take in.

abbonamento *m* subscription; season ticket; * ~rsi *vr* to subscribe.

abbondante *adj* abundant; plentiful.

abbondanza *f* abundance; affluence; plenty; fullness.

abbondare *vi* to abound.

abbordare *vt* to accost: — (marine) to assault a ship from another ship; to chat someone up.

abbozzare *vt* to draft.

abbracciare *vt* to embrace; to hug.

abbraccio *m* cuddle; embrace; hug.

abbreviare *vt* to abbreviate; abridge.

abbronzarsi *vr* to tan.

abbronzato *adj* tanned.

abbronzatura *f* suntan, tan.

abbrutire *vt* (from bruto, beast) to brutalise; to degrade; * ~rsi *vr* to become brutish.

abbruttire *vt* (from brutto, ugly) to make ugly, spoil.

abete *m* fir (tree), spruce.

abile *adj* able; adept; adroit; artful; deft; skilled; skilful.

abilità *f* ability; aptitude; knack; skill.

abilitazione *f* qualification.

abissale *adj* abysmal.

abisso *m* abyss.

abitabile *adj* habitable; inhabitable.

abitante *m* or *f* inhabitant.

abitare *vt* to inhabit; * *vi* to live.

abito *m* dress; gown: ~ da sera *m* evening dress.

abituare *vt* to accustom.

abituato *adj* accustomed.

abiurare *vt* to abjure.

abnegazione *f* self-sacrifice.

abolire *vt* to abolish.

abolizione *f* abolition.

abominevole *adj* abominable.

aborigeno *adj* aboriginal.

abortire *vt* to abort.

aborto *m* abortion.

abrasione *f* abrasion.

abrasivo *adj* abrasive.

abrogare *vt* to revoke; repeal.

abrogazione *f* repeal.

abside *f* apse.

abusare *vt* to misuse: ~ di to abuse.

abusivo *adj* unauthorised; unlawful.

abuso *m* abuse; misuse.

a.C. (avanti Cristo) BC (before Christ).

acacia *f* acacia.

accademia *f* academy.

accademico *adj* academic;
 * *m* academic, academician.

accadere *vt* to befall; * *vi* to
 befall; to happen; to occur;
 to pass.

accalappiacani *m* or *f* dog-
 catcher.

accalappiare *vt*, *vr* ~rsi (*sl*) to
 catch: — è riuscita ad ~ il
 merlo she managed to catch
 the fool (= she managed to get
 him to marry her); il merlo si
 è lasciato ~ the fool let himself
 get caught (= married).

accanirsi *vr* to rage; to persist.

accanto *prep* beside: ~ a next to.

accappatoio *m* bathrobe.

accampamento *m* camp.

accasciarsi *vr* to fall to the
 ground; to lose heart.

accarezzare *vt* to fondle; to
 pet; to stroke.

accecare *vt* to blind.

accedere a *vi* to assent to; to
 attain (office); to adhere
 (to); to access.

accelerare *vt* to accelerate; to
 hasten; to precipitate; * *vi* to
 accelerate.

accendere *vt* to switch on; to
 turn on; to put on; to light.

accendino *m* cigarette lighter.

accensione *f* ignition: —
 chiave di ~ *f* ignition key.

accento *m* accent.

accertarre *vt* ascertain.

acceso *adj* on, alight.

accessibile *adj* accessible.

accesso *m* access; fit: —
 divieto di ~ no entry.

accessori *mpl* fittings; trim-
 mings.

accessorio *m* accessory;
 attachment; fitment.

accettabile *adj* acceptable.

accettare *vt* to accept; to
 take.

accettazione *f* acceptance;
 reception.

acciaio *m* steel.

accidente *m* accident: — bad
 cold; something bad: — che ti
 venga un ~! go to hell! — che
 mi venga un ~! Well, I'll be
 damned!

acclammare *f* to acclaim.

acclimatare *vt* to acclimatise;
 * ~rsi *vr* to acclimatise
 oneself.

accoglienza *f* acceptance.

accompagnamento *m* accompaniment.

accordo *m* agreement: —
 essere d'~ con to agree with.

accoccolarsi *vr* to nestle.

accogliere *vt* to welcome.

accollarsi *vr* to shoulder.

accomodante *adj* easy-going.

accompagnare *vt* to accompany.

accompagnato *adj* accompanied.

acconsentire *vt* to consent.

accontentare *vt* to indulge; to
 humour; to please.

accoppiare *vt* to mate; * ~rsi
 vr to copulate; to mate.

accordare *vt* to grant; to tune.

accordo *m* agreement; deal;
 settlement.

accorgersi *vr* to notice.

accreditare *vt* to credit.

accrescere *vt* to increase;
 * ~rsi *vr* to increase.

accumulare *vt* to accumulate.

accuratezza *f* accuracy.

accurato *adj* accurate; careful.

accusa *f* accusation; charge;
 prosecution (law).

accusare *vt* to accuse; to
 charge.

accusato *m* accused.

accusatore *m* accuser.

aceto *m* vinegar.

acido *adj* acid; caustic; sour; * *m* acid.

acne *f* acne.

acqua *f* water: ~ dolce fresh water: — tirare l'~ to flush the toilet.

acquaio *m* kitchen sink.

acquatico *adj* aquatic.

acquazzone *m* cloudburst; downpour; shower.

acquedotto *m* aqueduct.

acquerello *m* watercolour.

acquirente *m* or *f* purchaser.

acquisire *vt* to acquire.

acquistare *vt* to purchase.

acro *m* acre.

acute *adj* acute.

adatto *adj* appropriate; right; fit; suitable; becoming.

adattare *vt* to suit.

addestramento *m* training.

addestrare *vt* to train; to school.

addetto *m* attaché; employee.

addio *m* farewell; goodbye.

addirittura *adv* quite: — really!

additivo *m* additive.

addizionare *vt* to add.

addizione *f* addition.

addolcire *vt* to sweeten.

addolorato *adj* sorrowful; pained.

addome *m* abdomen.

addomesticamento *m* domestication.

addominale *adj* abdominal.

addormentarsi *vr* to fall asleep.

addossarsi *vr* to take on.

adeguatamente *adv* suitably.

adeguato *adj* adequate.

aderire *vi* to adhere.

adesivo *m* adhesive; sticker.

adesso *adv*, *conj* now.

adolescenza *f* adolescence.

adolescente *m* or *f* adolescent; teenager.

adorabile *adj* adorable; lovable.

adorare *vt* to adore; to worship.

adorato *adj* beloved.

adottare *vt* to adopt.

adulterare *vt* to adulterate; to doctor.

adultero *adj* adulterous; * *m* adulterer.

adulterio *m* adultery.

adulto *adj* adult; * *m* adult, grown-up.

aereo *adj* aerial.

aeronautica *f* air force.

aeroporto *m* airport.

affabile *adj* affable; amiable; good-natured.

affarista *m* or *f* speculator.

affamato *adj* hungry; starving; famished.

affare *m* affair; deal; bargain; snip.

affari *mpl* business: — uomo *m* or donna *f* d'~ businessman or woman.

affascinare *vt* to fascinate; to charm; * affascinante *adj* fascinating; glamorous.

affaticare *vt* to fatigue; to strain.

aftermativo *adj* affirmative.

affettare *vt* to slice; to affect.

affettato *adj* affected.

affetto *m* affection; fondness.

affilare *vt* to sharpen.

affilato *adj* sharp.

affiliazione *f* affiliation.

affinché *conj* so that.

affinità *f* affinity.

affittare *vt* to lease; to let; to rent.

affitto *m* rent: — proprietà in ~ *f* leasehold: — contratto d'~ *m* tenancy agreement.

affluente *m* tributary.

affogare *vt*, *vi* to drown.

affollare *vt* to crowd; to throng; * ~rsi *vr* to cram.

affrancatura *f* postage.
affresco *m* fresco.
affrettare *vt* to quicken;
   * ~rsi *vr* to hurry, make haste.
affrontare *vt* to broach; to
   confront; to deal with,
   tackle; to face.
affumicato *adj* smoked.
afoso *adj* close; sultry; muggy.
afrodisiaco *m* aphrodisiac.
agenda *f* diary.
agente *m* or *f* agent:
   ~ immobiliare *m* estate agent.
agenzia *f* agency: ~ di viaggi *f*
   travel agency.
agganciare *vt* to hook.
aggettivo *m* adjective.
aggiungere *vt* to add.
agghiacciante *adj* gruesome;
   spine-chilling.
aggiornare *vt* to update; to
   write up.
aggiudicare *vt* to award;
   * ~rsi *vr* to win.
aggiustare *vt* to adjust; to
   mend, repair.
agglomerato *m* agglomerate:
   — built-up area, urban centre.
aggravamento *m* aggravation.
aggrapparsi *vr* to cling to; to
   get hold of.
aggravare *vt* to aggravate.
aggraziato *adj* graceful.
aggredire *vt* to mug.
aggressione *f* aggression.
aggrovigliare *vt* to entangle;
   * ~rsi *vr* to get entangled.
agiato *adj* well-to-do
agile *adj* agile; lithe; nimble.
agilità *f* agility.
agiografia *f* hagiography.
agitare *vt* to agitate; to stir;
   * ~rsi *vr* to fidget; to wriggle.
agitato *adj* flustered.
agitazione *f* agitation.
aglio *m* garlic; * spicchio d'~ *m*
   clove of garlic.

agnello *m* lamb.
ago *m* needle.
agonia *f* agony.
agosto *m* August.
agricolo *adj* agricultural.
agricoltore *m* farmer.
agricoltura *f* agriculture;
   farming.
agrodolce *adj* bitter-sweet;
   sourish.
ahi! *excl* ouch!
AIDS *m* AIDS.
aiuola *f* flower bed.
aiutante *m* or *f* assistant;
   help: ~ di campo aide-de-
   camp.
aiutare *vt* to assist; aid; help.
aiuto *m* aid; assistance; help.
ala *f* wing; winger.
alabastro *m* alabaster.
alba *f* dawn; daybreak;
   sunrise.
albergo *m* hotel.
albero *m* tree; mast; (marine)
   spar.
albicocca *f* apricot.
album *m* album.
alchimia *f* alchemy.
alcolico *m* alcoholic drink:
   — bevande alcoliche *fpl*
   strong spirits; * *adj* alcoholic.
alcolismo *m* alcoholism.
alcool *m* alcohol, (*sl*) booze:
   ~ denaturato *m* methylated
   spirits.
alcoolizzato *m*, *adj* alcoholic.
alcuno *adj*, *pron* some(one).
alfabetico *adj* alphabetical:
   — in ordine ~ in alphabetical
   order.
alfabeto *m* alphabet: ~ Morse
   m Morse code.
algebra *f* algebra.
alghe *fpl* algae; seaweed.
alias *adv* alias.
alibi *m* alibi.
alimentare *vt* to feed; * *m* food:

8

— negozio di ~ *m* grocery;
* *adj* related to food.
aliscafo *m* hydrofoil.
alito *m* breath.
allacciare *vt* to tie; to lace; to
buckle; * ~rsi *vr* to buckle,
fasten.
allarme *m* alarm; alert: —
falso ~ *m* false alarm.
alleanza *f* alliance.
alleato *adj* allied; * *m* ally.
allegato *m* enclosure.
alleggerire *vt* to lighten; to
relieve.
allegoria *f* allegory.
allegria *f* gaiety; merriment.
allegro *adj* cheerful; jolly;
merry; perky.
allegrone *m* jolly fellow.
allenare *vt* to train.
allenamento *m* training.
allestire *vt* to prepare, to fit
out.
allergia *f* allergy.
allergico *adj* allergic.
alleviare *vt* to alleviate; to
ease; to relieve.
alligatore *m* alligator.
allodola *f* lark; skylark:
— felice come un'~ as happy
as a lark.
alloggiare *vt* to accommodate;
to house; * *vi* to lodge; to stay.
alloggio *m* accommodation.
allora *adv* then: — da ~ since.
alloro *m* bay, laurel.
alludere *vt* to hint.
alluminio *m* aluminium.
allungare *vt* to elongate; to
lengthen.
almeno *adv* at least.
alpinismo *m* climbing;
mountaineering.
alpinista *m* or *f* climber;
mountaineer.
alpino *adj* alpine.
alquanto *adv* somewhat.

altare *m* altar.
alternativa *f* alternative.
alternativamente *adv* alter-
natively.
alternato *adj* alternate.
altezza *f* height; headroom;
highness: — essere all'~ to be
up to.
altitudine *f* altitude.
alto *adj* high; tall: — il più ~
topmost: — verso l'~ up-
wards; * *adv* in ~ overhead.
altoparlante *m inv* loudspeaker; speaker.
altrettanto *adv* just as; likewise.
altrimenti *adv* else; otherwise.
altro *pron*: — un ~ another;
other: — l'un l'~ one another;
* *adj* other; more.
alzare *vt* to heighten; to rise;
to turn up; * ~rsi *vr* to rise;
to stand up.
amaca *f* hammock.
amante *m* or *f* lover; *f* mistress.
amare *vt* to love.
amaro *adj* bitter.
ambasciata *f* embassy.
ambasciatore *m* ambassador.
ambedue *adj* both.
ambidestro *adj* ambidextrous.
ambientale *adj* environmental.
ambientalista *m* or *f*
conservationist.
ambientarsi *vr* to find one's
feet.
ambiente *m* environment;
setting: ~ sociale *m* milieu.
ambiguo *adj* ambiguous;
dubious.
ambito *m* scope.
ambizione *f* ambition.
ambulanza *f* ambulance.
ambulatorio *m* surgery.
ametista *f* amethyst.
amica *f* girlfriend.
amichevole *adj* amicable;
friendly.

amicizia *f* friendship.
amico *m* friend; pal: ~ del cuore bosom friend.
ammaliare *vt* to bewitch.
ammazzare *vt* to kill.
ammettere *vt* to accept, admit: — bisogna ~ che admittedly.
ammiccare *vi* to wink.
amministrare *vt* to administer.
amministrativo *adj* administrative.
amministratore *m* administrator; trustee: ~ delegato managing director.
ammirare *vt* to admire.
ammiratore *m* admirer; well-wisher.
ammirazione *f* admiration.
ammissibile *adj* admissible; allowable.
ammissione *f* acknowledgement; admission; entrance.
ammobiliato *adj* furnished.
ammonitorio *adj* cautionary.
ammuffire *vt* to grow musty; * *fig* to languish.
ammutinamento *m* mutiny.
amnesia *f* amnesia.
amnistia *f* amnesty.
amorale *adj* amoral.
amore *m* love: — fare l'~ to make love.
amorfo *adj* amorphous.
ampio *adj* ample.
ampliare *vt* amplify; to enlarge; to widen.
ampolla *f* cruet.
amputare *vt* amputate.
anacronismo *m* anachronism.
analcolico *m* soft drink; * *adj* non-alcoholic.
analfabeta *m* or *f*, *adj* illiterate.
analisi *f inv* analysis.
analista *m* or *f* analyst: ~ di sistemi *m* systems analyst.
analitico *adj* analytic(al).
analizzare *vt* to analyse.

ananas *m inv* pineapple.
anarchia *f* anarchy.
anatomia *f* anatomy.
anca *f* hip.
ancestrale *adj* ancestral.
anche *adv* also; too; as well.
ancora *adv* again; another; even; still; already.
ancora *f* anchor.
andare *vi* to go.
andata *f*: — biglietto di ~ *m* single ticket.
anello *m* ring.
anemia *f* anaemia.
anemico *adj* anaemic.
anemone *m* anemone.
anestetico *m* anaesthetic.
anfiteatro *m* amphitheatre.
angelo *m* angel.
anglicismo *m* anglicism.
anglicizzare *vt* anglicise.
angolo *m* angle; corner.
angoscia *f* anguish; distress; * ~rsi *vr* to agonise over.
anguilla *f* eel.
anguria *f* watermelon.
angusto *adj* cramped; poky.
anice *m* aniseed.
anima *f* soul.
animale *adj* animal; * *m* animal: ~ da compagnia pet: — *mpl* animali da cortile farm animals; animali nocivi vermin.
animare *vt* to animate; to pep up.
animiosità *f inv* animosity.
annegare *vt*, *vi* to drown.
anniversario *m* anniversary.
anno *m* year; session: — A. Nuovo *m* New Year: ~ luce *m* light year: — all'~ per annum.
annoiare *vt* to bore; * ~rsi *vr* to be (get) bored.
annotare *vt* to annotate; to record.
annuale *adj* yearly.

annunciare *vt* to announce.
annunciatore *m* newscaster.
annuncio *m* advertisement;
announcement.
ano *m* anus.
anonimato *m* anonymity;
obscurity.
anonimo *adj* anonymous;
unnamed.
anoressia *f* anorexia.
anormale *adj* abnormnal;
freak.
anormalità *f* abnormality.
ansia *f* anxiety.
ansioso *adj* nervous; solicitous.
antagonismo *m* antagonism.
antartico *adj* antarctic.
antecedente *adj* antecedent.
antenna *f* aerial; antenna;
feeler.
anteriore *adj* anterior; fore.
antibiotico *m* antibiotic.
antichità *f* antiquity.
anticipo *m* advance; down
payment.
antico *adj* ancient; antique.
anticoncezionale *adj*, *m*
contraceptive.
antidolorifico *m* pain-killer.
antidoto *m* antidote.
antifurto *m inv* burglar alarm.
antilope *f* antelope.
antincendio *adj*: — allarme ~ *f*
fire alarm.
antipasto *m* hors d'oeuvres,
starters.
antipatico *adj* objectionable;
unlovable.
antipodi *mpl* antipodes.
antiquato *adj* antiquated;
dated; old-fashioned; stuffy.
antisemitico *adj* anti-semitic.
anziano *adj* aged; elderly; old;
* *m* elder.
aorta *f* aorta.
apartheid *f* apartheid.
ape *f* bee.

aperitivo *m* aperitif.
aperto *adj* open; broad-minded;
open-minded; gaping:
— all'~ outdoor.
apertura *f* aperture; opening;
spread.
apostrofo *m* apostrophe.
appagare *vt* to quench.
apparecchio *m* set; appliance:
~ acustico *m* hearing aid.
apparenza *f* semblance.
apparire *vi* to appear:
~ indistintamente to loom.
appartamento *m* apartment;
flat; suite.
appartenere *vi* to belong.
appassionante *adj* gripping.
appassionato *adj* devotee;
enthusiastic; passionate;
* *m* enthusiast.
appellante *m* or *f* appellant.
appena *adv* barely, just; hardly;
fresh, freshly; scarcely; just.
appendere *vt* to hang.
appetito *m* appetite.
appisolarsi *vr* to doze off.
applaudire *vt* to applaud; to
clap.
applauso *m* applause; acclaim;
clapping.
applicare *vt* to enforce;
* ~rsi *vr* to apply oneself, to
try to do something.
appoggiare *vt* to back; to lean;
to support.
apporre *vt* affix; append.
apprezzare *vt* to appreciate.
appropriato *adj* apt; proper;
suitable.
approvare *vt* to approve; to
assent.
appuntamento *m* appoint-
ment; date; rendezvous.
apribottiglie *m inv* bottle-
opener.
aprile *m* April.
aprire *vt* to open; to unlock.

apriscatole *m inv* tin-opener.
aquila *f* eagle.
arabo *adj*, *m* Arab.
arachide *f* peanut.
arancia *f* orange.
aranciata *f* orangeade.
archeologia *f* archeology.
archeologico *adj* archaeo-
logical.
archeologo *m* archaelogist.
architettare *vt* to engineer.
architetto *m* architect.
architettura architecture.
arco *m* arch; bow: — tiro con
l'~ archery; * ad ~ *adj* arched.
arcobaleno *m* rainbow.
area *f* area.
argento *m* silver.
argomento *m* argument;
subject; topic.
Ariete *m* Aries.
aristocrazia *f* aristocracy.
aritmetica *f* arithmetic.
aritmetico *adj* arithmetical.
arma *f* weapon: ~ da fuoco
firearm.
armadio *in* cupboard.
armare *vt* to arm.
armato *adj* armed.
armonia *f* concord; harmony.
armonica *f* harmonica; mouth
organ.
aroma *in* aroma.
arrabbiare *vt* fare ~ to make
someone angry; to enrage.
arrabbiato *adj* angry; rabid:
— un cane ~ a rabid dog.
arrampicatore (arrampicatrice)
sociale *m(f)* social climber.
arredare *vt* to furnish.
arrivare *vi* to arrive; to turn up.
arrivederci *excl* goodbye.
arrogante *adj* arrogant.
arroganza *f* arrogance.
arrosto *m* roast.
arte *f* art; craft: — le belle arti
fpl the fine arts.

articolo *m* article; item; story.
artigiano *m* craftsman;
artisan.
artiglicre *m* gunner.
asciugacapelli *m inv* hair-dryer.
asciugamano *m* towel.
asciugare *vt* to dry; to blot
(ink).
ascoltare *vt* to listen to.
asma *f* asthma.
asmatico *adj* asthmatic.
aspettare *vt* to await; to
expect; * *vi* to wait.
aspirina *f* aspirin.
assaggiare *vt* to taste; to
sample.
assassinare *vt* to assassinate;
to murder.
assassinio *m* assassination;
murder; foul play.
assassino *m adj* assassin.
asse *f* board; axis: ~ da stiro
ironing board.
assegnare *vt* to assign; to
award; to set.
assemblea *f* assembly.
assicurare *vt* to assure; to
insure; to secure.
assistenza *f* help; aid:
~ sociale social services.
assomigliare *vi* to look like;
to take after.
assorbente *m* sanitary towel;
* *adj* absorbent.
assurdità *f* (an) absurdity.
assurdo *adj* absurd;
preposterous.
astratto *adj* abstract.
astringente *adj*, *m* astringent.
astrologia *f* astrology.
astronauta *m* or *f* astronaut;
spaceman or woman.
astronomia *f* astronomy.
astronomico *adj* astronomical.
atavico *adj* ancestral.
ateismo *m* atheism.
ateo *m* atheist.

atipico *adj* atypical.

atlante *m* atlas.

atleta *m* or *f* athlete.

atletico *adj* athletic.

atmnosfera *f* atmosphere.

atomico *adj* atomic.

atomo *m* atom.

atrocità *f inv* atrocity; enormity; outrage.

atrofia *f* atrophy.

attaccare *vt* to affix; (military) to charge; to attach, attack; to hitch up.

attacco *m* (also med) attack, stroke, fit: ~ cardiaco heart attack: — strike; onslaught; bout.

attento *adj* careful; observant; watchful: — stare ~ to beware.

attenuante *adj* extenuating.

attenzione *f* attention; care; heed; caution: — fare ~ to pay attention.

atterraggio *m* landing: ~ forzato forced landing: ~ di fortuna emergency landing.

atterrare *vi* to land; * *vt* to take or pull to the ground.

attesa *f* wait; waiting: — lista d'~ waiting list: — sala d'~ waiting room.

attestare *vt* to certify; to attest.

attestato *m* certification.

attirare *vt* to attract; to draw.

attività *f* activity; business; pursuit.

atto *m* act: — deed.

attore *m* actor; plaintiff.

attrattiva *f* attraction.

attraversare *vt* to cross; to span.

attraverso *prep* across; through.

attrazione *f* attraction; pull.

attrezzo *m* tool: — cassetta degli attrezzi *f* toolbox.

attribuire *vt* attribute; ascribe;

apportion; to give.

attrice *f* actress.

attuale *adj* current; present; prevailing; up-to-date.

attualità *fpl* news

audacia *f* audacity; boldness; daring; temerity.

auditorio *m* auditorium.

augurare *vt* to wish.

augurio *m* wish.

augusto *adj* august.

aula *f* classroom.

aumentare *vt* to increase; * *vi* increase; to rise.

aumento *m* raise; gain; increase; rise: ~ di valore *m* appreciation.

ausiliario *adj*, *m* ancillary.

autenticità *f* authenticity.

autentico *adj* authentic.

autista *m* chauffeur; *m* or *f* driver.

autoaffondare *vt* to scuttle.

autoarticolato *m* articulated lorry.

autobiografia *f* autobiography.

autoblinda *f* armoured car.

autobus *m* bus.

autocarro *m* lorry: ~ della nettezza urbana *m* dust-cart.

autodifesa *f* self-defence.

autodisciplina *f* self discipline.

autografo *m* autograph.

automobile *f* car: ~ sportiva sports car.

autopsia *f* autopsy; post-mortem.

autore *m* author; writer.

autorimessa *f* garage.

autorità *f* authority.

autoritratto *m* self-portrait.

autorizzare *vt* to authorise.

autorizzazione *f* authorisation; clearance; permit; licence.

autostop *m* hitchhiking: — fare l'~ to hitch (a lift), hitchhike.

autostrada *f* motorway.
autrice *f* authoress.
autunnale *adj* autumnal.
autunno *m* autumn.
avanguardia *f* avant-garde;
  forefront: * d'~ *adj* avant-garde.
avanti *adv* ahead; forwards: —
  d'ora in ~ from now onwards;
  forwards: — più ~ further on,
  farther.
avaro *adj* avaricious; mean;
  * *m* miser.
avere *vt* to have.
aviazione *f* aviation.
avido *adj* greedy; grasping.
avorio *m*, *adj* ivory.
avvalersi *vr*: ~ di to avail
  oneself of.
avvallamento *m* subsidence.
avvelenare *vt* to poison.
avvenimento *m* event;
  happening; incident.
avventura *f* adventure; affair.
avverbio *m* adverb.
avversario *m* adversary;
  opponent; * *adj* opposing.
avvertimento *m* warning.
avvisare *vt* advise.
avviso *m* notice; advice.
avvocato *m* advocate; lawyer;
  solicitor; attorney, barrister,
  counsel.
avvolgere *vt* to wind; to
  envelop; to coil; to swathe;
  to shroud.
avvoltoio *m* vulture.
azalea *f* azalea.
azienda *f* company.
azione *f* action; deed; share:
  — società per azioni joint-stock company.
azionista *m* or *f* shareholder.
azzurro *adj* azure; blue.

B

babà (cookery) baba.
babbo *m* (*sl*) pa(pa), dad(dy).
babbeo *m* blockhead.
babbuino *m* baboon.
bacca *f* berry.
baccalà *m* stockfish (dried
  salted cod).
baccano *m* uproar.
bacchettone *m* (*sl*) bigot.
baciare *vt* to kiss.
baciapile *m* (*sl*) bigot.
bacio *m* kiss.
baffo *m* (baffi *mpl*) moustache;
  (*sl*) whiskers.
bagaglio *m* baggage; bagagli
  mpl luggage.
bagigi *mpl* peanuts.
bagnante *m* or *f* bather.
bagnare *vt* to wet, to bathe.
bagnato *adj* wet, soggy.
bagnino *m* lifeguard.
bagno *m* bath.
baia *f* bay; cove.
balcone *m* balcony.
balbettare *vi* to stammer.
balbuziente *m* stammerer
baldacchino *m* canopy: —
  letto a ~ four-poster (bed).
balena *f* whale.
balia *f* (wet) nurse.
ballare *vt* to dance.
balla *f* bale; * (*sl*) lie: — contar
  balle to tell lies; (*sl*) balle!
  nonsense! (*vulg*) bullshit!; (*sl*)
  rompiballe, rompipalle
  inopportune person, pain in
  the arse: — (*sl*) che balle, che
  palle! what a bore!: — (*sl*)
  drunken state: — essere in ~
  to be drunk: — avere una ~ to
  be drunk: — andare in ~ to
  get drunk.
ballo *m* dance.
balneare *adj* bathing:

— stazione ~ seaside resort.
bambina(o) f(m) child.
bambola f doll.
banca f bank.
bancarella f stall.
banchetto m banquet.
banco m bench.
bandito m bandit.
bara f coffin.
baracca f hut.
barba f beard: — (sl) che ~!
  what a bore!
barbiere m barber.
barbone m tramp; poodle.
barbuto adj bearded.
barca f boat.
barzelletta f joke.
bassorilievo m bas-relief.
bastione m rampart.
battaglia f battle.
battello m boat.
battere vt to beat: ~ le mani to
  clap hands.
batteria f battery.
battibecco m squabble.
bava f slaver.
beccare vt to peck; to catch;
  * ~rsi vr (sl) to catch something (a disease).
becco m beak; billy-goat;
  cuckold.
beffa f mockery.
bega f quarrel.
beghina f (sl) bigot.
bella(o) f(m) adj beautiful
bellezza f beauty.
bellico adj related to war.
bellicoso adj warlike.
belva f wild beast.
benda f bandage.
bene m good: — per il tuo ~ for
  your sake: — voler ~ to love;
  * adv well.
beni mpl goods, property.
beniamino m darling; favourite.
bernoccolo m bump.
berretto m cap.

bersaglio m target: — tiro al ~
  target shooting.
bestemmia f swear-word.
bestia f beast: — mandare in ~
  to madden someone.
bestiame m livestock.
bettola f tavern.
bevanda f drink.
bianco adj and m white.
Bibbia f Bible.
bibliografia f bibliography.
biblioteca f library.
bicchiere m glass.
bicocca f hut.
bidello m porter.
bidone m can: — (sl) tirare un
  ~ a qualcuno to swindle
  someone.
bifolco m boor.
biglietteria f booking office;
  box office.
biglietto m ticket: ~ da visita
  visiting card.
bigodino m hair-curler.
bilancia f balance, scales.
bilancio m budget: — fare il ~
  to strike the balance.
biografia f biography.
biondo adj fair.
birbone m rouge.
birichino m urchin;
  * adj naughty.
biro f ballpoint pen.
birreria f beer-house; brewery.
biscia f snake.
bisestile adj anno ~ leap year.
bislacco adj odd.
bisnonna(o) f(m) great-grand-
  mother(father).
bisogno m need: — avere ~ to
  need.
bisticcio m squabble.
bistrattare vt to ill-treat.
bizzarro adj strange.
blaterare vi to prate.
boa f (marine) buoy; m boa

constrictor.

bocca *f* mouth.

boccaccia *f* grimace.

boccia *f* bowl: — giocare a ~ to play bowls.

bocciare *vt* to reject.

boia *m* executioner.

bolgia *f* (*fig*) bedlam: ~ infernale hell pit.

bollente *adj* boiling; steaming hot.

bolletta *f* bill: — essere in ~ to be penniless.

bollire *vt* to boil.

bollito *m* boiled meat.

bollo *m* stamp.

bonario *adj* good-natured.

bonaccione *adj* good-natured.

bontà *f* goodness.

borbottare *vt* to mumble.

bordello *m* brothel.

bordo *n* board; * a ~ *adv* on board.

borgata *f* village.

borghese *adj* middle-class; * *m* or *f* middle-class person: — in ~ to dress in civilian clothes.

borghesia *f* middle-classes: — alta ~ upper middle-classes: — bassa or piccola ~ lower middle-classes.

borgo *m* village.

boria *f* arrogance.

borioso *adj* arrogant.

borsa *f* bag; briefcase.

borseggiare *vt* to pick pockets.

borseggiatore *m* pick-pocket.

borsellino *m* purse.

borsetta *f* handbag.

bosco *m* wood.

botta *f* blow: — dare le ~ to spank.

botte *f* barrel.

bottiglia *f* bottle.

botto *m* cracker; firework.

bottone *m* button; (*sl*)

attaccare un ~ a qualcuno to bore someone with a long story: — un attaccabottoni *m* and *f* chatterer, bore.

boaro, bovaro *m* cowherd; cowboy: — (*sl*) boorish person, boor, lout.

bovini *mpl* cattle; livestock.

bozza *f* draft.

bozzetto *m* sketch.

braccio *m* arm.

bracco *m* hound.

bracconaggio *m* poaching.

bracconiere *m* poacher.

brache *fpl* trousers: — (*sl*) calare le ~ to surrender.

brasato *m* braised beef.

bravata *f* bravado.

bravo *adj* clever, good: — (che) ~! good boy! — su, da ~! be a good boy!

brefotrofio *m* foundling hospital.

bricco *m* kettle, pot.

bricconata *f* roguish trick.

briccone *m* rouge.

brigadiere *m* police officer.

brigante *n* robber.

brillo *adj* (*sl*) tipsy.

brina *f* frost.

brindare *vi* to toast.

brindisi *m inv* toast: — qui ci vuole un brindisi! this calls for a drink!

brio *m* liveliness.

britannico *adj* British.

brizzolato *adj* grizzled.

brocca *f* jug; pitcher.

broccato *m* brocade.

brodo *m* broth; stock; consommé: — (*sl* and *fig*) andare in ~ to melt.

broglio *m* intrigue: ~ elettorale gerrymander.

bronchiale *adj* bronchial.

bronchite *f* bronchitis.

broncio *m* pout; * tenere il ~ *vi*

to sulk: — fare il ~ to pout.
broncopolmonite *f* broncho-
  pneumonia.
brontolare *vt*, *vi* to grumble;
  to grouse; to rumble.
brontolone *m* grumbler.
bronzo *m* bronze.
bruciare *vt* to burn; * *vi* to
  smart; to sting; to rankle.
bruciato *m* burning.
brufolo *m* pimple, spot.
brullo *adj* bare.
bruma *f* mist.
bruna, brunetta *f* brunette.
bruno *m* brown.
bruscamente *adv* sharply;
  abruptly.
brusco *adj* abrupt, brusque,
  bluff, blunt, offhand, curt;
  sharp; unceremonious; rude.
bruscolo *m* grain of dust:
  — avere un ~ nell'occhio to
  have something in the eye.
brusio *m* buzz.
brutale *adj* brutal.
brutalità *f* brutality.
brutalmente *adv* roughly.
bruto *m*, brute; * *adj* brute.
bruttezza *f* ugliness.
brutto *adj* ugly.
bùbbola *f* (*sl*) lie.
bubbone *m* bubo; lump; swelling.
bubbonico *adj* bubonic: — la
  peste bubbonica bubonic
  plague.
buca *f* pit: — buca di sabbia *f*
  sandpit.
bucaneve *m inv* snowdrop.
bucare *vt* to hole; to prick.
bucato in washing.
buccia *f* peel; skin; rind; zest.
buco *m* hole: — (*sl*) fare un ~
  nell'acqua to achieve nothing,
  to fail.
bucolico *adj* bucolic.
budello *m* gut: — le budella *fpl*
  the guts.

budino *m* pudding.
bue *m* ox.
bufalo *m* buffalo.
bufera *f* gale: ~ di neve
  blizzard.
buffo *adj* funny, comic.
buffonata *f* joke.
buffone *m* buffoon; fool;
  jester.
bugia *f* lie: ~ pietosa *f* white lie.
bugiardo *adj* lying; * *m* liar,
  fibber.
buio *adj* dark; gloom; * *m*
  dark, darkness.
bulbo *m* bulb: ~ oculare *m*
  eyeball.
bullo *m* (*sl*) swaggerer; tough.
bullone *m* bolt.
buoi *mpl* oxen.
buongustaio *m* epicure;
  gourmet.
buongusto *m* good taste.
buono *adj* good.
buono *m* coupon; token:
  ~ premio gift voucher.
buonsenso *m* commom sense.
buontempone *m* merry fellow.
buonumore *m* good mood.
buonuomo *m* good fellow;
  simple man.
burattino *m* puppet.
burattinaio *m* puppeteer.
burbero *adj* gruff; surly.
burino *m* and *adj* (*sl*) boor
burla *f* prank.
burlone *m* joker; tease.
burocrate *m* or *f* bureaucrat.
burocrazia *f* bureaucracy; (*fig*)
  red tape.
burrasca *f* storm.
burrascoso *adj* rough; stormy;
  tempestuous.
burro *m* butter.
burrone *m* ravine.
buscarsi *vt* to get: — (*sl*) ~ le
  busse to get a thrashing.
bussare *vi* to knock; to tap;

* *vt* to rap.

busse *fpl* blows: — (*sl*) buscarsi or prendere le ~ to get a thrashing.

bussola *f* compass.

bussolotto *m* tin can, dice box.

busta *f* envelope.

bustarella *f* (*sl*) backhander; bribe.

bustina *f* sachet.

busto *m* bust; girdle, corset.

butano *m* butane.

buttare *vt* to throw: — buttar fuori to turf out: — buttar via to throw away.

buttafuori *m inv* bouncer.

C

cabina *f* booth; (lorry) cab; (plane) cabin; cubicle.

cacao *m* cocoa.

cacca *f* (*sl*) poop: — fare la ~ to poop.

cacciare *vi* to hunt.

cadavere *m* corpse.

cadaverico *m* of a corpse: deve essere molto malato, ha un aspetto ~ he must be very ill, he looks like a corpse.

cadere *vi* to fall; to topple over; to slump.

caffè *m* café.

caffettiera *f* coffee pot.

cagnolino *m* little dog.

calamaro *m* squid.

calare *vt* to drop; to wane: ~ le brache (*sl*) to surrender.

calcagno *m* heel.

calcare *m* limestone.

calce *f* lime: — calce viva quicklime; bianco di ~ whitewash.

calcestruzzo *m* concrete.

calciatore *m* footballer.

calcificare *vt* to calcify.

calcio *m* kick; calcium; football; soccer.

calcolare *vt* to calculate; to compute; to reckon.

calcolatore *m* calculator.

caldo *adj* hot, warm.

caleidoscopio *m* kaleidoscope.

calendario *m* calendar.

calendola *f* marigold.

callo *m* corn.

calma *f* calm; cool; composure.

calmiante *adj* soothing; sedative; * *m* sedative.

calmare *vt* to calm; to lull; to pacify; to steady; to soothe.

caloroso *adj* warm, appreciative.

calmo *adj* calm; cool.

calo *m* fall; drop.

calore *m* heat; warmth.

calvo *adj* bald.

calza *f* stocking: — calze *fpl* hosiery.

calzettone *m* sock.

calzoni *mpl* trousers.

calzoncini *mpl* shorts.

cambiamento *m* change; shift: ~ continuo flux.

cambiare *vt* to change.

cambio *m* change; exchange: — gearbox.

camelia *f* camellia.

camera *f* room; chamber: — (political) house: ~ da letto bedroom.

cameriere *m* waiter.

camicetta *f* blouse.

camicia *f* shirt: ~ di forza *f* straitjacket.

camino *m* chimney.

camion *m inv* lorry, truck.

cammeo *m* cameo.

camminare *vi* walk.

campagna *f* country, countryside; campaign.

campagnolo *m* countryman.

campana *f* bell.

campanello *m* bell; doorbell.
campanile *m* belfry; steeple.
campeggiare *vi* to camp.
campione *m* champion.
campo *m* ground, field; pitch.
cancellare *vt* to cancel.
cancro *m* cancer.
candela *f* candle; spark plug.
candidato *m* candidate.
candidatura *f* candidacy.
cane *m* dog: ~ per ciechi *m*
  guide dog: — un lavoro da
  cani a dog job: — una vita da
  cani a dog's life: — solo come
  un ~ utterly alone, desper-
  ately lonely: — figlio d'un ~
  son of a bitch.
canna *f* cane.
canoa *f* canoe.
canottiera *f* vest.
cantante *m* or *f* singer.
cantare *vi* to sing.
canto *m* song; chant: ~ funebre
  m dirge.
canzone *f* song.
capacità *f* capability.
capelli *mpl* hair.
capezzolo *m* nipple.
capire *vt* to understand; to
  comprehend.
capitale *f* capital (city).
capitano *m* captain, skipper.
capo *m* boss, chief;
  commander; leader.
Capodanno *m* New Year's Day.
cappa *f* cape; cloak.
cappella *f* chapel.
cappellaio *m* hatter.
cappellano *m* chaplain.
cappello *m* hat.
capra *f* goat.
capretto *m* kid.
caprone *m* billy-goat: —
  puzzare come un ~ to stink
  like a goat.
Capricorno *m* Capricorn.
carattere *m* character; type.

caratteristica *f* feature; trait.
carbone *m* coal; charcoal.
carciofo *m* artichoke.
cardiaco *adj* cardiac.
carenza *f* shortage.
caricare *vt* to load.
carino *adj* sweet.
carità *f* charity.
carne *f* meat; flesh.
caro *adj* dear; darling; expensive.
carota *f* carrot.
carta *f* paper; charter; map.
cartellino *m* docket.
cartello *m* placard; cartel:
  ~ stradale *m* road sign.
cartolina *f* postcard.
cartone *m* cardboard.
casa *f* house; home.
casalinga *f* housewife.
casco *m* helmet, crash helmet.
caserma *f* barracks: ~ dei
  pompieri fire station.
casinó *m* casino
casino *m* (*sl*) brothel.
caso *m* (medical, grammati-
  cal) case; chance: — per ~ by
  accident, by chance.
cassetto *m* drawer.
cassettone *m* chest of drawers.
castagna *f* chestnut.
castello *m* castle.
castigare *vt* to castigate; to
  chasten; to discipline.
catacombe *fpl* catacombs.
catalizzatore *m* catalyst.
catalogo *m* catalogue.
categoria *f* category.
cattedrale *f* cathedral.
cattivo *adj* bad; ill; evil; nasty.
cattolicesimo *m* Catholicism.
cattolico *adj*, *m* Catholic,
  Roman Catholic.
caucciù *m* rubber.
causa *f* cause; lawsuit.
causare *vt* to cause.
cavalletta *f* grasshopper.
cavallo *m* horse; horsepower.

caverna *f* cave, cavern.
caviglia *f* ankle.
cavolfiore *m* cauliflower.
cavolino *m*: — cavolini di
  Bruxelles Brussels sprouts.
cavolo *m* cabbage.
cazzo *m* (*vulg*) prick; testa di ~
  dickhead: — non capisco un ~
  I don't understand a thing.
cazzotto *m* (*sl*) punch; sock: —
  fare a cazzotti con qualcuno
  to have a punch-up with
  someone.
celebrazione *f* celebration.
cena *f* dinner, supper.
cenere *f* ash.
cenotafio *m* cenotaph.
centesimo *m* cent; hundredth;
  * *adj* hundredth.
centigrado *adj* centigrade.
centilitro *m* centilitre.
centimetro *m* centimetre.
cento *adj*, *m* hundred.
centrale *adj* central; middle.
centro *m* centre; middle.
ceramica *f* ceramic; pottery.
cercare *vt* to try; to look for.
cerchio *m* circle.
cerniera *f* zip.
certamente *adv* definitely.
certo *adj* certain; some; sure;
  * certi *pron* some.
certosino *m* Carthusian.
cervello *m* brain; mastermind.
cervo *m* deer.
cesareo *adj* Caesarian.
cespuglio *m* bush, shrub.
cessare *vt* to cease; * *vi* to
  cease, stop.
cesso *m* (*vulg*) toilet.
cestino *m* basket.
cetriolo *m* cucumber.
champagne *m inv* champagne.
che *rel pron* that; which; who,
  whom; * *conj* that; then;
  * *adj* what.
checca *f* (*sl*) gay man.

chi *pron* who, whom.
chiappa *f* (*sl*) buttock:
  — muovere le chiappe! move!
chiacchierare *vi* to chat,
  chatter; to gossip; to jabber.
chiamare *vt* to call; to name:
  ~ alle armi to muster in.
chiamata *f* call.
chiarimento *m* explanation.
chiave *f* key.
chiavaiolo *m* locksmith;
  * (*vulg*) stud.
chiavare *vt* (*vulg*) to fuck.
chiavata *f* (*vulg*) fuck, screw.
chiaro *adj* clear; articulate;
  fair; light; straightforward.
chiedere *vt* to ask.
chiesa *f* church.
chilo *m* kilo.
chilogrammo *m* kilo-gramme.
chilometraggio *m* mileage.
chilometro *m* kilometre.
chimica *f* chemistry.
chimico *adj* chemical;
  * *m* chemist.
chiocciola *f* snail.
chiostro *m* cloister.
chirurgo *m* surgeon.
chitarra *f* guitar.
chiudere to close; to shut;
  * ~rsi *vr* to shut.
chiunque *pron* anyone; who.
chiuso *adj* closed.
ci *pron* us.
ciao *interj* hello, goodbye.
ciascuno *adj*, *pron* each (one).
cibo *m* food.
cicatrice *f* scar.
ciclo *m* cycle.
ciclomotore *m* moped.
cicogna *f* stork.
cieco *adj* and *m* blind.
cielo *m* heaven; sky.
ciglio *m* eyelash, lash; side.
ciliegia *f* cherry.
cima *f* crown (of hill); peak;
  summit; top.

cimitero *m* cemetery; churchyard; graveyard.

cinema *m inv* cinema.

cinghiale *m* boar.

cinquanta *m, adj* fifty.

cinque *m, adj* five.

cintura *f* belt: ~ di sicurezza seatbelt, safety belt.

cioccolato *m* chocolate.

cioè *adv* ie; namely.

cipolla *f* onion.

cipresso *m* cypress.

circa *adv* around; some; somewhere.

circolo *m* club; clubhouse.

circostanza *f* circumstance.

citofono *m* entryphone.

citrico *adj* citric.

città *f inv* city, town.

cittadino *m* citizen; national.

civilizzare *vt* to civilise.

classe *f* class, form; style.

classico *adj* classic(al); standard.

clemente *adj* clement.

clero *m* clergy.

cliente *m or f* client, customer.

clima *m* elimate.

climatizzato *adj* air-conditioned.

clinica *f* clinic; nursing home.

cloro *m* chlorine.

club *m* club.

coagulare *vi* to coagulate.

coalizione *f* coalition.

cobalto *m* cobalt.

cocco *m* coconut; darling: ~ di mamma mummy's boy.

coccola *f* cuddle.

coccolare *vt* to cuddle.

coccolone *m* person (animal) who loves a cuddle.

cocomero *m* watermelon.

coda *f* queue; tail, tailback.

cogliere *vt* to pluck; to pick; to seize.

coglione *pl* (~i *mpl, vulg*) testicles; balls: — (*vulg*) rompere i ~ a qualcuno to pester someone: — (*vulg*) togliti dai! fuck off! — (*vulg*) un rompicoglioni a bore, a pain in the arse: — (*vulg*) è un ~ he is an arsehole, an idiot: — (*vulg*) avere i ~ (quadrati) to have guts: — (*vulg*) essere senza ~ to be feckless, weak.

coglionata *f* (*vulg*) nonsense; rubbish: ma non dire coglionate! stop talking nonsense!

cognata(o) *f(m)* sister (brother)-in-law.

cognome *m* surname.

coincidere *vi* to coincide; to concur.

colazione *f*: — prima ~ breakfast: — seconda ~ lunch.

colibrì *m inv* humming-bird.

collaboratore *m* collaborator.

collaborazione *f* collaboration.

collasso *m* collapse.

collaudare *vt* to test.

collaudo *m* test.

collina *f* hill; foothill.

collirio *m* eyedrops.

collo *m* collar; neck; instep.

collocare *vt* to locate; to site.

colombo *m* dove.

colonia *f* colony.

colorante *m* dye; stain.

colorare *vt* to colour.

colpevole *adj, m or f* guilty.

colpire *vt* to hit; to knock.

coltellata *f* stab.

coltello *m* knife: ~ a serramanico jack-knife.

coltivare *vt* to cultivate; to grow, farm, till.

coltivazione *f* crop; cultivation.

colto *adj* cultured, learned, educated.

comandamento *m* commandment.

comandare *vt* to command.

comando *m* control; command; order.

comatoso *adj* comatose.

combattente *m* or *f* combatant; fighter.

combattere *vt* to fight.

combattimento *m* battle, combat, fight.

combinare *vt* to combine.

combinazione *f* combination.

combustibile *adj* combustible; * *m* fuel.

combustione *f* combustion.

come *conj* (such) as; * *adv* how; * *prep* like.

cometa *f* comet.

comico *adj* comic; * *m* comedian.

comignolo *m* chimney stack.

cominciare *vt* to begin, commence.

comitato *m* committee: ~ elettorale *m* caucus.

comizio *m* rally: ~ elettorali *mpl* hustings.

commando *m* commando.

commedia *f* comedy; play.

commemorare *vt* to commemorate.

commentare *vt* to commentate.

commento *m* comment; commentary.

commerciale *adj* commercial; trading.

commercialista *m* chartered acountant.

commerciante *m* or *f* dealer, merchant, trader.

commerciare *vi* to trade.

commercio *m* commerce, trade, trading.

commessa(o) *f*(*m*) saleswoman(man).

commestibile *adj* edible, eatable.

commettere *vt* to commit.

commiserazione *f* commiseration.

commissariato *m* commissariat.

commissario *m*: ~ di bordo *m* purser.

commissionare *vt* to commission.

commissione *f* commision; board; errand.

commosso *adj* affected, touched.

commovente *adj* appealing, moving, touching, emotive.

commozione *f* emotion: ~ cerebrale *f* concussion.

commuovere *vt* to move, touch.

commutare *vt* to commute.

comodità *f* convenienee.

comodo *adj* comfortable; convenient; bandy.

compagnia *f* company, society.

compagno *m* companion; comrade; mate: ~ di classe (scuola) *m* class (school)mate: ~ di viaggio *m* fellow-traveller.

comparativo *adj* comparative.

comparire *vi* to appear.

comparsa *f* appearance.

compassione *f* compassion, pity.

compassionevole *adj* compassionate.

compasso *m* compass: ~ a punte fisse *m* dividers.

compatibile *adj* compatible.

compatire *vt* to pity; * *vi* to sympathise.

compatriota *m* or *f* compatriot, fellow countryman.

compatto *adj* compact.

compendiare *vt* abridge.

compensare *vt* to compensate.

compensato *m* plywood.

compenso *m* compensation.

competente *adj* competent, proficient.

competenza *f* competence, proficiency.
competere *vi* to compete.
compiacente *adj* compliant.
compiacimento *m* complacency.
compiaciuto *adj* complacent; smug, self-righteous.
compiere *vt* to do; to accomplish; to fulfil.
compilare *vt* to compile.
compilazione *f* compilation.
compimento *m* fulfilment.
compito *m* homework; job; task.
compleanno *m* birthday.
complementare *adj* complementary; subsidiary.
complemento *m* complement.
complessità *f inv* complexity; intricacy.
complessivo *adj* aggregate.
complesso *m* complex; ensemble; entirety: — nel ~ all together.
completamente *adv* completely, fully.
compietamento *m* completion; accomplishment.
completare *vt* to complete; to fill in (form, etc).
completo *adj* complete.
complicare *vt* to complicate.
complicato *adj* complicated, elaborate; involved.
complicazione *f* complication.
complice *m* or *f* accomplice, accessory.
complicità *f* complicity.
complimentarsi *vr* to compliment.
complimento *m* compliment.
complottare *vi* to plot.
complotto *m* plot.
componente *adj* component; * *m* component; constituent.
comporre *vt* to compose.
comportamento *m* behaviour.
comportare *vt* to entail; * ~rsi *vr* to behave.

composito *adj* composite.
compositore *m* composer.
composizione *f* composition.
composto *m* compound; * *adj* composed.
comprare *vt* to buy.
compratore *m* buyer.
comprendere *vt* to comprise; to comprehend; to encompass.
comprensibile *adj* comprehensible, understandable.
comprensione *f* comprehension, appreciation, understanding.
comprensivo *adj* understanding, sympathetic.
compressa *f* compress; tablet.
comprimere *vt* to compress.
compromesso *m* compromise.
comprovare *vt* to substantiate.
computer *m* compute.
comune *adj* common; ordinary; * *m* municipality; borough; town-hall.
comunemente *adj* commonly.
comunicare *vt* to communicate; to impart; to commune.
comunicazione *f* communication; via di ~ connection.
comunione *f* communion.
comunismo *m* communism.
comunista *m* or *f* communist.
comunità *f inv* community.
comunque *adv* anyhow; * *conj* however.
con *prep* with.
conato *m* spasm, effort: ~ di vomito spasm of vomiting.
concavo *adj* concave.
concedere *vt* to allow.
concentramento *m* concentration: — campo di ~ *m* concentration camp.
concentrare *vt* to concentrate.
concentrato *m* concentrate; strong.
concentrazione *f* concentration.

concentrico *adj* concentric.
concepibile *adj* conceivable.
concepimento *m* conception.
concepire *vt* to conceive.
concerto *m* concert.
concessione *f* concession, franchise.
concetto *m* concept.
conchiglia *f* shell.
conciare *vt* to cure.
conciliabile *adj* reconcilable.
conciliare *vt* to accommodate (differences).
conciliante *adj* accommodating, amenable.
conciliatorio *adj* conciliatory.
conciliazione *f* conciliation.
concimare *vt* to manure.
concime *m* compost, manure.
conciso *adj* concise.
concittadino *m* fellow-citizen.
concludere *vt* to conclude; to clinch.
conclusione *f* conclusion.
conclusivo *adj* conclusive; closing.
concomitante *adj* concomitant.
concordanza *f* concordance.
concordare *vt* to agree.
concorrente *m* or *f* competitor, entrant.
concorrenza *f* competition.
concorrenziale *adj* competitive.
concorso *m* competition, contest.
concreto *adj* concrete.
concubina *f* concubine.
concupire *vt* to covet.
condanna *f* conviction, sentence.
condannare *vt* to condemn; to sentence.
condensare *vt* to condense.
condensato *adj* potted.
condensazione *f* condensation.
condiglianze *fpl* condolences.
condimento *m* dressing, seasoning.

condire *vt* (cookery) to dress, season.
condiscendente *adj* condescending; acquiescent.
condiscendenza *f* compliance.
condividere *vt* to share.
condizionale *adj* conditional.
condizionare *vt* to condition.
condizionato *adj* qualified.
condizione *f* condition, term.
condotta *f* conduct.
conducente *m* driver.
condurre *vt* to conduct; to lead.
conduttività *f* conductivity.
conduttore *m* conductor.
conduttura *f* conduit; pipeline.
conduzione *f* conduction.
confederarsi *vr* to confederate.
confederato *adj* confederate.
confederazione *f* confederacy.
conferenza *f* talk; lecture; ~ stampa press conference.
conferire *vt* to bestow, confer.
conferma *f* confirmation.
confermare *vt* to confirm.
confessare *vt* to confess.
confessionale *m* confessional.
confessione *f* confession; denomination.
confessore *m* confessor.
confezionare *vt* to package; to tailor.
conficcare *vt* to stick; to plunge; to jab.
confidare *vt* to confide.
confidente *m* confidant.
confidenziale *adj* private.
configurazione *f* configuration.
confinare *vt* to intern; to confine: — * ~ con *vi* to border with.
congedare *vt* to dismiss.
congedo *m* dismissal; furlough.
congegno *m* device; contrivance.
congelamento *m* freezing, frostbite.
congelare *vt* to freeze; * ~rsi *vr* to freeze.

congelato *adj* frozen, frost-bitten.

congelatore *m* (deep-)freezer.

congenito *adj* congenital, inbred.

congestionato *adj* congested.

congestione *f* congestion.

congettura *f* conjecture, surmise, guesswork.

congetturare *vt* to conjecture, surmise.

congiuntivo *adj*, *m* subjunctive.

congiuntura *f* conjuncture; juncture.

congiunzione *f* conjunction.

congiura *f* conspiracy.

congiurare *vi* to conspire.

conglomerato *m* conglomerate.

congratularsi *vr* to congratulate.

congratulazioni *fpl* congratulations.

congregazione *f* congregation.

congresso *m* congress.

congruità *f* congruity.

congruo *adj* congruous.

coniare *vt* to mint.

conico *adj* conic(al).

conifera *f* conifer.

conifero *adj* coniferous.

conigliera *f* rabbit hutch.

coniglio *m* rabbit.

coniugale *adj* conjugal, matrimonial, marital.

coniugare *vt* to conjugate.

coniugato *adj* married.

coniugazione *f* conjugation.

connivente *adj*: — essere ~ in to connive.

connivenza *f* connivance.

cono *m* cone.

conoscente *m or f* acquaintance.

conoscenza *f* acquaintance; knowledge; consciousness.

conoscere *vt* become acquainted with; to know.

conosciuto *adj* familiar.

conquista *f* conquest.

conquistare *vt* to conquer; to win.

conquistatore *m* conqueror.

consacrare *vt* to consecrate, hallow.

consacrazione *f* consecration.

consapevole *adj* aware; mindful.

consapevolezza *f* awareness.

consapevolmente *adv* wittingly.

consciamente *adv* knowingly.

consecutivo *adj* consecutive; successive.

consegna *f* delivery.

consegnare *vt* to consign; to hand over; to deliver; to turn in.

conseguente *adj* consequent.

conseguenza *f* consequence: — * di ~ *adv* consequently.

consenso *m* consensus; acquiescence.

conserva *f* preserve.

conservante *m* preservative.

conservare *vt* to conserve, preserve; to retain.

conservatore *m* conservative; * *adj* conservative.

conservatorio *m* conservatory.

conservazione *f* conservation, preservation.

considerare *vt* to consider; to regard; to deliberate; to treat.

considerazione *f* consideration.

considerevole *adj* considerable, handsome, sizeable.

consigliabile *adj* advisable.

consigliare *vt* advise; to recommend.

consigliere *m* adviser; counsellor.

consiglio *m* advice; council, counsel: — C~ dei Ministri the Cabinet.

consistenza *f* consistency; texture.

consistere *vi* to consist.

consociato *adj* associate.

consolare *adj* consular; * *vt* to console.

consolato *m* consulate.
consolazione *f* consolation, comfort, solace.
console *m* consul.
consolidare *vt* to consolidate; * ~rsi *vr* to strengthen.
consolidazione *f* consolidation.
consonante *f* consonant.
consorte *m* or *f* consort.
consorzio *m* consortium.
consueto *adj* customary.
consuetudine *f* custom.
consulente *m* or *f* adviser, consultant.
consulenza *f* consultancy.
consultare *vt* to consult; * ~rsi *vr* to confer.
consultazione *f* consultation.
consultivo *adj* advisory.
consumare *vt* to consummate; to consume; to wear; * ~rsi *vr* to wear away.
consumato *adj* threadbare, worn.
consumatore *m* consumer.
consumazione *f* consummation.
consumista *adj* consumerist.
consumo *m* consumption: — beni di ~ *mpl* consumer goods.
consunto *adj* worn-out.
consunzione *f* (medical) consumption.
contabile *m* or *f* accountant, book-keeper.
contabilità *f* accountancy, book-keeping.
contachilometri *m inv* mile-ometer.
contadino *m, adj* peasant, rustic.
contagioso *adj* catching, contagious.
contagocce *m inv* dropper.
contaminare *vt* to contaminate.
contaminato *adj* tainted.
contaminazione *f* contamina-tion.

contanti *mpl* in ~ in cash.
contare *vt* to count: ~ su to depend on, rely on; to number; * *vi* to count.
contatore *m* meter.
contattare *vt* to contact.
contatto *m* contact, touch: — lenti a ~ contact lenses.
conte *m* count, earl.
contea *f* county, shire.
conteggio *m* count.
contegno *m* demeanour.
contegnoso *adj* demure.
contemplare *vt* to contemplate.
contemplativo *adj* contemplative.
contemplazione *f* contemplation.
contemporaneo *adj* contempo-rary.
contendente *m* or *f adj* contender.
contendere *vt* to contend; * ~rsi *vr* to vie.
contenere *vt* to contain.
contenitore *m* container, holder.
contentare *vt* to suit.
contentezza *f* contentment. happiness.
contento *adj* content; con-tented; glad; happy; pleased.
contenuto *m* contents.
contenzioso *adj* contentious.
contessa *f* countess.
contestare *vt* to contest; to dispute; to query.
contestatore *m* protestor.
contesto *m* context.
contiguo *adj* contiguous; adjoining.
continentale *adj* continental.
continente *m* continent; mainland.
contingente *m* contingent.
contingenza *f* contingency.
continuare *vt* to carry on,

continue; * *vi* to continue; to go on.

continuazione *f* continuance, continuation.

continuità *f* continuity.

continuo *adj* continual; continuous; constant; non-stop.

conto *m* account; bill: —
rendere ~ a qualcuno to be responsible to someone:
— tenere ~ di to consider:
— per ~ di on behalf of:
~ in banca bank account:
~ scoperto overdraft:
— estratto ~ statement:
~ spese expense account:
* rendersi ~ di *vr* to realise, to understand.

contorcere *vt* to contort;
* ~rsi *vr* to squirm; to writhe.

contorno *m* contour, outline.

contorsione *f* contortion.

contrabbandare *vt* to smuggle.

contrabbandiere *m* smuggler.

contrabbando *m* contraband; smuggling.

contraccambiare *vt* to reciprocate; to requite.

contraccezione *f* contraception, birth control.

contraddire *vt* to contradict.

contraddittorio *adj* conflicting, contradictory; inconsistent.

contraddizione *f* contradiction.

contrafatto *adj* counterfeit.

contraffare *vt* to counterfeit, forge.

contrariare *vt* to put out.

contrariato *adj* disgruntled.

contrario *m* contrary, opposite; * *adj* contrary:
— al ~ conversely.

contrarre *vt* to contract; to incur.

contrarsi *vr* to twitch.

contrastante *adj* contrasting.

contrastare *vt* to contrast.

contrasto *m* contrast.

contrattare *vt* to bargain, haggle.

contrattempo *m* contretemps, accident.

contratto *m* contract:
~ d'affitto lease.

contrattuale *adj* contractual.

contravvenire *vt* to contravene; to flout.

contravvenzione *f* contravention.

contrazione *f* contraction.

contribuente *m* or *f*, *adj* taxpayer.

contribuire *vt*, *vi* to contribute.

contribuzione *f* contribution.

contro *prep* against, versus.

controbilianciare *vt* to counterbalance.

controcuitura *f* underground.

controfigura *f* stand-in.

controfiletto *m* sirloin.

controfirmare *vt* countersign.

controllare *vt* to check; to inspect; to control; to test.

controllo *m* control; inspection.

controproducente *adj* counterproductive.

controversia *f* controversy, dispute.

controverso *adj* controversial.

contusione *f* contusion.

conurbazione *f* conurbation.

convalescente *adj*, *m* or *f* convalescent.

convalescenza *f* convalescence; recuperation.

convalescenziario *m* sanatorium.

convalidare *vt* to authenticate; to validate.

convegno *m* conference.

convenire *vi* to convene, to agree.

convento *m* convent.

convenuto *adj* agreed;

* *m* respondent.
convenzionale *adj* conventional.
convenzione *f* convention.
convergente *adj* convergent.
convergenza *f* convergence.
convergere *vi* to converge.
conversare *vi* to converse.
conversazione *f* talk; conversation.
conversione *f* conversion.
convertibile *adj* convertible.
convertire *vt* to convert.
convertito *m* convert.
convertitore *m* converter.
convincente *adj* convincing; cogent; forcible.
convincere *vt* to convince; to coax.
convinzione *f* conviction; belief.
convocare *vt* to summon; to convoke; to convene.
convoglio *m* convoy.
convulsione *f* convulsion.
convulso *adj* convulsive.
cooperare *vi* to co-operate.
cooperativa *f* co-operative.
cooptare *vt* to co-opt.
coordinamento *m* co-ordinate;
  * *vt* to co-ordinate.
coordinata *f* co-ordinate
coperchio *m* cover, lid.
coperta *f* blanket; deck.
coperto *adj* covered; cloudy, overcast.
copertura *f* cover, covering.
copia *f* copy.
copiare *vt* to copy; to crib.
copioso *adj* profuse.
coppia *f* couple, pair, twosome.
coprire *vt* to cover; to defray.
coraggio *m* courage, bravery; pluck; spirit; valour.
coraggioso *adj* brave, courageous, plucky, valiant.
corale *adj* choral.

corallino *m* coral reef.
corallo *m* coral.
corda *f* cord; string; rope; chord.
cordiale *m* cordial;
  * *adj* cordial, genial.
cordialità *f* friendliness.
cordone *m* cord: ~ ombelicale
  m umbilical cord.
coreografia *f* choreography.
coreografo *m* choreographer.
coriaceo *adj* thick-skinned.
coriandoli *mpl* confetti.
coriandolo *m* coriander.
corista *m* or *f* chorister.
cornacchia *f* crow.
cornamusa *f* bagpipes:
  — suonatore di ~ piper.
cornea *f* cornea.
cornetto *m* croissant; cornet.
cornice *f* frame.
cornicione *m* cornice.
corno *m* horn.
coro *m* choir; chorus.
corona *f* crown.
corpo *m* body; corps.
correggere *vt* to correct; to emend; to right; to mark.
correre *vi* to race; to run.
correttezza *f* fair play.
correzione *f* correction; emendation.
corrida *f* bullfight.
corridoio *m* corridor.
corridore *m* runner; racer.
corriera *f* coach.
corriere *m* carrier; courier.
corrispondente *m* or *f* corrispondent; penfriend;
  * *adj* corresponding.
corrispondenza *f* correspondence.
corrispondere *vt* to correspond; to match; * *vt* to correspond.
corroborare *vt* to corroborate.
corrodere *vt* to corrode;
  * ~rsi *vr* to corrode.
corrompere *vt* to corrupt; to bribe; to debauch.

corrosione *f* corrosion.
corrosivo *adj* corrosive.
corrotto *adj* corrupt.
corruttibile *adj* corruptible.
corruzione *f* corruption;
  bribery.
corsa *f* dash; race; run; racing.
corsia *f* ward.
corsivo *adj* italic.
corso *m* course: ~ serale *m*
  evening class: — in ~ ongoing.
corte *f* court: ~ marziale *f*
  court-martial.
corteccia *f* bark.
corteggiare *vt* to court, woo.
corteggiatore *m* suitor.
corto *adj* short.
cosa *f* thing.
coscia *f* thigh; haunch; leg:
  ~ di pollo *f* drumstick.
cosciente *adj* conscious.
così *adv* so: — così così so-so.
cosmetico *adj*, *m* cosmetic.
costa *f* coast.
costare *vt* to cost.
costituzione *f* constitution.
costo *m* cost.
costola *f* rib.
costoletta *f* chop.
costoso *adj* costly, expensive.
costrizione *f* compulsion;
  constraint; constriction.
costruire *vt* to construct, build.
costruttore *m* builder.
cotoletta *f* cutlet.
cotone *m* cotton: ~ idrofilo *m*
  cotton wool.
cotto *adj* cooked.
cranio *m* skull.
cravatta *f* tie.
creazione *f* creation; brainchild.
credenziali *fpl* credentials.
credere *vt* to believe; to feel;
  to reckon; to understand.
credibilità *f* credibility.
credito *m* credit: — lettera di ~
  letter of credit.

creditore *m* creditor.
credo *m* creed.
credulo *adj* credulous.
credulone *adj* gullible.
crema *f* cream.
crepa *f* crack.
crepatura *f* crack.
crepare *vi* (*vulg*) to die: — crepa!
  go to hell! * ~rsi *vr* to crack.
crepuscolo *m* dusk, nightfall,
  twilight.
crescente *adj* growing;
  increasing; rising.
crescere *vi* to grow.
cresima *f* confirmation.
cresimare *vt* to confirm.
criminale *m* or *f* and *adj*
  criminal, felon.
crimine *m* or *f* crime.
criniera *f* mane.
cristallizzare *vt* to crystallise:
  * ~rsi *vr* to crystallise.
cristianesimo *m* Christianity,
  Christendom.
cristiano *adj* Christian.
Cristo *m* Christ.
criticare *vi* to criticise; to
  fault; to slate.
critico *m* critic, critique:
  * *adj* critical.
croccante *adj* crisp, crunchy.
croce *f* cross.
crociata *f* crusade.
crociato *m* crusader.
crociera *f* cruise.
crocifisso *m* crucifix.
croco *m* crocus.
cronico *adj* chronic.
cronista *m* reporter.
crostata *f* tart.
cruciverba *m inv* crossword.
crudeltà *f* cruelty.
crudo *adj* raw; uncooked.
crumiro *m* blackleg; scab:
  — strikebreaker.
cucchiaio *m* spoon.
cucciolo *m* pup, cub.

cucina *f* cooker, cookery;
  kitchen.
cucitrice *f* stapler.
cucitura *f* seam.
cuculo *m* cuckoo.
cugino *m* cousin.
cui *pron*: — il ~ whose.
culla *f* crib, cradle, cot.
cullare *vt* to rock (a baby).
culatta *f* (cookery) rump.
culattone *m* (*sl*) gay man.
culo *m* (*vulg*) bum, arse: —
  prendere or trattare a calci
  in ~ to kick someone in the
  arse (also *fig*): — prendere
  per il ~ to take the mickey
  out of.
culto *m* cult.
cultura *f* culture, learning,
  edification.
cuocere *vt* to cook: ~ al forno
  to bake: ~ in bianco to poach.
cuoco *m* cook.
cuoio *m* hide, leather:
  ~ capelluto *m* scalp.
cuore *m* heart: — prendere a ~ to
  take to heart: — di ~ heartily.
cupola *f* dome.
cura *f* cure: — * aver ~ di *vt* to
  groom.
curare *vt* to care for; to tend;
  to treat.
curiosità *f inv* curio; curiosity.
curioso *adj* curious; inquisitive, nosey.
curriculum vitae *m inv*
  curriculum vitae.
curva *f* curve, bend, turn,
  turning.
cuscinetto *m* pad.
cuscino *m* cushion.
custode *m* or *f* custodian,
  attendant.
custodia *f* case; custody.
cute *f* skin.

D

da *prep* to; out; off; since;
  from, by, for.
dalia *f* dahlia.
daltonico *adj* colour-blind.
damigella *f* damsel: ~ d'onore
  bridesmaid.
dannazione *f* damnation.
danneggiare *vt* to damage,
  hurt; to impair.
danno *m* damage.
danzare *vt*, *vi* to dance.
danza *f* dance.
dappertutto *adv* everywhere;
  throughout.
dapprima *adv* at first.
dare *vt* to give: ~ su to over-
  look: ~ la colpa a qualcuno to
  lay the blame on someone:
  ~ da dormire, ~ da mangiare
  or ~ da bere a qualcuno to
  offer someone a bed, food or
  drink: ~ alle fiamme to burn :
  ~ allo stomaco to sicken:
  ~ da pensare to make someone
  concerned: ~ un esame to take
  an examination: ~ ragione or
  ~ torto a qualcuno to prove
  that someone is right or
  wrong: ~ qualcuno per morto
  to hold that someone is dead:
  — darsi arie to boast.
data *f* date.
dati *mpl* data.
dattilografa(o) *f*(*m*) typist.
davanti *adv* ahead; * *prep* by;
  * *m* front, fore.
davvero *adv* really.
d.C. (dopo Cristo) AD (anno
  domini, the year of our Lord).
dea *f* goddess.
debole *adj* weak, frail, feeble;
  * *m* or *f* penchant; foible.
debosciato *adj* debauched,
  dissolute.

debutto *m* debut.
decaffeinato *adj* decaffeinated.
decennio *m* decade.
decente *adj* decent, proper.
decentramento *m* decentralisation, devolution.
decidere *vt* to decide; to elect; to resolve.
decimo *adj*, *m* tenth.
decisione *f* decision.
decollare *vi* to take off.
decorativo *adj* decorative.
decrepito *adj* decrepit.
dedizione *f* dedication.
deficiente *m* or *f*, *adj* deficient; fool, idiot.
definire *vt* to define; to class; to settle; to finalise.
definitivo *adj* definitive, definite; firm.
deflazione *f* deflation.
deformità *f* deformity.
delfino *m* dolphin.
delinquente *m* or *f* delinquent.
delirio *m* delirium.
delitto *m* crime.
delizia *f* delight.
deludente *adj* disappointing.
deludere *vt* to disappoint.
demolire *vt* to demolish, pull down, knock down; to scrap.
demonio *m* demon, fiend.
dente *m* tooth; cog.
dentiera *f* dentures.
dentifricio *m* toothpaste.
dentista *m* or *f* dentist.
dentro *prep* into; within; inside; * *adv* inside: — (*sl*) essere ~ to be in jail: — finire ~ to end up in jail.
depressione *f* depression.
depresso *adj* depressed.
deprimente *adj* depressing.
deputazione *f* deputation.
derivare *vt* to derive.
dermatite *f* dermatitis.
dermatologia *f* dermatology.

descrivere *vt* to describe.
deserto *m* desert; wilderness.
desiderare *vt*, *vi* to desire; to wish; to want; to long for; to lust after.
desiderio *m* desire; wish.
desolato *adj* bleak, desolate, dreary.
destinatario *m* recipient.
destino *m* destiny, fate, lot; doom.
destra *f* right.
detective *m* or *f* detective.
detenzione *f* detention; custody.
deterioramento *m* deterioration.
detersivo *m* detergent; soap powder.
detestare *vt* to detest, loathe.
detonare *vt* to detonate.
dettaglio *m* detail: — vendere al ~ to retail.
detto *m* saying.
devoto *adj* devoted, devout.
di *prep* of; any.
diabetico *m* or *f*, *adj* diabetic.
diabolico *adj* devilish, diabolical, fiendish.
diagnosi *f* diagnosis.
diagnosticare *vt* to diagnose.
diagonale *adj* diagonal.
diagramma *m* diagram.
dialetto *m* dialect.
dialogo *m* dialogue.
diamante *m* diamond.
diapositiva *f* slide, transparency.
diario *m* diary.
diarrea *f* diarrhoea.
diatriba *f* diatribe.
diavoleria *f* (*sl*) trick; devilry.
diavoletto *m* imp.
diavolo *m* devil.
dibattere *vt* to debate; * ~rsi *vr* to flounder.
dicembre *m* December.
dichiarazione *f* declaration.
diciannove *m* nineteenth.
diciassette *m* seventeen.

31

diciassettesimo *adj* seventeenth.

diciottesimo *adj* eighteenth.

diciotto *adj* eighteen.

dieci *m* ten.

dieta *f* diet: — seguire una ~ or essere a ~ to diet.

dietro *prep* behind; * *adv* back.

difendere *vt* to defend; to champion; to plead.

differenza *f* difference.

difficile *adj* difficult, hard, tricky, stiff.

difficoltà *f* difficulty.

digeribile *adj* digestible.

digerire *vt* to digest.

digestione *f* digestion.

dignità *f* dignity.

dilemma *m* dilemma.

diligente *adj* diligent, industrious.

diluire *vt* to dilute.

diluvio *m* deluge.

dimagrante *adj* slimming.

dimensione *f* dimension.

dimesso *m* modest; shabby.

dimenticare *vt* to forget.

diminuire *vt* to diminish; to decrease; to lessen.

diminuzione *f* decrease.

dimissioni *fpl* resignation: — dare le ~ to hand in one's resignation.

dimostrare *vt* to demonstrate; to prove.

dinamite *f* dynamite.

dinastia *f* dynasty.

dinosauro *m* dinosaur.

dio *m* god: — per l'amor di D~! (*excl*) for God's sake!

dipendente *m* or *f* employee.

dipendere *vi* to depend; to be contingent on.

dipingere *vt* to paint.

diploma *m* diploma, degree.

diplomatico *m* or *f*, *adj* diplomat(ic).

dire *vt* to speak; to tell; to

say: — va detto che admittedly.

direttamente *adv* directly; squarely; straight.

diretto *adj* direct; first hand; non-stop.

direttore *m* director; editor; ~ d'orchestra (musical) conductor.

direttrice *f* manageress.

direzione *f* direction, way; leadership.

dirigere *vt* to direct; to administer; (musical) to conduct; to run.

diritto *m* right; law.

diritti *mpl* dues: ~ d'autore *mpl* royalties.

disapprovare *vt* to disapprove.

disarmo *m* disarmament.

disattenzione *f* carelessness.

discesa *f* descent: — in ~ downhill.

dischetto *m* floppy disk.

disciplina *f* discipline.

disco *m* disc, discus; record: ~ volante *m* flying saucer.

discorsivo *m* discursive.

discorso *m* discourse, speech, address.

discoteca *f* disco; record library.

disegnare *vt* to draw.

disgraziato *adj* unlucky; wretched.

disgustare *vt* to disgust.

disinfettante *m* disinfectant.

disoccupato *adj* unemployed, jobless.

disorganizzato *adj* disorganised, unorganised.

dispari *adj* odd.

dispensario *m* dispensary.

disperare *vi* to despair.

disponibile *adj* available; disposable.

disprezzare *vt* to despise; to scorn.

disputa*f* dispute, contention.
disputare*vt* to dispute;
* ~rsi*vr* to dispute.
dissenteria*f* dysentery.
dissentire*vi* to dissent.
dissertazione*f* dissertation.
dissolvere*vt* to dissolve.
distante*adj* distant, far;
* *adv* far off.
distanza*f* distance: — a ~ with
distance, with hindsight:
— in ~ far away.
distanziare*vt* to move away;
to space out; * ~rsi da*vr* to
take distance from.
disteso*adj* recumbent;
outstretched.
distinto*adj* distinct.
distinzione*f* distinction:
— * senza distinzioni*adv*
regardless.
distorcere*vt* to distort.
distorsione*f* distorsion.
distribuzione*f* distribution.
distruggere*vt* to destroy; to
wreck.
disturbare*vt* to disturb; to
trouble.
disturbo*m* disturbance;
nuisance: — fare azione di ~
to heckle.
disubbidiente*adj* disobedient,
naughty.
disubbidienza*f* disobedience.
disubbidire*vt* to disobey.
disuguale*adj* unequal.
disuso*m* disuse: — essere in ~
to be in abeyance: — cadere
in ~ to fall into disuse.
ditale*m* thimble.
dito*m* finger (*pl* dita): — dita
dei piedi *mpl* toes.
ditta*f* firm.
dittatore*m* dictator.
dittatoriale*adj* dictatorial.
dittatura*f* dictatorship.
dittongo*m* diphthong.

diuretico*adj* diuretic.
divagare*vi* to digress, ramble.
divampare*vi* to blaze, flame.
divano*m* sofa, couch, settee.
divenire*vi* to become.
diventare*vi* to become: —
diventare grande*to* grow up.
divergente*adj* divergent.
divergenza*f* divergence.
divergere*vt* to diverge.
diversamente*adv* differently,
other than.
diversificare*vt* to diversify.
diversità*f* diversity.
diverso*adj* different;
* ~rsi*adj* sundry.
divertente*adj* amusing,
entertaining.
divertimento*m* amusement,
enjoyment, fun.
divertire*vi* amuse; * ~rsi *vr* to
enjoy oneself, have a good time.
dividendo*m* dividend.
dividere*vt* to divide, split, share.
divieto*m* ban.
divinità*f* divinity, godhead,
deity.
divino *adj* divine, heavenly,
godlike.
divisa*f* uniform, strip.
divisibile *adj* divisible.
divisione*f* division.
diviso *adj* divided.
divisore *m* divisor.
divo *m* star: ~ del cinema*m*
film-star.
divorare *vt* to devour, wolf.
divorziare *vt*, *vi* to divorce.
divorziato *adj* divorced;
* *m* divorcee.
divorzio *m* divorce.
divulgare *vt* to divulge; to leak.
dizionario *m* dictionary: ~ dei
sinonimi thesaurus.
dizione *f* diction, elocution.
doccia *f* shower: — fare la ~ to
shower.

33

docente *adj* teaching; * *m*
~ universitario lecturer, don.

docile *adj* docile.

documentare *vt* to document.

documentairio *adj*, *m* documentary.

documento *m* document.

dodicesimo *adj* twelfth.

dodici *m* twelve.

dogana *f* customs: — esente da ~ duty-free.

doganiere *m* customs officer.

doglie *fpl* labour: — avere le ~ to be in labour.

dogma *m* dogma.

dogmatico *adj* dogmatic, opinionated.

dolce *adj* sweet; gentle; soft:
— dalla voce ~ soft-spoken;
* *m* sweet, pudding.

dolcemente *adv* gently.

dolcezza *f* sweetness.

dolcificante *m* sweetener.

dolciumi *mpl* confectionery.

dollaro *m* dollar.

dolo *m* fraud.

doloso *adj* fraudulent.

dolore *m* ache, pain; grief, sorrow, woe.

doloroso *adj* painful, sore.

domanda *f* question; inquiry; query; application: — fare ~ to apply.

domandarsi *vr* to wonder.

domani *adv*, *m* tomorrow.

domare *vt* to tame.

domenica *f* Sunday.

domestico *adj* domestic;
* *m* servant.

domicilio *m* domicile, abode.

dominante *adj* dominant, uppermost.

dominare *vt* to dominate; to control; to subdue; to master.

dominazione *f* domination.

dominio *m* dominion, domain,

domino.

donare *vt* to donate.

donatore *m* contributor; donor.

donazione *f* endowment, donation.

dondolare *vt* to swing; to dangle; * *vi* to swing; to rock.

dondolo *m* swindle: — sedia a ~ *f* rocking chair: — cavallo a ~ rocking horse.

dongiovanni *m* ladykiller.

donna *f* woman: ~ d'affari *f* businesswoman: ~ di malaffare, ~ di facili costumi prostitute.

donnaiolo *m* ladies' man; womaniser; philanderer.

donnola *f* weasel.

dono *m* gift: ~ dei cielo *m* godsend.

dopo *prep* after; * *adv* after; next: — dopotutto after all; afterwards.

dopobarba *m* aftershave.

doppiamente *adv* doubly.

doppiare *vt* to dub.

doppio *adj* dual, double; twofold:
— camera doppia *f* double room.

dorare *vt* to gild.

doratura *f* gilding, gilt.

dormire *vi* to sleep, slumber.

dormitorio *m* dormitory.

dorso *m* backstroke.

dosare *vt* to dose.

dose *f* dose.

dotare *vt* to endow.

dotato *adj* gifted.

dote *f* dowry: — doti *fpl* abilities.

dotto *adj* scholarly.

dottore *m* doctor.

dottrina *f* doctrine.

dottirinale *m* doctrinal.

dove *adv* where, whereabouts;
* *conj* where.

dovere *vb* must; to have to; to be to; to owe.

E

dovunque *conj* wherever.
dovuto *adj* due.
dozzina *f* dozen.
draga *f* dredge.
dragare *vt* to drag, dredge.
drago *m* dragon.
dragoncello *m* tarragon.
drammatico *adj* dramatic.
dramma *m* drama.
drammatizzare *vt* to dramatise.
drammaturgo *m* playwright, dramatist.
drappeggiare *vt* to drape.
drappo *m* cloth.
drastico *adj* drastic.
drenaggio *m* drain, drainage.
drenare *vt* to drain.
dribbling *m* dribble.
dritto *adj* erect; * *adv* straight.
droga *f* drug, dope; spice.
drogare *vt* to drug; to spice.
drogato *m* drug addict, junkie.
dubbio *adj* dubious; * *m* doubt.
dubitare *vt* to doubt.
duca *m* duke.
duchessa *f* duchess.
due *m* two; * *adj* two: — tutti e ~ both: — a ~ porte two-door.
duello *m* duel.
duetto *m* duet.
duna *f* dune.
duomo *m* cathedral.
duplicare *vt* to duplicate.
duplicato *m* duplicate.
duplice *adj* dual.
duplicità *f* duplicity.
durante *prep* during.
durare *vi* to last, wear.
durata *f* length, duration.
duraturo *adj* enduring, lasting.
durevole *adj* durable.
durevolezza *f* durability.
durezza *f* hardness.
duro *adj* hard, stiff; trying: ~ d'orecchio hard of hearing: ~ di cuore hard-hearted.

e *conj* and.
è *vi* he, she or it is.
ebano *m* ebony.
ebete *adj* half-witted; stupid.
ebbrezza *f* drunkenness; intoxication.
ebbro *adj* drunk: ~ di libertà drunk with freedom: ~ d'ira mad with anger: ~ di gioia beside oneself with joy: — d'amore drunk with love.
ebraico *adj* Hebrew; Jewish; of the Jewish creed.
ebrea *f* Jewess.
ebreo *m* Jew.
ecatombe *f* massacre.
eccedenza *f* excess.
eccedere *vt* to exceed.
eccellente *adj* excellent.
eccentricità *f* eccentricity.
eccentrico *m* eccentric; crank; freak; * *adj* eccentric.
eccesso *m* excess.
eccetto *prep* except.
eccezionale *adj* exceptional.
eccezione *f* exception.
eccitare *vt* to excite.
eccitante *adj* exciting.
eccitato *adj* excited, aroused.
ecclesiastico *adj* ecclesiastical.
eco *m* or *f* echo.
ecologia *f* ecology.
economia *f* economy, economics.
economico *adj* economical, inexpensive.
eczema *m* eczema.
edera *f* ivy.
edificio *m* building, edifice.
editore *m* publisher.
editoria *f* publishing house.
editoriale *m* editorial.
edizione *f* edition.
edonismo *m* hedonism.
educare *vt* to educate.

educato *adj* polite.

educazione *f* education; politeness; upbringing: —buona ~ breeding, good manners: —educazione fisica *f* physical education.

effeminato *adj* effeminate.

effetto *m* effect; spin.

effettuare *vt* to effect.

effigie *f* effigy.

effimero *adj* ephemeral.

egli *pron* he.

ego *m* ego.

egocentrico *adj* self-centred.

egoismo *m* selfishness.

egoista *m* or *f* egoist; * *adj* selfish.

egualitario *adj* egalitarian.

eiaculare *vt* to ejaculate.

elaborare *vt* to elaborate; to evolve; to hatch (a plot).

elasticità *f* elasticity.

elastico *adj* elastic; resilient; * *m* elastic; rubber band.

elefante *m* elephant.

elegante *adj* elegant; dressy; smart.

eleganza *f* elegance, smartness.

eleggere *vt* to elect.

eleggibile *adj* elegible.

elementare *adj* elementary.

elemento *m* element.

elencare *vt* to list.

elenco *m* list; directory: ~ telefonico *m* telephone directory.

elettorato *m* electorate.

elettricità *f* electricity.

elevare *vt* to elevate.

elezione *f* election.

elica *f* propeller.

elicoidale *adj* helicoidal.

elicottero *m* helicopter.

eliminare *vt* to eliminate; to remove.

elio *m* helium.

élite *f inv* élite.

ella *pron* she.

eloquente *adj* eloquent.

emancipare *vt* to emancipate.

emblema *m* emblem.

emblematico *adj* emblematic.

emendare *vt* amend.

emergenza *f* emergency.

emergere *vi* to emerge.

emigrante *m* or *f* emigrant.

emigrare *vi* to emigrate.

emigrazione *f* emigration.

emisfero *m* hemisphere.

emittente *f* transmitter.

emofilia *f* haemophilia.

emorroidi *fpl* haemorrhoids, piles.

emotivo *adj* emotional (person).

emozionante *adj* exciting, emotive (of films, plays, arts).

emozione *f* emotion.

enciclopedia *f* encyclopaedia.

endovenoso *adj* intravenous.

energia *f* energy.

energico *adj* energetic, spirited; strenuous.

enfasi *f* emphasis, stress.

enigma *m* enigma.

enigmatico *adj* enigmatic, cryptic.

enorme *adj* enormous, huge, tremendous, terrific.

ente *m* corporation.

entità *f inv* entity.

entrare *vi* to enter, go in, come in: —lasciare or fare ~ to admit: —questo non c'entra this doesn't enter into it.

entrata *f* entrance, entry, hall.

entroterra *m* inland.

epatite *f* hepatitis.

epidemia *f* epidemic.

Epifania *f* Epiphany.

epilessia *f* epilepsy.

epilettico *adj*, *m* epileptic.

episodio *m* episode, incident.

epoca *f* epoch, day, age.

equatore *m* equator.

equatoriale *adj* equatorial.

equazione *f* equation.

equino *m* horse; * *adj* of horses, equine: — una faccia ~ a horsy face: — una risata ~ horsy laughter.

equipaggiamento *m* equipment.

equipaggiare *vt* to fit out.

equipaggio *m* crew.

equità *f* equity.

equitazione *f* riding; horse-manship: — scuola di ~ *f* riding school.

equivalente *m* or *f* counterpart; * *adj* equivalent.

equivoco *m* misapprehension; * *adj* equivocal.

era *f* era, age, time; * *vi* he, she or it was.

erba *f* grass.

ereditare *vt* to inherit.

erezione *f* erection.

ergastolo *m* life imprisonment.

ergastolano(a) *m(f)* convict serving a life sentence.

ermellino *m* ermine, stoat.

erodere *vt* to erode.

eroe *m* hero.

eroico *adj* heroic.

eroina *f* heroine (female hero); heroin (drug).

erotico *adj* erotic.

errore *m* error; mistake; fallacy.

eruttare *vt* to erupt.

eruzione *f* eruption: — essere in ~ to erupt.

esagerare *vt* to exaggerate; to overstate.

esagonale *adj* hexagonal.

esagono *m* hexagon.

esame *m* examination; test.

esaminare *vt* to examine; to vet; to survey.

esattamente *adv* exactly.

esattezza *f* accuracy, exactness, exactitude.

esatto *adj* exact, accurate, spot-on.

esattore *m* collector: ~ delle imposte *m* tax collector.

esauriente *adj* exhaustive, comprehensive.

esaurientemente *adv* at length.

esaurimento *m* exhaustion: ~ nervoso *m* nervous break-down.

esaurire *vt* to deplete; to exhaust.

esaurito *adj* exhausted; spent; out of print.

esca *f* bait.

escandescenza *f* outburst of rage: — dare in escandescenze to flare up; to fly off the handle.

eschimese *adj* Eskimo: — * cane ~ *m* husky (dog).

esclamare *vt* to exclaim.

esclamazione *f* exclamation.

escludere *vt* to exclude, debar, except.

esclusione *f* exclusion.

esclusivo *adj* exclusive, select, sole.

escursionista *m* or *f* rambler.

esecutivo *adj* executive.

esecutore *m* executor.

esempio *m* example, instance.

esemplare *adj* exemplary.

esentare *vt* to exempt.

esenzione *f* exemption.

esercitare *vt* to exercise; to drill; to exert; to ply; * ~rsi *vr* to practise.

esercitazione *f* drill.

esercito *m* military, army.

esercizio *m* exercise, practice.

esibirsi *vr* to appear; to perform.

esibizionista *m* or *f* show-off; (medical) flasher.

esigente *adj* exacting, demanding.

esigenza *f* requirement.

esigere *vt* to expect; to demand; to exact.

esilio *m* exile.

esistenza *f* existence.

esistere *vi* to exist.

esitante *adj* hesitant; tentative.

esitare *vi* to hesitate; to dither.

esitazione *f* hesitation.

esodo *m* exodus.

esofago *m* oesophagus.

esonerare *vt* to excuse.

esorbitante *adj* exorbitant; extortionate.

esorcismo *m* exorcism.

esorcizzare *vt* to exorcise.

esortare *vt* to exhort.

esoterico *adj* esoteric.

esotico *adj* exotic.

esotismo *m* exoticism.

espandere *vt, vr* ~rsi, to expand.

espansione *f* expansion.

espansivo *adj* expansive, effusive, gushing; demonstrative.

espatriato *adj, m* expatriate.

espediente *m* expedient.

espellere *vt* to expel; to eject.

esperienza *f* experience.

esperimentare *vt* to experience.

esperimento *m* experiment.

esperto *adj* accomplished; experienced; expert; * *m* expert; adept; troubleshooter; pundit.

espirare *vt* to exhale.

esplicativo *adj* explanatory.

esplicito *adj* explicit.

esplodere *vi* to expode; * *vt* to blow up.

esplorare *vt* to explore; to prospect.

esploratore *m* explorer.

esplorazione *f* exploration.

esplosione *f* explosion; blast.

esplosivo *adj, m* explosive.

esponente *m* or *f* exponent.

esportare *vt* to export.

esportazione *f* export.

espositore *m* exhibitor.

esposizione *f* display, exposition; show; exposure.

esposto *adj* exposed.

espressione *f* expression.

espressivo *adj* expressive.

espresso *adj* express.

esprimere *vt* to express; to air; to phrase; to voice; * ~rsi *vr* to express oneself.

espropriare *vt* to expropriate.

esproprio *m* expropriation.

espulsione *f* expulsion, ejection.

essenza *f* essence.

essenziale *adj* essential.

essenzialmente *adv* essentially.

essere *vi* to be; * *m* being.

essi *pers pron* they.

essiccare *vt* to dry.

essiccato *adj* dried; desiccated.

esistenza *f* being.

esso *pers pron* it.

est *m* east; * verso ~ *adv* eastwards.

estasi *f inv* ecstasy; rapture: — * mandare in ~ *vt* to entrance.

estasiare *vt* to enrapture; to ravish.

estasiato *adj* rapturous.

estate *f* summer: — mezza ~ midsummer: — piena ~ the height of summer.

estatico *adj* ecstatic.

estendersi *vr* to reach; to range.

estensione *f* extent.

estenuante *adj* gruelling; wearisome.

esterno *adj* external, exterior; outside; outward; outer.

estero *adj* foreign; overseas; * all'~ *adv* overseas: — andare all'~ to go abroad.

esteso *adj* extensive.

estetico *adj* aesthetic.

estinguere *vt* to extinguish; to

write off.
estinto *adj* extinct.
estintore *m* (fire) extinguisher.
estinzione *f* extinction.
estirpare *vt* to extirpate.
estorcere *vt* to extort.
estorsione *f* extortion.
estradare *vt* to extradite.
estradizione *f* extradition.
estramurale *adj* extramural.
estraneo *adj* foreign; alien;
  extraneous; * *m* outsider.
estrarre *vt* to extract; to
  mine; to draw.
estratto *m* excerpt.
estrazione *f* extraction; draw:
  ~ mineraria *f* mining.
estremamente *adv* extremely.
estremista *m* or *f* extremist.
estremità *f* end, extremity.
estremo *adj* far; extreme;
  uttermost; * *m* extreme.
estrinseco *adj* extrinsic.
estrogeno *m* oestrogen.
estro *m* fancy; inspiration; bent;
  (zoological) oestrus, heat.
estroso *adj* inspired; freakish.
estroverso *adj*, *m* extroverted.
estuario *m* estuary.
esuberante *adj* exuberant.
esuberanza *f* exuberance.
esule *m* or *f* exile.
esultante *adj* elated, jubilant.
esultanza *f* elation, jubilation.
esultare *vi* to exult.
esumare *vt* to exhume.
età *f inv* age.
etere *m* ether.
eternamente *adv* forever.
eternità *f* eternity.
eterno *adj* eternal; everlasting;
  timeless.
eterodosso *adj* heterodox.
eterogeneo *adj* heterogeneous.
eterosessuale *adj*, heterosexual; (*sl*) straight.
etica *f* ethics.

etichetta *f* label; tag; etiquette.
etico *adj* ethical.
etimologia *f* etymology.
etimologico *adj* etymological.
etnico *adj* ethnic.
etrusco *m* Etruscan;
  * *adj* Etruscan.
eucalipto *m* eucalyptus.
Eucaristia *f* Eucharist.
eufemismo *m* euphemism.
euforia *f* euphoria.
euforico *adj* euphoric.
eunuco *m* eunuch.
eutanasia *f* euthanasia.
evacuare *vt* to evacuate.
evacuazione *f* evacuation.
evadere *vt* to escape; to break
  out; to abscond; * *vt* to evade:
  ~ le tasse, ~ le imposte to
  evade taxes.
evangelico *adj* evangelic(al).
evangelista *m* evangelist.
evaporare *vi* to evaporate.
evaporazione *f* evaporation.
evasione *f* evasion; escape;
  breakout; escapism.
evasivo *adj* evasive; non-
  committal.
evaso *m* escaped prisoner;
  runaway.
evasore fiscale *m* tax evader.
evento *m* occurrence.
eventuale *adj* eventual.
eventualità *f* eventuality.
evidente *adj* evident; plain;
  overt.
evirare *vt* to castrate.
evitabile *adj* avoidable.
evitare *vt* to avoid; to shun; to
  miss; to eschew.
evocare *vt* to evoke.
evocativo *adj* evocative.
evoluzione *f* evolution.
evolversi *vr* to evolve.
extra *adj* extra.
extra-coniugale *adj* extra-
  marital.

extrasensoriale *adj* extrasensory.

extraterrestre *m* alien.

F

fa *adv* ago: —quanto tempo fa? how long ago? * *vt* he, she or it does.

fabbisogno *m* needs

fabbrica *f* factory; mill; works.

fabbricante *m* manufacturer.

fabbricare *vt* to manufacture; to make; to fabricate.

fabbro *m* blacksmith.

facchino *m* (railway) porter.

faccia *f* face; side: — perdere la ~ to lose face.

facciata *f* façade.

facile *adj* easy; effortless.

facilità *f* facility; easiness.

facilitare *vt* to facilitate; to ease.

facilmente *adv* easily.

facoltà *f* faculty; school.

facoltativo *adj* optional.

facsimile *m* facsimile; fax.

factotum *m* factotum; jack of all trades.

faggio *m* beech.

fagiano *m* pheasant.

fagiolo *m* bean: ~ bianco *m* haricot.

fagiolino *m* French bean.

faglia *f* (geological) fault.

fai da te *m* do-it-yourself

faida *f* feud.

falce *f* scythe, sickle.

falco *m* hawk, falcon: ~ pescatore *m* osprey.

falconeria *f* falconry.

falconiere *m* falconer.

fallico *adj* phallic.

fallire *vi* to go bankrupt; to fail; * *vt* to miss: — (*sl*) ~ il colpo to miss the mark, to

muff the shot.

fallo *m* fault; phallus.

falò *m* bonfire.

falsario *m* forger; coiner.

falsificare *vt* to falsify, fake.

falso *adj* false, fake.

fama *f* fame.

fame *f* hunger.

famiglia *f* family, household.

famoso *adj* famous, famed, noted.

fanatico *adj* fanatic.

fanciulla *f* girl.

fanciullesco *adj* boyish.

fanciullo *m* boy.

fannullone *m* idler.

fango *m* mud.

fantasia *f* fantasy.

fantasma *m* ghost, apparition, phantom.

fantino *m* jockey.

fantoccio *m* puppet.

faraone *m* Pharoah.

farcire *vt* to stuff.

fare *vt* to do; to make: ~ lo stupido to act the fool: ~ male to hurt: ~ una passeggiata to go for a walk: · colazione to have breakfast: — che tempo fa? what's the weather like? — fa freddo it's cold.

farfalla *f* butterfly; bow tie.

farina *f* flour; meal.

farmaceutico *adj* pharmaceutical.

farmacia *f* pharmacy.

farmacista *m* or *f* chemist, pharmacist.

faro *m* lighthouse; beacon.

fascia *f* band; bandage.

fasciare *vt* to bind (up).

fascino *m* glamour, fascination, allure, charm, mystique.

fascio *m* sheaf.

fascismo *m* fascism.

fascista *m* or *f* fascist.

fase *f* phase.
fastidio *m* annoyance.
fastidioso *adj* troublesome.
fasto *m* pomp.
fasullo *adj* bogus, fake, phoney.
fata *f* fairy.
fatale *adj* fatal; vital.
fatalismo *m* fatalism.
fatica *f* fatigue; toil.
faticare *vi* to labour, toil, slog.
faticata *f* slog.
faticoso *adj* strenuous, uphill,
  tough, tiring, laborious.
fatidico *adj* fateful.
fatiscente *adj* derelict.
fattibile *adj* workable.
fattibilità *f* feasibility.
fatto *m* fact; * *pp* done;
  * ben ~ *adj* shapely.
fattore *m* bailiff; factor.
fattoria *f* farm.
fattorino *m* errand boy.
fattura *f* bill, invoice.
fatturare *vt* to invoice.
fatuo *adj* fatuous.
fauna *f* fauna.
fautore *m* campaigner.
fava *f* broad bean.
favo *m* honeycomb.
favola *f* fable.
favoloso *adj* fabulous.
favore *m* favour: — a ~ di for.
favorevole *adj* favourable;
  auspicious.
favorire *vt* to favour, further,
  farther; to advance; to be
  conducive to.
favoritismo *m* favouritism.
favorito *adj* favoured, favourite.
fax *m* fax.
fazione *f* faction.
fazioso *adj* factious.
fazzolettino *m*: ~ di carta
  tissue.
fazzoletto *m* handkerchief:
  — un ~ di terra a small
  allotment.

fazzolettone *m* bandanna.
febbraio *m* February.
febbre *f* fever.
febbrile *adj* feverish.
feccia *f* dregs, scum (also *fig*).
feci *fpl* faeces.
fecondare *vt* to fertilise.
fecondo *adj* fertile: — in età ~
  of childbearing age.
fede *f* faith, belief; wedding
  ring.
fedele *adj* faithful; true;
  regular; accurate; * *m* or *f*
  churchgoer, worshipper.
fedeltà *f* faithfulness, fidelity;
  accuracy.
fegato *m* liver: — avere ~ to be
  brave.
fegatoso *adj* (*sl*) brave,
  courageous.
felice *adj* happy.
femmina *adj*, *f* female.
femminismo *m* feminism.
fenice *f* phoenix.
fenicottero *m* flamingo.
feriale *adj* working; * giorno ~
  m weekday.
ferire *vt* to hurt, injure,
  wound.
ferita *f* wound; injury.
fermaglio *m* clip, paperclip.
fermare *vt* to wait; to stop; to
  stay.
fermata *f* stop; halt:
  ~ dell'autobus bus stop.
fermo *adj* firm; still.
feroce *adj* ferocious, fierce.
ferocia *f* ferocity, fierceness;
  savagery.
ferragosto *m* August bank
  holiday period (1-15 August)
  and 15 August in particular.
ferro *m* iron.
ferrovia *f* railway.
fertile *adj* fertile.
fesseria *f* nonsense: non dire ~!
  don't talk any nonsense!

41

m or *f*, *adj* idiot.
fessura *f* crack; slot.
festa *f* party, feast, festival; festivity, bank holiday: — * di ~ *adj* festive.
festeggiamenti *mpl* rejoicings.
fetido *adj* foetid.
feto *m* foetus.
fetta *f* slice.
fettuccia *f* tape.
feudale *adj* feudal.
feudo *m* fief.
fiamma *f* flame; pennant.
fiammifero *m* match.
fianco *m* side; flank.
fiasco *m* flask, fiasco; flop.
fibbia *f* buckle.
ficcanaso *m* or *f* nosey-parker; busybody; meddler.
fico *m* fig.
fica *f* (*vulg*) *see* figa.
fidanzamento *m* engagement; betrothal.
fidanzare *vt* to betroth.
fiera *f* fair; show.
figa *f* (*vulg*) pussy.
figata *f* (*vulg*) fun, great thing.
figlia *f* daughter.
figlio *m* son.
figo *m* (*sl*) a nice fellow, a good character.
figura *f* figure.
filamento *m* filament.
filantropia *f* philanthropy.
filantropo *m* philanthropist.
filastrocca *f* nursery rhyme.
filatelia *f* philately.
filetto *m* fillet.
filigrana *f* filigree; watermark.
film *m inv* film, motion picture, movie.
filmare *vt* to film.
filo *m* thread; string; wire; flex; (*sl*) fare il ~ a una ragazza to court a girl.
filologia *f* philology.
filosofia *f* philosophy.

filosofo *m* philosopher.
filtrare *vt* to percolate; to filter.
filtro *m* filter: — * con ~ *adj* filter-tipped.
finale *adj* final; eventual; finale.
finalista *m* or *f* finalist.
finalmente *adv* at last.
finanza *f* finance.
finanziare *vt* to finance; to fund.
finanziario *adj* financial.
finché *conj* until.
fine *adj* fine; acute; * *f* end; close; ending; finish: —senza ~ endless.
finemente *adv* finely.
finestra *f* window: ~ a saliscendi *f* sash window.
finezza *f* finesse.
fingere *vi* to fake, pretend; to sham.
finire *vt* to finish, to end.
finito *adj* over; through; finite.
fino *adj* fine; * ~ a *prep* until.
finocchio *m* fennel; (*sl*) gay man.
finto *adj* dummy, mock.
finzione *f* fiction, make-believe.
fionda *f* sling.
fiore *m* flower; bloom.
firma *f* signature.
firmare *vt* to sign, autograph.
fisarmonica *f* accordion.
fiscale *adj* fiscal.
fisica *f* physics.
fischio *m* whistle: —prendere fischi per fiaschi to get hold of the wrong end of the stick.
fisco *m* national revenue; tax office.
fisiologico *adj* physiological.
fisioterapia *f* physiotherapy.
fisso *adj* fixed; set; steady.

fittizio *adj* fictitious.

fiume *m* river, stream.

flaccido *adj* flabby, flaccid.

flanella *f* flannel.

flautista *m* or *f* flautist.

flauto *m* flute, recorder.

flemma *f* phlegm.

flessibile *adj* flexible; supple, limber.

flipper *m* pinball machine.

flora *f* flora.

floscio *adj* floppy.

fluido *adj*, *m* fluid.

fluire *vi* to flow.

fluorescente *adj* fluorescent.

fluoruro *m* fluoride.

fluttuare *vi* to fluctuate.

fobia *f* phobia.

foca *f* seal.

focale *adj* focal.

focena *f* porpoise.

focoso *adj* fiery, hot.

foglia *f* leaf.

foglio *m* folio, leaf (of paper), sheet.

fohn *m* hairdrier.

fondamentale *adj* fundamental, basic; seminal.

fondare *vt* to establish, found.

fondo *m* fund; bottom; sediment.

fondi *mpl* grounds.

fontana *f* fountain.

fonte *m* spring, source.

forbici *fpl* scissors: ~ per potare secateurs.

forca *f* gallows.

forchetta *f* fork.

foresta *f* forest.

forestale *adj* forest: —guardia ~ forester.

forfora *f* dandruff.

forma *f* shape; fitness; form: — in ~ fit.

formattare *vt* to format.

formazione *f* formation; education; background.

formica *f* ant; Formica.

formidabile *adj* formidable.

formoso *adj* curvaceous.

fornello *m* gas ring.

fornire *vt* to furnish, provide, supply.

fornitore *m* supplier, stockist, tradesman, purveyor.

fornitura *f* supply, provision.

forno *m* oven.

foro *m* forum; hole; market: ~ boario cattle market.

forse *adj* perhaps; * *adv* maybe.

forsennato *adj* frenzied; berserk.

forte *m* hard; loud; strong; (musical) forte.

fortezza *f* fortress, stronghold, strength.

fortificare *vt* to fortify.

fortificato *adj* walled.

fortiricazione *f* fortification.

fortuna *f* luck; fortune.

forza *f* force; might; power; strength.

forzato *m* convict to hard labour; * *adj* forced.

fossa *f* ditch.

fossile *m*, *adj* fossil.

foto *f inv* photo.

fotocopia *f* photocopy.

fotografare *vt* to photograph, snap.

fotografia *f* photograph, photography.

fottere *vt* (*vulg*) to fuck.

fra *prep* between.

frac *m* tailcoat.

fracasso *m* fracas, crash, smash, noise, racket.

fragile *adj* fragile, breakable, brittle.

fragola *f* strawberry.

fragranza *f* fragrance.

fraintendere *vt* to misunderstand.

frana *f* landslide.

franco *m* franc, frank;

* *adj* candid; straightforward.

francobollo *m* stamp, postage stamp.

frangetta *f* fringe.

frasario *m* phrase book.

frase *f* sentence; phrase.

frassino *m* (botanical) ash.

fratello *m* brother.

fraterno *adj* brotherly.

fratricida *m* or *f* fratricide; * *adj* fratricidal.

frattempo *adv*: —nel ~ in the meantime, meanwhile.

frattura *f* fracture.

fraudolento *adj* fraudulent.

frazione *f* fraction.

freccia *f* arrow; indicator: —mettere la ~ to indicate.

frecciata *f* gibe: —lanciare frecciate a qualcuno to gibe at someone.

freddo *adj* cold, chill; stand-offish; * *m* cold, chill.

fregare *vt* (*vulg*) to pinch, nick; to cheat; * *vr* (*sl*) ~rsene: —me ne frego! I don't give a damn!

fregata (marine) frigate; (*sl*) swindle, disappointment: *see* fregatura.

fregatura *f* rubbing; (*sl*) swindle; disappointment: —dare una ~ a qualcuno to swindle someone: —prendersi una ~ to be swindled; to be ripped off: —che ~! what a disappointment!

frenare *vt* to curb; to control; to brake.

freno *m* brake; curb.

frequente *adj* frequent.

fresco *adj* fresh; crisp; chilly; cool: — (of food) mettere in ~ to chill; essere in ~ to be in the fridge: — (of a person) essere al ~ to be in jail; finire al ~ to end up in jail.

fretta *f* hurry, haste, rush.

frigo *m* fridge.

frigorifero *m* refrigerator.

frittata *f* omelette.

frivolezza *f* frivolity; triviality; levity.

frizzante *adj* sparkling.

frizzare *vi* to fizz.

frodare *vt* to cheat; to defraud.

frode *f* fraud.

frodo *m*: —cacciare di frodo to poach.

fronte *m* front; *f* forehead.

frontiera *f* frontier.

frusta *f* whip.

frustrare *vt* to frustrate; to foil.

frutta *f* fruit.

fruttare *vi* to yield.

frutteto *m* orchard.

fruttifero *adj* fruitful.

fruttivendolo *m* fruiterer, greengrocer.

frutto *m* fruit: —frutti di mare *mpl* seafood.

fruttuoso *adj* fruitful.

fucilare *vt* to execute by shooting.

fucilazione *f* execution by shooting.

fucile *m* gun, rifle: ~ ad aria compressa air gun: ~ da caccia *m* shotgun.

fucina *f* smithy.

fuco *m* drone.

fucsia *f* fuchsia.

fuga *f* flight; escape; fugue: ~ romantica *f* elopement: ~ precipitosa *f* stampede.

fuggifuggi *m* stampede; scramble; rush.

fuggire *vt*, *vi* to flee; to abscond; to elope.

fuggitivo *adj*, *m* fugitive, runaway.

fulcro *m* hub, fulcrum.

fuliggine *f* soot: —granellino

di ~ *m* smut.

fulminare *vt* to electrocute:
~ con lo sguardo to wither
someone (with a glance).

fulmine *m* lightning, bolt of
lightning, thunderbolt.

fulmineo *adj* lighting; instant.

fulvo *m*, *adj* fawn.

fumante *adj* smoking.

fumare *vt* to smoke:
— vietato ~ no smoking.

fumatore *m* smoker.

fumetti *mpl* comics.

fumo *m* smoke; smoking.

fumoso *adj* smoky.

fune *f* rope.

funebre *adj* funeral; * carro ~
m hearse.

funerale *m* funeral.

funereo *adj* funereal.

fungo *m* mushroom:
~ velenoso *m* toadstool: ~ del
legno *m* dry rot.

funivia *f* cable-car.

funzionale *adj* functional.

funzionamento *m* function:
— cattivo ~ or malfunzion-
amento *m* malfunction.

funzionare *vi* to function; to
work: — far ~ to operate.

funzionario *m* official: ~ del
fisco tax assessor.

funzione *f* function; service.

fuoco *m* fire; focus: — al ~!
fire! fire! — (military)
~ incrociato crossfire;
cessate il ~ ceasefire; fuoco!
fire! — * resistente al ~ *adj*
fireproof: — fuochi
d'artificio fireworks: —
(medical, *sl*) fuoco di
Sant'Antonio or fuoco sacro
herpes zoster, shingles.

fuori *adv* outside; out; * *prep*
out: * ~ di *adj* outside.

fuoribordo *adj* outboard.

fuorigioco *adv* (sport) offside.

fuorilegge *m* outlaw.

fuoristrada *m* all-terrain
vehicle.

furberia *f* shrewdness.

furbizia *f* shrewdness.

furbo, furbastro, furbone *adj*
shrewd, cunning, artful.

furetto *m* ferret.

furfante *m* knave.

furgone *m* van.

furia *f* fury, rage.

furibondo *adj* wild, livid.

furiere *m* quartermaster.

furioso *adj* furious; raging:
— rendere ~ to infuriate.

furtivamente *adv* by stealth:
— procedere ~ to sidle.

furtivo *adj* furtive, stealthy,
surreptitious.

furto *m* theft; snatch; larceny:
~ con scasso burglary.

fusa *fpl* purr; * fare le ~ *vi* to
purr.

fusciacca *f* sash.

fusibile *m* fuse: — scatola dei
fusibili *f* fusebox.

fusione *f* fusion; merger:
— punto di ~ *m* melting point.

fuso *m* spindle; * *adj* molten.

fusoliera *f* fuselage.

fustigazione *f* flogging.

fusto *m* (botanical) stalk,
stem, trunk; * (*sl*) he-man.

futile *adj* futile, self-defeating.

futilità *f* futility.

futuro *adj* future; prospective;
coming; * *m* future.

G

gabbamondo *m* swindler.

gabbare *vt* to swindle.

gabbia *f* cage; hutch:
— * mettere in ~ *vt* to cage.

gabbiano *m* (sea)gull.

gabinetto *m* lavatory.

gagà *m* dandy.

gaglioffo *m* rascal.

gaio *adj* cheerful.

galante *adj* gallant.

galassia *f* galaxy.

galateo *m* book of good manners.

galeotto *m* convict; galley slave.

galera *f* galley; * (*sl*) jail.

galleggiare *vi* to float.

galleria *f* gallery, arcade; tunnel: ~ d'arte art gallery.

Galles *m* Wales.

Gallese *m* Welshman or woman; Welsh language; * *adj* Welsh.

gallina *f* hen.

gallismo *m* cocksure behaviour towards women.

gallo *m* cock, rooster.

gallone *m* gallon.

galoppare *vi* to gallop.

galoppo *m* gallop.

galvanizzare *vt* to galvanise.

gamba *f* leg: — in ~ smart, clever.

gambero, gamberetto *m* shrimp.

gancio *m* hook; catch; clasp.

ganghero *m* hinge: —andare fuori dai ~ to lose one's temper: —mandare fuori dai ~ to madden.

garage *m inv* garage.

garantire *vt* to guarantee; to ensure; to warrant; to go bail for.

garanzia *f* warranty.

garbato *adj* polite.

gargolia *f* gargoyle.

garofano *m* carnation.

gargarismo *m* gargle.

garrulo *adj* happy and talkative.

garza *f* gauze.

garzone *m* shop-boy, apprentice.

gasolio *m* diesel.

gassato *adj* carbonated:

— non ~ still.

gastronomia *f* gastronomy.

gatta *f* she-cat.

gattabuia *f* (*sl*) jail.

gattino *m* kitten.

gatto *m* cat, tomcat.

gazza *f* magpie.

gazzarra *f* din.

gazzetta *f* gazette.

gelare *vt, vi* to freeze.

gelataio *m* ice-cream vendor.

gelato *m* ice cream; * *adj* icy, frozen.

gelido *adj* icy.

gelo *m* frost.

gelosia *f* jealousy.

Gemelli *mpl* Gemini; twins.

gemello *adj, m* twin.

gemma *f* gem.

gendarme *m* policeman.

gene *m* gene.

generico *adj* generic.

generalità *f inv* generality.

generalizzare *vt* to generalise.

genere *m* gender; kind, sort, genus.

generosità *f* generosity.

gengiva *f* gum.

geniale *adj* brilliant, brainy.

genio *m* genius.

genitali *mpl* genitals.

genitore *m* parent.

gennaio *m* January.

genocidio *m* genocide.

gente *f* people, folk.

gentildonna *f* lady; gentle-woman.

gentile *adj* kind, nice, good.

gentilezza *f* kindness; polite-ness.

gentiluomo *m* gentleman.

genuino *adj* genuine, sterling.

geografia *f* geography.

geranio *m* geranium.

gerarchia *f* hierarchy.

germe *m* germ.

germicida *m* germicide;

* *adj* germicidal.
gesso *m* chalk; plaster; (medical) cast.
gestazione *f* gestation.
gesticolare *vi* to gesticulate; to wave.
gesto *m* gesture, sign.
gestore *m* manager.
Gesù *m* Jesus.
gettare *vt* to throw; to chuck; to sprout; to cast.
gettone *m* token.
ghetto *m* ghetto.
ghiacciaio *m* glacier.
ghiaccio *m* ice: ~ invisibile *m* black ice.
ghiacciolo *m* icicle; ice lolly.
ghiaia *f* gravel.
ghianda *f* acorn.
ghiandola *f* gland.
ghigliottina *f* guillotine.
ghirlanda *f* garland, wreath.
ghiotto *adj* greedy; gluttonous; (of food) delicious.
ghiottone *adj* glutton; gourmand; * *m* (zoological) wolverine.
già *adv* already; yet.
giacca *f* jacket: ~ a vento *f* anorak, windcheater.
giacinto *m* hyacinth.
giada *f* jade.
giallo *adj*, *m* yellow; (traffic lights) amber.
giardinaggio *m* gardening.
giardino *m* garden.
giarrettiera *f* garter.
gigante *m* giant.
gigantesco *adj* gigantic, monster.
giglio *m* lily.
ginecologo *m* gynaecologist.
ginepro *m* juniper.
ginocchio *m* knee.
giocare *vt*, *vi* to play.
giocatore *m* player: ~ d'azzardo gambler.

giocattolo *m* toy.
gioco *m* game; play.
gioia *f* joy, glee.
gioielliere *m* jeweller.
gioiello *m* jewel: — gioielli *mpl* jewellery.
giornale *m* (news)paper: ~ radio *m* news.
giornaliero *adj* daily.
giornalismo *m* journalism.
giornalista *m* or *f* journalist, columnist.
giornata *f* day.
giorno *m* day, daytime: ~ per ~ day by day: — di ~ by day: — buon ~ good morning; * un ~ *adv* sometime.
giostra *f* merry-go-round, carousel.
giovane *adj* young.
giovanotto *m* young man.
giovedì *inv* Thursday.
gioventù *f* youth.
giovinastro *m* hooligan.
giovincella *f* wench.
giovincello *m* lad.
giraffa *f* giraffe.
giramondo *m* or *f* globetrotter; wanderer.
girare *vt* to revolve; to spin; to turn.
girasole *m* sunflower.
girino *m* tadpole.
giro *m* tour; round; circuit; turn; walk; ride; run.
gita *f* jaunt; excursion; trip.
giù *adv* down: — in ~ downwards.
giubbotto *m* heavy jacket; coat.
giubileo *m* jubilee.
giubilo *m* exultation.
giudicare *vt* to judge; to deem; to adjudicate.
giudice *m* judge.
giugno *m* June.
giungla *f* jungle, wilderness.

giunta *f* junta.

giuntare *vt* to splice.

giuntura *f* join.

giuramento *m* oath.

giurare *vt* to swear, vow; * *vi* to swear.

giurato *m* juror.

giustamente *adv* right.

giustificare *vt* to justify.

giustificazione *f* justification.

giustizia *f* justice.

giustiziare *vt* to execute.

giusto *adj* right; just; fair; proper.

gli *art* the.

gli *pron* him, to him: ~ mando un libro I'm sending him a book; it, to it.

globale *adj* global; comprehensive; blanket.

globo *m* globe.

gnocco *m* dumpling.

gnomo *m* gnome.

gnu *m inv* gnu.

gobba *f* hump; humpbacked woman.

gobbo *m* humpbacked man; humpbacked.

goccia *f* drop, drip.

godere *vt* to enjoy.

godereccio *adj* pleasure-loving.

godinento *m* enjoyment.

gol *m inv* goal.

gola *f* throat, gullet; gorge.

golf *m* golf; (*sl*) sweater, pullover.

goloso *adj* greedy, glutton.

gomito *m* elbow.

gomma *f* rubber.

gonfiabile *adj* inflatable.

gonfiare *vt* to inflate; to swell.

gonfio *adj* swollen; puffy, bloated; * essere ~ di *vi* to bulge.

gonna *f* skirt.

gonorrea *f* gonorrhoea.

gonzo *m* dupe.

gorgogliare *vi* to gurgle.

gorilla *m inv* gorilla.

gotico *adj* gothic.

gotta *f* gout.

gradasso *m* boaster; braggart: fare il ~ to brag.

gradevole *adj* pleasant: ~ al palato palatable.

gradiente *m* gradient.

gradino *m* step.

gradito *adj* welcome; acceptable: — non ~ unwelcome.

grado *m* degree; grade; rank.

graduale *adj* gradual.

gradualmente *adv* little by little.

graduare *vt* to grade.

graffio *m* scratch.

graffiti *mpl* graffiti.

grafica *f* graphics.

grafico *adj* graphic(al); * *m* graph.

grammatica *f* grammar.

grammo *m* gramme.

grammofono *m* gramophone.

gramo *adj* miserable, wretched: tempi grami wretched times.

grana *f* grain; (*sl*) money.

grancassa *f* drum.

granchio *m* crab: — prendere un ~ to make a mistake.

grande *adj* big, large, great.

grandine *f* hail.

grandiosità *f* grandeur.

granito *m* granite.

grano *m* corn, wheat: — campo di ~ *m* wheatfield.

grasso *m* grease.

grasso *m* fat: ~ dell'arrosto *m* dripping: ~ di balena blubber; * *adj* fat, fatty: — piante grasse *fpl* succulent plants.

grassoccio *m*, *adj* plump.

gratis *adv* gratis.

gratitudine *f* gratitude, thankfulness.

grato *adj* grateful; apprecia-

tive; thankful.
grazia *f* grace; mercy.
grattacapo *m* (*fig*) headache.
grattacielo *m* skyscraper.
gratuito *adj* free; gratuitous.
grave *adj* grave; serious; acute.
gravità *f* gravity.
gravitare *vi* to gravitate.
gravitazione *f* gravitation.
grazia *f* grace
grazie *fpl* thanks.
greco *adj* and *m* Greek.
greggio *adj* unrefined, raw.
grembo *m* lap, womb.
grettezza *f* meanness.
gretto *adj* mean, narrow-
  minded.
grida *fpl* shouting.
gridare *vt*, *vi* to cry, shout.
grido *m* cry; shout: ~ di
  incoraggiamento *m* cheer.
griffone *m* griffin.
grigio *m* grey; * *adj* grey, drab.
griglia *f* grill: — cuocere alla
  ~ to grill.
grigliare *vt* to grill.
grigliata *f* mixed grill;
  barbecue.
grilletto *m* trigger.
grillo *m* cricket.
grinta *f* drive.
grondare *vt* to stream.
groppa *f* rump.
grossa *f* gross.
grossista *m* or *f* wholesaler.
grosso *adj* big; thick.
grossolanamente *adv* roughly.
grossolano *adj* gross; crude;
  earthy.
grotta *f* grotto; cave.
grottesco *adj* grotesque.
groviglio *m* entanglement,
  tangle.
gru *f inv* crane.
gruccia *f* crutch: —
  camminare con le ~ to walk
  on crutches; (coat)hanger.

grugnire *vi* to grunt.
grugnito *m* grunt.
grumo *m* clot, lump.
gruppo *m* group; cluster; batch:
  ~ sanguineo blood group.
gruzzolo *m* hoard; nest egg.
guadagnare *vt* to earn; to gain.
guadagno *m* gain; return:
  — guadagni *mpl* earnings.
guadare *vt* to ford.
guado *m* ford.
guai *mpl* trouble.
guaina *f* sheath.
guaio *m* scrape, fix.
guaire *vi* to whine.
guaito *m* whine.
guancia *f* cheek.
guanciale *m* pillow.
guanto *m* glove.
guantoni *mpl* boxing gloves.
guardacaccia *m inv* game-
  keeper.
guardacoste *m inv* coastguard.
guardalinee *m inv* linesman.
guardare *vt* to look; to watch:
  ~ i bambini to babysit.
guardaroba *m inv* wardrobe;
  cloakroom.
guardia *f* guard; watch: ~ del
  corpo bodyguard: — corpo di ~
  guardroom: ~ forestale
  ranger: — cane da ~ watch-
  dog: — fare la ~ to guard.
guardiano *m* watchman;
  keeper.
guaribile *adj* curable.
guarigione *f* recovery; cure.
guarire *vi* to recover; * *vt* to
  cure; to heal.
guarnigione *f* garrison.
guarnire *vt* to garnish.
guarnizione *f* gasket.
guastafeste *mf inv* spoilsport,
  killjoy.
guastare *vt* to vitiate; * ~rsi *vr*
  to go off, spoil.
guasto *m* breakdown.

guerra *f* war: ~ civile *f* civil
war.
guerriero *m* warrior.
guerriglia *f* guerrilla warfare.
guerrigliero *m* guerrilla.
gufo *m* owl.
guglia *f* spire.
guida *f* leader; guide; guidebook; driving; guidance;
runner.
guidare *vt* to drive; to guide;
to steer; to lead.
guidatore *m* driver.
guinzaglio *m* leash, lead.
gulasch *m inv* goulash.
guru *m inv* guru.
guscio *m* shell; husk: ~ d'uovo
m eggshell: ~ di noce *m*
nutshell.
gustare *vt* to relish.
gusto *m* flavour; taste; relish:
mangiare di ~ or ridere di ~
to eat or laugh heartily:
— di (buon) ~ tasteful: — di
cattivo ~ tasteless.
gustoso *adj* tasty.
gutturale *adj* guttural.

H

habitat *m inv* habitat; home.
hamburger *m inv* hamburger.
handicap *m* handicap.
handicappato *adj* handicapped.
harem *m inv* harem.
hascisc *m* hash(ish).
herpes *m inv* cold sore:
— herpes zoster *m* (medical)
shingles.
hi-fi *m inv* hi-fi.
hobby *m inv* hobby.
hockey *m* hockey.
hostess *f inv* stewardess.
hot dog *m inv* hot dog.
hotel *m inv* hotel.
house boat *f inv* houseboat.

I

ibrido *adj, m* hybrid.
iceberg *m inv* iceberg.
icona *f* icon.
idea *f* idea; notion.
ideare *vt* to conceive, to devise.
ideale *adj, m* ideal.
identico *adj* identical.
identificare *vt* to identify; to
equate.
ideologia *f* ideology.
idillico *adj* idyllic.
idiota *m* or *f* idiot; moron.
idoneità *f* fitness.
idrante *m* hydrant.
idrogeno *m* hydrogen.
iella *f* bad luck.
iellato *adj* unlucky
iena *f* hyena.
ieri *adv* yesterday.
igiene *f* hygiene.
ignizione *f* ignition.
ignorante *adj* ignorant.
il *def art* the.
illegale *adj* illegal.
illeggibile *adj* illegible.
illustrare *vt* to illustrate, to
show.
illustrazione *f* illustration.
imballaggio *m* packing.
imbarazzante *adj* embarrassing,
awkward.
imbarcare *vt* to embark; to
ship; * ~rsi *vr* to board.
imbecille *m* imbecile.
imbiancare *vt* to whitewash.
imboscata *f* ambush.
imboscato *adj* and *m* shirker;
draft-dodger.
imboschimento *m* afforestation.
imboschire *vt* to afforest.
imbottigliare *vt* to bottle;
(*fig*) to block.
imbottigliato *adj* bottled;
blocked: ~ nel traffico stuck

in the traffic jam.
imbottigliare *vt* to bottle.
imitare *vt* to imitate, imper-
sonate, copy, mimic.
immaginazione *f* imagination.
immagine *f* image.
immangiabile *adj* inedible,
unpalatable.
immaturo *adj* immature;
callow.
immediato *adj* immediate,
instant.
immenso *adj* immense.
immergere *vt* to immerse, to
sink; * ~rsi *vr* to to plunge or
dive into.
immerso *adj* immersed,
soaked, submerged.
immigrato *m* immigrant.
immigrazione *f* immigration.
immorale *adj* immoral.
immoralità *f* immorality.
immune *adj* immune.
imparare *vt* to learn.
imparziale *adj* impartial, fair,
unbiased, detached.
impaziente *adj* impatient.
impazienza *f* impatience.
impazzire *vi* to go mad:
— far ~ to madden.
impedire *vt* to stop, hinder.
impegnare *vt* to pledge, pawn;
* ~rsi *vr* to covenant.
impegno *m* commitment;
bond; engagement.
imperativo *adj* imperative.
imperatore *m* emperor.
imperatrice *f* empress.
imperdonabile *adj*
unforgivabie, inexcusable.
imperfetto *adj* imperfect.
imperiale *adj* imperial.
impermeabile *adj* impermeable;
waterproof; *m* mackintosh,
raincoat.
impero *m* empire.
impersonale *adj* impersonal.

impervio *adj* impervious.
impestare *vt* to foul.
impianto *m* plant: ~ elettrico
m wiring; *mpl* fixtures.
impiccione *m and adj* meddler;
busybody; nosey-parker.
impiegare *vt* to employ.
impiegato *m* clerk, office
worker.
impiego *m* job, position; use.
implicare *vt* to implicate,
imply.
implicazione *f* implication.
implicito *adj* implicit.
implorare *vt* to implore.
imponente *adj* imposing,
impressive, awe-inspiring.
imponibile *adj* taxable.
importante *adj* important;
momentous; weighty:
— il più ~ foremost.
importanza *f* importance:
— avere più ~ di to outweigh.
importare *vt* to import; * *vi* to
matter: — non importa it
doesn't matter: — non mi
importa I don't care.
importatore *m* importer.
importazione *f* import,
importation.
importo *m* amount.
impossibile *adj* impossible;
hopeless.
impossibilità *f* impossibility.
imposta *f* tax; levy.
impostazione *f* layout.
impotente *adj* impotent,
powerless.
impotenza *f* impotence.
impraticabile *adj*
impracticable.
impreciso *adj* imprecise.
impregnare *vt* to impregnate,
steep.
imprenditore *m* entrepreneur.
impresa *f* enterprise; deed;
exploit: — è un'~ it's no easy

task; firm.

impressionabile *adj* impressionable.

impressione *f* impression, feeling, hunch: — fare ~ to impress, to upset.

imprevedibile *adj* unforeseeable, unpredictable.

imprigionare *vt* to imprison, incarcerate.

imprimere *vt* to imprint.

improbabile *adj* improbable, unlikely.

improbabilità *f* improbability, unlikelihood.

improduttivo *adj* unproductive.

improvvisamente *adv* all at once.

improvvisare *vt* to improvise.

improvvisato *adj* improvised, impromptu.

improvviso *adj* sudden, snap.

impulsivo *adj* impulsive.

impulso *m* impulse, urge.

impunemente *adv* with impunity.

impunito *adj* unpunished.

impurità *f inv* impurity.

impuro *adj* impure.

imputare *vt* to indict.

imputato *m* defendant, accused.

imputazione *f* charge, indictment.

in *prep* in; into: — * in vettura *adv* aboard.

inabilità *f* inability.

inabitabile *adj* uninhabitable.

inaccessibile *adj* inaccessible.

inadatto *adj* inappropriate, unfit, unsuitable.

inadeguato *adj* inadequate.

inafferrabile *adj* elusive.

inalare *vt* to inhale.

inalterabile *adj* unalterable.

inammissibile *adj* inadmissible.

inanimato *adj* inanimate.

inatteso *adj* unexpected.

inattività *f* inactivity.

inattuabile *adj* unworkable.

inaugurale *adj* inaugural, maiden.

inaugurare *vt* to inaugurate.

inazione *f* inaction.

incandescente *adj* incandescent, white-hot.

incantare *vt* to enchant.

incantevole *adj* enchanting, ravishing.

incanto *m* charm.

incapace *adj* incapable, unable.

incarnazione *f* incarnation, embodiment.

incartare *vt* to wrap.

incassare *vt* to cash.

incendio *m* fire, blaze.

incenso *m* incense.

incertezza *f* uncertainty, suspense.

incerto *adj* unsure, uncertain, touch-and-go.

inchiesta *f* inquest, inquiry.

inchinarsi *vr* to bow.

inchiostro *m* ink.

incidente *m* accident.

incidenza *f* incidence.

incidere *vt* to incise; to engrave; to cut.

incidere su *vt* affect; to engrave on.

incinta *adj* pregnant, expecting.

incivile *adj* uncivil.

inclinare *vt* to tilt, slant.

includere *vt* to include.

incollare *vt* to glue, stick.

incolpare *vt* to blame.

incolto *adj* uncultivated, fallow; uneducated.

incomodare *vt* to inconvenience.

incomparabile *adj* incomparable.

incompatibile *adj* incompatible.

incompetente *adj* incompetent.

incompetenza *f* incompetence.

inconfondibile *adj* unmistakable.

inconscio *adj, m* unconscious.

incontestato *adj* unchallenged.

incontrare *vt* to meet, encounter.

incontro *m* encounter; meeting; match; (boxing) bout.

inconveniente *m* drawback.

incoraggiare *vt* to encourage.

incorniciare *vt* to frame.

incoronare *vt* to crown.

incorporare *vt* to incorporate.

incorruttibile *adj* incorruptible.

incredibile *adj* incredible, unbelievable.

incriminare *vt* to incriminate.

incrociare *vt* to cross.

incrocio *m* crossing, crossroads, junction; crossbreed.

incubo *m* nightmare.

incurabile *adj* incurable, terminal.

indagare *vt* to investigate, inquire (into).

indagine *f* investigation; survey.

indebolire *vt* to weaken, enfeeble; * ~rsi *vr* to weaken.

indecente *adj* indecent, rude.

indeciso *adj* undecided; indecisive; doubtful.

indecoroso *adj* unseemly.

indelebile *adj* indelible.

indennità *f* allowance; compensation.

indennizzare *vt* to indemnify.

indicazione *f* indication.

indice *m* index; forefinger, index finger.

indietro *adv* behind; back, backwards.

indifeso *adj* defenceless, unprotected.

indifferente *adj* indifferent, cold, uninterested, unmoved.

indigeno *adj* indigenous, native.

indigestione *f* indigestion.

indignato *adj* indignant.

indignazione *f* indignation.

indipendente *adj* independent; self-contained.

indiretto *adj* indirect.

indirizzare *vt* to address.

indirizzo *m* address.

indiscreto *adj* indiscreet.

indiscrezione *f* indiscretion.

indispensabile *adj* indispensable.

indistinto *adj* indistinct.

indistruttibile *adj* indestructible.

individuale *adj* individual, one-man.

indolenza *f* indolence, lethargy.

indossare *vt* to wear; to model.

indovinare *vt* to guess.

indubbiamente *adv* doubtless.

indubbio *adj* undoubted.

indulgenza *f* indulgence.

industria *f* industry, trade.

industrioso *adj* industrious.

inebriare *vt* to intoxicate.

inefficace *adj* ineffective, ineffectual.

inefficiente *adj* inefficient.

ineguaglianza *f* inequality.

ineguale *adj* uneven.

inesperto *adj* inexperienced; unskilful.

inespressivo *adj* expressionless.

inesprimibile *adj* inexpressible.

inetto *adj* inept.

infame *m or f, adj* infamous.

infamia *f* infamy.

infangare *vt* to soil (also *fig*); to taint.

infantile *adj* infantile, babyish, childish.

infanzia *f* infancy, childhood:
— prima ~ *f* babyhood.
infastidire *vt* to annoy,
bother.
infaticabile *adj* indefatigable,
untiring.
infatti *adv* indeed.
infatuazione *f* infatuation.
infedele *adj* unfaithful,
infidel; * *m* or *f* infidel.
infedeltà *f inv* unfaithfulness,
infidelity.
infelice *adj* unhappy, miserable.
infelicità *f* unhappiness.
inferiore *adj* inferior, lower.
infermiera *f* female nurse.
infermiere *m* male nurse.
infermo *adj* infirm; patient.
inferno *m* hell.
infestare *vt* to infest.
infettare *vt* to infect.
infettivo *adj* infectious.
infezione *f* infection.
infilare *vt* to thread; to string.
infiltrare *vt* to infiltrate;
* ~rsi *vr* to infiltrate (oneself).
infilzare *vt* to spike.
infine *adv* lastly.
infinità *f* infinity.
infinitivo *adj* infinitive.
inflazione *f* inflation.
inflessibile *adj* inflexible;
adamant.
influenza *f* influence; influenza.
informale *adj* informal, casual.
informare *vt* to inform.
informatica *f* computer
science.
informato *adj* knowledgeable.
informazione *f* information.
inframmezzare *vt* to inter-
sperse.
infrangere *vt* to infringe.
infrarosso *adj* infra-red.
infrastruttura *f* infrastructure.
infrazione *f* (minor) offence,
infraction.

infrequente *adj* infrequent.
infruttuoso *adj* unfruitful,
barren.
infusione *f* infusion:
— * lasciare in ~ *vt* to infuse.
infuso *m* infused; brew;
tisaned; (herbal) tea.
ingaggiare *vt* to engage.
ingannare *vt* to deceive, fool,
hoax, trick.
inganno *m* trick, deceit,
deception: — * trarre in ~ *vt* to
mislead.
ingegnere *m* engineer: ~ civile
m civil engineer.
ingegneria *f* engineering.
ingegnoso *adj* ingenious.
ingenuo *adj* naïve, ingenuous,
artless, simple.
ingiustizia *f* injustice.
ingiusto *adj* wrong, wrongful,
unfair, unjust.
ingoveirnabile *adj*
ungovernable.
ingozzare *vt* to guzzle.
ingrandimento *m* enlargement.
ingrandire *vt* to enlarge,
magnify.
ingrassare *vt* to fatten; * *vi* to
gain weight.
ingratitudine *f* ingratitude.
ingraziarsi *vr* to ingratiate
(oneself).
ingrediente *m* ingredient.
ingresso *m* entrance; admission,
admittance.
ingrosso *adj*: — * all'~ *adv*
wholesale.
inguine *m* groin.
inibire *vt* to inhibit.
inibizione *f* inhibition.
iniettare *vt* to inject.
iniezione *f* injection, shot.
inimicarsi *vr* to antagonise.
inimicizia *f* enmity.
inimmaginabile *adj* unimaginable, inconceivable.

inintelligibile *adj*
unintelligible.
ininterrotto *adj* unbroken,
uninterrupted.
iniquità *f* iniquity.
iniziale *f, adj* initial.
iniziare *vt* to begin, start; to
initiate; * *vi* to begin.
iniziativa *f* initiative, enterprise.
inizio *m* beginning.
innaffiare *vt* to water,
innamorare *vt* to enamour;
* ~rsi *vr* to fall in love.
innato *adj* innate, inborn.
innervosire *vt* to fluster.
inno *m* hymn, anthem.
innocente *adj* innocent.
innocenza *f* innocence.
innocuo *adj* innocuous,
harmless.
innovazione *f* innovation.
innumerevole *adj* innumerable,
countless.
inoculare *vt* to inoculate.
inoculazione *f* inoculation.
inodore *adj* odourless,
scentless.
inoffensivo *adj* harmless,
inoffensive.
inoltre *adv* furthermore,
besides, moreover.
inondare *vt* to inundate, flood,
swamp.
inondazione *f* inundation,
flood.
inopportuno *adj* inopportune,
unsuitable; ill-timed.
inorganico *adj* inorganic.
inorridire *vt* to horrify.
inorridito *adj* horrified;
shocked; appalled.
inospitale *adj* inhospitable.
inquietante *adj* disturbing;
disquieting; worrying;
alarming.
inquieto *adj* uneasy; nervous.

inquilino *m* tenant, occupant,
occupier.
inquinamento *m* pollution.
inquinare *vt* to pollute.
insalata *f* salad.
insalatiera *f* salad bowl.
insalubre *adj* unhygienic.
insegnamento *m* teaching.
insegnante *m* or *f* teacher;
m master, schoolmaster.
insegnare *vt* to teach.
inseguire *vt* to chase, pursue.
inseminazione *f* insemination.
insensibile *adj* insensitive,
unfeeling, callous.
inseparabile *adj* inseparable.
inserire *vt* to insert.
inserviente *m* attendant; odd-
job man; server.
insetto *m* insect.
insicurezza *f* insecurity.
insidioso *adj* insidious.
insieme *adj, adv* together.
insignificante *adj* insignificant.
insincerità *f* insincerity.
insincero *adj* insincere.
insinuare *vt* to insinuate;
* ~rsi *vr* to worm.
insipido *adj* insipid, flavour-
less, tasteless.
insistente *adj* insistent.
insoddisfacente *adj* unsatisfying.
insoddisfatto *adj* dissatisfied.
insolazione *f* sunstroke.
insolito *adj* uncommon,
unusual.
insolubile *adj* insoluble.
insonnia *f* insomnia.
insopportabile *adj* insuffer-
able, unendurable.
insormontabile *adj* insur-
mountable.
insostenibile *adj* untenable.
inspiegato *adj* unexplained.
instillare *vt* to instil.
insufficiente *adj* insufficient,

unsatisfactory.
insufficienza *f* insufficiency, deficiency.
insulare *adj* insular.
insulina *f* insulin.
insultare *vt* to insult, abuse; to revile.
insulto *m* insult.
insuperato *adj* unequalled.
insurrezione *f* insurrection, uprising.
intaglio *m* carving.
intarsiare *vt* to inlay.
integerrimo *adj* of the utmost integrity.
integrale *adj* complete, integral, (bread) wholemeal.
integrante *adj* integral.
intelletto *m* intellect.
intellettuale *m* or *f*, *adj* intellectual.
intelligente *adj* intelligent, clever.
intelligenza *f* intelligence, cleverness, wit.
intendere *vt* to intend, mean.
intenditore *m* connoisseur.
intensivo *adj* intensive.
intenzionale *adj* intentional.
intercettare *vt* to intercept; to tap.
interessante *adj* interesting.
interessare *vt* to interest; * ~rsi di *vr* to care about, to have an interest in something or someone.
interferire *vt* to interfere.
interiezione *f* interjection.
interiore *adj* inner, inward.
interlocutore *m* speaker.
intermediario *m* intermediary, go-between.
intermedio *adj* intermediate, in-between.
intero *adj* entire, whole.
interporre *vi* to interpose.
interpretare *vt* to interpret;

to render; to act.
interpretazione *f* interpretation, performance.
interprete *m* or *f* interpreter.
interrogare *vt* to interrogate, cross-examine; to quiz, question.
interrompere *vt* to interrupt.
interurbano *adj* long-distance.
intervallo *m* interval, interlude, break, recess.
intervenire *vt* to intervene.
intervista *f* interview.
intesa *f* understanding.
intestino *m* intestine; bowels; gut.
intimidire *vt* to intimidate.
intimità *f* intimacy.
intimo *adj* intimate.
intonacare *vt* to plaster.
intonaco *m* plaster.
intorno *adv* around; * ~ a *prep* about, around; round.
intorpidimento *m* numbness.
intossicazione *f* poisoning: ~ alimentare *f* food poisoning.
intraducibile *adj* untranslatable.
intralcio *m* hindrance.
intransigenza *f* intransigence.
intransitabile *adj* impassable.
intransitivo *adj* intransitive.
intrepido *adj* intrepid, fearless.
intricato *adj* intricate.
intrigo *m* intrigue.
intrinseco *adj* intrinsic, inherent.
introdurre *vt* to introduce.
introduzione *f* introduction.
introiti *mpl* income; revenue.
intromettersi *vr* to intrude, interfere.
introverso *m* introvert.
intrusione *f* intrusion.
intruso *m* intruder, inter-

loper, gate-crasher.
intuire *vt* to sense, divine.
intuito *m* intuition.
inumanità *f* inhumanity.
inumano *adj* inhuman.
inumidire *vt* to damp, dampen, moisten.
inutile *adj* useless, unnecessary.
inutilità *f* uselessness.
inutilizzato *adj* unused.
invalido *adj* disabled; invalid;
 * *m* invalid.
invano *adv* to no avail.
invariabile *adj* invariable.
invariato *adj* unchanged.
invasare *vt* to pot; to possess:
 — essese invasato dal
 demonio to be possessed by
 the devil.
invasione *f* invasion.
invasore *m* invader.
invece *adv* instead: ~ di in lieu
 of.
invecchiare *vi* to age; * *vt* to
 make old; to age: ~ il vino to
 age the wine.
inveire *vi* to rail (against).
invendibile *adj* unsaleable.
invenduto *adj* unsold.
inventare *vt* to invent; to make
 up; to concoct (a story).
inventario *m* inventory,
 stocktaking.
inventivo *adj* inventive.
inventore *m* inventor.
invenzione *f* invention.
invernale *adj* winter, wintry.
inverno *m* winter: — pieno ~
 the depth of winter.
inverosimile *adj* unlikely.
inversione *f* inversion,
 reversal.
inverso *m* converse;
 * *adj* inverse, reverse.
invertebrato *m* invertebrate.
invertire *vt* to reverse; to
 switch.

investigatore *m* investigator,
 detective.
investimento *m* investment.
investire *vt* to invest.
inveterato *adj* inveterate,
 confirmed.
invettiva *f* invective.
inviare *vt* to send, dispatch.
inviato *m* envoy.
invidia *f* envy.
invidiabile *adj* enviable:
 — poco ~ unenviable.
invidiare *vt* to grudge,
 begrudge.
invidioso *adj* envious.
invincibile *adj* invincible,
 unconquerable.
invio *m* dispatch.
inviolabile *adj* inviolable.
invisibile *adj* invisible.
invitante *adj* inviting.
invitare *vt* to invite; to ask
 out; to take out.
invitato *m* guest.
invito *m* invitation.
invocare *vt* to invoke.
involontario *adj* involuntary.
involontario *adj* inadvertent,
 accidental, unwitting,
 unintentional.
involtino (di carne) *m* (meat)
 roulade.
involontario *adj* unintentional.
invulnerabile *adj* invulnerable.
inzuppare *vt* to drench, soak,
 dunk.
inzuppato *adj* waterlogged.
inzuppare *vt* to soak; to dip.
io *pron* I.
iodio *m* iodine.
iperbole *f* hyperbole.
iperbolico *adj* hyperbolic(al).
ipersensibile *adj* hypersensitive.
ipersensibilità *f* hyper-
 sensitivity.
ipermercato *m* hypermarket.

ipersensibile *adj* hypersensitive.
ipertensione *f* hypertension.
ipnosi *f* hypnosis.
ipnotizzare *vt* to hynotise.
ipocondria *f* hypochondria.
ipocondriaco *adj* hypochondrial.
ipocrisia *f* hypocrisy.
ipocrita *adj, m* or *f* hypocrite.
ipoteca *f* mortgage.
ipotesi *f* hypothesis.
ipotetico *adj* hypothetical.
ippica *f* horse-racing.
ippico *adj* related to horse-racing.
ippocastano *m* horse-chestnut tree.
ippodromo *m* racecourse.
ippopotamo *m* hippopotamus.
ira *f* anger; rage.
iracondo *adj* choleric; irascible; quick-tempered.
irascibile *adj* irascible.
iride *f* iris.
ironia *f* irony.
ironico *adj* ironic.
irraggiungibile *adj* unattainable.
irragionevole *adj* unreasonable.
irrazionale *adj* irrational.
irreale *adj* unreal.
irrealizzabile *adj* unattainable; unrealisable.
irreconciliabile *adj* irreconcilable.
irrecuperabile *adj* irretrievable.
irregolare *adj* irregular.
irreligioso *adj* irreligious.
irremovibile *adj* unshakable.
irreparabile *adj* irreparable.
irreperibile *adj* untraceable.
irreprensibile *adj* blameless.
irrequieto *adj* restless; uneasy.
irresistibile *adj* irresistible.
irresoluto *adj* hesitating.
irresponsabile *adj* irresponsible, feckless.

irreversibile *adj* irreversible.
irriconoscibile *adj* unrecognisable.
irrigare *vt* to irrigate.
irrilevante *adj* immaterial.
irrisorio *adj* derisory; trifling: — un prezzo ~ a ridiculously low price.
irritante *adj* irritating.
irritare *vt* to irritate.
irritazione *f* irritation.
irriverente *adj* irreverent, disrespectfui, flippant.
irriverenza *f* irreverence.
iscrivere *vt* to enrol; * ~rsi *vr* to register.
iscritto *adj* enrolled; * *m* member.
iscrizione *f* inscription; enrolment; membership.
Islam *m inv* Islam.
isola *f* island, isle.
isolamento *m* insulation; isolation, seclusion.
isolare *vt* to insulate; to isolate.
isolato *m* block; * *adj* isolated: insulated.
ispirare *vt* to inspire.
ispirazione *f* inspiration.
isreliano *m* Israeli man; * *adj* Israeli.
israelita *m* Jew; * *adj* Jewish.
istante *m* instant.
isterico *adj* hysteric(al).
istigare *vt* to instigate.
istigazione *f* instigation.
istinto *m* instinct.
istituire *vt* to institute, establish.
istituto *m* institute.
istituzione *f* institution, establishment.
istmo *m* isthmus.
istrione *m* quack.
istruire *vt* to instruct, educate.

istruttivo *adj* instructive.
istruzione *f* instruction, education.
itinerario *m* itinerary, route.
IVA *f* (Imposta sul Valore Aggiunto) VAT.

J

jazz *m* jazz.
jeans *mpl* jeans; tessuto jeans *m* denim.
jeep *f inv* jeep.
jet *m inv* jet.
jolly *m* joker.
judo *m* judo.
juke-box *m inv* jukebox.

K

K.O. *m inv* knockout.
karate *m* karate.
ketchup *m* ketchup.
kilt *m inv* kilt.
kolossal *m* spectacular.

L

la *def art* the; * *pron* her.
là *adv* there.
labbro *m* lip.
labirinto *m* labyrinth, maze.
laboratorio *m* laboratory.
laborioso *m* laborious.
lacca *f* lacquer, hairspray.
laccio *m* (shoe)lace.
lacerare *vt* to lacerate.
lacrima *f* tear: — in ~e *fpl* in tears.
lacuna *f* gap.
lacunoso *adj* imperfect.
ladro *m* thief.
lago *m* lake, (Scottish) loch.
lagnanza *f* complaint.

lagnarsi *vr* to complain.
laguna *f* lagoon.
laicato *m* laity.
laico *m*, *adj* lay.
laim *m* lime.
lama *f* blade.
lamentare *vt* to lament.
lampada *f* lamp.
lampadina *f* lightbulb.
lampeggiare *vi* to flash.
lampo *m* flash; lightning.
lampone *m* raspberry, raspberry bush.
lana *f* wool.
lancia *f* lance, spear.
lanciare *vt* to throw.
lanterna *f* lantern.
lapide *f* gravestone; tablet.
lapis *m* pencil.
larghezza *f* width, breadth.
largo *adj* broad, wide.
laringe *f* larynx.
larva *f* larva.
lasciapassare *m inv* pass.
lasciare *vt* to leave.
laser *m inv* laser.
lassativo *m* laxative.
lastricare *vt* to pave.
lastricato *m* paving.
laterale *adj* lateral, side.
latifondo *m* large landed estate.
latifondista *m* landowner.
lato *m* side.
latrina *f* lavatory.
latta *f* can.
lattaio *m* milkman.
lattante *mf* suckling (baby); * *adj* unweaned.
latte *m* milk.
latteria *f* dairy.
latteo *adj* milky: — Via Lattea *f* Milky Way.
lattina *f* can, tin.
lattuga *f* lettuce.
laureato *m* graduate.
lavabo *m* washbasin.

lavagna *f* blackboard.
lavandino *m* basin.
lavare *vt* to wash.
lavastoviglie *f inv* dishwasher.
lavatrice *f* washing machine.
lavorare *vi* to work; * *vt* to carve: — lavorato a mano hand-carved.
lavoratore *m* worker.
lavoro *m* work.
leader *m* leader.
lebbra *f* leprosy.
lebbrosario *m* leper hospital.
lecca lecca *m inv* lollipop.
leccapiedi *m* or *f* bootlicker.
leccare *vt* to lick, lap.
lega *f* league.
legale *adj* legal, lawful.
legalità *f* legality.
legalizzare *vt* to legalise.
legare *vt* to tie.
legatoria *f* bookbinder's establishment.
legge *f* law.
leggenda *f* legend.
leggere *vt* to read.
leggero *adj* light, flimsy.
leggibile *adj* legible, readable.
legione *f* legion.
legislativo *adj* legislative: — corpo ~ *m* legislature.
legislazione *f* legislation.
legittimare *vt* to legitimise.
legittimità *f* legitimacy.
legittimo *adj* legitimate.
legna *f* wood.
legname *m* timber.
legno *m* wood.
lei *pron* her, she: — di lei hers: — Lei *pers pron* you (formal).
lenone *m* pimp.
lente *f* lens.
lentiggine *f* freckle.
lento *adj* slow.
lenzuolo *m* sheet.
leoncino *m* lion cub.
leone *m* lion.

leonessa *f* lioness.
leopardo *m* leopard.
lepre *f* hare.
lesbica *f* lesbian.
lesione *f* lesion; hurt.
lessare *vt* to boil.
lesso *adj* boiled; * *m* boiled meat.
lessico *m* lexicon.
letale *adj* lethal.
letame *m* muck.
letargico *adj* lethargic.
lettera *f* letter.
letterale *adj* literal.
letterario *adj* literary.
letteratura *f* literature.
lettino *in* cot.
letto *m* bed.
lettore *m* reader.
leucemia *f* leukaemia.
leva *f* lever; call-up, conscription: — soldati di ~ conscripts.
levataccia *f* early rising.
levatrice *f* midwife.
levriero *m* greyhound.
lezione *f* lesson.
li *pers pron* them.
lì *adv* there.
libbra *f* pound.
libellula *f* dragonfly.
liberale *adj* liberal.
liberare *vt* to liberate.
libero *adj* free, unattached, unoccupied.
libertà *f* liberty.
libertino *m*, *adj* libertine.
libidine *f* lust, lustfulness.
libido *f* lustfulness.
libraio *m* bookseller.
libreria *f* bookshop; bookcase.
libretto *m* libretto; booklet.
libro *m* book.
licenza *f* licence; leave.
licenziamento *m* dismissal.
licenziare *vt* to dismiss; * ~rsi *vr* to give up one's job.
licenzioso *adj* licentious.

lichene *m* lichen.
lieto *adj* pleased, glad, joyful, joyous.
lievitare *vi* to rise.
lievito *m* yeast.
lignaggio *m* lineage.
lillà *m inv* lilac.
lima *f* file.
limare *vt* to file.
limitare *vt* to limit.
limitazione *f* limitation, check.
limite *m* limit: ~ di velocità *m* speed limit.
limiti *mpl* bounds.
limonata *f* lemonade.
limone *m* lemon.
limousine *f inv* limousine.
limpido *adj* limpid.
lince *f* lynx.
linea *f* line; figure.
linfa *f* sap, lymph.
lingua *f* language; tongue.
linguaggio *m* language, speech.
linguetta *f* flap, tab.
linguista *m or f* linguist.
linguistica *f* linguistics.
linguistico *adj* linguistic.
linimento *m* liniment.
linoleum *m* linoleum.
liquidare *vt* to liquidate.
liquidazione *f* liquidation.
liquido *adj, m* liquid.
liquore *m* liqueur.
liquori *mpl* spirits.
lirico *adj* lyrical; operatic.
lisca *f* fishbone.
lisciare *vt* to smooth.
liscio *adj* smooth.
litania *f* litany.
lite *f* row.
litigare *vi* to argue.
litigio *m* quarrel.
litigioso *adj* litigious, quarrelsome.
litografia *f* lithograph, lithography.

litorale *m* coast.
litro *m* litre.
liturgia *f* liturgy.
liuto *m* lute.
livellare *vt* to level; to equalise.
livello *m* level.
livido *m* bruise; * *adj* livid:
— farsi un ~ *vt* to bruise.
livrea *f* livery.
lo *pron* him.
lobo *m* lobe.
locale *adj* local.
locali *mpl* premises.
località *f inv* locality.
localizzare *vt* to localise:
~ con esatezza to pinpoint.
locanda *f* inn.
locandiere *m* innkeeper.
locomotiva *f* locomotive, engine.
locusta *f* locust.
lodevole *adj* laudable.
logica *f* logic.
logo *m inv* logo.
logoramento *m* wear.
logorarsi *vr* to wear out.
logoro *adj* effete.
lombata *f* loin.
lombrico *m* earthworm.
longevità *f* longevity.
longitudine *f* longitude.
lontananza *f* distance.
lontano *adj* distant, far, faraway: — più ~ farthest.
lontra *f* otter.
loquace *adj* loquacious, talkative.
loquacità *f* loquacity.
loro *pers pron* you; them; * *poss adj* your(s), their; your(s).
lordo *adj* gross.
losanga *f* lozenge.
losco *adj* shifty.
lotta *f* fight.
lottare *vt* to fight, struggle.
lottatore *m* wrestler.
lotteria *f* lottery, draw.

lotto *m* lot.
lozione *f* lotion.
lubrificante *m* lubricant.
lubrificare *vt* to lubricate,
  grease.
lucchetto *m* padlock.
luccicare *vi* to glisten.
luccichio *m* gleam.
luccio *m* pike.
lucciola *f* firefly; (*sl*) prostitute.
luce *f* light.
lucente *adj* shining.
lucentezza *f* gloss, shine,
  sheen.
lucernario *m* skylight.
lucertola *f* lizard.
lucidare *vt* to polish, buff.
lucidato *adj* polished.
lucidata *f* polish.
lucido *adj* shiny, glossy; lucid;
  * *m* polish: ~ da scarpe boot
  polish.
lucrativo *adj* lucrative.
luglio *m* July.
lugubre *adj* lugubrious,
  mournful.
lui *pron* him, he.
lumaca *f* slug.
luminosità *f* brightness.
luminoso *adj* luminous,
  bright.
luna *f* moon.
lunare *adj* lunar.
lunatico *adj* moody.
lunedì *m inv* Monday.
lunghezza *f* length.
lungo *adj* long.
lungomare *m* esplanade,
  seafront.
luogo *m* place.
lupara *f* shotgun (originally
  used to shoot wolves).
lupanare *m* brothel.
lupo *m* wolf.
lupacchiotto *m* wolf cub.
lupetto *m* wolf cub.
luppolo *m* hop.

lusingare *vt* to flatter.
lussare *vt* (medical) to dislocate.
lussazione *f* dislocation.
lusso *m* luxury.
lussuoso *adj* luxurious.
lussureggiante *adj* lush,
  luxuriant.
lustrare *vt* to shine, polish.
lustrino *m* sequin, spangle.
lustro *m* lustre.
lutto *m* mourning; bereavement:
  — * in ~ *adj* bereaved.
luttuoso *adj* mournful.

M

ma *conj* but; yet.
macabro *adj* macabre; grim;
  sick.
macadam *m*: ~ al catrame *m*
  tarmac.
macerie *f* rubble.
machiavellico *adj*
  Machiavellian.
machiavellismo *m*
  Machiavellianism.
maccheroni *mpl* macaroni.
macchia *f* spot, smudge, stain.
macchiare *vt* to mark, stain.
macchiato *adj* spotted.
macchietta *f* little spot; (*sl*)
  eccentric person, character;
  oddball.
macchina *f* machine; car:
  ~ fotografica *f* camera.
macchinari *mpl* machinery.
macchinazione *f* machination.
macchinista *m* engine driver.
macedonia *f* fruit salad.
macellaio *m* butcher.
macellare *vt* to butcher,
  slaughter.
macelleria *f* butcher's shop.
macello *m* shambles.
macigno *m* boulder.
madre *f* mother.

madrelingua *f* native language.
madreperla *f* mother-of-pearl;
  nacre.
madrina *f* godmother.
maestà *f* majesty.
maestra *f* teacher, schoolmistress.
maestria *f* craftsmanship.
maestro *m* maestro; teacher,
  schoolmaster.
mafia *f* mafia.
mafioso *m* mafia man;
  * *adj* related to mafia.
maga *f* sorceress.
magazzino *m* warehouse.
maggio *m* May.
maggioranza *f* majority.
maggiordomo *m* butler.
maggiore *adj* elder, eldest;
  senior.
magia *f* magic.
magico *adj* magic.
magistrale *adj* masterly.
magistrato *m* magistrate.
maglia *f* jersey.
maglieria *f* knitwear.
maglietta *f* T-shirt.
maglione *m* jumper, sweater.
magnaccia *m* (*sl*) pimp.
magnanimità *f* magnanimity.
magnanimo *adj* magnanimous.
magnate *m* magnate, tycoon.
magnesio *m* magnesium.
magnetico *adj* magnetic.
magnificenza *f* magnificence.
magnifico *adj* magnificent,
  grand.
mago *m* magician, wizard.
magro *adj* thin, lean.
mai *adv* never, ever.
maiale *m* pig, pork.
maionese *f* mayonnaise.
maiuscola *f* capital letter.
malaria *f* malaria.
malato *adj* ill, sick, diseased.
malattia *f* illness, sickness,
disease, malady.
malavita *f* the underworld;
  the world of crime.
malavitoso *m* gangster;
  * *adj* criminal.
malcontento *adj*, *m* malcontent.
male *m* harm, wrong, evil.
maledetto *adj* damned,
  accursed, bloody.
maledire *vt* to curse.
maledizione *f* curse.
maleducato *adj* bad mannered,
  ill-bred.
maleducazione *f* rudeness.
malevolenza *f* ill-will.
malevolo *adj* malevolent,
  acrimonious.
malfamato *adj* low, seamy.
malgrado *prep* despite;
  * *conj* in spite of.
malinconia *f* melancholy.
malizia *f* malice.
malleabile *adj* malleable,
  pliable.
malloppo *m* swag.
malsano *adj* unhealthy.
malsicuro *adj* insecure.
malto *m* malt.
maltolto *m* ill-gotten property.
maltrattare *vt* to maltreat,
  mistreat.
malva *f* mallow; * *adj* mauve.
malvone *m* hollyhock.
mamma *f* (infant's) mummy.
mammalucco *m* (*sl*) simpleton.
mammella *f* breast; udder.
mammifero *m* mammal.
mammut *m inv* mammoth.
mancante *adj* missing,
  deficient.
mancanza *f* lack; deficiency.
mancare *vi* to miss; * *vi* to
  lack.
mancia *f* tip; gratuity.
manciata *f* handful.
mancino *adj* left-handed.
mandare *vt* to send.

mandarino *m* mandarin.

mandolino *m* mandolin.

mandorla *f* almond.

mandria *f* herd.

maneggevole *adj* manageable.

maneggio *m* riding school.

manesco *adj* rough; aggressive.

manette *fpl* handcuffs.

manganello *m* truncheon.

manganese *m* manganese.

mangereccio *adj* edible.

mangiabile *adj* edible.

mangiare *vt* to eat: — dare da
  ~ a to feed.

mangiata *f* feed.

mangiatoia *f* manger, crib,
  trough.

mangiucchiare *vt* to nibble.

mango *m* mango.

mania *f* mania, craze.

maniaco *adj* manic;
  * *m* maniac: ~ sessuale sex
  maniac.

manica *f* sleeve: — la M~ the
  English Channel.

manichino *m* dummy.

manico *m* handle.

manicure *f inv* manicure.

maniera *f* manner.

manifestare *vt* to demonstrate,
  manifest, evince.

manifestazione *f* demonstration,
  manifestation, show.

manifesto *m* manifesto,
  poster.

manipolare *vt* to manipulate.

maniscalco *m* farrier.

mano *f* hand.

manoscritto *m* manuscript.

manovra *f* manoeuvre.

manovrare *vt* to manoeuvre.

mansarda *f* attic.

mantella *f* cloak.

mantello *m* cape.

mantenere *vt* to maintain; to
  support.

mantenimento *m* maintenance.

manuale *m* handbook.

manutenzione *f* maintenance.

manzo *m* beef.

mappa *f* map.

mappamondo *m* globe.

maratona *f* marathon.

marca *f* make, brand.

marcato *adj* pronounced;
  rugged.

marcatore *m* marker.

marchiare *vt* to brand.

marchio *m* hallmark, trade-
  mark.

marciapiede *m* pavement.

marciare *vi* to march.

marco *m* mark (currency).

mare *m* sea.

marca *f* tide.

margarina *f* margarine.

marginale *adj* marginal.

margine *m* border, margin.

marijuana *f* marijuana.

marina *f* navy.

marinaio *m* sailor.

marinare *vt* (cookery) to
  marinade: ~ la scuola to
  bunk off school.

marino *adj* marine.

marito *m* husband.

marketing *m* marketing.

marmellata *f* jam: ~ di arance
  f orange marmalade.

marmo *m* marble.

marmocchio (*sl*) child.

marrone *adj* brown.

marsupiale *m*, *adj* marsupial.

marsupio *m* pouch.

martedì *m inv* Tuesday:
  ~ grasso *m* Shrove Tuesday.

martello *m* hammer.

martin pescatore *m* king-
  fisher.

martire *m* martyr.

martirio *m* martyrdom.

marzapane *m* marzipan.

marziale *adj* martial.

marzo *m* March.

mascalzone*m* scoundrel;
rascal; bastard.

mascara*m inv* mascara.

mascella*f* jaw.

maschera*f* mask.

mascherare*vt* to mask; to
disguise.

mascherata*f* masquerade.

maschiaccio*m* tomboy.

maschile*adj* male, masculine;
* *m* masculine.

maschilismo*m* male chauvinism.

maschilista*m* male chauvinist.

maschio*adj, m* male; (zoology)
buck.

masochista*m* or *f* masochist.

mass media*mpl* mass media.

massa*f* mass, body, bulk.

massacro*m* massacre,
slaughter.

massaggiare*vt* to massage.

massaggiatore*m* masseur.

massaggiatrice*f* masseuse.

massiccio*adj* massive.

massimo*adj* utmost, maximum.

masticare*vt* to masticate,
chew.

mastro*m* master: — libro ~ *m*
ledger.

masturbarsi*vr* to masturbate.

masturbazione*f* masturbation.

matassa*f* skein.

matematica*f* mathematics,
maths.

matematico*adj* mathematical;
* *m* mathematician.

materasso*m* mattress.

materia*f* matter; subject.

materiale*adj* material.

materialismo*m* materialism.

maternità*f* motherhood,
maternity.

matinée*f inv* matinée.

matita*f* pencil.

matrice*f* stencil.

matrigna*f* stepmother.

matrimoniale*adj* matrimonial: — letto ~ *m* double bed.

matrimonio*m* marriage.

mattatoio*m* slaughterhouse.

matterello*m* rolling pin.

mattina*f* morning, forenoon.

matto*adj* crazy: ~ da legare
crazy.

mattone*m* brick.

mattonella*f* tile.

mattutino*m* matins.

maturare*vi* to ripen.

maturità*f* maturity.

mausoleo*m* mausoleum.

mazzo*m* bunch.

mazzolino*m* posy, spray.

me*pron* me.

meccanica*f* mechanics.

meccanico*m* mechanic.

meccanismo*m* mechanism.

meccanizzaire*vt* to mechanise.

mecenate*m* or *f* patron.

medaglia*f* medal.

medaglione*m* medallion;
locket.

media*mpl* media; * *f* average;
* sopra la ~ *adj* above average.

mediatore*m* mediator; broker.

medicare*vt* to medicate.

medicato*adj* medicated.

medicina*f* medicine; drug.

medicinale*adj* medicinal;
* *m* drug.

medico*m* doctor.

medievale*adj* medieval.

medio*adj* average.

mediocre*adj* mediocre.

mediocrità*f* mediocrity.

meditare*vt* to meditate,
cogitate.

meditativo*adj* meditative.

meditazione*f* meditation.

mediterraneo*adj* Mediterranean.

medusa*f* jellyfish.

megalomane*m* or *f* megalo-
maniac.

meglio *adv* better, best.
mela *f* apple.
melagrana *f* pomegranate.
melanzana *f* aubergine.
melassa *f* treacle, molasses.
melma *f* slime.
melmoso *adj* slimy.
melodia *f* melody, tune.
melodioso *adj* melodious, tuneful.
melodramma *m* melodrama.
melone *m* melon.
membrana *f* membrane.
membro *m* member, fellow.
memorabile *adj* memorable.
memorandum *m inv* memorandum.
memoria *f* memory.
mendicante *m* or *f* beggar.
mendicare *vt* to beg.
meno *prep* less; minus.
menopausa *f* menopause.
mensa *f* canteen.
mensile *adj* monthly.
mensola *f* bracket; cantilever.
menta *f* mint.
mentale *adj* mental.
mentalità *f inv* mentality.
mentalmente *adv* mentally.
mente *f* mind: — di mente aperta *adj* open-minded.
mentire *vi* to lie.
mento *m* chin.
mentore *m* mentor.
mentre *conj* as, whereas, while.
menù *m inv* menu.
menzione *f* mention.
meraviglia *f* marvel.
meraviglioso *adj* marvellous, great, smashing.
mercato *m* market.
merce *f* merchandise.
mercé *f* mercy: — essere alla ~ di qualcuno to be left to the mercy of someone.
mercenario *adj*, *m* mercenary.
merceria *f* haberdashery.

merciaio *m* haberdasher.
merci *fpl* goods.
mercoledì *m inv* Wednesday.
mercurio *m* mercury, quicksilver.
merda *f* (*vulg*) shit.
merdaio *f* (*vulg*) dunghill; filthy place, pigsty.
meretrice *f* prostitute.
meridiana *f* sundial; * *adj*, *m* meridian.
meridionale *adj* south.
meringa *f* meringue.
meritare *vt* to merit, deserve.
merito *m* merit.
merlo *m* blackbird; very naïve person; fool, booby, dolt: — che ~! what a fool!
merluzzo *m* cod.
mescolanza *f* mix.
mescolare *vt* to mix.
mescolata *f* shuffle.
mese *m* month.
messa *f* mass.
messaggero *m* messenger.
messaggio *m* message.
mestolo *m* ladle, scoop.
mestruazione *f* menstruation.
metà *f inv* half.
metabolismo *m* metabolism.
metafisica *f* metaphysics.
metafora *f* metaphor.
metaforico *adj* metaphoric(al).
metallo *m* metal.
metallurgia *f* metallurgy.
metamorfosi *f inv* metamorphosis.
metano *m* methane.
meteora *f* meteor.
meteorite *m* meteorite.
meteorologia *f* meteorology.
meticcio *m* half-caste.
metodico *adj* methodical.
metodo *m* method.
metrico *adj* metric.
metro *m* metre.
metrò *m inv* underground

railway.
metropolitana *f* underground
  railway.
mettere *vt* to put.
mezzacalzetta *m* or *f* (*sl*)
  mediocre, feckless person.
mezzana *f* procuress; bawd.
mezz'ora *f* half-hour.
mezzaluna *f* half-moon,
  crescent.
mezzanino *m* mezzanine.
mezzanotte *f* midnight.
mezzo *m* middle, medium.
mezzogiorno *m* noon, midday.
mi *pron* me.
mia *poss adj* my.
microbo *m* germ, microbe.
microfono *m* microphone.
microonda *f* microwave.
microscopio *m* microscope.
midollo *m* marrow.
miele *m* honey.
miglio *m* mile; millet.
migliorare *vt* to improve; to
  better; * *vi* to improve.
migliore *adj* better, best,
  topmost; * *m* best.
migrare *vi* to migrate.
migrazione *f* migration.
milionario *m* millionaire.
milione *m* million.
milionesimo *m* millionth.
militante *m* or *f* militant.
militare *adj* military; * *vi* to
  militate.
mille *adj*, *m* thousand.
millennio *m* millennium.
millepiedi *m inv* centipede,
  millipede.
millesimo *adj*, *m* thousandth.
milligrammo *m* milligramme.
millilitro *m* millilitre.
millimetro *m* millimetre.
milza *f* spleen.
mimare *vt*, *vi* to mime.
mimo *m* mime.
mina *f* mine.

minaccia *f* threat, menace.
minacciare *vt* to threaten,
  menace.
minare *vt* to mine; to undermine.
minato *m*: — campo ~ mine-
  field.
minatore *m* miner, coalminer.
minerale *m* mineral.
minestra *f* soup.
mingherlino *m* weakling;
  * *adj* thin, skinny.
miniatura *f* miniature.
miniera *f* mine.
minima *f* minimum.
minimo *adj* least; minimal.
ministeriale *adj* ministerial.
ministero *m* ministry.
ministro *m* minister; clergyman: — Primo M~ *m* Prime
  Minister.
minoranza *f* minority.
minore *adj* minor, lesser,
  younger.
minuscolo *adj* tiny, minute.
minuto *adj* minute, tiny.
minuzioso *adj* thorough.
mio *poss adj* my; * *poss pron*
  mine.
miope *adj* short-sighted, near-
  sighted, myopic.
miopia *f* short-sightedness,
  myopia.
miracolo *m* miracle, wonder.
miraggio *m* mirage.
mirino *m* viewfinder, sight.
mirra *f* myrrh.
mirtillo *m* blueberry.
mirto *m* myrtle.
misantropo *m* misanthropist.
miscela *f* mixture, blend.
miscellanea *f* miscellany.
mischiare *vt* to blend.
miseria *f* poverty, want,
  misery.
misericordia *f* mercy.
misero *adj* poor.

misogino *m* misogynist.
missile *m* missile.
missionario *m* missionary.
missione *f* mission.
misterioso *adj* mysterious.
mistero *m* mystery.
misto *adj* mixed.
mistura *f* mixture.
misura *f* size; measure.
misurare *vt* to measure; to
  gauge.
mito *m* myth.
mitologia *f* mythology.
mitra *f* mitre.
mittente *m* or *f* sender.
mobile *adj* mobile, moving.
mobili *mpl* furniture, furnishings.
mobilità *f* mobility.
moccio *m* snot.
moccioso *m* snotty boy; brat;
  urchin; * *adj* snotty.
moda *f* fashion.
modellare *vt* to model,
  fashion.
modello *m* pattern; model;
  mock-up.
moderato *adj* moderate;
  sparing.
moderazione *f* moderation.
modernizzare *vt* to modernise.
moderno *adj* modern.
modestia *f* modesty.
modesto *adj* modest, unassuming.
modifica *f* modification.
modificare *vt* to modify.
modo *m* way; mode.
moffetta *f* skunk.
mogano *m* mahogany.
moglie *f* wife.
mohair *m* mohair.
molare *m* molar.
molecola *f* molecule.
molestare *vt* to molest.
molla *f* spring; * a ~ *adj*
  clockwork.

molle *adj* limp.
mollusco *m* mollusc.
molo *m* jetty, quay.
moltiplicare *vt* to multiply.
moltitudine *f* host, throng,
  multitude.
molto *adj* much.
molti *pron* many.
momento *m* moment.
monaco *m* monk.
monarca *m* monarch.
monarchia *f* monarchy.
monastero *m* monastery.
monastico *adj* monastic.
mondiale *adj* world, worldwide.
mondo *m* world.
monello *m* urchin; little
  scoundrel.
moneta *f* coin; currency.
mongolfiera *f* hot air balloon.
monolocale *adj*: —
  (appartamento) ~ *m* studio
  apartment.
monopolio *m* monopoly.
monotonia *f* monotony;
  sameness; flatness.
montaggio *m* assembling;
  (cinema) editing; (photo)
  montage.
montagna *f* mountain:
  — montagne russe big dipper.
montagnoso *adj* mountainous.
montare *vt* to assemble; to
  mount.
monte *m* mount: ~ di pietà *m*
  pawnshop.
montone *m* ram; sheepskin; *m*
  mutton.
monumentale *adj* monumental.
monumento *m* monument,
  memorial.
moquette *f* (fitted) carpet.
mora *f* bramble; blackberry;
  (*sl*) brunette.
morale *adj* moral.
moraleggiante *adj* sanctimo-
  nious.

moraleggiare *vi* to moralise.
moralità *f* morality.
morbido *adj* soft, smooth.
morbillo *m* measles.
morboso *adj* morbid.
mordere *vt* to bite.
morrina *f* morphine.
morire *vi* to die.
mortale *adj* mortal; deadly.
mortalità *f* mortality.
morte *f* death; dying.
morto *adj* dead.
mosaico *m* mosaic.
mosca *f* fly.
moscerino *m* gnat.
moschea *f* mosque.
moscone *m* bluebottle.
mostra *f* display; exhibition.
mostrare *vt* to show.
mostro *m* monster.
motel *m inv* motel.
motivo *m* reason, motive.
moto *f inv* (*sl*) motorbike.
motocicletta *f* motorcycle.
motolancia *f* launch.
motore *m* motor, engine.
motoscafo *m* motorboat.
motto *m* motto.
mousse *f inv* mousse.
movibile *adj* movable.
movimentato *adj* eventful, hectic.
movimento *m* movement,
  motion.
mucca *f* cow.
mucchio *m* heap, pile, mound,
  stack.
muco *m* mucus.
muffa *f* fungus, mildew, mould.
mughetto *m* lily of the valley.
mugnaio *m* miller.
mulino *m* mill: ~ a vento *m*
  windmill.
mulo *m* mule.
multa *f* fine: ~ per sosta
  vietata *f* parking ticket.
multare *vt* to fine.
multiplo *adj*, *m* multiple.

moltiplicazione *f* multiplication.
mummia *f* mummy.
municipale *adj* municipal.
municipio *m* town hall.
muovere *vt* to move.
murale *adj* mural.
muratore *m* bricklayer,
  builder, mason.
muro *m* wall.
musa *f* muse.
muschio *m* moss; musk.
muscolare *adj* muscular.
muscolo *m* muscle.
muscoso *adj* mossy.
museo *m* museum, gallery.
musicale *adj* musical.
musicista *m* or *f* musician.
mutabile *adj* fickle.
mutande *fpl* pants, knickers.
mutandine *fpl* panties, briefs.
mutante *adj*, *m* mutant.
mutare *vt* to change.
mutazione *f* mutation: —
  subire una ~ to mutate.

N

nailon *m* nylon.
naïf *adj* naïve.
nano *m* midget, dwarf.
narciso *m* narcissus.
narcotico *adj*, *m* narcotic.
narice *f* nostril.
narrativa *f* fiction.
nasale *adj* nasal.
nascita *f* birth.
nascondere *vt* to hide.
naso *m* nose.
nastro *m* ribbon; tape.
Natale *m* Christmas
natica *f* buttock.
nativo *m* native.
natura *f* nature.
naturale *adj* natural; unaffected.

naturalista *m* or *f* naturalist.
naufragio *m* (ship)wreck.
nausea *f* nausea.
nauseato *adj* sick, disgusted.
nautico *adj* nautical.
navale *adj* naval.
navata *f* nave, aisle.
nave *f* ship, boat.
nave scuola *f* training ship;
(*sl*) lady known for 'introduc-
ing' young men to the
secrets of Eros.
navetta *f* shuttle.
navigare *vt* to navigate.
navigazione *f* navigation.
nazionale *adj* national.
nazionalità *f inv* nationality.
nazione *f* nation.
né *conj* neither, nor.
nebbia *f* fog.
necessario *adj* necessary.
necrologio *m* obituary.
negare *vt* to deny.
negativa *f* (photographic)
negative.
negativo *adj* negative.
negligente *adj* negligent.
negoziante *m* or *f* shopkeeper.
negozio *m* shop.
negra *f* negress.
negro *adj*, *m* negro.
nemmeno *conj* neither.
neon *m* neon: —insegna al ~ *f*
neon light.
neonato *adj* newborn, baby.
nepotismo *m* nepotism.
neppure *conj* neither.
nero *adj*, *m* black.
nervo *m* nerve.
nervoso *adj* nervous, jumpy.
nessuno *pron* none, nobody.
netturbino *m* dustman.
neutrale *adj* neutral.
neve *f* snow.
nevicare *vi* to snow.
nicotina *f* nicotine
nido *m* nest.

niente *pron* none.
ninfea *f* waterlily.
ninnananna *f* lullaby, cradle
song: —cantare una ~ to sing
a lullaby.
nipote *m* nephew, *f* niece; *m* or
f grandchild.
nipotina *f* granddaughter.
nipotino *m* grandson.
nitido *adj* clear, sharp.
no *adv* no.
nobile *adj*, *m* noble.
nobiltà *f* nobility.
nocciola *f* hazelnut; * *adj* hazel.
nocciolina *f* peanut.
noce *f* walnut; *m* walnut tree.
nocivo *adj* noxious, harmful.
nodo *m* knot, crux.
nodulo *m* lump.
noi *pers pron* us, we.
noia *f* bore; boredom.
noioso *m* bore; * *adj* dull,
boring; annoying, troublesome.
nome *m* name, first name.
non *adv* not.
nondimeno *adv* nonetheless.
nonna *f* grandmother, granny.
nonno *m* grandfather,
granddad.
nono *adj*, *m* ninth.
nonostante *conj* in spite of.
nord *adj* north.
nordest *m* northeast.
nordovest *m* northwest.
norma *f* norm.
nostro *adj* our; * *pron* ours.
notaio *m* notary (public).
notifica *f* notification.
noto *adj* well-known; distinguished.
notorietà *f* notoriety.
notte *f* night.
notturno *adj* nocturnal.
novantesimo *adj*, *m* ninetieth.
nove *adj*, *m inv* nine.
novembre *m* November.

novità *f* novelty.
novizio *m* novice.
nozze *fpl* wedding.
nube *f* cloud.
nucleare *adj* nuclear.
nudista *adj*, *m* or *f* nudist.
nudità *f* nudity.
nudo *adj* nude, naked, bare.
numerale *m* numeral.
numerare *vt* to number.
numerico *adj* numerical.
numero *m* number.
nuocere *vt* to harm.
nuora *f* daughter-in-law.
nuotare *vi* to swim.
nuotata *f* swim.
nuovo *adj* new.
nutriente *adj* nourishing,
  nutritious.
nutrimento *m* nourishment.
nutrire *vt* to nourish.
nuvola *f* cloud.
nuvoloso *adj* cloudy.
nuziale *adj* nuptial, bridal.

O

o *conj* or, either.
oasi *f inv* oasis.
obbligatorio *adj* mandatory.
obbligo *m* obligation.
obeso *adj* obese, markedly
  overweight.
oblungo *adj* oblong.
oboe *m* oboe.
obsoleto *adj* obsolete.
oca *f* goose; silly girl or
  woman.
occasionale *adj* occasional.
occasione *f* occasion.
occhiali *mpl* glasses, spectacles.
occhiata *f* look, glance.
occhio *m* eye.
occidentale *adj* western.
occorrente *adj*, *m* requisite.
occupare *vt* to take up, occupy.

occuparsi *vr* to deal with, look
  after.
occupato *adj* busy; engaged.
oceano *m* ocean.
ocra *f* ochre.
oculista *m* or *f* oculist.
odiare *vt* to hate.
odioso *adj* hateful, horrid,
  odious.
odissea *f* odyssey.
odontoiatria *f* dentistry.
odore *m* odour, smell.
offendere *vt* to offend.
offensivo *adj* offensive.
offerta *f* bid, offer.
offesa *f* offence.
officina *f* garage, workshop.
offrire *vt* to offer.
offuscare *vt* to blur.
oggetto *m* object.
oggi *adv*, *m inv* today.
oggigiorno *adv* nowadays.
ogni *adj* every, each.
ognuno *pron* each, everybody.
oleandro *m* oleander.
oleoso *adj* oily.
olfatto *m* sense of smell.
oliare *vt* to oil; to lubricate
  with oil.
oliatore *m* oilcan.
olio *m* oil.
oliva *f* olive.
olmo *m* elm.
olocausto *m* holocaust.
oltre *prep* besides, aside from.
oltremare *adv* overseas.
oltremarino *adj*, *m* ultramarine.
omaggio *m* homage:
  — in ~ complimentary.
ombelico *m* navel.
ombra *f* shade, shadow.
ombrello *m* umbrella.
ombretto *m* eyeshadow.
omeopatia *f* homoeopathy.
omettere *vt* to omit.
omicida *m* or *f* murderer;
  * *adj* homicidal.

omicidio *m* murder, homicide.
omissione *f* omission.
omogeneità *f* homogeneity.
omogeneo *adj* smooth, homogenous.
omonimo *m* homonym, namesake.
omosessuale *adj*, *m* or *f* homosexual; gay.
onda *f* wave.
ondulato *adj* corrugated.
onere *m* burden, onus.
onestà *f* honesty.
onesto *adj* honest.
onnivoro *adj* omnivorous.
onorare *vt* to honour; to respect.
onorario *adj* honorary fee, retainer.
onore *m* honour.
onorevole *adj* honourable; ** m* or *f* member of Parliament.
opaco *adj* opaque, matt.
opale *m* or *f* opal.
opera *f* work, opera.
operaio *adj* blue-collar (worker).
operazione *f* operation, transaction.
operoso *adj* industrious.
opinione *f* opinion, belief.
oppio *m* opium.
opporsi *vr* to oppose.
opportunista *m* or *f* opportunist.
opportuno *adj* fitting, timely.
opposizione *f* opposition.
opprimente *adj* oppressive, heavy.
opprimere *vt* to oppress, burden.
optare *vt* to opt (for).
opulento *adj* opulent.
opzione *f* option.
ora *adv*, *conj* now; ** f* hour, time.
oracolo *m* oracle.
orale *adj*, *m* oral.
oralmente *adv* orally.

orario *m* timetable.
orbitare *vi* to orbit.
orchestra *f* orchestra.
orchidea *f* orchid.
ordinare *vt* to order; to ordain; to reserve; to book.
ordine *m* order, command; reservation.
orecchino *m* earring.
orecchio *m* ear.
orfano *adj*, *m* orphan.
organigramma *m* flow chart.
organismo *m* organism.
organista *m* or *f* organist.
organizzare *vt* to organise.
organo *m* organ.
orgasmo *m* orgasm, climax.
orgia *f* orgy.
orgoglio *m* pride.
orientale *adj* oriental, easterly, eastern.
orientare *vt* to orientate.
oriente *m* east.
orifizio *m* orifice.
origano *m* oregano.
originale *adj*, *m* original.
originalità *f* originality.
origine *f* origin.
orina *f* urine.
orinare *vi* to urinate.
orizzontale *adj* horizontal.
orizzonte *m* horizon.
ormone *m* hormone.
ornamentale *adj* ornamental.
ornato *adj* ornate.
ornitologo *m* bird watcher.
oro *m* gold.
orologio *m* clock.
oroscopo *m* horoscope.
orribile *adj* horrible, hideous.
orrore *m* horror.
orsetto *m* bear cub; teddy bear.
orsacchiotto *m* bear cub; teddy bear.
orso *m* bear.
ortensia *f* hydrangea.
orticaria *f* rash.

orticoltura*f* horticulture.
orto*m* vegetable garden,
  kitchen garden.
ortodossia*f* orthodoxy.
ortografia*f* spelling.
orzo*m* barley.
oscenità*f* obscenity.
oscillazione*f* swing.
oscurità*f* dark, darkness,
  blackness.
oscuro*adj* obscure.
ospedale*m* hospital.
ospitare*vt* to give hospitality.
ospite*m* or *f* host, guest,
  visitor.
osservanza*f* observance.
osservare*vt* to remark,
  observe.
osservatore*m* observer.
osservazione*f* remark,
  observation, comment.
ossidare*vt* to tarnish, oxidise.
ossigeno*m* oxygen.
osso*m* bone (*pl* [human] ossa,
  [animal] ossi); (*sl*) kernel:
  — essere all' ~ to have nothing:
  — ridurre qualcuno all' ~ to
  ruin someone: — essere pelle
  e ossa to be only skin and
  bones: — rompersi l' ~ del
  collo to break one's neck, to
  kill oneself (by accident):
  — in carne e ~ in flesh and
  blood, in person: — farsi le
  ossa to gain experience:
  — sputa l' ~! tell the truth!
ostia*f* (Christian) Host.
ostacolo*m* hurdle, obstacle.
ostaggio*m* hostage.
ostello*m* hostel.
osteopatia*f* osteopathy.
ostetrica*f* midwife.
ostile*adj* hostile, unfriendly.
ostilità*f* hostility.
ostinato*adj* obstinate, wilful.
ostinazione*f* wilfulness.
ostracizzare*vt* to ostracise.

ostrica*f* oyster.
ostruire*vt* to obstruct.
ottanta*adj, m* eighty.
ottantesimo*adj* eightieth.
ottavo*adj* eighth.
ottenere*vt* to gain, get, obtain.
otto*adj, m* eight.
ottobre*m* October.
ottone*m* brass.
ovaia*f* ovary.
ovale*adj, m* oval.
overdose*f inv* overdose.
ovest*m, adv* west, westward.
ovvio*adj* obvious.
oziare*vi* to laze.
ozono*m* ozone.

P

pace*f* peace, calm.
padella*f* frying pan; bedpan.
padre*m* father.
padrino*m* godfather.
padrona*f* mistress.
padrone*m* boss, master.
paesaggio*m* scenery, landscape.
paese*m* land, country, village.
paesino*m* hamlet.
pagamento*m* payment.
pagano*m* heathen.
pagare*vt* to pay.
pagina*f* page.
paglia*f* straw.
pagliaccio*m* clown.
paio*m* pair.
pala*f* shovel.
palazzo*m* palace, mansion;
  block of flats or offices.
palco*m* stage.
palestra*f* gym.
palla*f* ball: — (*vulg*) palle
  testicles: — ne ho le palle
  piene I can't stand it any
  longer; *see also* balla.
palloso*adj* (*fam* and *vulg*)
  boring.

pallacanestro *f* basketball.
pallavolo *f* volleyball.
pallido *adj* pale, wan.
pallone *m* ball.
paio *m* stake, goalpost.
pancetta *f* bacon.
pancia *f* belly, tummy.
panciotto *m* waistcoat.
pane *m* bread, loaf.
panificio *m* bakery.
panino *m* roll, sandwich.
panna *f* cream: ~ montata *f*
  whipped cream.
pantaloni *mpl* trousers.
pantofola *f* slipper.
panza *f* (*sl*) tummy: — che ~!
  what a tummy!
panzana *f* lie, tall story.
panzone *m* (*sl*) a (man with a)
  big tummy.
papà *m* (*inf*) dad(dy).
papero (a) *m* or *f* duck: — fare
  una ~ to make a slip.
Paperino Donald Duck.
pappa *f* mush, feed.
parabrezza *m inv* windscreen.
paragonare *vt* to liken,
  compare.
parare *vt* to shade.
parasole *m* sunshade.
parassita *m* or *f* parasite,
  hanger-on.
parcheggio *m* parking place.
parco *m* park: ~ comunale *m*
  common.
parecchio *adj* a lot; *pl* several;
  * *adv* a lot.
pareggiare *vt* to equalise,
  draw, tie.
pareggio *m* equalisation;
  balance; draw, tie.
parente *m* or *f* relation,
  relative.
parentesi *f inv* bracket.
parere *vi* to seem, to appear:
  — mi sembra che it seems to
  me that : — pare che it

appears that ; * *m* opinion:
  — a mio ~ in my opinion.
pari *adj* equal, even.
paria *m inv* untouchable.
parlamentare *m* or *f* member
  of Parliament.
parlare *vt, vi* to talk, tell, speak.
parodia *f* parody, travesty.
parola *f* word.
parolaccia *f* swearword.
parrucca *f* wig.
parrucchiere *m* hairdresser.
parsimonioso *adj* thrifty.
parte *f* part, share, side.
partecipare *vi* to participate.
partenza *f* departure.
particolare *adj* particular,
  special, especial, detail.
partire *vi* to leave, depart,
  start.
partita *f* lot, consignment;
  match, game.
parvenu *m inv* upstart.
Pasqua *f* Easter.
passare *vi* to pass, go by.
passatempo *m* hobby.
passeggiare *vi* to walk.
passeggiata *f* walk.
passeggiatrice *f* prostitute.
passerella *f* gangway, foot-
  bridge.
passero *m* sparrow.
passionale *adj* passionate,
  sultry.
passo *m* step, pace.
pastello *m* crayon.
pasticceria *f* cake shop.
pasticciere *m* confectioner.
pasticcino *m* cake.
pasticcio *m* pie.
pastiglia *f* lozenge.
pastore *m* shepherd; clergyman,
  vicar.
patata *f* potato.
patatina *f* crisp.
patente *f* licence: ~ di guida *f*
  driving licence.

patria *f* homeland.

patrigno *m* stepfather.

patrimonio *m* heritage, estate, wealth.

pattinare *vi* to skate.

paura *f* fear; * avere ~ di *vt* to fear: — mi fa ~ it scares me.

pauroso *adj* fearful, timid; cowardly.

pausa *f* pause, stop, rest.

pavimento *m* floor.

pazzo *adj* demented, mad, insane, lunatic.

pazzesco *adj* crazy; absurd; incredible.

peccare *vi* to sin.

peccato *m* shame, sin.

peccatore *m* sinner.

pecora *f* ewe, sheep.

peculiarità *f inv* idiosyncracy.

pederasta *m* paederast.

pedofilo *m* paedophile.

peggio *adj*, *adv*, *m* or *f* worse, worst.

peggiorare *vt* to worsen, compound.

peggiore *adj*, *m* or *f* worse, worst.

pelle *f* skin, leather.

pellicola *f* film.

pelo *m* hair, fur.

pena *f* punishment.

pendere *vi* to slant, hang, lean.

penna *f* pen; feather.

pennello *m* brush.

pennino *m* nib.

pensare *vt*, *vi* to think, expect: ~ a to think of, about.

pensiero *m* thought.

pensione *f* pension, retirement.

Pentecoste *f* Whit Sunday.

pentola *f* saucepan.

penzolare *vi* to swing.

pepe *m* pepper.

per *prep* for, from, to, through.

percepibile *adj* discernible, noticeable.

perchè *conj* why, because, what for.

perciò *adv* thus.

perdere *vt* to lose; to miss.

perdersi *vr* to get lost, go astray.

perdonare *vt* to forgive, condone.

perfetto *adj* perfect, flawless.

pericolo *m* danger.

pericoloso *adj* dangerous, unsafe.

periferia *f* suburbia, outskirts.

periferico *adj* outlying.

periodico *m* journal.

periodo *m* period, spell, time.

perizia *f* expertise, survey.

perlina *f* bead.

permanente *adj* permanent.

permesso *m* leave.

permettere *vt* to allow.

permissività *f* laxity.

permissivo *adj* lax.

pernacchia *f* raspberry: — fare una ~ to blow a raspberry.

perplesso *adj* puzzled, bemused.

persiana *f* shutter.

persistente *adj* lingering, niggling.

personaggio *m* character.

personale *m* staff.

persuadere *vt* to persuade, induce.

pesante *adj* heavy, hefty.

pesare *vt* to weigh.

pesca *f* fishing.

pescare *vt* to fish.

pesce *m* fish: — pesce rosso *m* goldfish.

pescecane *m* shark.

pescivendolo *m* fishmonger.

peso *m* weight, encumbrance.

pessimo *adj* wretched, lousy.

peste *f* plague; terror, scamp: — una ~ di ragazzo a pest of a boy.

pestifero *adj* pestilential;
stinking: —un bambino ~ a
pest of a child.
pestilenziale *adj* pestilential;
stinking.
peto *m* breaking wind.
petroliera *f* oil tanker.
petrolio *m* petroleum, oil.
pettinare *vt* to comb.
pettine *m* comb.
pettirosso *m* robin.
petto *m* breast, chest.
pezzo *m* piece, bit: —
un ~ d'uomo a big, tall man.
piacere *vt* to please: —mi
piace I like: —mi dispiace I
am sorry.
piacevole *adj* nice, agreeable.
piaga *f* cold sore; wound; (*sl*)
nuisance, pain in the neck.
piangere *vt*, *vi* to cry, weep.
piano *m* floor, storey.
pianta *f* map; plant.
pianto *m* cry.
piastrella *f* tile.
piastrellare *vt* to tile.
piattino *m* saucer.
piatto *m* plate, dish; turntable.
piazza *f* square; (*sl*) essere in ~
to have a bald head.
piazzale *m* forecourt.
piccante *adj* spicy, hot.
picchio *m* woodpecker.
piccione *m* pigeon:
~ viaggiatore *m* carrier
pigeon.
piccolino *adj* smallish.
piccolo *adj* small, little.
piede *m* foot.
piega *f* crease, fold, twist.
piegare *vt* to bend, fold;
* ~rsi *vr* to bend, fold.
pieno *adj* full.
pietanza *f* dish.
pietoso *adj* sorry.
pietra *f* stone.
pietrisco *m* grit.

pigna *f* pine-cone: —avaro
come una ~ very stingy.
pignolo *adj* fastidious, fussy.
pigro *adj* lazy, idle.
pila *f* battery, torch.
pilota *m* pilot.
pino *m* pine tree.
pinolo *m* pine-seed; pine kernel.
pioggia *f* rain.
pioimbo *m* lead.
piovere *vi* to rain.
piovra *f* octopus.
pipa *f* pipe.
pipì *f* (*sl*) pee: —far ~ to pee.
pipistrello *m* bat.
pisciare *vt* (*vulg*) to piss.
pisciata *f* (*vulg*) a piss: —fare
una ~ to take a piss.
pisciatoio *m* (*vulg*) urinal.
piscina *f* swimming pool,
baths.
pisolino *m* doze, nap: —fare
un ~ to take a nap.
pista *f* scent; track: ~ di
decollo take-off strip.
pistola *f* pistol, gun.
pittoresco *adj* scenic; picturesque.
più *adv*, *adj* more, most.
piuma *f* feather: —piume *fpl*
down.
piumino, piumone *m* duvet.
piuttosto *adv* rather.
pizzicare *vt* to nip, sting.
placenta *f* afterbirth.
plastica *f* plastic.
poco *m* a little; pochi *mpl* few.
podio *m* podium; platform.
poesia *f* verse.
poggiare *vi* to rest.
poi *adv* then.
poichè *conj* inasmuch as, for,
as, since.
polemico *adj* argumentative.
polena *f* (marine) figurehead.
polenta *f* maize porridge.
polizia *f* police.

poliziotto(a) *m(f)* policeman-(woman).

polizza *f* policy: —polizza d'assicurazione *f* insurance policy.

pollame *m* fowl.

pollice *m* inch; thumb.

pollo *m* chicken; (*sl*) naïve person: *see* merlo.

polmone *m* lung.

polo *m* pole: — P~ Nord *m* North Pole.

polso *m* wrist.

poltrona *f* armchair.

poltrone *m* lazy, indolent person; lazybones.

polvere *f* dust, powder.

polveroso *adj* dusty.

pomeriggio *m* afternoon.

pomodoro *m* tomato.

pompa *f* pump; pomp.

pompelmo *m* grapefruit.

pompiere *m* fireman.

ponente *m* west: — * di ~ *adj* westerly.

ponte *m* bridge.

popolo *m* people.

poppa *f* stern.

porcata *f* obscenity: — revolting food.

porcellana *f* china.

porcellino *m* piglet.

porcheria *f* filth, muck; obscenity; revolting food.

porcile *m* pigsty (also *fig*).

porco *m* pig, hog (also *fig*).

porta *f* door, gateway.

portacenere *m inv* ashtray.

portachiavi *m* key ring.

portaerei *f* aircraft carrier.

portafoglio *m* wallet.

portafortuna *m inv* mascot.

portare *vt* to wear; to carry; to take; to bring.

portauovo *m* eggcup.

portavoce *m inv* spokesman.

portiere *m* porter, doorman.

porto *m* port, harbour.

porzione *f* helping.

posizione *f* position.

possessore *m* holder.

possibile *adj* possible.

posta *f* post, mail: ~ aerea airmail.

posteggio *m* parking.

posteriore *adj* hind, hindquarters.

posto *m* seat.

potabile *adj* drinkable.

potere *vi* to be able to; * *m* power.

poveraccio *m* (*sl*) poor devil.

povero *m, adj* poor.

pozzo *m* well.

pranzare *vi* to dine.

pranzo *m* lunch, feast.

prato *m* meadow, lawn.

preavvertire *vt* to forewarn.

preavviso *m* notice.

precedente *adj* former.

preciso *adj* accurate.

precoce *adj* precocious.

prego *excl* not at all.

preferire *vt* to prefer.

prefisso *m* dialling code.

prematuro *adj* untimely, early; premature: — un bambino ~ a premature baby.

premere *vt* to squeeze.

premiare *vt* to reward.

premio *m* prize, award.

premura *f* rush.

prendere *vt* to take.

prenotare *vt* to reserve, book.

prenotazione *f* reservation.

preoccupare *vt* to worry, trouble.

presentatore *m* announcer, TV host, compère.

presentare *vt* to introduce.

presente *adj, m* present.

presentimento *m* foreboding.

preservativo *m* condom, sheath.

presidente *m* president, chairman.
pressione *f* pressure.
prestare *vt* to lend.
prestito *m* loan; * prendere in ~ *vt* to borrow.
presto *adv* early, soon.
pretendere *vt* to expect, claim.
prevalere *vi* to prevail.
prevedere *vt* to foresee, forecast.
prezioso *adj* valuable.
prezzo *m* price.
prigione *f* prison.
prima *adv* before.
primavera *f* spring, springtime.
primo *adj* first, early, former.
principale *adj* main, chief.
principe *m* prince.
principiante *m* or *f* beginner, learner.
principio *m* beginning, inception; principle, tenet.
privare *vt* to deprive.
probabile *adj* probable, likely.
problema *m* problem.
procedere *vi* to proceed.
processo *m* trial, process.
prodotto *m* product, commodity.
produzione *f* production, output, generation.
professionale *adj* professional, vocational.
professore *m* professor, teacher.
profilattico *m* condom; * *adj* prophylactic.
profondo *adj* deep.
pròfugo *m adj* refugee.
profumare *vt* to scent.
profumo *m* scent, smell.
progenitori *mpl* forefathers.
progettare *vt* to design.
progetto *m* design.
programma *m* programme, syllabus, schedule.

progresso *m* progress.
proiettile *m* bullet.
prolungare *vt* to lengthen, extend.
promotore *m* sponsor.
pronto *adj* ready: — pronto! *excl* (telephone) hello.
propenso *adj* inclined.
proporzionale *adj* proportional.
proporzionato *adj* commensurate.
proposito *m* intention.
proprietà *f* ownership.
proprietario *m* owner, landlord.
proprio *adj* own.
prosciutto *m* ham.
prossimo *adj* next.
proteggere *vt* to shield.
protestare *vt* to protest.
protezione *f* guard.
prova *f* test.
provare *vt* to rehearse; to feel; to try.
provenire *vi* to derive.
provvisorio *adj* temporary, interim.
prudente *adj* careful, cautious.
prurito *m* itch.
pubblicare *vt* to publish, issue.
pubblicazione *f* publication.
pubblicità *f* commercial, advertisement.
pubblico *m* audience.
pugnale *m* dagger.
pugno *m* fist.
pulce *f* flea: — il mercatino delle ~ car boot sale.
pulire *vt* to clean.
pulito *adj* clean.
pulsare *vi* to pulsate.
punire *vt* to chastise, discipline.
punta *f* tip.
punteggio *m* score.
punto *m* dot, point, stop, stitch.

pupazzo *m* puppet.

puro *adj* pure, sheer.

purtroppo *adv* unluckily.

putrefarsi *vr* to decay.

puttana *f* prostitute, whore.

puzzare *vi* to smell, stink, reek.

puzza *f* stench, reek, stink, smell: — fare una ~ to make a smell.

puzzle *m* (jigsaw) puzzle.

puzzo *m* see puzza.

puzzola *f* polecat.

puzzolente *adj* smelly, rank.

Q

qua *adv* here.

quacchero *adj, m* Quaker.

quaderno *m* exercise book.

quadrangolo *m* quadrangle.

quadrante *m* dial, face (of watch, etc), quadrant.

quadrato *adj, m* square.

quadrilatero *adj, m* quadrilateral.

quadro *m* painting, picture.

quadruplo *adj* quadruple, fourfold.

quaglia *f* quail.

qualche *adj* some.

qualcosa *pron* something.

qualcuno *pron* anybody, somebody.

quale *adj* what, which.

qualificare *vt* to qualify.

qualità *f* quality.

qualsiasi *adj* any; * ~ cosa *pron* whatever.

quantità *f inv* quantity.

quantitativo *adj* quantitative.

quanto *adj* how much; quanti how many.

quaranta *m inv* forty.

quarantena *f* quarantine.

quarantesimo *adj, m* fortieth.

quartetto *m* quartet.

quartiere *m* quarter.

quarto *m* quarter, fourth.

quarzo *m* quartz.

quasi *adv* almost, nearly.

quattordicesimo *adj, m* fourteenth.

quattordici *adj, m* fourteen.

quattro *adj, m* four.

quel *adj* that; * quelli *pron* those.

quercia *f* oak.

questo *dem adj, dem pron* this: — questi *dem adj, dem pron* these.

questione *f* question, matter.

qui *adv* here.

quietare *vt* to hush.

quindi *adv* therefore, consequently.

quindicesimo *adj* fifteenth.

quindici *adj, m* fifteen: — quindici giorni *m* fortnight.

quintetto *m* quintet.

quinto *adj, m* fifth.

quiz *m inv* quiz.

quota *f* quota, dues.

quotare *vt* to quote.

quotazione *f* quotation.

quotidiano *adj* daily; * *m* daily (newspaper).

R

rabbia *f* rabies; anger; * con ~ *adv* angrily.

rabbino *m* rabbi.

rabbioso *adj* rabid; angry, furious.

racchetta *f* racket.

raccogliere *vt* to collect.

raccolta *f* collection, set.

raccomandabile *adj* advisable.

raccomandare *vt* to recommend.

raccomandato *adj* recommended: — un ~ di ferro a

candidate who has friends in high places.

raccomandazione*f* recommendation.

raddoppiare*vt* to double.

raddrizzare*vt* to straighten, right.

radersi*vr* to shave.

radiante*adj* radiant.

radiatore*m* radiator.

radicale*adj* radical.

radicare*vi* to root.

radicato*adj* entrenched.

radice*f* root.

radio*f* radio.

radiografia*f* X-ray, radiography.

rafano*m* horseradish.

raffica*f* gust.

raffinare*vt* to refine.

raffinato*adj* polished, cultured; refined.

raffreddare*vt* to cool.

raffreddore*m* cold.

ragazza*f* girl.

ragazzo*m* boy, lad; boyfriend.

raggiante*adj* radiant, very happy.

raggio*m* spoke; radius; ray.

raggiungere*vt* to hit, reach.

raggruppare*vt* to group.

ragionare*vi* to reason.

ragione*f* reason, sense.

ragioniere*m* or *f* accountant.

ragnatela*f* web, spider web.

ragno*m* spider.

ramato*adj* auburn.

rame*m* copper.

ramo*m* branch, bough.

ramoscello*m* sprig, twig.

rampa*f* ramp.

rampante*adj* rampant.

rampicante*adj* creeper, climber; * *m, f* climbing tree.

rana*f* frog: — uomo ~frogman.

ranch*m inv* ranch.

rancido*adj* rancid, rank.

rancore*m* grudge, ill feeling, rancour.

rango*m* standing.

rantolo*m* rattle.

ranocchio*m* frog: — il principe ~ frog prince.

ranuncolo*m* buttercup.

rapa*f* turnip: — una testa di ~ a blockhead.

rapporto*m* report, relation, rapport.

rappresentare*vt* to represent.

rappresentativo*adj* representative.

rapsodia*f* rhapsody.

raramente*adv* seldom.

rarità*f* rarity.

raro*adj* rare.

raschiare*vt* to scrape.

raso*m* satin.

rasoio*m* razor: ~ elettrico*m* shaver.

rassegnato*adj* resigned.

rassicurare*vt* to reassure.

rata*f* instalment.

ratifica*f* ratification.

ratificare*vt* to ratify.

ratto*m* rat; abduction; rape: — il ~ delle Sabine the abduction or rape of the Sabine women.

rattristare*vt* to sadden.

ravanello*m* radish.

ravvivare*vt* to liven up.

razionalità*f* rationality.

razionare*vt* to ration.

razione*f* ration.

razza*f* race, strain, breed.

razzismo*m* racism.

razzista*m* or *f* racist.

razzo*m* rocket.

re*m inv* king.

reagire*vi* to react.

reale*adj* real, actual, royal.

reali*mpl* royalty.

realistico*adj* realistic, lifelike.

realizzabile *adj* feasible.

realizzare *vt* to realise, accomplish.

realtà *f* reality: — in realtà in fact.

reazionario *m* reactionary.

reazione *f* reaction.

rebus *m* puzzle.

recensire *vt* to review.

recensore *m* reviewer.

recente *adj* recent.

reception *f inv* reception.

recessione *f* recession.

recintare *vt* to enclose, fence.

recinto *m* fence.

recipiente *m* vessel, receptacle.

reciproco *adj* mutual, reciprocal.

reciso *adj* cut.

recitare *vt, vi* to recite.

reclamizzare *vt* to publicise.

reclusione *f* imprisonment, confinement.

recluso *adj* recluse.

record *m inv* record.

recriminare *vt* to recriminate.

redattore *m* editor.

redazionale *adj* editorial.

redditività *f* profitability.

reddito *m* income, revenue.

Redentore *m* Redeemer.

redenzione *f* redemption.

redigere *vt* to edit.

redine *f* rein.

referendum *m inv* referendum.

referenza *f* reference.

refettorio *m* refectory.

refrigerante *m* coolant.

refrigerare *vt* to refrigerate.

refrigerio *m* refreshment, coolness; relief, comfort.

regalare *vt* to give.

regale *adj* regal.

regalo *m* gift.

regata *f* regatta.

reggimento *m* regiment.

reggiseno *m* bra; brassière.

regime *m* regime.

regina *f* queen.

regionale *adj* regional.

regione *f* region.

registrare *vt* to register, record.

registratore *m* tape recorder, recorder.

regnare *vi* to rule, reign.

regno *m* kingdom.

regola *f* rule.

regolare *vt* to regulate.

regressivo *adj* regressive.

reincarnazione *f* reincarnation.

reintegrare *vt* to reinstate.

reinvestire *vt* to plough back.

reiterare *vt* to reiterate.

relativo *adj* relative.

relax *m* relaxation.

relazione *f* paper; relation, relationship.

religione *f* religion.

religioso *adj* religious, holy.

reliquia *f* relic.

relitto *m* wreck.

reminiscenza *f* reminiscence.

remissione *f* remission.

remo *m* oar.

remoto *adj* remote.

rena *f* sand.

renale *adj* renal.

rendere *vt* to render.

rene *m* kidney.

renna *f* reindeer.

reparto *m* unit, department.

reperto *m* exhibit.

repertorio *m* repertory, repertoire.

replica *f* repeat, replica.

reportage *m inv* report.

repressione *f* suppression, repression.

reprimere *vt* to suppress.

repubblica *f* republic.

reputazione *f* reputation.

requisire *vt* to commandeer, requisition.

rescindere *vt* to rescind.

residente*adj, m* resident.
residuo*m* reside; ** adj* residual.
resina*f* resin.
resinoso*adj* resinous.
resistente*adj* tough,
hardwearing.
resistere*vt* to resist, withstand.
respingente*m* buffer.
respingere*vt* to repulse, repel,
spurn, quash.
respirare*vt* to breathe.
respiro*m* breath.
responsabile*adj* responsible,
reliable.
responsabilità*f* responsibility,
liability.
restare*vt* to stay, remain.
restaurare*vt* to restore.
resti*mpl* remains.
restio*adj* reluctant.
restituire*vt* to give back.
resto*m* rest, change.
restringere*vt* to narrow;
* ~rsi *vr* to shrink.
restrittivo*adj* restrictive.
retata*f* roundup, catch, haul.
rete*f* net, network, grid.
rètina*f* retina.
retína*f* thin net.
rètore*m* orator.
retorica*f* rhetoric.
retorico*adj* rhetorical.
retribuzione*f* retribution.
retro*m* back.
retrodatare*vt* to backdate.
retrogrado*adj* retrograde.
retromarcia*f* reverse.
retrospettiva*f* retrospective.
retrovisore*adj* rear-view:
~ specchietto*m* rear-view
mirror.
rettangolo*m* rectangle,
oblong.
rettificare*vt* to rectify.
rettile*m* reptile.
rettilineo*adj* rectilinear.
rettitudine*f* righteousness,

rectitude.
retto*adj* straight; upright:
— intestino ~rectum.
rettore*m* vice-chancellor,
rector.
reumatico*adj* rheumatic.
revisione*f* review, service.
rianimare*vt* to revive.
riaprire*vt* to reopen.
riarso*adj* parched.
riassunto*m* summary,
résumé.
ribaltabile*adj* reclining.
ribattino*m* rivet.
ribellarsi*vr* to revolt, rebel.
ribelle*adj* rebel.
ribellione*f* rebellion.
ribes*m inv* redcurrant.
ricadere*vi* to relapse.
ricamare*vt* to embroider.
ricambiare*vt* to repay,
exchange.
ricaricare*vt* to recharge.
ricattare*vt* to blackmail.
ricchezza*f* wealth, richness.
riccio*m* hedgehog; ** adj* curly.
ricciolo*m* curl.
ricco*adj* wealthy, rich.
ricerca*f* research.
ricetta*f* prescription, recipe.
ricettario*m* cookery book.
ricevere*vt* to receive, get.
ricevimento*m* reception.
ricevuta*f* receipt.
richiedere*vt* to request,
require.
riconoscere*vt* to recognise,
know.
riconsiderare*vt* to reconsider.
ricoprire*vt* to recover, coat.
ricordare*vt* to recall, remember,
remind.
ricordo*m* souvenir.
ricorrente*adj* recurrent.
ricorrere*vi* to return.
ricorso*m* recourse, resort;
* far ricorso a*vt* to resort to.

ricreazione *f* recreation.
ricuperare *vt* to salvage, recover.
ridere *vi* to laugh, scoff.
ridicolo *m* ridicule;
  * *adj* ridiculous.
ridondante *adj* redundant.
ridotto *adj* diminished.
ridurre *vt* to reduce.
riduzione *f* cut, cutback, reduction.
riempire *vt* to fill, refill; to stuff.
rievocare *vt* to conjure up.
riferimento *m* reference.
riferirsi *vr* to refer.
rifiutare *vt* to refuse, turn down.
rifiuto *m* refusal.
rillessione *f* reflection.
riflessivo *adj* reflexive.
riflesso *m* reflection, reflex.
riflettere *vt* to think over, reflect.
riflettore *m* searchlight, floodlight, spotlight.
rifluire *vi* to ebb.
riflusso *m* ebb.
riforma *f* reform.
riformare *vt* to reform.
riformatorio *m* reform school; reformatory.
rifornire *vt* to stock.
rifugiato *m* refugee.
rifugio *m* shelter.
riga *f* stripe, line, (hair) parting.
rigare *vt* to streak, rule:
  ~ dritto to toe the line, to behave properly.
rigato *adj* lined.
rigetto *m* rejection.
righello *m* ruler.
rigidezza *f* rigidity.
rigidità *f* stiffness.
rigido *adj* rigid, stiff.
rigonfiamento *m* bulge.
rigore *m* rigour.

rigoroso *adj* stringent, rigorous.
riguadagnare *vt* to regain.
riguardare *vt* to regard, to reconsider.
rilasciare *vt* to release, issue.
rilassare *vt* to relax; * ~rsi *vr* to relax.
rilevamento *m* survey.
rilievo *m* relief.
riluttanza *f* reluctance, disinclination.
rima *f* rhyme.
rimanere *vi* to stay, remain.
rimbalzare *vi* to bounce, rebound.
rimborsare *vt* to refund.
rimediare *vt* to remedy.
rimedio *m* remedy.
rimettere *vt* to remit.
rimorso *m* remorse.
rimpiangere *vt* to regret.
rimunerazione *f* remuneration.
Rinascimento *m* Renaissance.
rincoglionire *vt* (*vulg*) to make someone become stupid or senile; * ~rsi *vr* to become stupid or senile.
rincoglionito *adj* (*vulg*) dazed; senile, gaga.
rinforzo *m* reinforcement.
rinfrescare *vt, vi* to freshen, refresh.
ringhiera *f* banisters.
ringraziare *vt* to thank.
rinnovare *vt* to refurbish, renovate.
rinoceronte *m* rhinoceros.
rinunciare *vt* to renounce, surrender.
rinvigorire *vt* to exhilarate.
riorganizzare *vt* to reorganise.
riparare *vt* to repair.
ripassare *vt* to revise.
ripasso *m* revision.
ripensare *vi* to think over.
ripetere *vt* to repeat.

ripiano *m* shelf.
ripido *adj* steep.
ripiegare *vt* to refold.
riposante *adj* restful.
riposare *vi* to rest, stand.
riprendersi *vr* to recover.
riprodurre *vt* to reproduce.
ripudiare *vt* lo repudiate.
ripugnante *adj* repulsive.
ripulsione *f* repulsion.
risata *f* laugh, laughter.
riscaldamento *m* heating.
rischiare *vt* to risk, venture.
rischio *m* risk, hazard, chance.
risciacquare *vt* to rinse, swill.
risciò *m inv* rickshaw.
riservare *vt* to reserve, book.
riso *m* rice; laughter.
risoluto *adj* resolute.
risparmiare *vt* to spare, save.
rispecchiare *vt* to reflect.
rispettare *vt* to respect.
rispondere *vi* to answer,
  respond.
risposarsi *vr* to remarry.
risposta *f* reply, response,
  retort.
ristagno *m* stagnation.
ristampa *f* reprint, reissue.
ristorante *m* restaurant.
ristrutturare *vt* to convert.
risultare *vi* to result, emerge.
risultato *m* result.
risuscitare *vt* to resuscitate.
risvolto *m* lapel.
ritagliare *vt* to clip.
ritardare *vt* to hold up, delay.
ritardato *adj* retarded.
ritardo *m* delay; * in ~ *adj* late.
ritirare *vt* to withdraw,
  retract.
ritiro *m* withdrawal.
ritmo *m* rhythm, beat, swing.
rito *m* rite, ceremonial.
ritornare *vi* to revert, go
  back.
ritornello *m* chorus, refrain.

ritorno *m* return.
ritratto *m* portrait.
rituale *adj, m* ritual.
riunione *f* meeting, reunion.
riunire *vt* to rally, reunite.
riuscire *vi* to succeed.
riva *f* bank (river): — riva del
  mare *f* seashore.
rivale *adj, m* rival.
rivedere *vt* to revise.
rivelare *vt* to give away,
  disclose, reveal.
rivestimento *m* facing, casing.
rivestire *vt* to cover.
rivista *f* magazine, review.
rivolta *f* revolt.
rivoltante *adj* revolting.
rivoltare *vt* to turn over
  (again); revolt; * ~rsi *vr* to
  revolt against.
rivoluzionario *adj, m* revolutionary.
rivoluzione *f* revolution.
rizzarsi *vi* to bristle.
roano *m* roan.
roba *f* stuff, things: — che ~!
  what a mess! ~ da chiodi! or ~
  da matti! madness! — robe da
  non credersi! unbelivable!
robot *m inv* robot.
robusto *adj* sturdy.
robustezza *f* sturdiness.
roccia *f* rock.
roditore *m* rodent.
rododendro *m* rhododendron.
rognone *m* kidney.
romantico *adj* romantic.
romanziere *m* novelist.
romanzo *m* novel.
rompere *vt* to snap, break.
rompicoglioni *m (vulg) see*
  palle
rompipalle *m (vulg) see* palle
rondella *f* washer.
rondine *f* swallow.
rondone *m* swift.
rosa *f* rose; * *adj* pink.

rosario *m* rosary.
rosbif *m* roast beef.
rosicchiare *vt* to gnaw, nibble.
rosmarino *m* rosemary.
rospo *m* toad.
rossetto *m* lipstick.
rosso *adj*, *m* red.
rosticceria *f* (roasts) take-away.
rotare *vi* to rotate.
rotatoria *f* roundabout.
roteare *vi* to gyrate.
rotella *f* caster, roller.
rotolare *vt*, *vi* to roll; * ~rsi *vr*
  to wallow.
rotondo *adj* round.
rotula *f* kneecap.
roulotte *f inv* caravan.
round *m inv* round.
routine *f* routine.
rovente *adj* red-hot, glowing.
rovescia *f* lapel; * alla ~ *adj*
  inside-out.
rovina *f* ruin, undoing,
  downfall.
rovinare *vt* to spoil, ruin.
rovo *m* bramble bush.
rubacuori *m* lady-killer,
  charmer; heart-breaker.
rubare *vt* to steal.
rubinetto *m* tap, (water) cock.
rublo *m* rouble.
rubrica *f* rubric.
rudere *m* ruin(s).
rudimentale *adj* rough and
  ready.
rudimento *m* rudiment.
ruffiano *m*, *adj* pimp; go-
  between; toady.
ruga *f* wrinkle, line.
rugby *m* rugby.
ruggire *vi* to roar.
rugiada *few*.
rullino *m* film, roll.
rum *m inv* rum.
rumore *m* noise, sound.
ruolo *m* role.
ruota *f* wheel.

rurale *adj* rural.
russare *vi* to snore.
russo *m* Russian.
rustico *adj* rustic.
ruttare *vi* to belch, burp.
rutto *m* burp, belch.
ruvidità *f* roughness.
ruvido *adj* rough, coarse.
ruzzolare *vi* to tumble.

S

sabato *m* Saturday, Sabbath.
sabbia *f* sand.
sabbioso *adj* sandy.
sabotaggio *m* sabotage.
sabotare *vt* to sabotage.
saccarina *f* saccharin.
saccheggiare *vt* to sack, raid,
  pillage.
sacchetto *m* carrier bag, bag.
sacco *m* sack: ~ a pelo *m*
  sleeping bag.
sacerdote *m* priest.
sacramento *m* sacrament.
sacrificare *vt* to sacrifice.
sacrificio *m* sacrifice.
sacrilegio *m* sacrilege.
sacro *adj* sacred.
sadico *m* sadist.
sadico *adj* sadistic.
sadismo *m* sadism.
safari *m inv* safari.
saga *f* saga.
saggio *adj* wise; * *m* essay;
  sage.
Sagittario *m* Sagittarius.
sagoma *f* silhouette, tem-
  plate.
sagrestano *m* sacristan.
sagrestia *f* vestry.
sala *f* room, hall.
salame *m* salami, sausage.
salare *vt* to salt, cure.
salariato *m* wage-earner.
salato *adj* savoury, salty.

saldare *vt* to weld, solder; to settle.

saldarsi *vr* to set.

saldo *adj* steady, firm.

sale *m* salt.

salice *m* willow.

salicone *m* pussy willow.

saliente *adj* salient.

saliera *f* salt cellar.

salino *adj* saline.

salire *vi* to ascend.

salita *f* rise, climb, slope.

saliva *f* saliva.

salivare *vi* to salivate.

salma *f* corpse.

salino *m* psalm.

salmone *m* salmon.

salnitro *m* saltpetre (potassium nitrate).

salone *m* salon, saloon, lounge, hall.

saloon *m inv* saloon.

salopette *f inv* dungarees.

salotto *m* parlour, sitting room.

salsa *f* sauce: ~ indiana *f* chutney.

salsiccia *f* sausage.

saltare *vt, vi* to jump.

saltatore *m* jumper.

saltuario *adj* casual (labour).

salubre *adj* wholesome, salubrious.

salumeria *f* delicatessen.

salutare *adj* salutary; * *vt* to salute, greet.

salute *f* health.

saluto *m* greeting, salute.

salva *f* salvo.

salvadanaio *m* piggy bank.

salvaguardare *vt* to safeguard.

salvare *vt* to save, rescue.

salvatore *m* saviour.

salvia *f* sage.

sambuco *m* cider.

San Silvestro *m*: — la notte *f* di San Silvestro New Year's Eve.

sandalo *m* sandal.

sandwich *m* sandwich.

sangue *m* blood.

sanguinaccio *m* black pudding.

sanguinare *vi* to bleed.

sanguisuga *f* leech, bloodsucker *(also fig)*.

sanità *f* soundness.

sano *adj* healthy, sound.

santificare *vt* to sanctify.

santo *m* saint.

santuario *m* sanctuary, shrine.

sanzione *f* sanction.

sapere *vt* to know: ~ di to smell or taste (of).

sapone *m* soap.

sapore *m* taste, favour, savour: ~ forte *m* tang.

saporito *adj* tasty.

saracinesca *f* shutter.

sarcasmo *m* sarcasm.

sarcofago *m* sarcophagus.

sardina *f* sardine, pilchard.

sassofono *m* saxophone.

Satana *m* Satan.

satanico *adj* satanic.

satellite *m* satellite.

satira *f* satire, lampoon.

satiro *m* satyr.

saturo *adj* saturated.

saturare *vt* to saturate.

saziare *vt* to satiate.

sazio *adj* satiated, satisfied.

sbaciucchiarsi *vr* to smooch.

sbadigliare *vi* to yawn.

sbadiglio *m* yawn.

sbagliare *vt* to make a mistake.

sbagliato *adj* wrong.

sbaglio *m* mistake, slip.

sbalordire *vt* to stagger, astound.

sbaragliare *vt* to rout.

sbarcare *vi* to disembark, land.

sbarra *f* rail, bar.

sbarramento *m* barrage.

sbiadirsi*vr* to fade.

sbiancare*vt* to whiten.

sbigottire*vt* to dumbfound.

sbirciare*vi* to peek, peep.

sbloccare*vt* to unblock.

sborsare*vt* to disburse, fork out.

sbottonare*vt* to unbutton.

sbrigare*vt* to deal with, polish off.

sbrinare*vt* to defrost.

sbrodolare*vt* to dribble.

sbrogliare*vt* to untangle, disentangle.

sbronzo*adj* drunk, tight.

sbucciapatate*m* potato peeler.

sbucciare*vt* to peel, skin.

scacchi*mpl* chess: — giocare a ~ to play chess.

scacchiera*f* chessboard.

scacco*m* check (chess): — scacco matto*m* checkmate.

scadente*adj* shoddy, third-rate, ropey.

scadenza*f* expiry, deadline.

scadere*vi* to fall due, lapse, expire.

scaduto*adj* out-of-date, overdue.

scaffalatura*fpl* shelving.

scaglia*f* scale, flake.

scala*f* scale, ladder, staircase.

scalare*vt* to scale, climb.

scaldabagno*m* water heater, geyser.

scaldare*vt* to warm, heat.

scalino*m* stair.

scalogno*m* shallot.

scalpello*m* chisel.

scambiare*vt* to swap, exchange.

scambio*m* exchange, swap.

scampare*vt* to escape.

scampolo*m* remnant.

scanalatura*f* slot.

scandagliare*vt* to plumb.

scandalizzare*vt* to scandalise, shock.

scandalo*m* scandal.

scansare*vt* to shirk.

scappare*vi* to escape, abscond.

scappatoia*f* loophole.

scarabeo*m* beetle.

scarabocchio*m* scribble, doodle.

scarafaggio*m* cockroach.

scaramuccia*f* skirmish.

scardinare*vt* to unhinge.

scarica*f* discharge.

scaricare*vt* to dump, unload.

scarico*m* drain, plughole, outlet.

scarlattina*f* scarlet fever.

scarlatto*adj, m* scarlet.

scarpa*f* shoe.

scarpetta*f* bootee.

scarpone*m* boot, brogue.

scarsità*f* dearth, scarcity.

scarto*m* reject.

scassato*adj* dilapidated.

scatenare*vt* to trigger (off).

scatola*f* tin, box; *pl* scatole (*vulg*); *see* palle.

scattare*vi* to click.

scatto*m* click.

scavare*vt* to excavate, dig.

scavezzacollo*m* daredevil.

scavo*m* excavation.

scegliere*vt* to single out, select, choose.

sceicco*m* sheik.

scemo*m* nit, twit.

scendere*vt, vi* to come down, descend.

sceneggiatura*f* screenplay.

sceriffo*m* sheriff.

scetticismo*m* scepticism.

scheda*f* index card.

scheletro*m* skeleton.

schematico*adj* schematic.

scherma*f* fencing.

schermo*m* screen.

scherno*m* mockery.

scherzare*vi* to joke.

scherzo*m* joke, lark, trick.

schiaccianoci *m inv* nut-
crackers.
schiaffeggiare *vt* to smack.
schiaffo *m* slap, smack.
schiavitù *f* slavery.
schiavo *m* slave.
schiena *f* back.
schietto *adj* frank, outright,
forthright.
schifo *m* repugnance, disgust:
— fare ~ to be disgusting.
schifoso *adj* lousy, rotten.
schiuma *f* froth, foam, lather.
schiumoso *adj* frothy.
schizofrenia *f* schizophrenia.
schizzare *vt* to splash, squirt;
to sketch.
sci *m inv* ski, skiing.
sciacallo *m* jackal.
sciacquare *vt* to rinse.
sciarpa *f* scarf.
sciatica *f* sciatica.
scientifico *adj* scientific.
scienza *f* science.
scimmia *f* monkey, ape.
scimpanzé *m inv* chimpanzee.
scintilla *f* spark.
scintillare *vi* to twinkle,
sparkle, glint.
scioccare *vt* to shock.
sciocco *m* fool.
sciogliere *vt* to melt, dissolve.
scioltezza *f* fluency.
scioperare *vi* to strike.
sciopero *m* strike, stoppage.
sciovinismo *m* chauvinism.
sciovinista *m* or *f* chauvinist.
scisma *m* schism.
scissione *f* split.
sciupare *vt* to mar.
scivolare *vi* to slide, slip.
scivolo *m* slide, chute.
scivolone *m* slide.
sclerosi *f* sclerosis.
scoiato *adj* skinned.
scoiattolo *m* squirrel.
scollato *adj* low-cut.

scollatura *f* cleavage.
scommessa *f* wager, bet.
scommettere *vt* to bet, wager.
scomodità *f* inconvenience.
scomodo *adj* uncomfortable,
inconvenient.
scompartimento *m*
compartment.
scomunicare *vt* to excom-
municate.
scongelare *vt* to thaw.
sconosciuto *adj* strange,
unknown.
sconsiderato *adj* thoughtless.
sconsolato *adj* disconsolate,
forlorn.
sconto *m* discount.
scontrarsi *vr* to crash, collide,
clash.
scontro *m* clash, smash.
sconvolgere *vt* to convulse.
scooter *m inv* scooter.
scopa *f* broom.
scopare *vt*, *vi* to sweep, brush.
scoperta *f* discovery, detection,
find.
scoperto *adj* exposed.
scoppiare *vi* to burst, break out.
scoppiettare *vi* to sputter,
crackle.
scoprire *vt* to uncover, find out.
scoraggiamento *m* discourage-
ment.
scorbutico *adj* grumpy.
scorbuto *m* scurvy.
scoreggia *f* fart.
scoreggiare *vi* to fart.
Scorpione *m* Scorpio.
scorpione *m* scorpion.
scorrettezza *f* impropriety.
scorretto *adj* incorrect,
improper.
scorrevole *adj* sliding, fluent.
scorso *adj* last.
scortare *vt* to escort.
scortese *adj* discourteous,
unkind, impolite.

scotch *m inv* whisky; adhesive tape, sellotape.

scotennare *vt* to scalp.

scottare *vt* to scald, blanch.

scottato *adj* scalded, blanched; sunburnt.

scovolino *m* pipe cleaner.

scozzese *adj* Scottish; *tessuto ~ *m* plaid, tartan.

screditare *vt* to discredit; *~rsi *vr* to cheapen oneself.

scremato *adj* skimmed.

scriba *m* scribe.

scribacchiare *vt* to scrawl.

scricciolo *m* wren.

scrigno *m* casket.

scrittore *m* writer.

scrittura *f* writing, handwriting.

scrivania *f* desk, writing desk.

scrivere *vt*, *vi* to write.

scroccare *vi* to sponge, scrounge.

scroccone *m* or *f* scrounger, sponger.

scrollata *f* shaking.

scroto *m* scrotum.

scrupolo *m* scruple, qualm.

scrutare *vt* to scan, peer, eye, scrutinise.

scuderia *f* stable.

scudo *m* shield.

sculacciare *vt* to spank.

scultore *m* sculptor.

scultura *f* sculpture.

scuola *f* school.

scuro *adj* dark.

scusa *f* excuse.

scusare *vt* to excuse: — *~rsi *vr* to apologise.

sdegnare *vt* to disdain.

sdentato *adj* toothless.

sdraiarsi *vr* to lie down.

sdrucciolevole *adj* slippery.

se *conj* if, whether.

se stessi *pers pron* themselves.

secca *f* shallow; * in ~ *adv* aground.

seccare *vt* to dry: — to bother, to be inopportune.

seccatore *m* inopportune person, time-waster.

seccatura *f* bother.

secco *adj* dry, arid.

secernare *vt* to secrete.

secondario *adj* secondary, incidental.

secondino *m* prison guard, jailer, warder.

secondo *prep* according to, under.

secretaire *m* bureau.

secrezione *f* secretion, discharge.

sedano *m* celery.

sedativo *m*, *adj* sedative.

sede *f* seat, head office.

sedentario *adj* sedentary.

sedere *vi* to sit.

sedia *f* chair, seat.

sedicesimo *adj*, *m* sixteenth.

sedici *adj*, *m* sixteen.

sedile *m* seat.

sedimento *m* sediment, lees.

seducente *adj* glamorous, seductive.

sedurre *vt* to seduce.

sega *f* saw.

segale *f* rye.

segare *vt* to saw.

seggiolone *m* high chair.

seghetto *m* hacksaw.

segmento *m* segment.

segnalare *vt*, *vi* to signal.

segnale *m* signal, sign.

segualibro *m* bookmark.

segnare *vt* to show, write down, mark.

segnatura *f* signature.

segnavento *m inv* weather vane.

segno *m* indicator, token, tick, sign, mark.

segregazione *f* segregation.

segretario *m* secretary.

segreteria telefonica*f* answering machine.
segreto*adj* secret, sneaking; * *m* secret.
seguire*vt* to follow; * *vi* to ensue.
sei*adj*, *m* six.
selezionare*vt* to select.
self service*adj inv* self-service.
sella*f* saddle.
selvaggio*adj* uncivilised, wild, savage.
selvatico*adj* wild.
semaforo*m* traffic lights.
semantica*f* semantics.
sembianza*f* guise.
sembrare*vi* to seem, appear.
seme*m* seed, pip.
semestrale*adj* half-yearly.
semicerchio*m* semi-circle.
semifinale*f* semi-final.
semiprezioso*adj* semi-precious.
semolino*m* semolina.
semplice*adj* simple, plain.
sempre*adv* always, ever.
sempreverde*m* or *f* evergreen.
senato*m* senate.
senile*adj* senile.
seno*m* bosom, breast; sinus.
sensibile*adj* tender, sensitive.
senso*m* sense, feeling.
sensuale*adj* sensual.
sentenza*f* sentence.
sentiero*m* track, trail, path.
sentimentale*adj* sentimental.
sentire*vt* to feel, hear.
senza*prep* without, apart from.
separabile*adj* separable.
separare*vt* to separate, part.
sepolcro*m* sepulchre.
seppellire*vt* to bury, inter.
seppia*f* cuttlefish.
sera*f* evening.
serata*f* evening.
serenata*f* serenade.

serenità*f* serenity, equanimity.
serie*f inv* succession, series, run.
serigrafia*f* silk-screen printing.
serio*adj* serious, earnest.
sermone*m* sermon.
serpente*m* snake, serpent.
serra*f* hot-house.
serratura*f* lock.
servile*adj* servile; menial.
servire*vi* to wait, serve, dish.
servizio*m* service.
sessanta*adj*, *m* sixty.
sessantesimo*adj*, *m* sixtieth.
sessismo*m* sexism.
sesso*m* sex.
sessuale*adj* sexual.
sessualità*f* sexuality.
sestante*m* sextant.
sesto*adj*, *m* sixth.
set*m inv* set.
seta*f* silk.
sete*f* thirst.
setola*f* bristle.
setta*f* sect.
settanta*adj*, *m* seventy.
settantesimo*adj*, *m* seventieth.
settario*adj* sectarian.
sette*adj*, *m* seven.
settembre*m* September.
settentrionale*adj* northern.
settentrione*m* north.
setter*m inv* setter.
setticemia*f* septicaemia.
settico*adj* septic.
settimana*f* week: — fine settimana*m inv* weekend.
settimanale*adj*, *m* weekly.
settimo*adj*, *m* seventh.
settore*m* sector.
severità*f* strictness, harshness, severity.
severo*adj* severe, harsh, strict.
sexy*adj inv* sexy.

sezionamento *m* dissection.
sezionare *vt* to dissect.
sezione *f* section, department.
sfacelo *m* dilapidation.
sfarzo *m* pageantry.
sfavorevole *adj* unfavourable, adverse.
sfera *f* sphere.
sfidante *m* or *f* challenger.
sfidare *vt* to defy.
sfiga *f* (*vulg*) bad luck.
sfigato *adj* (*vulg*) unlucky.
sfigurare *vt* to disfigure.
sfilare *vt* to unthread; * *vi* to parade.
sfilata *f* parade, march past.
sfinge *f* sphinx.
sfocato *adj* fuzzy, hazy.
sfoderato *adj* unlined.
sfogare *vt* to vent.
sformato *adj* baggy.
sfortuna *f* bad luck, adversity.
sfortunatamente *adv* unfortunately, unhappily.
sforzarsi *vr* to strive, exert oneself.
sforzo *m* stress, exertion, effort.
sfregare *vt* to rub, chafe.
sfrontato *adj* unashamed, brash.
sfruttamento *m* exploitation.
sfruttare *vt* to tap, exploit.
sfumatura *f* tint, nuance.
sgabello *m* stool.
sgangherato *adj* ramshackle.
sgargiante *adj* garish.
sgocciolare *vi* to drip.
sgonfiare *vt* to deflate.
sgorgare *vi* to well up, gush.
sgradevole *adj* undesirable, distasteful, nasty.
sgranare *vt* to shell.
sgualdrina *f* tart, slut.
sguardo *m* look, gaze.
shampoo *m inv* shampoo.
shock *m inv* shock.

show-room *m inv* showroom.
si *pers pron* itself, themselves.
sì *adv*, *m* yes, yeah.
sibilo *m* hiss.
siccità *f* drought.
siccome *conj* since.
sicomoro *m* sycamore.
sicurezza *f* safety, security.
sidro *m* cider.
siepe *f* hedge.
siero *m* serum.
sifilide *f* syphilis.
sifone *m* siphon.
sigaretta *f* cigarette, (*sl*) fag.
sigaro *m* cigar.
sigillare *vt* to seal.
sigillo *m* seal.
sigla *f* abbreviation: ~ editoriale imprint.
significare *vt* to signify, mean.
significativo *adj* meaningful, significant.
significato *m* meaning, significance.
signora *f* lady, madam, Mrs.
signore *m* sir, gentleman, lord, Mr.
signorina *f* Miss.
silenzio *m* silence, quiet, hush.
silice *f* flint.
sillaba *f* syllable.
silo *m* silo.
simbolo *m* symbol.
simile *adj* similar, comparable.
similitudine *f* simile.
simmetria *f* symmetry.
simpatia *f* liking, fellow-feeling.
simpatico *adj* likeable, nice, congenial.
simposio *m* symposium.
simulare *vt* to simulate, feign.
simulato *adj* simulated.
simulazione *f* simulation.
simultaneo *adj* simultaneous, concurrent.
sinagoga *m* synagogue.

sincerità *f* sincerity.
sincronizzare *vt* to synchronise.
sindacato *m* syndicate, trade union, union.
sindrome *f* syndrome.
sinfonia *f* symphony.
singolare *adj* singular, quaint.
singolo *adj* single; * *m* singles (tennis).
sinistra *f* left hand; * a ~ *adv* on the left.
sinistro *adj* left; eerie, sinister, spooky.
sinodo *m* synod.
sinonimo *m* synonym, byword; * *adj* synonymous.
sinossi *f inv* synopsis.
sintassi *f* syntax.
sintesi *f inv* synthesis.
sintomo *m* symptom.
sirena *f* siren, hooter; mermaid.
siringa *f* syringe.
sistema *m* system.
sistemare *vt* to settle, position.
sistematico *adj* systematic.
situare *vt* to place.
situato *adj* situated.
situazione *f* situation.
skate-board *m inv* skateboard.
slang *m* slang.
slitta *f* sled, sledge, sleigh.
slittare *vi* to skid.
slogan *m inv* slogan.
slogare *vt* to wrench, strain.
smaltare *vt* to enamel.
smalto *m* enamel, glaze.
smarrire *vi* to mislay.
smeraldo *m* emerald.
smettere *vi* to quit, stop.
smistare *vi* to sort, shunt.
smog *m inv* smog.
smontare *vi* to take down, dismantle.
smorfia *f* grimace.
smorto *adj* pasty.
smottamento *m* landslip.
snazionalizzare *vi* to

denationalise.
snello *adj* trim, slender.
sniffare *vt* to sniff (drugs).
snob *m* or *f invar* snob.
snobbare *vt* to snub, slight.
sobborgo *m* suburb.
sobrietà *f* sobriety.
sobrio *adj* sober.
socchiuso *adj* ajar.
soccombere *vi* to succumb.
soccorrere *vi* to help, aid.
soccorso *m* help: — pronto ~ first aid.
socialismo *m* socialism.
socialista *m* or *f* socialist.
società *f inv* society, company, corporation.
socio *m* partner, member.
sociologia *f* sociology.
sociologo *m* sociologist.
soda *f* soda.
soddisfacente *adj* satisfactory.
soddisfare *vi* to satisfy, content.
sodo *adj* hard, solid, compact, firm: — uovo ~ hard-boiled egg.
sofà *m inv* sofa.
soffiare *vt* to puff, blow.
soffice *adj* soft.
soffitta *f* attic, loft.
soffitto *m* ceiling.
soffocante *adj* sweltering, overpowering.
soffocare *vt*, *vi* to suffocate, stifle, choke.
soffrire *vt*, *vi* to suffer.
sofisticare *vi* to adulterate.
sofisticato *adj* sophisticated.
soggetto *m* subject.
soggiorno *m* living room; stay.
sognare *vt*, *vi* to dream.
sogno *m* dream, fantasy.
soia *f* soya.
solamente *adv* only.
solare *adj* solar.
solarium *m inv* solarium.
solco *m* rut, groove, furrow.

soldato *m* soldier.
soldo *m* penny, cent: — soldi *mpl* money.
solenne *adj* solemn.
solfato *m* sulphate.
solido *adj* solid, sturdy.
solista *m* or *f* soloist.
solitario *adj* solitary, lonely.
solitudine *f* solitude, loneliness.
sollecitare *vi* to solicit, invite.
sollevare *vi* to raise, lift, uplift.
solo *adj* alone, single; lonely.
solstizio *m* solstice.
soltanto *adv* only, just.
solubile *adj* soluble, (coffee) instant.
soluzione *f* solution.
solvente *adj*, *m* solvent.
solvenza *f* solvency.
somiglianza *f* similarity, resemblance.
somigliare *vi* to resemble.
somma *f* sum, amount.
sommare *vt* to add.
somministrare *vi* to dose, administer.
somministrazione *f* administration.
sonata *f* sonata.
sondare *vt* to sound, probe.
sonetto *m* sonnet.
sonnambulismo *m* sleepwalking.
sonnambulo *m* sleepwalker.
sonnifero *m* sleeping pill.
sonno *m* slumber, sleep.
sontuoso *adj* palatial, sumptuous.
sopportabile *adj* bearable, endurable.
sopportare *vt* to bear, stand, endure.
sopprimere *vt* to suppress, put down.
sopra *prep* over, above, on.
sopracciglio *m* eyebrow.

sopraggiungere *vi* to intervene.
soprammenzionato *adj* above-mentioned.
soprannaturale *adj*, *m* supernatural.
soprattutto *adv* above all.
sopravvivenza *f* subsistence.
sorbetto *m* sorbet, sherbet.
sordido *adj* sordid.
sordità *f* deafness.
sordo *adj* deaf.
sordomuto *adj* deaf and dumb.
sorella *f* sister.
sorgere *vi* to rise, spring.
sorprendente *adj* surprising, startling, astonishing.
sorprendere *vt* to surprise, catch.
sorpresa *f* surprise.
sorpresina *f* treat, little surprise.
sorridere *vi* to smile.
sorriso *m* smile.
sorsata *f* draught.
sorseggiare *vt* to sip.
sorso *m* sip.
sorte *f* fate, lot.
sorteggio *m* draw.
sorveglianza *f* supervision, watch.
sorvegliare *vt* to supervise, invigilate, oversee.
S.O.S. *m* S.O.S.
sosia *m inv* double.
sospendere *vt* to suspend.
sospensione *f* suspension.
sospettare *vt* to suspect.
sospettoso *adj* suspicious.
sospirare *vi* to sigh.
sospiro *m* sigh.
sosta *f* stop, stopover, halt.
sostantivo *adj* substantive.
sostanza *f* substance.
sostanziale *adj* substantial.
sostegno *m* support, prop, mainstay.
sostenere *vt* to support.

sostentamento *m* livelihood.
sostituire *vt* to substitute.
sostituzione *f* substitution.
sottaceti *mpl* pickles.
sotterfugio *m* subterfuge.
sotterraneo *adj* subterranean, underground.
sottile *adj* subtle, thin, fine.
sottilmente *adv* subtly.
sotto *adv*, *prep* under.
sottobicchiere *m* coaster.
sottobosco *m* undergrowth.
sottolineare *vt* to underline, emphasise.
sottomettere *vt* to subdue.
sottopassaggio *m* subway, underpass.
sottoporre *vt* to subject.
sottoprodotto *m* by-product.
sottoscrivere *vt* to sign, underwrite.
sottosegretario *m* under-secretary.
sottosopra *adj*, *adv* topsy-turvy, upside down.
sottosviluppato *adj* under-developed.
sottotitolo *m* subtitle, caption.
sottovento *adj* lee, leeward.
sottoveste *f* slip, petticoat.
sottrarre *vt* to subtract.
sottrazione *f* subtraction.
soufflé *m inv* soufflé.
souvenir *m inv* souvenir.
soviet *m inv* soviet.
sovrabbondanza *f* surfeit, glut.
sovraffollato *adj* overcrowded.
sovranità *f* sovereignty.
sovrano *m* ruler, sovereign.
sovrapporsi *vr* to overlap.
sovrastruttura *f* superstructure.
sovrumano *adj* superhuman.
sovvenzionare *vt* to subsidise.
sovvenzione *f* grant, subsidy.
sovvertire *vt* to subvert.
spaccare *vt* to split, chop.
spacco *m* slit, vent, split.

spaccone *m* braggart.
spada *f* sword; * pesce ~ *m* swordfish.
spaghetti *mpl* spaghetti.
spago *m* string.
spalare *vt* to shovel.
spalla *f* shoulder.
spallina *f* strap.
spaniel *m inv* spaniel.
spanna *f* span.
sparare *vt* to fire, shoot.
sparato *adj* shot; shirtfront: — partire ~ to be off like a shot: — andare ~ to belt along.
spareggio *m* disparity.
sparlare *vi* to backbite.
sparo *m* shot, gunshot.
spartano *adj* spartan.
spartizione *f* share-out.
sparviero *m* sparrowhawk.
spasmo *m* spasm.
spassionato *adj* dispassionate.
spassoso *adj* hilarious.
spastico *m*, *adj* spastic.
spatola *f* spatula.
spavalderia *f* bravado.
spaventapasseri *m inv* scarecrow.
spaventare *vt* to frighten, startle, scare.
spaventoso *adj* frightening, abysmal, horrific.
spaziale *adj* spatial.
spazio *m* room, space, gap.
spazzacamino *m* chimney sweep.
spazzare *vt* to sweep.
spazzatura *f* trash, rubbish.
spazzola *f* brush: ~ per capelli *f* hairbrush.
spazzolare *vt* to brush.
spazzolino *m* small brush: ~ da denti *m* toothbrush.
specchio *m* mirror.
speciale *adj* special.
specialista *m* or *f* (medical) consultant, specialist.

specialità *f inv* speciality.
specializzato *adj* specialist, skilled.
specie *f inv* sort, species.
specificare *vt* to specify.
specificazione *f* specification.
specifico *adj* specific.
specioso *adj* specious.
speculare *vi* to speculate, profiteer.
speculativo *adj* speculative.
speculatore *m* profiteer.
spedire *vt* to ship, send, dispatch.
spedizione *f* trek, expedition, dispatch.
spegnere *vt* to switch off, extinguish.
spellare *vt* to skin.
spendere *vt* to spend, expend.
spennare *vt* to pluck.
spensierato *adj* happy-go-lucky.
spento *adj* dull, off.
speranza *f* hope.
sperare *vt* to hope.
sperduto *adj* god-forsaken.
spericolato *adj* reckless.
sperimentare *vt* to test.
sperma *in* sperm, semen.
speronem *m* spur.
sperperare *vt* to squander.
spesa *f* expense, shopping, groceries.
spesso *adj* thick; * *adv* often.
spettacolo *m* spectacle, show.
spettare *vi* to be due, appertain.
spettatore *m* spectator, onlooker.
spettinato *adj* uncombed.
spettrale *adj* ghost-like, spookish, spectral.
spettro *m* ghost, spectre; spectrum.
spezie *fpl* spices.
spezzato *adj* broken.
spia *f* spy.

spiacevole *adj* unpleasant, disagreeable.
spiaggia *f* seaside, beach.
spianare *vt* to smooth, level.
spiare *vt* to peep, spy.
spiccioli *mpl* small change.
spiedino *m* kebab.
spiedo *m* spit, skewer.
spiegabile *adj* explicable.
spiegare *vt* to unfold, spread; to explain.
spiegazione *f* explanation, elucidation.
spietato *adj* pitiless, ruthless, remorseless.
spifferare *vt* to blab, to tell, to shoot one's mouth.
spiffero *m* draught.
spilla *f* brooch: ~ di balia *f* safety pin.
spillo *m* pin.
spilungone *adj* lanky man or woman; spindleshanks.
spina *f* plug, thorn, prickle.
spinaci *mpl* spinach.
spinale *adj* spinal.
spinello *m* joint.
spingere *vt* to push.
spinta *f* push, impetus, boost.
spinto *adj* suggestive.
spionaggio *m* spying, espionage.
spioncino *m* peephole.
spione *m* telltale, sneak.
spirale *adj* spiral.
spirare *vi* to expire.
spiritista *m* or *f* spiritualist.
spirito *m* spirit.
spiritoso *adj* humorous.
spirituale *adj* spiritual.
splendido *adj* splendid, stunning, gorgeous.
splendore *m* radiance, splendour.
spogliare *vt* to undress, despoil.
spogliarellista *m* or *f* stripper.
spogliarello *m* striptease.

spoglio *adj* bare.
spola *f* shuttle.
spolverare *vt, vi* to dust.
sponda *f* shore.
sponsorizzare *vt* to sponsor.
sponsorizzazione *f* sponsorship.
spontaneità *f* spontaneity.
spontaneo *adj* unstudied,
  spontaneous.
spopolare *vt* to depopulate.
sporadico *adj* sporadic.
sporcare *vt* to soil, foul.
sporcizia *f* dirtiness.
sporco *adj* dirty, smutty;
  * *m* dirt.
sporgere *vi* to protrude.
sport *m inv* sport.
sportello *m* door.
sposa *f* bride, wife.
sposare *vt* to wed, marry.
sposato *adj* married.
sposo *m* spouse, bridegroom.
spostare *vt* to budge, shift.
spot *m inv* spotlight, (TV)
  commercial.
spratto *m* sprat.
spray *m inv* spray.
sprecare *vt* to fritter (away),
  waste.
sprecato *adj* misspent.
spreco *m* wastage, waste.
spregevole *adj* contemptible,
  despicable.
spregiativo *adj* derogatory.
spremere *vt* to squeeze.
sprint *m inv* sprint.
spronare *vt* to spur, urge on.
sprone *m* yoke, boost, spur.
sproporzionato *adj* dispropor-
  tionate.
sprovvisto *adj* lacking.
spruzzare *vt* to spray, squirt.
spruzzatina *f* sprinkling.
spruzzo *m* splash, spray.
spudorato *adj* shameless.
spugna *f* towelling, sponge.
spugnoso *adj* spongy.

spumoso *adj* foamy.
spuntare *vt* to tick, trim.
spuntino *m* snack.
sputtanare *vt* (*vulg*) to expose,
  to shame; * ~rsi *vr* to shame
  oneself, to lose face.
sputacchiare *vi* to splutter.
sputare *vt, vi* to spit.
sputo *m* spit, spittle.
squadra *f* team, side.
squadrare *vt* to square; to
  look up and down; to study,
  to measure.
squadrone *m* troop, squadron.
squalificare *vt* to disqualify.
squallido *adj* seedy, sleazy,
  squalid, dingy.
squallore *m* squalor.
squalo *m* shark.
squash *m* squash.
squaw *f inv* squaw.
squilibrato *adj* unbalanced.
squilibrio *m* imbalance.
squillo *m* ring.
squisito *adj* exquisite.
squittio *m* squeak.
squittire *vi* to peep, squeak.
sradicare *vt* to eradicate,
  uproot.
sragionare *vt* to rave; to talk
  nonsense.
stabile *adj* stable.
stabilimento *m* establishment,
  plant.
stabilire *vt* to establish.
stabilità *f* stability.
stabilito *adj* set.
stabilizzare *vt* to stabilise.
staccabile *adj* detachable.
staccare *vt* to unplug,
  disconnect.
staccato *adj* unattached,
  detached.
stadio in stage, stadium.
staffa *f* stirrup.
stagionare *vt* to season.
stagionato *adj* ripe.

stagione *f* season.
stagnare *vi* to stagnate.
stagno *adj* watertight; * *m* tin.
stalagmite *f* stalagmite.
stalattite *f* stalactite.
stalla *f* stable, stall, barn, cowshed.
stallo *m* stalemate.
stallone *m* stud, stallion.
stame *m* stamen.
stampa *f* press, print, printing.
stampante *m* printer.
stampare *vt* to print.
stampato *m* print.
stampella *f* crutch.
stampo *m* cast, mould.
stancare *vi* to tire.
stanchezza *f* tiredness, weariness, fatigue.
stanco *adj* weary, tired: —
stanco morto *adj* dead tired.
stantio *adj* stale, musty.
stanza *f* room.
stanziamento *m* allocation.
stanziare *vt* to station.
stappare *vt* to uncork.
stare *vi* to stay, stand, to be.
starnutire *vi* to sneeze.
starnuto *m* sneeze.
starter *m inv* starter.
stasera *adv* tonight.
statico *adj* static.
statista *m* statesman.
statistica *f* statistics.
stato *m* status, state.
statua *f* statue.
statuario *adj* statuesque, statuary.
statura *f* stature.
status *m* status.
statuto *m* statute, charter.
stazionario *adj* stationary.
stazione *f* station.
steeplechase *m inv* steeple-chase.
stella *f* star.
stelo *m* stem.

stendardo *m* banner.
stendibiancheria *m inv* clothes horse.
stenografia *f* stenography, shorthand.
stentato *adj* laboured.
sterco *m* dung.
stereo *m inv* stereo, hi-fi.
stereofonia *f* stereo.
stereotipo *m* stereotype.
sterile *adj* barren, sterile.
sterilità *f* sterility.
sterilizzare *vt* to sterilise.
sterlina *f* pound (sterling).
sterminare *vt* to exterminate.
sterno *m* sternum, breastbone.
sterzo *m* lock.
stesso *adj* self, same, self-same, very.
stetoscopio *m* stethoscope.
steward *m inv* steward.
stigma *m* stigma.
stigmatizzare *vt* to stig-matise.
stile *m* style, panache.
stiletto *m* stiletto.
stima *f* esteem, valuation, estimation.
stimabile *adj* reputable.
stimare *vt* to treasure, esteem.
stimolante *m* stimulant.
stimolare *vt* to stimulate, whet, arouse.
stimolo *m* stimulus.
stinco *m* shank, shin.
stipato *adj* crammed.
stipendio *m* wages, salary.
stipulazione *f* stipulation.
stirare *vt* to press, iron.
stirpe *f* stock.
stitichezza *f* constipation.
stitico *adj* constipated.
stivale *m* boot.
stivare *vt* to stow.
stock *m* stock.
stoffa *f* fabric, cloth.

stola *f* stole.
stomaco *m* stomach.
stonato *adj* flat, off-key.
stop *m* stop sign.
stoppa *f* tow.
stoppino *m* wick.
stordito *adj* light-headed, in a daze, dazed.
storia *f* story, history.
storico *adj* historic(al).
storione *m* sturgeon.
storno *adj* starling.
storpiare *vt* to maim.
storta *f* retort.
storto *adj* crooked, awry.
strabico *adj* cross-eyed.
strabismo *m* squint, cast.
stracciare *vt* to shred.
stracciato *adj* ragged.
straccio *m* duster, rag.
strada *f* street, road, way.
stradina *f* lane.
strage *f* slaughter.
strambo *adj* odd, strange.
strangolare *vt* to strangle.
straniero *m* alien, foreigner.
strano *adj* strange, peculiar, odd.
straordinario *adj* extraordinary.
strapazzare *vt* to overwork; to mistreat.
strappare *vt* to tear, rip.
straripare *vi* to flood.
strascicare *vt* to shuffle, drawl.
stratagemma *m* stratagem, ploy.
strategia *f* strategy.
strato *m* stratum.
strattone *m* tug, wrench.
stravagante *adj* extravagant.
stravaganze *f* extravagance.
stravedere *vi* to dote.
stravolto *adj* distraught.
straziante *adj* harrowing,
strega *f* witch.
stregare *vt* to bewitch,

stregone *m* sorcerer.
stregoneria *f* witchcraft, sorcery.
stremare *vt* to exhaust.
stress *m* stress.
stressante *adj* stressful.
stretta *f* squeeze.
stretto *adj* tight, strict, narrow.
striare *vt* to streak.
stricnina *f* strychnine.
stridere *vi* to screech.
strillare *vi* to yell.
strillo *m* scream, shriek.
stringa *f* shoelace.
stringente *adj* stringent.
stringere *vt* to tighten, grip.
striscia *f* streak, strip, band.
strisciare *vi* to creep, trail.
striscione *m* banner.
strizzare *vt* to squeeze, wring.
strizzata *f* squeeze.
strizzatina *f* wink: — dare una ~ d occhio to wink.
strofinaccio *m* dish-cloth.
strofinare *vt* to scrub, rub.
stroneare *vt* to scotch, quash.
stronza *f* (*vulg*) bitch.
stronzo *m* (*vulg*) turd; pig.
stropicciare *vt* to wrinkle.
strozzare *vt* to throttle, strangle.
struggente *adj* poignant.
strumentale *adj* instrumental.
strumento *m* instrument, tool.
struzzo *m* ostrich.
stucchevole *adj* sickly.
stucco *m* stucco, putty.
studente *m* student.
studiare *vt*, *vi* to study, read.
studio *m* studio, study.
studioso *adj* studious.
stufa *f* fire, heater, stove.
stufare *vt* to stew.
stufato *m* stew.
stufo *adj* fed-up.
stunt-man *m inv* stuntman.

stupendo *adj* stupendous.
stupidità *f* stupidity.
stupido *adj* stupid.
stupire *vt* to stupefy, amaze.
stupore *m* wonder, astonishment, amazement.
stuprare *vt* to rape.
stupratore *m* rapist.
stupro *m* rape.
stuzzicadenti *m inv* toothpick.
su *adv* up, above; * *prep* over, on.
subacqueo *adj* underwater.
subaffittare *vt, vi* to sublet.
subalterno *adj, m* subordinate.
subappaltare *vt* to subcontract.
subconscio *m* subconscious.
subcosciente *adj* subconscious.
subdolo *adj* devious.
subire *vt* to undergo, sustain.
subito *adv* at once, straight away.
sublimare *vt* to sublimate.
sublime *adj* sublime.
subnormale *adj* subnormal.
subordinare *vt* to subordinate.
suburbano *adj* suburban.
succedere *vi* to happen.
successione *f* succession, sequence.
successivo *adj* subsequent.
successo *m* success, hit.
successone *m* smash.
successore *m* successor.
succhiare *vt, vi* to suck.
succo *m* juice, gist.
succoso *adj* juicy.
succulento *adj* succulent.
sud *adj, m* south.
sudare *vt, vi* to sweat.
sudario *m* shroud.
suddetto *adj* aforementioned.
suddito *m* subject.
suddividere *vt* to subdivide.
sudicio *m* filth.
sudiciume *m* grime, filth.
sudore *m* sweat.
sufficiente *adj* sufficient.

suffragetta *f* suffragette.
suffragio *m* suffrage.
suggerimento *m* tip, suggestion.
suggerire *vt* to suggest, prompt.
suggeritore *m* prompter.
sughero *m* cork.
sugo *m* sauce.
suicidio *m* suicide.
suite *f inv* suite.
sultanina *f* sultana.
sultano *m* sultan.
suo *poss adj, pron* your(s), her(s), his, its.
suocera *f* mother-in-law.
suocero *m* father-in-law.
suola *f* sole.
suonare *vt, vi* to sound, play, ring; (*sl*) spank: — se non la smetti, te le suono! give it up, or I'll spank you!
suonata *f* ringing; (*sl*) thrashing, beating, rip-off: — che ~! what a rip-off!
suono *m* sound.
suora *f* nun, sister.
superare *vt* to pass, top, excel, surpass.
superbo *adj* superb, haughty.
superficiale *adj* superficial.
superficie *f* top, surface.
superfluo *adj* superfluous.
superiore *adj* upper, senior.
superiorità *f* superiority.
superlativo *adj, m* superlative.
supermercato *m* supermarket.
superpetroliera *f* supertanker.
superpotenza *f* superpower.
supersonico *adj* supersonic.
superstite *m* or *f* survivor.
superstizione *f* superstition.
superuomo *m* superman.
supino *adj* supine.
supplemento *m* supplement.
supplica *f* supplication.
supplicare *vt* to beg, appeal.
supportabile *adj* tolerable,

bearable.
supportare *vt* to bear.
supporto *m* strut.
supposizione *f* assumption, supposition, guess.
supposta *f* suppository.
suppurare *vt* to suppurate, to fester.
supremazia *f* supremacy.
supremo *adj* ultimate, crowning.
surf *m* surfboard.
surgelare *vt* to freeze.
surplus *m inv* surplus.
surrealismo *m* surrealism.
surrogato *adj, m* surrogate.
suscettibilità *f* susceptibility, sensibility.
susina *f* plum, damson.
suspense *m* suspense.
sussidiario *m* subsidiary.
sussidio *m* help.
sutura *f* suture.
svago *m* leisure.
svalutazione *f* devaluation.
svanire *vi* to vanish.
svantaggio *m* disadvantage.
svantaggioso *adj* disadvantageous.
svariato *adj* diverse, multifarious.
svasato *adj* flared.
svastica *f* swastika.
sveglia *f* waking-up, waking-up time; alarm clock.
svegliare *vt* to awake, rouse.
svelare *vt* to unveil.
svelto *adj* agile, smart.
svendita *f* sale.
svenire *vi* to swoon, faint.
sventolare *vt* to wave.
sventrare *vt* to gut.
sventurato *adj* luckless, wretched.
sverniciare *vt* to strip.
svilire *vt* to debase.
sviluppare *vt* to develop.

sviluppo *m* development, twist.
svista *f* oversight, lapse.
svitare *vt* to unscrew.
svogliato *adj* half-hearted.
svolazzare *vi* to flit, flutter.
svolazzo *m* flourish.
svolgere *vt* to perform.
svuotare *vt* to drain.
swing *m* swing.

T

tabaccaio *m* tobacconist.
tabacco *m* tobacco.
tabella *f* chart.
tabellone *m* billboard, scoreboard.
tabb *m inv* taboo.
tacca *f* notch.
taccagno *adj* miserly.
taccheggiare *vi* to shoplift.
taccheggiatore *m* shoplifter.
tacchino *m* turkey.
tacco *m* heel.
taccuino *m* notebook.
tachimetro *m* speedometer.
tacito *adj* tacit, unwritten.
tafano *m* horsefly.
taffettà *m* taffeta.
taglia *f* size: ~ forte *f* outsize.
tagliaboschi *m inv* woodcutter.
tagliaerba *m inv* lawnmower.
taglialegna *m inv* lumberjack.
tagliare *vt* to cut.
tagliatelle *fpl* noodles.
tagliaunghie *m* clippers.
taglicre *m* chopping board, bread board.
taglio *m* cut, cutback, slash.
talco *m* talc, talcum powder.
tale *adj* such.
talento *m* talent.
talpa *f* mole.
tamburino *m* tambourine.

tamburo *m* drum.
tampone *m* tampon, wad.
tanga *m inv* thong, G-string.
tangente *f* tangent.
tangibile *adj* tangible.
tanto *adj, pron* so much, so many.
tappa *f* stage.
tappare *vt* to bung, cap, cork, plug.
tappetino *m* mat.
tappeto *m* carpet, rug.
tappezzare *vt* to paper.
tappezzeria *f* upholstery.
tappo *m* top, bung, stopper.
tarantola *f* tarantula.
tardi *adj* late.
tariffa *f* rate, tariff.
tarlo *m* woodworm.
tarma *f* moth.
tartan *m inv* tartan.
tartaro *m* tartar.
tartaruga *f* tortoise.
tartufo *m* truffle.
tasca *f* pocket.
tascabile *m* paperback.
tassa *f* duty, tax.
tassare *vt* to tax.
tassativo *adj* imperative.
tassazione *f* taxation.
tassista *m* or *f* taxi-driver.
tasso *m* rate; badger; yew.
tastare *vt* to feel.
tastiera *f* keyboard.
tasto *m* key.
tattica *f* tactic, tactics.
tattico *adj* tactical.
tatto *m* touch, tact, feel.
tatuaggio *m* tattoo.
tatuare *vt* to tattoo.
tautologia *f* tautology.
tautologico *adj* tautological.
taverna *f* tavern.
tavola *f* table, plank.
tavolino *m* coffee table.
tavolo *m* table.
taxi *m inv* taxi, cab.

tazza *f* cup.
tazzone *m* mug.
te *m inv* tea.
teatrale *adj* theatrical.
teatro *m* theatre.
tecnica *f* skill, technique.
tecnico *m* technician.
tecnologia *f* technology.
tedio *m* tedium.
teenager *m* or *f inv* teenager.
tela *f* web, canvas.
telaio *m* frame, loom.
telecomando *m* remote control.
telecomunicazioni *fpl* telecommunications.
telecronaca *f* commentary.
telecronista *m* or *f* commentator.
telefonare *vi* to phone, ring, call.
telefonata *f* telephone call.
telefonista *m* or *f* telephonist.
telefono *m* telephone.
telegiornale *m* TV news.
telegrafo *m* telegraph.
telegramma *m* telegram.
telenovella *f* soap opera.
telepatia *f* telepathy.
telescopio *m* telescope.
telespettatore *m* viewer.
televisione *f* television.
televisore *m* television set.
telex *m inv* telex.
telone *m* tarpaulin.
tema *m* theme.
temerario *adj* foolhardy.
temere *vt, vi* to fear, dread.
tempera *f* distemper.
temperamatite *m inv* sharpener.
temperamento *m* temperament, temper.
temperare *vt* to sharpen.
temperato *adj* temperate.
temperatura *f* temperature.
temperino *m* penknife.
tempesta *f* tempest, storm.

tempia *f* temple.
tempio *m* temple.
tempo *m* time; weather; tense.
temporale *m* storm.
temporaneamente *adv* temporarily.
tenace *adj* tenacious, dogged.
tenacia *f* tenacity.
tenda *f* tent, curtain.
tendenza *f* tendency.
tender *m inv* tender.
tendere *vt* to tend, stretch.
tendine *m* tendon, sinew.
tendone *m* awning.
tenente *m* lieutenant.
tenere *vt* to keep.
tenerezza *f* tenderness, gentleness.
tenero *adj* tender, endearing.
tenia *f* tapeworm.
tennis *m* tennis.
tennista *m* or *f* tennis player.
tenore *m* tenon.
tensione *f* tension, stress.
tentacolo *m* tentacle.
tentare *vt* to tempt, attempt.
tentazione *f* temptation.
teologia *f* theology.
teorema *m* theorem.
teoretico *adj* theoretical.
teoria *f* theory.
teorico *m* theorist.
teorizzare *vt* to theorise.
terapeutico *adj* therapeutic.
terapia *f* therapy.
tergicristallo *m* windscreen wiper.
tergo *m* back; * a ~ *adv* overleaf.
termale *adj* thermal; *stazione termale *f* spa, watering place.
terminale *adj*, *m* terminal.
terminare *vt*, *vi* to end, terminate.
termine *m* term, limit, end.
termite *f* termite.
termometro *m* thermometer.
termosifone *m* radiator.

termostato *m* thermostat.
terra *f* land, ground, earth.
terrazza *f* patio, terrace.
terremoto *m* earthquake.
terreno *m* ground, land, terrain.
terrestre *adj* terrestrial.
terribile *adj* terrible.
terrier *m inv* terrier.
terrificare *vt* to terrify.
territoriale *adj* territorial.
terrore *m* terror, dread.
terrorismo *m* terrorism.
terrorista *m* or *f* terrorist.
terzo *adj*, *m* third.
teschio *m* skull.
tesi *f inv* thesis, contention.
tesoro *m* treasure; exchequer; darling, sweetheart
tessera *f* card.
tessere *vt*, *vi* to weave.
tessile *adj* textile.
tessitura *f* weaving.
tessuti *mpl* textiles.
tessuto *f* fabric, cloth, tissue, material.
test *m* test.
testa *f* head.
testamento *m* testament, will.
testicolo *m* testicle.
testimone *m* witness.
testimoniare *vi* to testify, witness.
testo *m* text.
tetano *m* tetanus.
tetro *adj* bleak.
tetta *f (sl)* tit, boob.
tettarella *f* teat.
tetto *m* roof.
thermos *m inv* vacuum flask.
thriller *m inv* thriller.
tibia *f* shinbone.
tic *m inv* tic, twitch.
tiepido *adj* tepid, lukewarm.
tifo *m* typhus.
tifone *m* typhoon.
tifoso *m* fan, supporter.

tigre *f* tiger, tigress.
timbrare *vt* to stamp.
timbro *m* stamp.
timidezza *f* timidity.
timido *adj* shy, diffident.
timo *m* thyme.
timore *m* fear.
timpano *m* eardrum.
tingere *vt* to stain.
tinta *f* paint, hue.
tintoria *f* dyeworks.
tintura *f* dye.
tipico *adj* typical.
tipo *m* type.
tirannia *f* tyranny.
tirare *vi* to pull.
tiroide *f* thyroid.
titolare *m* bearer, occupant, occupier.
titolo *m* title.
toccare *vt* to touch.
toga *f* gown.
togliere *vi* to take away, remove.
toilette *f inv* toilet, dressing table.
tollerare *vt* to tolerate, suffer.
tomba *f* tomb, grave.
tombola *f* bingo.
tomo *m* tome.
tonaca *f* frock, habit.
tonalità *f* shade.
tonare *vi* to thunder.
tonico *f* tonic.
tonificante *adj* invigorating, bracing.
tonnellaggio *m* tonnage.
tonnellata *f* ton.
tonno *m* tuna.
tono *m* tone.
tonsilla *f* tonsil.
tonsillite *f* tonsillitis.
tonsura *f* tonsure.
tonto *adj* stupid.
topazio *m* topaz.
topo *m* mouse.
topografla *f* topography.

Topolino Mickey Mouse.
toporagno *m* shrew.
torace *m* thorax.
torbido *adj* murky.
torcia *f* torch.
tordo *m* thrush.
torero *m* bullfighter.
tormentare *vt* to torment.
tormento *m* torment.
tornado *m inv* tornado.
tornare *vi* to return.
torneo *m* tournament.
tornire *vt* to turn.
toro *m* bull.
Toro *m* Taurus.
torre *f* tower.
torrefare *vt* to roast (coffee).
torrente *m* torrent.
torrenziale *adj* torrential.
torretta *f* turret.
torrido *adj* torrid.
torrone *m* nougat.
torso *m* torso.
torsolo *m* stalk, core.
torta *f* pie, cake.
tortora *f* turtledove.
tortuoso *adj* circuitous, tortuous.
tortura *f* torture.
torturare *vt* to torture.
tosse *f* cough.
tossico *adj* toxic.
tossicodipendente *m* or *f* drug addict.
tossicodipendenza *f* drug addiction.
tossicomane *m* or *f* drug addict.
tossina *f* toxin.
tossire *vi* to cough.
tostare *vt* to toast.
totale *adj* total.
totalità *f* totality.
totalitario *adj* totalitarian.
tovaglia *f* tablecloth.
tovagliolo *m* napkin, serviette.
tra *prep* between.
traccia *f* smear, trace.

tracciare *vt* to chart, trace.
trachea *f* trachea, windpipe.
tracolla *f* strap.
tradimento *m* betrayal, treason.
tradire *vt* to betray, shop.
traditore *m* traitor.
tradizionale *adj* traditional.
tradizione *f* tradition.
tradurre *vt* to translate.
traduttore *m* translator.
traduzione *f* translation.
trafficante *m* or *f* trafficker.
trafficare *vi* to traffic.
traffico *m* traffic.
tragedia *f* tragedy.
traghetto *m* ferry.
tragico *adj* tragic.
tragicommedia *f* tragi-comedy.
tragitto *m* haul, run.
tram *m inv* tram.
trama *f* story, plot, weave.
trambusto *m* commotion.
tramontare *vi* to set.
tramonto *m* sundown, sunset.
tramortire *vt* to stun.
trampolino *m* springboard, diving board.
trance *f inv* trance.
tranquillamente *adv* happily.
tranquillante *m* tranquilliser.
tranquillità *f* ease.
tranquillo *adj* leisurely.
transatlantico *m* liner.
transatlantico *adj* transatlantic.
transistor *m inv* transistor.
transito *m* transit.
transitorio *adj* transient.
transizione *f* transition.
trapano *m* drill.
trapezio *m* trapeze.
trapiantare *vt* to transplant.
trappola *f* trap, snare.
trascorrere *vi* to elapse, spend.
trascrizione *f* transcription.

trascurabile *adj* unimportant.
trascurare *vt* to neglect.
trasferire *vt* to shift, transfer.
trasformare *vt* adapt.
trasfusione *f* transfusion.
trasgredire *vt* to transgress.
trasgressione *f* misdemeanour.
trasgressore *m* offender.
traslocare *vt*, *vi* to move.
trasloco *m* removal, move.
trasmettere *vt* to transmit.
trasparente *adj* transparent.
traspirare *vt* to perspire.
trasportare *vt* to convey, transport.
trasporto *m* transport.
tratta *f* illegal trade; (bank) draft.
trattamento *m* treatment.
trattare *vt* to treat.
trattato *m* treaty, treatise.
trattino *m* dash, hyphen.
trattore *m* tractor.
trauma *m* trauma.
trave *f* beam, girder.
traveller's cheque *m inv* traveller's cheque.
traversata *f* crossing.
traverso *adj* cross.
travestire *vt* to disguise.
travestito *m* transvestite.
tre *adj*, *m* three.
treccia *f* plait, braid.
treccina *f* pigtail.
tredicesimo *adj*, *m* thirteenth.
tredici *adj*, *m inv* thirteen.
tredimensionale *adj* three-dimensional.
tregua *f* respite.
tremare *vi* to quiver.
tremendo *adj* dreadful.
trementina *f* turpentine.
tremolare *vi* to flicker.
trench *m inv* trench coat.
treno *m* train.
trenta *adj*, *m* thirty.
trentesimo *adj*, *m* thirtieth.

trepidazione f trepidation.
treppiede m tripod.
tresca f intrigue.
triangolare adj triangular.
triangolo m triangle.
tribale adj tribal.
tribolazione f tribulation.
tribù f tribe.
tribunale m law court, tribunal.
tributo m tribute.
tricheco m walrus.
triciclo m tricycle.
tricorizia f ringworm.
trigonometria f trigo-
  nometry.
trillare vi to trill.
trillo m trill.
trilogia f trilogy.
trimestrale adj quarterly.
trimestre m term.
trincea f trench.
Trinità f Trinity.
trio m trio.
trionfo m triumph.
triplicare vt to treble.
triplo adj triple, treble.
trippa f tripe.
triste adj sad, woeful.
tristezza f misery, sadness.
tritacarne m inv mincer.
tritare vt to mince.
tritone m newt.
trofeo m trophy.
tromba f trumpet.
trombare vt (sl) to fail, to
  reject (at school); (vulg) to
  screw, to fuck.
trombone m trombone;
  daffodil.
trombosi f thrombosis.
tronco m log, trunk.
trono m throne.
tropicale adj tropical.
troppo adv too.
trota f trout.
trottare vi to trot.
trotto m trot.

trottola f top.
trovare vt to find.
trovata f gimmick.
trucco m trick.
truffare vt to swindle.
tu pers pron you.
tuba f tuba.
tubature fpl piping.
tubercolosi f tuberculosis.
tubo m tube, pipe.
tuffarsi vr to plunge, dive.
tulipano m tulip.
tumore m tumour.
tumultuare vi riot.
tumultuoso adj tumultuous.
tunica f robe, tunic.
tunnel m inv tunnel.
tuo poss adj, pron your(s).
tuono m thunder.
tuorlo m yolk.
turbina f turbine.
turbolenza f turbulence.
turchese adj, m turquoise.
turismo m sightseeing,
  tourism.
turista m or f tourist.
turno m shift, turn.
tutela f guardianship.
tutore m guardian.
tuttavia conj however, yet, all
  the same.
twist m twist.

U

ubbidire vt, vi to obey.
ubicazione f site.
ubriachezza f drunkenness.
ubriaco adj drunk, inebriated.
uccelliera f aviary.
uccellino m fledgling.
uccello m bird.
uccidere vt to kill.
udibile adj audible.
udito m hearing.
ufficiale adj official.

ufficiare *vi* to officiate.
ufficio *m* office, bureau.
uguaglianza *f* equality.
uguagliare *vt* to touch,
  match, equal.
uguale *m* or *f* match; * *adj* equal.
ulcera *f* ulcer.
ulivo *m* olive tree.
ulteriore *adj* ulterior.
ultimamente *adv* lately.
ultimatum *m inv* ultimatum.
ultimo *adj* last.
ululare *vi* to howl (of wolves).
umanamente *adv* humanly.
umanista *m* or *f* humanist.
umanità *f* humanity, mankind.
umanitario *adj* humanitarian,
  humane.
umano *adj* human.
umidità *f* humidity.
umido *adj* damp, humid.
umile *adj* lowly, humble.
umiliare *vt* to demean,
  humiliate.
umiltà *f* humility.
umore *m* mood, frame of mind,
  humour.
unanime *adj* unanimity.
unanimità *f* unanimity.
undicesimo *adj*, *m* eleventh.
undici *adj*, *m* eleven.
ungere *vt* to anoint.
unghia *f* fingernail, nail, claw.
unguento *m* ointment, salve.
unico *adj* sole.
unicorno *m* unicorn.
unificante *adj* cohesive.
unificare *vt* to unify, unite.
uniforme *adj* uniform.
uniformemente *adv* evenly.
uniformità *f* uniformity.
unilaterale *adj* one-sided,
  unilateral.
unione *f* union, unity.
unire *vt* to join, unify.
unisono *m* unison.
unità *f inv* unit, unity.

unito *adj* united.
universale *adj* universal.
università *f* university.
universo *m* universe.
uno *adj*, *m* one.
unto *m* grease.
unzione *f* function.
uomo *m* (*pl* uomini) man.
uovo *m* egg.
uragano *m* hurricane.
uranio *m* uranium.
urbano *adj* urban; urbane.
urgente *adj* urgent.
urgenza *f* urgency.
urlare *vt*, *vi* to howl (of human
  beings).
urlo *m* scream, yell.
urna *f* urn.
urogallo *m* grouse.
usabile *adj* expendabile.
usanza *f* usage.
usare *vt* to use.
uscente *adj* outgoing.
usciere *m* usher.
uscire *vi* to go out.
uscita *f* exit, release.
usignolo *m* nightingale.
uso *m* usage, use.
usurpare *vt* to usurp, encroach.
utensile *m* utensil.
utero *m* uterus, womb.
utile *adj* useful, helpful.
utilità *f* usefulness, utility.
utilizzare *vt* to utilise.
uva *f* grapes.
uvetta *f* raisin.

V

vacanza *f* vacation, holiday.
vacca *f* cow.
vaccinare *vt* to vaccinate.
vaccinazione *f* vaccination.
vaccino *m* vaccine.
vacillare *vi* to totter, falter.
vacuo *adj* blank, vacant.

vaffanculo! *excl* (*vulg*) fuck off!
vagabondo *m* tramp, vagabond.
vagare *vi* to rove, drift.
vagina *f* vagina.
vaglia *m* draft.
vagliare *vt* to screen.
vago *adj* faint, woolly.
vagone *m* carriage.
vaiolo *m* smallpox.
valere *vi* to be worth.
validità *f* validity, soundness.
valido *adj* valid.
valutare *f* to appraise.
valigia *f* suitcase.
valle *f* valley.
valore *m* value, worth.
valorizzare *vt* to enhance.
valoroso *adj* valiant, manful.
valuta *f* currency.
valutare *vt* to value, assess, evaluate.
valutazione *f* valuation, appraisal.
valvola *f* valve.
valzer *m inv* waltz.
vampiro *m* vampire.
vandalizzare *vt* to vandalise.
vanga *f* spade.
vangare *vt* to dig.
vangelo *m* gospel.
vaniglia *f* vanilla.
vanità *f inv* vanity, conceit.
vanitoso *adj* vain, conceited.
vantaggio *m* advantage.
vantare *vt* to boast.
vapore *m* vapour, steam.
variare *vt*, *vi* to vary, range.
varicella *f* chickenpox.
varietà *f inv* variety.
variopinto *adj* mottled, motley.
vasaio *m* potter.
vasca *f* basin.
vaschetta *f* tub.
vasectomia *f* vasectomy.
vaselina *f* vaseline.
vasellame *m* crockery.

vasetto *m* pot.
vasino *m* potty.
vaso *m* vase.
vassoio *m* tray, salver.
vastità *f* magnitude.
vasto *adj* vast.
vecchiaia *f* old age.
vecchio *adj* old.
veci *f* duties.
vedere *vt*, *vi* to see.
vedova *f* widow.
vedovo *m* widower.
veduta *f* outlook, view.
vegetare *vi* to vegetate.
vegetariano *adj*, *m* vegetarian.
vegetazione *f* vegetation.
veglia *f* wake, vigil.
veicolo *m* vehicle.
vela *f* sail.
velare *vt* to veil.
veleno *m* poison, venom.
vello *m* fleece.
vellutato *adj* silky.
velluto *m* velvet.
velo *m* veil, ply.
veloce *adj* quick.
velocità *f* speed.
vena *f* vein, seam, streak.
venale *adj* venal.
vendere *vt* to sell.
vendetta *f* vendetta.
vendicare *vt* to avenge.
vendita *f* sale.
venditore *m* seller, vendor.
venerabile *adj* venerable.
venerare *vt* to venerate.
venerazione *f* veneration.
venerdì *m* Friday: — V~ Santo Good Friday.
venereo *adj* venereal.
veniale *adj* venial.
venire *vi* to come.
ventaglio *m* fan.
ventesimo *adj*, *m* twentieth.
venti *adj*, *m* twenty.
venticello *m* breeze.
ventilare *vt* to ventilate.

107

ventilatore *m* fan, ventilator.
ventilazione *f* ventilation.
vento *m* wind.
ventre *m* stomach.
veramente *adv* truly, really.
veranda *f* verandah, porch.
verbo *m* verb.
verde *adj*, *m* green.
verdetto *m* verdict.
verdura *f* greens.
vergine *adj*, *f* virgin.
Vergine *f* Virgo.
verginità *f* virginity.
vergogna *f* shame.
vergognare *vt* to shame.
verificare *vt* to verify, try, check.
verità *f inv* truth.
verme *m* worm.
vermut *m inv* vermouth.
vernice *f* paint, paintwork.
verniciare *vt* to paint.
vero *adj* true, real, veritable.
versare *vt* to spill.
versatile *adj* versatile.
versione *f* version.
verso *prep* toward(s); * *m* verse.
vertebra *f* vertebra.
verticale *adj*, *m* vertical.
vertigine *f* dizziness.
verve *f* verve.
vescica *f* blister, bladder.
vescovo *m* bishop.
vespa *f* wasp.
vespaio *m* wasps' nest:
— sollevare un ~ to stir up a hornets' nest.
vespasiano *m* urinal.
vestaglia *f* dressing gown.
vestire *m* dressing; * *vt* to clothe, dress.
vestito *m* dress.
veterano *m* veteran.
veterinario *adj* veterinary.
veto *m* veto.
vetraio *m* glazier.
vetrina *f* showcase, window.

vetro *m* glass, windowpane.
vetta *f* summit.
via *f* road: *prep* via, by.
viadotto *m* viaduct.
viaggiare *vi* to travel.
viaggio *m* journey.
viale *m* avenue.
vibrante *adj* vibrant.
vibrare *vi* to vibrate.
vibrazione *f* vibration.
vicepresidente *m* vice president.
viceversa *adv* vice versa.
vicinanza *f* proximity.
vicinato *m* neighbourhood.
vicino *m* neighbour.
vicolo *m* alley.
video *m inv* video.
vietare *vt* to prohibit.
vigilanza *f* vigilance.
vigilia *f* eve: — la ~ di Natale Christmas Eve.
vigliacco *m*, *adj* cowardly, craven, chicken.
vigna *f* vineyard.
vigneto *m* vineyard.
vignetta *f* cartoon.
vigore *m* vigour.
vigoroso *adj* vigorous.
vile *adj* base.
villa *f* villa.
villano *adj* rude.
vimine *m* wicker.
vincere *vt* to win.
vinite *m* vinyl.
vino *m* wine: ~ bianco white wine; ~ rosso red wine.
viola *m*, *adj* purple.
violare *vt* to violate.
violazione *f* breach.
violentare *vt* to rape.
violentatore *m* rapist.
violenza *f* violence.
violetto *adj*, *m* violet.
violinista *m* or *f* violinist
violino *m* violin, fiddle.
violoncello *m* violoncello,

cello.
vipera *f* viper, adder.
virare *vi* to turn.
virgola *f* comma, point.
virgoletta *f* inverted comma
virgolette *fpl* quotation
  marks.
virile *adj* manly, virile.
virilità *f* virility.
virtù *f inv* virtue.
virtuoso *adj* virtuous,
  righteous.
virus *m inv* virus.
vischio *m* mistletoe.
viscido *adj* slimy.
viscoso *adj* viscous.
visibile *adj* visible.
visione *f* vision.
visita *f* visit.
visitare *vt* to visit, examine.
viso *m* face.
visone *m* mink.
vispo *adj* frisky, bright.
vista *f* sight, vista.
vistoso *adj* showy.
vita *f* life.
vitamina *f* vitamin.
vite *f* vine, grapevine.
vitello *m* calf, veal.
vittima *f* victim.
vitto *m* board.
vittoria *f* victory.
vivace *adj* sprightly.
vivacità *f* liveliness.
vivere *vi* to live, subsist.
vivisezione *f* vivisection.
viziare *vt* to indulge, pamper.
viziato *adj* spoilt.
vizio *m* vice, fault.
vocabolario *m* vocabulary,
  dictionary.
vocale *f* vowel.
vocazione *f* vocation, calling.
voce *f* voice.
vodka *f inv* vodka.
voglia *f* fancy, inclination.
voi *pers pron* you.

volano *m* shuttlecock.
volantino *m* leaflet.
volare *vi* to fly.
volere *vt* to want, wish.
volgare *adj* coarse, vulgar.
volo *m* flight.
volontà *f* will.
volontario *m* volunteer.
volpe *f* fox.
volta *f* time; vault.
voltaggio *m* voltage.
voltare *vt* to turn, turn over.
volume *m* volume.
voluminoso *adj* bulky.
voluttuoso *adj* sensuous,
  voluptuous.
vomitare *vt* to vomit, be sick.
vomito *m* vomit.
vongola *f* clam.
vorace *adj* voracious.
vortice *m* whirl, whirlpool.
vostro *poss adj, pron* your(s).
votare *vt, vi* to vote.
votazione *f* poll, vote.
voto *m* mark, grade, vow.
vulcanico *adj* volcanic.
vulcano *m* volcano.
vulnerabile *adj* vulnerable.
vuotare *vt* to empty, bale out.
vuoto *m* vacuum, vacancy,
  void.

W

wagon-lit *m inv* sleeping car.
walzer *m inv* waltz.
WC *m inv* WC, toilet.
weekend *m inv* weekend.
würstel *m inv* frankfurter,
  sausage.

X

xilofono *m* xylophone.

Y

yacht *m inv* yacht.
yankee *mf inv* yankee.
yard *f inv* yard.
yen *m inv* yen.
yoga *m* yoga.
yogurt *m inv* yoghurt.
yuppy *m* or *f* yuppy.

Z

zafferano *m* saffron.
zaffiro *m* sapphire.
zampa *f* paw.
zampata *f* kick.
zanna *f* fang, tusk.
zanzara *f* mosquito, gnat.
zanzarone *m* daddy-long-legs.
zappa *f* hoe.
zar *m inv* czar.
zarina *f* czarina.
zattera *f* raft.
zebra *f* zebra.
zecca *f* tick, louse; mint:
— nuovo di ~ brand-new.
zecchino *m* sequin.
zelante *adj* zealous.
zelo *m* zeal.
zenit *m inv* zenith.
zenzero *m* ginger.
zerbino *m* doormat.
zero *m* nought, zero, nil.
zia *f* aunt.
zigomo *m* cheekbone.
zigzag *m inv* zigzag.
zinco *m* zinc.
zingaro *m* gypsy.
zio *m* uncle.
zip *m inv* zip.
zitella *f* spinster.
zizzania *f* darnel: — seminare ~
to sow discord, to make
mischief.
zoccola *f* whore.

zoccolo *m* hoof, clog.
zodiaco *m* zodiac.
zolfo *m* sulphur.
zolla *f* clod, sod.
zolletta *f* lump.
zona *f* zone.
zoo *m inv* zoo.
zoologico *adj* zoological.
zoologia *f* zoology.
zoom *m inv* zoom.
zoppicare *vi* to hobble, limp.
zoppo *m* cripple: — * *adj* lame.
zoster *m* herpes zoster,
shingles.
zotico *m* lout.
zoticone *m* oaf, boor.
zucca *f* pumpkin, marrow,
gourd: (*sl*) head.
zuccherare *vt* to sugar,
sweeten.
zucchero *m* sugar.
zucchetto *m* skullcap.
zucchina *f* courgette.
zuccone *m* blockhead.
zuffa *f* fray, dust-up, set-to.
zuppa *f* soup: ~ inglese
(cookery) trifle.
zuppiera *f* tureen.

ENGLISH ITALIAN
INGLESE ITALIANO

A

a *art* un, uno, una, un'; * *prep* a, per.

a.m. *adv* del mattino.

abandon *vt* abbandonare; to ~ all hope lasciare ogni speranza; * *n* disinvoltura *f*; brio *m*.

abase *vt* abbassare, umiliare, degradare; * to ~ oneself *vi* abbassarsi, umiliarsi, abruttirsi.

abbey *n* badia *f*, abbazia *f*.

abbot *n* abate *m*.

abbreviate *vt* abbreviare.

abbreviation *n* abbreviazione *f*.

abdicate *vt* abdicare a, rinunciare a.

abdication *n* abdicazione *f*.

abdomen *n* addome *m*.

ability *n* capacità *f*, abilità *f*; abilities *npl* doti *fpl*.

ablaze *adj* in fiamme.

able *adj* capace, abile, intelligente: — to be ~ to do poter fare.

able-bodied *adj* robusto, valido.

abnormal *adj* anormale.

abnormality *n* anormalità *f*, anomalia *f*.

aboard *adv* a bordo, in vettura.

abolish *vt* abolire.

abolition *n* abolizione *f*.

aboriginal *adj* aborigeno.

abortion *n* aborto *m*.

about *prep* intorno a.

above *prep* sopra; * *adv* al di sopra: ~ all soprattutto: ~-mentioned sopra menzionato.

abroad *adv* all'estero: — to go ~ andare all'estero.

abrupt *adj* brusco.

abscess *n* ascesso *m*.

absence *n* assenza *f*, mancanza *f*.

absent *adj* mancante, assente: ~-minded distratto.

absolute *adj* assoluto; totale; categorico; * ~ly *adv* assolutamente, completamente.

absorb *vt* assorbire, ammortizzare, assimilare.

absorbent *adj* assorbente.

abstain *vi* astenersi.

abstract *adj* astratto; * *n* riassunto *m*.

absurd *adj* assurdo, ridicolo.

absurdity *n* assurdità *f*, assurdo *m*.

abundance *n* abbondanza *f*, gran quantità *f*.

abundant *adj* abbondante: ~ in ricco di.

abuse *vt* insultare; abusare di.

abusive *adj* offensivo, ingiurioso.

academic *adj* accademico *m*.

academy *n* accademia *f*.

accelerate *vt*, *vi* accelerare.

acceleration *n* accelerazione *f*.

accelerator *n* acceleratore *m*.

accent *n* accento *m*.

accentuate *vt* accentuare; mettere in risalto.

accept *vt* accettare, ammettere.

acceptable *adj* accettabile; gradito.

acceptance *n* accettazione *f*, accoglienza *f*.

access *vt* accedere a; * *n* accesso *m*.

accessible *adj* accessibile; facilmente reperibile.

accident *n* incidente *m*, disgrazia *f*; caso *m*.

accidental *adj* fortuito; involontario; * ~ly *adv* per caso; senza volere.

acclimatise *vt* acclimatare; * *vi* acclimatarsi, adattarsi.

accommodate *vt* ospitare, alloggiare.

accommodation *n* sistemazione *f*, alloggio *m*.

accompaniment *n* accompagnamento *m*.

accompany *vt* accompagnare.

accomplish *vt* compiere, portare a termine, realizzare.

accomplished *adj* esperto.

accord *n* accordo *m*: — with one ~ all'unanimità: — of one's own ~ spontaneamente.

according to *prep* secondo, stando a; conforme a; * accordingly *adv* di conseguenza.

account *n* conto *m*; relazione *f*, resoconto *m*; considera-zione *f*: — on no ~ per nessun motivo; in nessun caso: — on ~ in acconto: — on ~ of a causa di; * ~ for *vt* rendere conto di; spiegare, giustificare.

account number *n* numero *m* di conto.

accountancy *n* ragioneria *f*, contabilità *f*.

accountant *n* ragioniere *m*, ragioneria *f*, contabile *m* or *f*.

accumulate *vt* accumulare; *vi* accumularsi.

accuracy *n* esattezza *f*, accuratezza *f*, precisione *f*, fedeltà *f*.

accurate *adj* accurato, esatto, preciso; corretto; fedele.

accusation *n* accusa *f*.

accuse *vt* accusare.

accused *n* accusato *m*, imputato *m*.

accuser *n* accusatore *m*, accusatrice *f*.

accustom *vt* abituare; *vt* abituarsi.

ace *n* asso *m*.

ache *n* dolore *m*; * *vi* far male.

achieve *vt* raggiungere; realizzare.

achievement *n* realizzazione *f*; raggiungimento *m*.

acid *adj* acido, caustico; * *n* acido *m*.

acknowledge *vt* riconoscere, ammettere; ricambiare.

acknowledgment *n* riconoscimento *m*, ammissione *f*; (of letter, etc) riscontro *m*.

acne *n* acne *f*.

acoustics *n* acustica *f*.

acquaintance *n* conoscenza *f*; conoscente *m* or *f*.

acquit *vt* assolvere.

acre *n* acro *m*.

across *adv* dall'altra parte; * *prep* attraverso.

act *vt* interpretare; * *vi* recitare; agire; comportarsi; * deed *n* atto *m*; (law) legge *f*, (theatre) atto *m*.

acting *adj* facente funzione: ~ manager facente funzione di direttore: ~ headmaster preside incaricato: ~ partner socio attivo.

action *n* azione *f*.

activity *n* attività *f*.

actor *n* attore *m*.

actress *n* attrice *f*.

actual *adj* reale, effettivo; * ~ly *adv* veramente, addirittura.

acute *adj* acuto; fine; intenso; grave; perspicace.

ad-lib *vt* improvvisare; * *adj* improvvisato.

adamant *adj* inflessibile.

adapt *vt* modificare; trasformare; adattare; * *vi* adattarsi a.

adaptation *n* adattamento *m*.

adaptor *n* presa multipla *f*,

riduttore m.

add vt aggiungere, sommare,
addizionare.

addict n tossicomane,
tossicodipendente m or f,
drogato m.

addictive adj che crea
dipendenza.

addition n aggiunta f,
addizione f: — there has been
an ~ to the family la famiglia
si è accresciuta.

additive n additivo m.

address vt indirizzare;
rivolgere; * n indirizzo m.

adequate adj sufficiente;
adeguato.

adhesive n adesivo m.

adhesive tape n nastro
adesivo m.

adjacent adj adiacente.

adjective n aggettivo m.

adjudicate vt giudicare;
decidere su; aggiudicare.

adjust vt regolare; modificare;
aggiustare.

adjustable adj regolabile.

adjustment n regolazione f,
modifica f, adattamento m.

administer vt dirigere,
gestire, amministrare;
somministrare.

administration n direzione f,
gestione f, amministrazione
f, somministrazione f.

administrative adj
amministrativo.

administrator n
amministratore m,
amministratrice f.

admirable adj ammirevole.

admiral n ammiraglio m.

admiration n ammirazione f.

admire vt ammirare.

admirer n ammiratore m,
ammiratrice f.

admission adj ammissione,

ingresso.

admit vt lasciar entrare;
ammettere.

adolescence n adolescenza f.

adolescent n adolescente m or f.

adopt vt adottare.

adopted adj adottato.

adoption n adozione f.

adorable adj adorabile.

adore vt adorare.

adult adj adulto; * n adulto m,
adulta f.

adulterer n adultero m.

adulteress n adultera f.

adulterous adj adultero.

adultery n adulterio m.

advance vt anticipare; favorire;
* vi avanzare; progredire.

advanced adj avanzato,
superiore.

advantage n vantaggio m:
— to take ~ of approfittare di.

adventure n avventura f.

adventurous adj avventuroso.

adverb n avverbio m.

advertise vt fare pubblicità,
reclamizzare.

advertisement n pubblicità f,
inserzione f, annuncio m.

advertising n pubblicità f.

advice n consiglio m; avviso m.

advisable adj consigliabile;
raccomandabile.

advise vt consigliare; avvisare.

adviser n consigliere m,
consulente m or f.

advisory adj consultivo.

aerial n antenna f; * adj aereo.

aerobics npl ginnastica
aerobica f.

aerosol n aerosol m.

affair n faccenda f, affare m;
relazione f, avventura f.

affect vt influire su, incidere su.

affected adj affettato;
commosso.

affection n affetto m.

affectionate *adj* affezionato.

affirm *vt* affermare, asserire.

affirmative *adj* affermativo.

affix *vt* apporre, attaccare.

affluence *n* ricchezza *f*, abbondanza *f*.

affluent *adj* ricco.

afford *vi* and *vt* permettersi.

aforementioned *adj* sunnominato.

afraid *adj*: — to be ~ aver paura; temere.

after *prep* dopo; * ~ all *adv* dopotutto; malgrado tutto.

after-effects *npl* ripercussione *f*, conseguenza *f*; reazione *f*.

afterlife *n* vita dell'aldilà *f*.

aftermath *n* conseguenze *fpl*.

afternoon *n* pomeriggio *m*.

aftershave *n* dopobarba *m*.

afterwards *adv* dopo, più tardi, in seguito.

again *adv* ancora, di nuovo, un'altra volta: ~ and ~ ripetutamente: — then ~ d'altra parte.

against *prep* contro.

age *n* età *f*, epoca *f*, era *f*; * under-~ *adj* minorenne; * *vi* invecchiare.

agency *n* agenzia *f*.

agent *n* agente *m* or *f*.

aggression *n* aggressione *f*.

aggressive *adj* aggressivo.

aggressor *n* aggressore *m*.

ago *adv* fa: — how long ~? quanto tempo fa?

agony *n* agonia *f*, dolore atroce *f*.

agree *vt* essere d'accordo con; (grammar) concordare.

agreeable *adj* piacevole.

agreed *adj* convenuto.

agreement *n* accordo *m*, consenso *m*.

agricultural *adj* agricolo.

agriculture *n* agricoltura *f*.

ahead *adv* avanti; davanti; in anticipo.

aid *vi* aiuto *m*; assistenza *f*.

AIDS *n* AIDS *m*.

aim *vi* puntare, mirare; * *n* mira *f*, scopo *m*, fine *m*.

air *n* aria *f*; * *vt* arieggiare; esprimere.

air-conditioning *n* aria condizionata *f*.

air force *n* aeronautica militare *f*.

air freshener *n* deodorante per l'ambiente *m*.

air terminal *n* terminale *m*.

aircraft *n* aeroplano *m*.

airlift *n* ponte aereo *m*.

airline *n* linea aerea *f*.

airport *n* aeroporto *m*.

aisle *n* navata *f*.

alarm *n* allarme *m*, sveglia *f*; * *vt* allarmare.

album *n* album *m*.

alcohol *n* alcool *m*.

alcoholic *adj* alcolico; * *n* alcolizzato *m*.

alcoholism *n* alcolismo *m*.

ale *n* birra *f*.

alert *adj* sveglio; vigile; * *n* allarme *m*; * *vt* avvertire.

alibi *n* alibi *m*.

alike *adj* simile.

alive *adj* vivo; to be ~ to essere conscio di, capire pienamente.

all *adj* tutto; in buone condizioni, a posto: — he is ~ right è a posto: ~ night tutta la notte: ~ around versatile: ~ inclusive comprensivo di tutto: — to be ~ in essere stremato: — All Fools' Day il primo di aprile: — All Hallows' Day Ognissanti; * ~ along *adv* fin dal principio: ~ right (tutto) bene.

all-time *adj* senza precedenti.

allegation *n* accusa *f*.

allergy n allergia f.
alley n vicolo m.
alliance n alleanza f.
allied adj alleato.
alligator n alligatore m.
allow vi permettere;
  concedere.
allowable adj ammissibile.
ally n alleato m; * vt allearsi.
almond n mandorla f.
almost adv quasi.
alone adj solo; * adv da solo:
  — to leave ~ lasciare in pace:
  — leave me ~! lasciami in
  pace!
along prep lungo.
alphabet n alfabeto m.
alphabetical adj alfabetico:
  * ~ly adv in ordine alfabetico.
alpine n alpino m.
already adv già.
also adv anche, pure.
altar n altare m.
alter vt modificare.
alteration n modifica f.
alternative n alternativa f.
although conj benché.
altogether adv tutto sommato.
always adv sempre.
amateur n dilettante m or f.
amaze vt stupire.
amazing adj sorprendente.
ambassador n ambasciatore m.
ambiguous adj ambiguo.
ambition n ambizione f.
ambitious adj ambizioso.
ambulance n ambulanza f.
amenities npl attrezzatura f.
America n America f.
American adj americano.
amnesia n amnesia f.
among(st) prep tra, in mezzo a.
amount n somma f, importo m;
  * vi ammontare a.
amphitheatre n anfiteatro m.
amputate vt amputare.
amuse vt divertire.

amusing adj divertente.
an indef art un, uno, una.
anaemia n anemia f.
anaemic adj anemico.
anaesthetic n anestetico m.
analysis n analisi f.
anchor n ancora f.
anchovy n acciuga f.
ancient adj antico.
and conj e: — faster ~ faster
  sempre più veloce.
angel n angelo m.
anger n rabbia f; * vt far
  arrabbiare.
angle n angolo m; * vt pescare
  con la lenza.
anglicism n anglicismo m.
angrily adv con rabbia.
angry adj arrabbiato,
  incollerito, in collera: — to
  be ~ at somebody for something essere in collera con
  qualcuno per qualcosa: — to
  be ~ with someone essere in
  collera con qualcuno: — to
  get ~ arrabbiarsi: — to make
  someone ~ fare arrabbiare
  qualcuno.
animal adj, n animale m;
  ~ husbandry zootecnica f;
  ~ spirits vivacità naturale f;
  ~ welfare society società per
  la protezione degli animali f.
ankle n caviglia f: ~ socks
  calzini mpl.
anniversary n anniversario m.
announce vt annunciare.
announcement n annuncio m.
annoy vt infastidire.
annoying adj irritante.
annual adj annuo.
anorak n giacca a vento f.
anorexia n anoressia f.
another adj un altro, ancora:
  — one ~ l'un l'altro.
answer vt rispondere;
  * n risposta f.

answering machine *n*
segreteria telefonica *f*.

ant *n* formica *f*.

antarctic *adj* antartico.

antenna *n* antenna *f*.

anthem *n* inno *m*.

antibiotic *n* antibiotico *m*.

anticipate *vt* prevedere.

anticipation *n* attesa *f*.

anti-clockwise *adj* antiorario;
* *adv* in senso antiorario.

antidote *n* antidoto *m*.

antihistamine *n*
antistaminico *m*.

antique *adj* antico; * *n* pezzo *m*
di antiquariato.

antiquity *n* antichità *f*.

antiseptic *adj*, *n* antisettico *m*.

anxiety *n* ansia *f*.

anxious *adj* preoccupato.

any *adj* del, dello, della, dei,
degli, delle, qualche, un po'.

apart *adv* a distanza; separatamente; a pezzi; a parte.

apartheid *n* apartheid *f*.

apartment *n* appartamento *m*.

ape *n* scimmia *f*: * to ~ *vt*
scimmiottare, imitare.

aperitif *n* aperitivo *m*.

apologetic *adj* (pieno) di scuse.

apologise *vt* scusarsi.

apology *n* scuse *fpl*.

apostrophe *n* apostrofo *m*.

apparatus *n* attrezzatura *f*.

apparent *adj* evidente; * ~ly
adv a quanto pare.

appeal *vi* (law) fare appello,
appellarsi; ricorrere;
attrarre; (law) appello *m*.

appealing *adj* attraente;
commovente.

appear *vi* apparire; comparire;
sembrare; esibirsi.

appearance *n* aspetto *m*;
comparsa *f*.

appease *vt* placare.

appetite *n* appetito *m*.

appetising *adj* appetitoso.

applaud *vi* applaudire.

applause *n* applauso *m*.

apple *n* mela *f*: — he is the ~ of
his mother's eye è il cocco *m*
delle mamma: ~ pie torta di
mele *f*.

appliance *n* apparecchio *m*.

applicable *adj* applicabile.

apply *vt* applicare; * *vi*
applicarsi; rivolgersi; fare
domanda.

appointment *n* appuntamento
m; nomina *f*.

appreciate *vt* apprezzare;
capire: — you will ~ that lei
capisce che; * *vi* aumentare
di valore.

appreciation *n* apprezzamento *m*.

apprehensive *adj* apprensivo,
timoroso.

approach *vt*, *vi* avvicinar(si) a;
* *n* approccio *m*.

appropriate *vt* appropriarsi di;
* *adj* adatto.

approval *n* approvazione *f*.

approve (of) *vt*, *vi* approvare.

approximate *adj*
approssimativo.

apricot *n* albicocca *f*: ~ tree
albicocco *m*.

April *n* aprile *m*.

aptitude *n* abilità *f*.

Aquarius *n* Acquario *m*.

Arab *n*, *adj* arabo *m*.

arcade *n* arcata *f*, galleria *f*.

arch *n* arco *m*; * *adj* principale;
malizioso.

archaeology *n* archeologia *m*.

arched *adj* arcuato, ad arco.

architect *n* architetto *m*.

architecture *n* architettura *f*.

archway *n* passaggio *m*, a volta.

area *n* area *f*.

arena *n* arena *f*.

argue *vt*, *vi* argomentare,
discutere, fare obiezione a:

— to ~ someone into something persuadere qualcuno a far qualcosa.

argument *n* discussione *f*.

Aries *n* Ariete *m*.

aristocracy *n* aristocrazia *f*.

arithmetic *n* aritmetica *f*.

arm *n* braccio *m*; * *vt* armare.

armchair *n* poltrona *f*.

armpit *n* ascella *f*.

army *n* esercito *m*.

around *prep* intorno; * *adv* circa.

arrange *vt* sistemare; organizzare; provvedere a; accomodare.

arrear *n* (of salary) arretrati *mpl*: — (of payments) in ~ in arretrato: — to be in ~ essere moroso.

arrest *n* arresto *m*; * *vt* arrestare.

arrival *n* arrivo *m*.

arrive *vt* arrivare.

arse *n* (*vulg*) culo *m*; what a pain in the ~! che rottura di scatole!

art *n* arte *f*: — arts *npl* lettere *fpl*, studi umanistici (*mpl*): — fine ~ belle arti (*mpl*): performing ~ arte dramatica *f*.

art gallery *n* galleria d'arte *f*.

artery *n* arteria *f*.

arthritis *n* artrite *f*.

arctic *adj* artico.

artichoke *n* carciofo *m*.

article *n* articolo *m*.

artificial *adj* artificiale.

artisan *n* artigiano *m*.

artist *m* artista *m* or *f*.

as *conj* mentre; come; ~ to, ~ for quanto a.

ascent *n* ascensione *f*.

ash *n* (botanical) frassino *m*; cenere *f*.

ashtray *n* portacenere *m*.

ask *vt* chiedere: ~ a question fare una domanda.

asleep *adj* addormentato.

asparagus *n* asparago *m*.

asphyxia *n* asfissia *f*.

aspire *vt* aspirare.

aspirin *n* aspirina *f*.

ass *n* asino *m*, somaro *m*: — to make an ~ of oneself fare la figura dello stupido: — to play the ~ fare lo stupido.

assassin *n* assassino *m*.

assault *n* assalto *m*; * *vt* assaltare.

assembly *n* assemblea *f*; montaggio *m*.

assignment *n* incarico *m*.

assist *vt* aiutare.

assistant *n* aiutante *m* or *f*.

associate *vt* associare; * *adj* consociato; * *n* collega *m* or *f*.

assurance *n* assicurazione *f*.

assure *vt* assicurare.

asthma *n* asma *f*.

asthmatic *adj* asmatico.

astrology *n* astrologia *f*.

astronomy *n* astronomia *f*.

asylum *n* asilo *m*; manicomio *m*.

at *prep* a: ~ once subito: ~ all affatto: ~ first dapprima: ~ last finalmente.

athlete *n* atleta *m* or *f*.

athletic *adj* atletico.

atlas *n* atlante *m*.

atmosphere *n* atmosfera *f*.

atmospheric *adj* atmosferico.

atom *n* atomo *m*.

attach *vt* attaccare, fissare, incollare, allegare.

attack *vt* attaccare, assalire, saltare addosso (*also fig*).

attempt *vt* tentare; * *n* tentativo *m*.

attend *vt* frequentare: ~ lessons frequentare lezioni; accudire: ~ to the animals accudire gli animali.

attendant *n* custode, aiutante *m* or *f*.

attention *n* attenzione *f*.

attic *n* soffitta *f*, mansarda *f*.

attract *vt* attirare.

attractive *adj* attraente.

attribute *vt* attribuire;
  * *n* attributo *m*.

aubergine *n* melanzana *f*.

auction *n* asta *f*.

audience *n* pubblico *m*;
  udienza *f*.

auditorium *n* auditorio *m*.

August *n* agosto *m*.

aunt *n* zia *f*.

austere *adj* austero.

authentic *adj* autentico.

author *n* autore *m*.

authority *n* autorità *f*.

automatic *adj* automatico.

autumn *n* autunno *m*.

available *adj* disponibile.

avenue *n* viale *m*.

average *n* media *f*; * *adj* medio.

avocado *n* avocado *m*.

avoid *vt* evitare.

awake *vt* svegliare;
  * *adj* sveglio.

award *vt* assegnare;
  * *n* premio *m*.

aware *adj* consapevole.

away *adv* lontano: — far and ~
  di gran lunga.

away game *n* partita *f* in
  trasferta.

awful *adj* terribile.

awkward *adj* imbarazzante;
  goffo.

axe *n* ascia; * *vt* ridurre
  drasticamente.

B

baby *n* bebè *m*, neonato *m*;
  bambino piccolo *m*, bimbo,
  bimbetto *m*: ~ food pappa da
  neonati *f*: ~ minder
  bambinaia *f*: ~ walker

passeggino *m*: ~ wipe
  salvietta igienica *f*:
  * ~ sit *vi* guardare i bambini.

baby-sitter *n* bambinaia *f*,
  baby sitter *m* or *f*.

bachelor *n* scapolo *m*; (of arts
  or science) laureato *m*,
  laureata *f*.

back *n* schiena *f*, dietro *m*;
  retro *m*: — behind someone's ~
  dietro le spalle di qualcuno:
  — *adj* posteriore: ~ wages
  salari arretrati *mpl*: ~ seat
  driver chi siede sul sedile
  posteriore e infastidisce
  l'autista con consigli di
  guida; * to know something
  ~wards and forwards *adv*
  conoscere qualcosa a menadito.

backbone *n* spina *f* dorsale.

backside *n* sedere *m*.

backward *adj* all'indietro;
  arretrato: — a ~ country un
  paese arretrato.

backwards *adv* indietro.

bacon *n* pancetta *f*.

bacteria *n* batteri *mpl*.

bad *adj* cattivo; brutto.

badge *n* distintivo *m*.

badminton *n* badminton *m*.

bag *n* borsa *f*, sacchetto *m*:
  — a bagful un carniere pieno
  m, un sacco *m*, un mucchio di
  cose *m*.

baggage *n* bagaglio *m*.

bail *n* cauzione *f*.

bake *vt* cuocereal forno:
  ~d potatoes patate arrosto.

baker *n* fornaio *m*.

bakery *n* panificio *m*.

balaclava *n* passamontagna *m*.

balance *n* equilibrio *m*;
  bilancio *m*.

balcony *n* balcone *m*.

bald *adj* calvo.

ball *n* palla *f*; ballo *m*.

ballad *n* ballata *f*.

ballerina *n* ballerina *f*.
ballet *n* danza *f* classica.
balloon *n* palloncino *m*: — hot
   air ~ mongolfiera *f*.
ballpoint (pen) *n* penna *f* a
   sfera.
ballroom *n* sala *f* da ballo.
balm *n* balsamo *m*.
bamboo *n* bambù *m*.
ban *n* divieto *m*; * *vt* proibire.
banana *n* banana *f*: ~ tree
   banano *m*.
band *n* banda *f*, striscia *f*.
bandage *n* fascia *f*.
bandit *n* bandito *m*.
bandstand *n* palco della-
   orchestra *m*.
bang *n* colpo *m*; * *vt*, *vi* sbattere.
banger *n* salsiccia *f*: ~s and
   mash salsicce (*fpl*) con puré
   di patate (*m*); petardo *m*.
bangle *n* braccialetto *m*.
banjo *n* banjo *m*.
bank *n* riva *f*, banca *f*:
   ~ account *n* conto in banca *m*:
   ~ holiday giorno festivo *m*:
   ~ hours orario di sportello *m*:
   ~ loan prestito *or* mutuo
   bancario *m*.
banker *n* banchiere *m*.
banknote *n* banconota *f*.
bankruptcy *n* bancarotta,
   fallimento *m*.
bankrupt *adj* fallito;
   * *n* fallito *m*, bancarottiere m.
bank statement *n* estratto *m*
   conto.
banner *n* stendardo *m*;
   striscione *m*.
banquet *n* banchetto *m*.
baptise *vt* battezzare.
bar *n* bar *m*; sbarra *f*:
   — a ~ of chocolate una
   tavoletta di cioccolata *f*;
   * *vt* sbarrare; * *prep* tranne.
barbecue *n* barbecue *m*.
barber *n* barbiere *m*.

bare *adj* nudo; spoglio;
   semplice: ~ bones pelle e
   ossa: — a ~ majority una
   maggioranza esigua; * to go ~
   vi essere scoperto, al verde;
   * *vt* scoprire, denudare: — to
   lay ~ mettere a nudo,
   svelare: — to ~ one's head
   scoprirsi il capo: — to ~ one's
   heart (soul) to someone
   aprire il cuore (l'anima) a
   qualcuno: — to ~ one's
   thoughts rivelare i propri
   pensieri: — to ~ one's teeth
   mostare i denti.
barely *adv* appena.
bargain *n* affare *m*: — it's a ~!
   è un affare! *or* affare fatto!
   * *vt*, *vi* contrattare,
   mercanteggiare.
bark *n* corteccia *f*; abbaiare *m*;
   * *vi* abbaiare.
barley *n* orzo *m*.
barmaid *n* barista *f*.
barman *n* barista *m*.
barn *n* stalla *f*.
barometer *n* barometro *m*.
baroque *adj* barocco.
barrel *n* barile *m*; canna *f*.
barrier *n* barriera *f*.
barrister *n* avvocato *m*.
bartender *n* barista *m*.
base *n* base *f*; * *vt* basare;
   * *adj* ignobile, vile.
baseball *n* baseball *m*.
basenient *n* seminterrato *m*.
bash *n* botta; * *vt* picchiare;
   * *vi* (*fig*) to ~ one's head
   against a brick wall sbattere
   la testa contro un muro.
basic *adj* fondamentale.
basil *n* basilico *m*.
basin *n* lavandino *m*.
basis *n* base *f*.
basket *n* cestino *m*.
basketball *n* pallacanestro *f*.
bass *adj* basso.

bassoon *n* fagotto *m*.

bastard *adj* bastardo.

bat *n* (zoology) pipistrello *m*;
(sport) mazza *f*.

bath *n* bagno *m*; * *vi* fare il
bagno a (un bambino, un
invalido); *vi* farsi il bagno,
lavarsi.

bathing cap *n* cuffia *f*.

bathing costume *n* costume *m*.

bathroom *n* (stanza da) bagno *m*.

baths *npl* piscine *f*; terme *f*,
bagni termali *mpl*.

batter *vt* colpire
violentemente; * *n* pastella *f*.

battery *n* pila *f*, batteria *f*.

battle *n* battaglia *f*, lotta *f*;
* *vi* lottare, combattere.

battleship *n* nave *f* da guerra.

bay *n* baia *f*; alloro *m*;
abbaiamento *m*, latrato *m*;
* *vi* abbaiare, latrare.

bayonet *n* baionetta *f*.

bazaar *n* bazar *m*.

be *vi* essere (io sono, tu sei, lui
[lei] è, noi siamo, voi siete,
loro sono).

beach *n* spiaggia *f*.

bead *n* perlina *f*.

beak *n* becco *m*.

bean *n* fagiolo *m*; chicco *m*.

bear *n* orso *m*; * *vt* portare;
sopportare; partorire.

bearable *adj* sopportabile.

beard *n* barba *f*.

beast *n* bestia *f*: ~ of burden
bestia da soma.

beastly *adj* bestiale, brutale,
insopportabile.

beat *vt* battere; * *vi* palpitare;
* *n* battito *m*; ritmo *m*.

beautiful *adj* bello; splendido.

beautify *vt* abbellire.

beauty *n* bellezza *f*: ~ spot neo *m*.

because *conj* perché.

become *vi* diventare; divenire.

becoming *adj* adatto.

bed *n* letto *m*.

bedclothes *npl* biancheria da
letto *f*.

bedroom *n* camera da letto *f*.

bee *n* ape *f*.

beef *n* manzo *m*.

beefsteak *n* bistecca (di manzo) *f*.

beer *n* birra *f*.

beetle *n* scarabeo *m*.

before *adv* prima di.

beg *vt* mendicare; supplicare.

beggar *n* mendicante *m* or *f*.

begin *vt*, *vi* cominciare,
incominciare, iniziare.

beginning *n* inizio *m*, principio *m*.

behave *vi* comportarsi.

behaviour *n* comportamento *m*.

behind *prep* dietro.

being *n* essere *m*, esistenza *f*.

belief *n* fede *f*; convinzione *f*,
opinione *f*.

believable *adj* credibile.

believe *vt*, *vi* credere.

bell *n* campanello *m*.

belly *n* pancia *f*.

belong *vi* appartenere.

belongings *npl* effetti *mpl*
personali.

below *prep*, *adv* sotto.

belt *n* cintura *f*; * *vt* prendere
a cinghiate, picchiare;
* *vi* (*sl*) filare via, sfrecciare.

bench *n* panchina *f*.

bend *vt* piegare; * *vi* piegarsi;
* *n* curva *f*.

beneath *adv*, *prep* sotto.

beneficial *adj* benefico.

beneficiary *n* beneficiario *m*.

benefit *n* vantaggio *m*;
* *vt* giovare a; * *vi* trarre
vantaggio da.

benign *adj* benevolo; benigno.

bent *n* inclinazione *f*; (*sl*)
finocchio *m*.

bereaved *adj* in lutto.

bereavement *n* lutto.

beret *n* berretto *m*.

berry *n* bacca *f*.
beside *prep* accanto a.
besides *prep* oltre a;
* *adv* inoltre.
best *adj* migliore; * *adv* meglio;
* *n* il migliore.
bestseller *n* bestseller *m*.
bet *vt, vi* scommettere;
* *n* scommessa *f*.
betray *vt* tradire.
betrayal *n* tradimento *m*.
betroth *vt* fidanzarsi con.
betrothal *n* fidanzamento *m*.
better *adj* migliore;
* *adv* meglio; * *vt* migliorare.
between *prep* tra, fra.
beware *vi* stare attento a, fare
attenzione a.
beyond *prep* oltre; al di là.
Bible *n* Bibbia *f*.
bicycle *n* bicicletta *f*.
bid *vt* offrire; * *vi* dichiarare;
* *n* offerto *m*; tentativo *m*.
big *adj* grande; grosso.
bikini *n* bikini *m*.
bile *n* bile *f*.
bilingual *adj* bilingue.
bill *n* becco *m*; fattura *f*, conto *m*.
billiards *npl* biliardo *m*.
billion *n* miliardo *m*.
bin *n* bidone *m*; * *vt* buttare via.
bind *vt* legare; rilegare.
bingo *n* tombola *f*.
binoculars *npl* binocolo *m*.
biographer *n* biografo *m*.
biography *n* biografia *f*.
biological *adj* biologico.
biology *n* biologia *f*.
bird *n* uccello *m*.
birth *n* nascita *f*; parto *m*.
birthday *n* compleanno *m*.
biscuit *n* biscotto *m*.
bishop *n* vescovo *m*; (chess)
alfiere *m*.
bison *n* bisonte *m*.
bit *n* punta *f*; pezzo *m*; morso *m*.
bitch *n* cagna *f*; (*vulg*) stronza *f*.

bite *vt* inordere; pungere:
~ the dust lasciarci la pelle;
* *n* morso *m*; puntura
(d'insetto) *f*.
bitter *adj* amaro; aspro; (*fig*)
amareggiato.
bitterly *adv* amaramente.
bizarre *adj* bizzarro.
black *adj* nero; * *n* nero;
* *vt* boicottare.
blackberry *n* mora *f*.
blackbird *n* merlo *m*.
blackboard *n* lavagna *f*.
blackhead *n* punto nero *m*.
blacklist *n* lista nera *f*.
blackmail *n* ricatto *m*;
* *vt* ricattare.
black sheep *n* pecora nera *f*.
blacksmith *n* fabbro *m*.
bladder *n* vescica *f*.
blade *n* lama *f*.
blame *vt* incolpare;
rimproverare; * *n* colpa *f*.
blameless *adj* irreprensibile.
bland *adj* blando.
blank *adj* bianco; vacuo;
* *n* vuoto *m*.
blank cheque *n* assegno in
bianco *or* a vuoto *m*.
blanket *n* coperta *f*;
* *adj* globale.
blaspheme *vi* bestemmiare.
blasphemous *adj* blasfemo.
blasphemy *n* bestemmia *f*.
blast *n* esplosione *f*, raffica *f*;
* *vt* far saltare; * *excl* ~!
mannaggia!
blaze *n* incendio *m*; * *vi* ardere;
divampare.
blazer *n* blazer *m*.
bleach *vt* candeggiare;
* *n* candeggina *f*.
bleak *adj* tetro; desolato.
bleed *vi* sanguinare;
* *vt* spurgare.
bleeding *n* emorragia *f*;
* *adj* sanguinante.

bless *vt* benedire.

blessed *adj* benedetto.

blessing *n* benedizione *f*.

blind *adj*, *n* cieco *m*;
* *vt* accecare: — venetian ~
tenda *f* avvolgibile.

blindness *n* cecità *f*.

blink *vt* battere le palpebre;
* *n* battito di ciglia *m*.

blister *n* vescica *f*.

blizzard *n* bufera *f* di neve.

block *n* blocco *m*: ~ade blocco:
— a ~ of tobacco un bloc-
chetto di tabacco *m*.

blond(e) *adj*, *n* biondo *m*.

blood *n* sangue *m*.

blossom *n* fiori *mpl*.

blouse *n* camicetta *f*.

blow *vi* soffiare: — to ~ one's
nose soffiarsi il naso;
* *vt* suonare; esplodere;
* *n* colpo *m*, attacco *m*, colpo
di mano *m*; to come to ~s
venire alle mani: — to
exchange ~s darsele.

blue *adj* azzurro, celeste.

bluebottle *n* moscone *m*.

blunder *n* gaffe *f*.

blunt *adj* non tagliente; brusco.

blush *n* rossore *m*; * *vi* arrossire.

bluster n furia *f*; bufera *f*;
sfuriata *f*; spacconata *f*.

board *n* asse *f*; (*chess*)
scacchiera; (*food*) vitto *m*;
commissione *f*; * *vt* imbarcarsi
su; salite su; * *vi* essere a
pensione da.

boast *vt* vantare; * *vi* vantarsi;
* *n* vanteria *f*.

boat *n* barca *f*; nave *f*.

bob *n* casco *m*; capelli a
caschetto *mpl*; peso del
pendolo *m*; moneta *f*;
* *vt* tagliare I capelli alla
maschietta; * *vi* ballonzolare.

body *n* corpo *m*; cadavere *m*;
massa *f*.

bogus *adj* fasullo.

boil *vi* bollire; * *vt* (far) lessare;
* *n* foruncolo *m*.

boisterous *adj* vivace, forte,
violento; (of children)
allegro e chiassoso.

bold *adj* audace.

bollard *n* colonnina *f*.

bolt *n* chiavistello *m*.

bomb *n* bomba *f*;
* *vt* bombardare.

bond *n* impegno *m*; legame *m*;
titolo *m*.

bone *n* (human) osso *m*; (fish)
lisca *f*.

bonfire *n* falò *m*.

bonus *n* gratifica *f*; premio *m*.

bony *adj* osseo.

boo *vt* fischiare, prendere a
fischi.

boob *n* sebmpliciotto *m*; gaffe
f; tetta *f*; ~less donna senza
tette, piatta *f*.

book *n* libro *m*; quaderno *m*;
* *vt* prenotare, riservare.

book-keeper *n* contabile *m* or *f*.

book-keeping *n* contabilità *f*.

booklet *n* opuscolo *m*.

bookshop *n* libreria *f*.

boom *n* boma *f*.

boot *n* stivale *m*, scarpone *m*,
scarponcino *m*.

booth *n* cabina *f*.

booze *vi* alzare il gomito;
* *n* alcool *m*.

boozer *n* osteria *f*.

bore *vt* trivellare; annoiare;
* *n* foro *m*; calibro *m*; noia *f*;
noioso *m*: — you are such a ~!
sei così noioso!

boredom *n* noia *f*.

boring *adj* noioso.

born *adj* nato.

borough *n* comune *m*.

borrow *vt* prendere in prestito.

bosom *n* petto *m*, seno *m*.

boss *n* capo *m*, padrone *m*.

botany *n* botanica *f*.
both *adj* entrambi; ambedue; tutti e due.
bother *vt* infastidire: * *n* una seccatura.
bottle *n* bottiglia *f*; * *vt* imbottigliare.
bottom *n* fondo *m*; sedere *m*.
bough *n* ramo *m*.
boulder *n* macigno *m*.
bound(s) *n* limiti *mpl*.
boundary *n* confine *m*.
bountiful *adj* abbondante; munifico.
bouquet *n* bouquet *m*.
bow *vi* chinare; * *vi* inchinarsi; * *n* inchino *m*; prua *f*.
bowl *n* scodella *f*; * *vt* lanciare.
box *n* scatola *f*: — palco *m*; * *vi* fare il pugile.
boxing *n* pugilato *m*: — B~ day Santo Stefano.
boxer *n* pugile *m*.
box office *n* botteghino *m*.
boy *n* ragazzo *m*; fanciullo *m*.
bra *n* reggiseno *m*.
bracelet *n* braccialetto *m*.
bracket *n* mensola *f*; parentesi *f*.
brain *n* cervello *m*.
brake *n* freno; * *vi* frenare.
bran *n* crusca *f*.
branch *n* ramo *m*; * *vi* diramarsi.
brand *n* marca *f*; * *vi* marchiare.
brandy *n* brandy *m*.
brass *n* ottone *m*.
brave *adj* coraggioso.
bread *n* pane *m*.
breadcrumbs *n* briciole di pane *fpl*; pangrattato *m*.
breadth *n* larghezza *f*.
break *vi* rompere; * *vi* rompersi.
breakable *adj* fragile.
breakdown *n* guasto *m*; esaurimento nervoso *m*.
breakfast *n* prima colazione *f*.
breast *n* petto *m*; seno *m*; mammella *f*.

breastbone *n* sterno *m*.
breath *n* fiato n; alito *m*.
breathe *vi* respirare.
breathing *n* respiro *m*, respirazione *f*.
breathless *adj* senza fiato.
breed *n* razza *f*; * *vt* allevare; * *vi* riprodursi.
breeze *n* brezza *f*, venticello *m*.
brewery *n* fabbrica di birra *f*.
bribe *n* bustarella *f*; * *vt* corrompere.
bribery *n* corruzione *f*.
brick *n* mattone *m*.
bride *n* sposa *f*.
bridegroom *n* sposo *m*.
bridesmaid *n* damigella d'onore *f*.
bridge *n* ponte *m*; bridge *m*.
brief *adj* breve; * *n* dossier; * *vt* dare istruzioni a.
briefcase *n* cartella *f*.
briefs *n* slip; mutandine *fpl*.
bright *adj* luminoso; vispo.
brightness *n* luminosità *f*.
brilliance *n* intensità *f*, intelligenza *f*.
brilliant *adj* brillant, scintillante.
bring *vt* portare.
brisk *adj* sbrigativo; attivo.
brittle *adj* fragile.
broad *adj* largo.
broadcast *n* trasmissione *f*; * *vt* trasmettere.
brochure *n* depliant *m*; brochure *f*.
broken *adj* rotto, spezzato.
brolly *n* ombrello *m*.
bronchitis *n* bronchite *f*.
bronze *n* bronzo *m*.
brooch *n* spilla *f*.
brood *vt* covare, rimuginare; * *n* covata *f*; prole *f*.
broom *n* scopa *f*; (botany) ginestra *f*.
broth *n* brodo *m*.

brothel *n* bordello *m*.
brother *n* fratello *m*.
brother-in-law *n* cognato *m*.
brotherly *adj* fraterno.
brown *adj* marrone.
bruise *vt* farsi un livido a;
* *n* livido *m*.
brush *n* spazzola *f*; * *vt* spazzolare; scopare; sfiorare.
brutal *adj* brutale.
bubble *n* bolla *f*.
bucket *n* secchio *m*.
buckle *n* fibbia *f*; * *vt* allacciare; * *vi* allacciarsi.
bud *n* bocciolo *m*.
Buddhism *m* buddismo *m*.
budgerigar *n* pappagallino *m*.
budget *n* bilancio *m*.
buffalo *n* bufalo *m*.
buffet *n* schiaffo; buffet *m*;
* *vt* sballottare.
bug *n* insetto *m*, germe *m*.
build *n* corporatura *f*;
* *vt* costruire.
builder *n* costruttore *m*;
muratore *m*.
building *n* costruzione *f*,
edificio *m*.
bulb *n* bulbo *m*; lampadina *f*.
bulk *n* volume *m*; massa *f*.
bull *n* toro *m*.
bulldozer *n* bulldozer *m*.
bullet *n* proiettile *m*,
pallottola *f*; fast as a ~
veloce come una scheggia.
bulletin *n* bollettino *m*.
bullet-proof *adj* a prova di
proiettile.
bullion *n* oro *m* in lingotti.
bully *n* bullo *m*; * *vt* fare il
prepotente.
bumblebee *n* bombo *m*,
calabrone *m*.
bump *n* botta *f*; bernoccolo *m*;
* *vt* sbattere.
bun *n* focaccia *f*; chignon *m*.
bunch *n* mazzo *m*; grappolo *m*.

bungalow *n* bungalow *m*.
bunion *n* (medical) cipolla *f*.
bunk *n* cuccetta *f*.
bunker *n* bunker *m*.
buoy *n* (marine) boa *f*.
buoyant *adj* galleggiante.
burden *n* carico *m*; onere *m*;
* *vt* opprirnere; oberare.
bureau *n* ufficio *m*;
secrétaire *m*.
bureaucracy *n* burocrazia *f*.
bureaucrat *n* burocrate *m* or *f*.
burglar *n* ladro *m*.
burgle *vt* svaligiare.
burial *n* sepoltura *f*.
burn *vt* bruciare; * *n* bruciatura
ustione *f*.
burp *n* rutto *m*; * *vi* ruttare.
burrow *n* tana *f*; * *vt* scavare.
bursar *n* amministratore,
tesoriere *m*.
bursary *n* borsa di studio *f*.
burst *vi* scoppiare.
bury *vt* seppellire.
bus *n* autobus *m*.
bush *n* cespuglio *m*.
busily *adv* alacremente.
business *n* affari *mpl*; attività *f*.
businessman *n* uomo di affari *m*.
bus-stop *n* fermata *f* dello
autobus.
bust *n* busto *m*; petto *m*.
busy *adj* occupato.
but *conj* ma; * *adv* solo;
* *prep* tranne.
butcher *n* macellaio *m*;
* *vt* macellare.
butcher's shop *n* macelleria *f*.
butler *n* maggiordomo *m*.
butt *n* botte *f*, mozzicone *m*;
* *vt* dare una testata.
butter *n* burro *m*.
buttercup *n* ranuncolo *m*.
butterfly *n* farfalla *f*.
buttock *n* natica *f*.
button *n* bottone *m*.
buy *vt* comprare.

by *adv* vicino; * *prep* vicino;
via; davanti.
bygone *adj* passato.
bypass *n* circonvallazione *f*;
* *vt* girare attorno.
by-product *n* sottoprodotto *m*.
byte *n* (computing) byte *m*.

C

cab *n* taxi *m*; cabina *f*.
cabbage *n* cavolo *m*.
cabin *n* capanna *f*, cabina *f*.
cabinet *n* armadietto *m*;
Consiglio *m* dei Ministri.
cable *n* cavo *m*.
cable car *n* funivia *f*.
cactus *n* cactus *m*.
café *n* caffè *m*; bar *m*.
caffeine *n* caffeina *f*.
cage *n* gabbia *f*; * *vt* mettere in
gabbia.
cake *n* torta *f*, pasticcino *m*;
tavoletta *f*, pezzo *m*: — a
piece of ~ una cosa facile *f*,
un gioco da ragazzi *m*; you
can't have your ~ and eat it
non si può avere la botte
piena e la moglie ubriaca;
~s and ale i piaceri
mondani *mpl*.
cake shop *n* pasticceria *f*.
calculate *vt* calcolare.
calculator *n* calcolatore *m*.
calendar *n* calendario *m*.
calf *n* vitello *m*.
call *n* chiamata *f*; grido *m*,
invocazione *f*; invito *m*;
richiesta *f*.
call *vt* and *vi* chiamare;
telefonare a; nominare;
gridare; to ~ someone's
attention richiamare
l'attenzione di qualcuno; to
~ a flight annunciare un
volo; to ~ someone into play

fare agire qualcuno; to feel
called upon to do something
sentirsi in dovere di fare
qualcosa.
calm *n* calma *f*, pace *f*.
calorie *n* caloria *f*.
camel *n* camello *m*.
camera *n* macchina *f* fotografica.
camomile *n* camomilla *f*.
camouflage *n* mimetizzazione *f*.
camp *n* accampamento *m*;
* *vi* campeggiare.
campaign *n* campagna *f*;
* *vi* fare una campagna.
camping *n* campeggio *m*.
campsite *n* campeggio *m*.
can *n* (barattolo di) latta *m*,
lattina *f*.
can *v aux* potere (io posso, tu
puoi, lui [lei] può, noi
possiamo, voi potete, loro
possono); *vt* inscatolare,
mettere in lattina.
canal *n* canale *m*.
cancel *vt* cancellare,
annullare, sospendere: to ~ a
football match sospendere
una partita di calcio; to ~ an
order (a booking) annullare
un'ordinazione (una
prenotazione); to ~ an
account (a debt) estinguere
un conto (un debito).
cancellation *n* cancellazione *f*.
cancer *n* cancro *m*.
Cancer *n* Cancro *m*.
candelabra *n* candelabro *m*.
candidate *n* candidato *m*.
candle *n* candela *f*.
candlestick *n* candeliere *m*.
cane *n* canna *f*, bastone *m*.
canine *adj* canino.
canister *n* barattolo *m*.
cannabis *n* canapa *f* indiana.
cannon *n* cannone *m*.
canoe *n* canoa *f*.

canteen *n* inensa *f*.
canvas *n* tela *f*.
canyon *n* canyon *m*.
cap *n* berretto *m*.
capability *n* capacità *f*.
capable *adj* capace.
capacity *n* capacità *f*.
cape *n* capo *m*; cappa *f*;
  mantello *m*.
capital *n* lettera maiuscola *f*,
  (city) capitale *f*; (economics)
  capitale *m*.
capitalism *n* capitalismo *m*.
capitalist *n* capitalista *m* or *f*.
Capricorn *n* Capricorno *m*.
captain *n* capitano *m*.
caption *n* sottotitolo *m*.
captivity *n* prigionia *f*;
  cattività *f*.
capture *n* cattura *f*.
car *n* macchina *f*, automobile *f*.
caramel *n* caramello *m*.
carat *n* carato *m*.
caravan *n* roulotte *f*.
carbonated *adj* gassato.
card *n* biglietto *m*; tessera *f*,
  carta *f*; playing ~ carta da
  gioco; to play ~s giocare a
  carte.
cardboard *n* cartone *m*.
card game *n* gioco di carte *m*.
cardiac *adj* cardiaco.
cardinal *adj* cardinale;
  * *n* cardinale *m*.
care *n* preoccupazione *f*; attenzione *f*; * *vi* interessarsi.
career *n* carriera *f*.
careful *adj* attento; accurato;
  prudente.
careless *adj* distratto; negligente.
caress *n* carezza *f*; * *vt*
  carezzare.
caretaker *n* portinaio *m*.
carnival *n* carnevale *m*.
carpet *n* tappeto *m*; moquette *f*.
carriage *n* carrozza *f*, vagone

m; portamento *m*.
carriageway *n* carreggiata *f*.
carrier *n* corriere *m*; (medical)
  portatore; portaerei *f*
  sacchetto *m*.
carrot *n* carota *f*.
carry *vt* portare; tenere;
  riportare; approvare.
cart *n* carretto *m*.
carton *n* cartone animato *m*;
  vignetta *f*.
cartoon *n* vignetta *f*; cartone
  m animato.
carve *vt* intagliere; incidere;
  scolpire.
case *n* valigia *f*, custodia *f*,
  astuccio *m*; cassa *f*; (grammar,
  medical) caso *m*: — in ~ caso
  mai.
cash *n* (soldi) contanti *mpl*;
  * *vt* incassare.
cashier *n* cassiere *m*.
cassette *n* cassetta *f*.
cassette recorder *n* registratore *m*.
cast *vt* gettare; lanciare;
  affidare; * *n* gesso *m*; cast *m*;
  stampo *m*; strabismo *m*.
castle *n* castello *m*.
casual *adj* casuale; informale;
  saltuario; indifferente.
casualty *n* vittima *f*.
cat *n* gatto *m*.
catalogue *n* catalogo *m*.
catarrh *n* catarro *m*.
catastrophe *n* catastrofe *f*.
catch *vt* afferrare; prendere;
  sorprendere; sentire.
category *n* categoria *f*.
cater *vi* provvedere a.
caterpillar *n* bruco *m*.
cathedral *n* cattedrale *f*;
  duomo *m*.
catholic *adj* cattolico.
Catholicism *n* cattolicesimo *m*.
cattle *n* bestiame *m*.
cauliflower *n* cavolfiore *m*.

cause *n* causa *f* motivo *m*;
 * *vt* causare.
caution *n* attenzione;
 prudenza *f*.
cautious *adj* cauto; prudente.
cave *n* caverna *f*.
caviar *n* caviale *m*.
cease *vt*, *vi* cessare.
ceasefire *n* cessate il fuoco *m*.
ceiling *n* soffitto *m*.
celebrate *vt* festeggiare.
celebrity *n* celebrità *f*.
celibacy *n* celibato *m*;
 astinenza sassuale *f*.
cell *n* cella *f*.
cellar *n* cantina *f*.
cello *n* violoncello *m*.
cellular *adj* cellulare.
cement *n* cemento *m*.
cemetery *n* cimitero *m*.
censorship *n* censura *f*.
centenary *n* centenario *m*.
centigrade *n* centigrado *m*.
centilitre *n* centilitro *m*.
centimetre *n* centimetro *m*.
centipede *n* millepiedi *m*.
central *adj* centrale.
century *n* secolo *m*.
ceramic *adj* di ceramica.
cereal *n* cereale *m*.
ceremony *n* cerimonia *f*.
certain *adj* certo; sicuro.
certainty *n* certezza *f*.
certificate *n* certificato *m*.
certify *vt* certificare;
 attestare.
cessation *n* cessazione *f*.
cesspit *n* pozzonero *m*.
chain *n* catena *f*; * *vt* incatenare.
chair *n* sedia *f*, poltrona *f*;
 * *vt* presiedere.
chairman *n* presidente *m*.
chalk *n* gesso *m*.
challenge *n* sfida *f*; * *vt* sfidare.
chamber *n* camera *f*.
chameleon *n* camaleonte *m*.
champagne *n* champagne *m*.

champion *n* campione *m*;
 * *vt* difendere.
chance *n* caso *m*; occasione *f*;
 probabilità *f*; rischio *m*;
 * *vi* rischiare.
chancellor *n* cancelliere *m*.
chandelier *n* lampadario *m*.
change *vt* cambiare;
 trasformare; * *vi* mutare;
 * *n* cambiamento *m*; resto *m*;
 spiccioli *mpl*.
channel *n* canale *m*;
 * *vt* incanalare.
chaos *n* caos *m*.
chapel *n* cappella *f*.
chapter *n* capitolo *m*.
character *n* carattere *m*;
 personaggio *m*.
charcoal *n* carbone *m*,
 carboncino *m*.
charge *vi* accusare; (military)
 attaccare; far pagare;
 * *n* imputazione *f*, (military)
 carica *f*, tariffa *f*.
charity *n* carità *f*, beneficenza *f*.
chase *vt* inseguire;
 * *n* inseguimento *m*; caccia *f*.
chat *vi* chiacchierare;
 * *n* chiacchierata *f*.
chauvinism *n* maschilismo *m*;
 sciovínismo *m*.
chauvinist *n* maschilista *m*;
 sciovinista *m* or *f*.
cheap *adj* a buon prezzo.
cheat *vt* imbrogliare;
 * *n* imbroglione *m*.
cheek *vi* verificare;
 controllare; * *n* limitazione *f*,
 controllo *m*; (chess) scacco *m*.
checkout *n* ora della partenza
 f, controllo finale *m*.
cheek *n* guancia *f*.
cheeky *adj* con la faccia tosta.
cheerful *adj* allegro.
cheese *n* formaggio *m*.
chef *n* chef *m*.
chemical *adj* chimico;

* *n* prodotto *m* chimico.
chemist *n* chimico *m*;
  farmacista *m* or *f*.
cheque *n* assegno *m*.
cherry *n* ciliegia *f*.
cherub *n* cherubino *m*.
chess *n* scacchi *mpl*; ~-game
  gioco degli scacchi *m*.
chessboard *n* scacchiera *f*.
chessman *n* pedina *f*.
chest *n* petto *m*; baule *m*.
chew *vt* masticare.
chewing gum *n* chewing-gum
  m, gomma da masticare.
chicken *n* pollo *m*.
chickenpox *n* varicella *f*.
chief *adj* principale; * *n* capo *m*.
child *n* bambino *m*.
chill *adj* freddo; * *n* freddo *m*;
  * *vt* mettere in fresco.
chilly *adj* fresco.
chimney *n* camino *m*.
chin *n* mento *m*.
chip *vi* scheggiare;
  * *n* frammento *m*; patatina
  fritta *f*; scheggiatura *f*.
chisel *n* scalpello *m*.
chlorine *n* cloro *m*; (*sl*)
  candeggina *f*.
chocolate *n* cioccolato *m*.
choice *n* scelta *f*; * *adj* di prima
  scelta.
choir *n* coro *m*.
choke *vt* soffocare; * *n* aria *f*.
cholera *n* colera *m*.
choose *vt* scegliere.
chop *vt* tagliare; spaccare;
  * *n* colpo *m* secco; costoletta *f*.
choral *adj* corale.
chord *n* corda *f*.
choreography *n* coreografia *f*.
chorus *n* coro *m*; ritornello *m*.
Christ *n* Cristo *m*.
christen *vt* battezzare.
Christian *adj*, *n* cristiano *m*.
Christianity *n* cristianesimo *m*.
Christmas *n* Natale *m*.

Christmas Eve *n* vigilia *f* di
  Natale.
chrome *n* metallo *m* cromato.
chronological *adj* cronologico.
chronology *n* cronologia *f*.
chum *n* amicone *m*.
chunk *n* bel pezzo *m*.
church *n* chiesa *f*.
churn *n* zangola *f*; * *vt* agitare.
chutney *n* salsa indiana *f*.
cider *n* sidro *m*.
cigar *n* sigaro *m*.
cigarette *n* sigaretta *f*.
cinema *n* cinema *m*.
circle *n* cerchio *m*;
  * *vt* accerchiare.
circuit *n* giro *m*; circuito *m*.
circular *adj* circolare;
  * *n* circolare *f*.
circulation *n* circolazione *f*.
circumference *n* circonferenza *f*.
circus *n* circo *m*.
citizen *n* cittadino *m*.
citrus *n* agrume *m*.
city *n* città *f*.
civic *adj* civico.
civil *adj* civile.
civilian *n* civile *m*, borghese *m*.
civilisation *n* civiltà *f*.
civilise *vt* civilizzare.
claim *vt* rivendicare;
  pretendere; * *n* pretesa *f*;
  affermazione.
clam *n* vongola *f*.
clamp *n* morsetto *m*;
  * *vt* stringere.
clap *vt* applaudire;
  * *n* battimano *m*.
claret *n* chiaretto *m*.
clarify *vt* chiarire.
clarinet *n* clarinetto *m*.
clarity *n* chiarezza *f*.
clasp *n* gancio *m*; * *vt* afferrare.
class *n* classe *f*, tipo *m*;
  categoria *f*; * *vt* definire.
classic(al) *adj* classico.
classification *n* classificazione *f*.

classify *vt* classificare.

classroom *n* aula *f*.

claustrophobia *n* claustrofobia *f*.

claw *n* unghia *f*; artiglio *m*;
 * *vt* graffiare.

clay *n* argilla *f*.

clean *adj* pulito; corretto *m*;
 * *vt* pulire.

clear *adj* chiaro; trasparente;
 nitido; sgombro.

clear *vt* chiarire: — to ~ one's
 mind chiarirsi le idee;
 sgombrare: — to ~ the
 ground sgombrare il terreno;
 disboscare: — to ~ the land
 disboscare il terreno;
 approvare, autorizzare: — to
 ~ a plan approvare un progetto;
 dichiarare innocente,
 prosciogliere: — he has been
 cleared è stato prosciolto.

clearly *adv* chiaramente.

clergy *n* clero *m*.

clergyman *n* sacerdote *m*;
 pastore *m*; ministro *m*.

clerk *n* impiegato *m*.

clever *adj* intelligente.

client *n* cliente *m* or *f*.

cliff *n* scogliera *f*.

climate *n* clima *m*.

climatic *adj* climatico.

climax *n* culmine *m*; orgasmo *m*.

climb *vt, vi* salire; arrampicarsi.

clinic *n* clinica *f*.

clip *n* sequenza *f*; fermaglio *m*;
 moletta *f*; * *vt* tosare;
 ritagliare.

cloak *n* cappa *f*, mantella *f*.

cloakroom *n* guardaroba *m*.

clock *n* orologio *m*.

clockwise *adv* in senso orario.

clockwork *adj* a molla.

close *vt* chiudere; * *adj, adv*
 vicino; * *n* fine *f*; chiusura *f*.

closed *adj* chiuso.

closely *adv* strettamente.

cloth *n* tessuto *m*, stoffa *f*.

clothe *vt* vestire.

clothes *npl* vestiti *mpl*.

cloud *n* nuvola *f*; nube *f*;
 * *vt* intorbidire.

clown *n* pagliaccio *m*.

club *n* randello *m*; mazza *f*;
 bastone *m*; circolo *m*; club *m*;
 (cards) fiori *mpl*.

clue *n* indicazione *f*, indizio *m*.

coach *n* corriera *f*, pullman *m*;
 carrozza *f*, allenatore *m*;
 * *vt* allenare.

coal *n* carbone *m*.

coalition *n* coalizione *f*.

coarse *adj* ruvido; volgare.

coast *n* costa *f*; litorale *m*;
 * *vt* andare/metere in folle.

coastal *adj* costiero.

coaster *n* sottobicchiere *m*.

coastline *n* litorale *m*.

coat *n* capotto *m*; mano *f*;
 * *vt* ricoprire.

coat hanger *n* gruccia *f*.

coax *vt* convincere.

cocaine *n* cocaina *f*.

cock *n* gallo *m*; rubinetto *m*.

cockerel *n* galletto *m*.

cockroach *n* scarafaggio *m*.

cocktail *n* cocktail *m*.

cocoa *n* cacao *m*.

coconut *n* noce *f* di cocco.

cod *n* merluzzo *m*.

code *n* codice *m*; * *vt* cifrare.

coffee *n* caffè *m*.

coffin *n* barra *f*.

cognac *n* cognac *m*.

coil *n* rotolo *m*; bobina *f*;
 spirale *f*; * *vt* avvolgere;
 * *vi* attorcigliarsi.

coin *n* moneta *f*.

coincide *vi* coincidere.

coincidence *n* coincidenza *f*.

cold *adj* freddo; indifferente;
 * *n* freddo *m*; raffreddore *m*.

cold sore *n* herpes *f*, piaga *f*.

coleslaw *n* insalata *f* di cavolo
 bianco.

colic n colica f.
collaborate vt collaborare.
collaboration n
  collaborazione f.
collaborator n collaboratore m.
collapse n crollo m; collasso m;
  * vi crollare.
collar n collo m.
colleague n collega m or f.
collect vt raccogliere;
  * vi radunarsi.
collection n raccolta f.
collector n esattore m;
  collezionista m or f.
college n college m; collegio m;
  istituto m superiore.
collision n scontro m.
colloquial adj familiare.
colon n (medical) colon m;
  (grammar) due punti mpl.
colonel n colonnello m.
colossal adj colossale.
colour n colore m; ~s bandiera
  f; * vt colorare; tingere.
column n colonna f.
coma n coma m.
comb n pettine m; * vt pettinare.
combat n lotta f, combattimento m; * vt combattere.
combination n combinazione f.
combine vt combinare.
come vi venire: — to ~ about
  accadere succedere:
  ~ across attraversare, dare
  l'impressione di:
  ~ after inseguire qualcuno:
  ~ again ritornare:
  ~ along! suvvia! coraggio!
  ~ apart andare a pezzi:
  ~ around passare:
  ~ at arrivare, raggiungere:
  ~ away venire via:
  ~ back ritornare:
  ~ before venire prima di:
  ~ by ottenere, procurarsi:
  ~ down venire giù:
  ~ down on piombare su:

~ down to scendere:
~ down with (an illness)
  prendersi una malattia:
~ forward venire avanti:
~ in(to) entrare:
~ on venir via:
~ out venire fuori:
~ over arrivare:
~ round riaversi, riprendersi,
  tornare in sè:
~ through comparire:
~ under essere catalogato sotto:
~ up venire su:
~ up to raggiungere, arrivare:
~ up with avere una trovata,
  tirare fuori qualcosa:
~ within fare parte di, rientrare
  nell'ambito di qualcosa.
comedian n comico m.
comedy n commedia f.
comet n cometa f.
comfort n consolazione f;
  conforto m; * vt confortare.
comfortable adj confortevole,
  comodo.
comic(al) adj comico; buffo.
coming adj prossimo; futuro;
  * n avvento m.
comma n virgola f.
command vt comandare;
  disporre di; * n ordine m;
  commando m.
commemorate vt commemorare.
comment n commento m;
  osservazione f.
commentary n commento m;
  telecronaca f.
commerce n commercio m.
commercial adj commerciale;
  * n pubblicità f, reclam f.
commission n commissione f;
  * vt commissionare;
  incaricare.
commit vt commettere.
commitment n impegno m.
committee n comitato m.
common adj comune;

* n parco comunale.

communication n comunicazione f.

communion n comunione f.

communism n comunismo m.

communist n comunista m or f.

community n comunità f.

commute vt commutare;
 * vi fare il pendolare.

compact adj compatto;
 * n portacipria m.

companion n compagno m.

companionship n cameratismo m.

company n compagnia f; società f.

comparable adj simile.

compare vt paragonare.

comparison n paragone m.

compartment n scompartimento m.

compass n bussola f; compasso m.

compassion n compassione f.

compete vt competere.

competent adj competente.

competition n concorrenza f; concorso m; gara f.

competitive adj competivo, agonistico; concorrenziale.

complain vi lamentarsi.

complaint n lamentela f.

complement n complemento m.

complete adj completo;
 * vt completare.

complex adj complesso.

complexion n carnagione f.

compliance n conformità f.

complicate vt complicare.

complication n complicazione f.

compliment n complimento m;
 * vi complimentarsi.

comply vi attenersi a.

component adj, n componente m.

compose vt comporre.

composer n compositore m.

composition n composizione f.

compound n composto m.

comprehend vt capire, comprendere.

comprehensive adj esauriente; globale.

compress vt comprimere;
 * n compressa f.

comprise vt comprendere.

compromise n compromesso m.

compulsory adj obbligatorio.

compute vt calcolare.

computer n elaboratore m; computer m.

comrade n compagno m.

concave adj concavo.

conceal vt nascondere.

conceive vt concepire.

concentrate vt concentrare.

concentration n concentrazione f.

concept n concetto m.

conception n concepimento m.

concern vi riguardare;
 * n preoccupazione f, impresa f.

concert n concerto m.

concession n concessione f.

concise adj conciso.

conclude vt, vi concludere.

conclusion n conclusione f.

conclusive adj conclusivo.

concrete n calcestruzzo m; cemento m; adj concreto; di calcestruzzo m.

concussion n commozione f cerebrale.

condemn vt condannare.

condensation n condensazione f.

condense vi condensare.

condiment n condimento m.

condition vi condizionare;
 * n condizione f.

conditional adj condizionale.

conditioner n balsamo m.

condom n preservativo m.

conduct vi condurre; (music) dirigere; * n condotta f.

conductor n (music) direttore; (electricity) conduttore m.

cone *n* cono *m*; pigna *f*.
confectioner *n* pasticciere *m*.
confectionery *n* dolciumi *mpl*.
confer *vt* conferire;
  * *vi* consultarsi.
conference *n* convegno *m*.
confess *vt* confessare.
confession *n* confessione *f*.
confide *vt* confidare.
confidence *n* fiducia *f*.
confident *adj* sicuro.
confidential *adj* riservato.
confirm *vt* confermare;
  (religion) cresimare.
confirmation *n* conferma *f*,
  (religion) cresima *f*.
confirmed *adj* inveterato.
confiscate *vt* confiscare.
confiscation *n* confisca *f*.
conflict *n* conflitto *m*.
conflicting *adj* contraddittorio,
  conflittuale.
conform *vi* conformarsi.
conformity *n* conforinità *f*.
confuse *vt* confondere.
confused *adj* confuso.
confusing *adj* sconcertante.
confusion *n* confusione *f*.
congested *adj* congestionato.
congestion *n* congestione *f*.
congratulate *vt* congratularsi
  con.
congratulations *npl*
  congratulazioni *fpl*.
congregation *n* congregazione *f*.
conical *adj* conico.
conifer *n* conifera *f*.
connect *vt* collegare.
connection *n* collegamento *m*.
conquer *vt* conquistare.
conqueror *n* conquistatore *m*.
conquest *n* conquista *f*.
conscience *n* coscienza *f*.
conscious *adj* cosciente.
consecutive *adj* consecutivo.
consent *n* benestare *m*;
  * *vi* acconsentire a.

consequence *n* conseguenza *f*.
consequent *adj* conseguente;
  * ~ly *adv* di conseguenza;
  quindi.
conservation *n* conservazione *f*.
conservationist *n*
  ambientalista *m* or *f*.
conservative *adj*, *n*
  conservatore *m*.
conservatory *n* serra *f*, (music)
  conservatore *m*.
conserve *vt* conservare.
consider *vt* considerare.
considerable *adj* considerevole.
considerate *adj* premuroso.
consideration *n*
  considerazione *f*.
considering *conj* visto che;
  * *adv* tutto sommato.
consign *vt* consegnare.
consignment *n* spedizione *f*,
  partita *f*.
consist *vi* consistere di.
consistency *n* consistenza *f*.
consistent *adj* coerente;
  * ~ly *adv* costantemente.
consolation *n* consolazione *f*.
consommé *n* brodo *m* ristretto.
consonant *n* (grammar)
  consonante *f*.
conspiracy *n* congiura *f*.
conspirator *n* cospiratore *m*.
constant *adj* continuo;
  costante.
constellation *n* costellazione *f*.
constipated *adj* stitico.
constipation *n* stitichezza *f*.
constituency *n* collegio *m*
  elettorale.
constituent *n* componente *m*;
  elettore *m*.
constitute *vt* costituire.
constitution *n* costituzione *f*.
constitutional *adj*
  costituzionale.
construct *vt* costruire.
construction *n* costruzione *f*.

consulate *n* consolato *m*.
consult *vt* consultare.
consume *vt* consumare.
consumer *n* consumatore *m*.
consumption *n* consumo *m*;
(medical) consunzione *f*, tisi *f*.
contact *n* contatto;
* *vt* contattare.
contact lenses *npl* lenti a
contatto *fpl*.
contagious *adj* contagioso.
contain *vt* contenere; self-
contained autonomo.
container *n* contenitore *m*.
contemporary *adj*
contemporaneo.
contempt *n* disprezzo *m*.
contemptible *adj* spregevole.
contemptuous *adj* sprezzante.
contender *n* contendente *m* or *f*.
content *adj* contento;
* *n* contentezza; * *vt* soddisfare.
contents *npl* contenuto *m*.
contest *vt* contestare; * *n* gara
f; concorso *m*.
context *n* contesto *m*.
continent *n* continente *m*.
continental *adj* continentale.
continual *adj* continuo.
continue *vt*, *vi* continuare.
continuity *n* continuità *f*.
continuous *adj* continuo.
contraception *n* contraccezione *f*.
contraceptive *adj*, *n*
anticoncezionale *f*.
contract *vt* contrarre;
* *n* contratto *m*.
contraction *n* contrazione *f*.
contradict *vt* contraddire.
contradiction *n* contraddizione.
contradictory *adj*
contraddittorio.
contrary *adj* contrario;
* *n* contrario *m*.
contrast *n* contrasto;
* *vt* contrastare.
contribute *vt*, *vi* contribuire.

contribution *n* offerta *f*
contribuzione *f*.
contrition *n* contrizione *f*.
control *n* controllo *m*,
comando *m*; * *vt* controllare,
frenare, dominare.
controversial *adj* controverso.
controversy *n* controversia *f*.
convalesce *vi* fare la convalescenza, essere convalescente.
convalescence *n*
convalescenza *f*.
convenience *n* comodità *f*.
convenient *adj* comodo,
conveniente.
convent *n* convento *m*.
convention *n* convenzione *f*.
conversation *n* conversazione *f*.
conversion *n* conversione *f*;
ristrutturazione *f*.
convert *vt* convertire; ristrutturare; * *n* convertito *m*.
convex *adj* convesso.
convey *vt* trasportare;
trasmettere.
convict *vt* riconoscere
colpevole; * *n* carcerato *m*.
conviction *n* condanna *f*;
convinzione *f*.
convince *vt* convincere.
convincing *adj* convincente.
cook *n* cuoco *m*; * *vt* cuocere;
(*sl*) falsificare.
cooker *n* cucina *f*.
cookery *n* cucina *f*.
cool *adj* fresco; calmo.
co-operate *vi* cooperare.
co-operation *n* cooperazione *f*.
co-operative *adj* cooperativo;
* *n* cooperativa *f*.
co-ordinate *vt* coordinare;
* *n* coordinata *f*.
co-ordination *n* coordinazione *f*.
cop *n* poliziotto *m*.
cope *vi* farcela, cavarsela.
copier *n* copiatrice *f*.
copper *n* rame; poliziotto *m*.

copy *n* copia; * *vt* imitare, copiare.
copyright *n* diritti d'autore *mpl.*
coral *n* corallo *m.*
coral reef *n* corallino *m.*
cord *n* corda *f.*
cork *n* sughero *m;* * *vt* tappare.
corkscrew *n* cavatappi *m.*
corn *n* grano *m;* frumento *m;* callo *m.*
corner *n* angolo *m;* * *vt* intrappolare.
cornet *n* (music) cornetta *f,* cornetto *m.*
coroner *n* coroner *m.*
corporal *adj* corporale; * *n* caporale *m.*
corporate *adj* collettivo.
corporation *n* società *f,* ente *m.*
correct *vt* correggere; * *adj* corretto.
correction *n* correzione *f.*
correspond *vt* corrispondere.
correspondence *n* corrispondenza *f.*
corridor *n* corridoio *m.*
corrosion *n* corrosione *f.*
corrupt *vt* corrompere; * *adj* corrotto.
corruption *n* corruzione *f.*
cosmetic *adj, n* cosmetico *m.*
cosmic *adj* cosmico.
cosmos *n* cosmo *m.*
cost *n* costo; * *vt* costare.
costly *adj* costoso.
costume *n* costume *m.*
cosy *adj* accogliente.
cot *n* lettino *m.*
cottage *n* cottage *m.*
cotton *n* cotone *m.*
cotton wool *n* cotone *m,* idrofilo.
couch *n* divano *m.*
couchette *n* cuccetta *f.*
cough *n* tosse *f;* * *vi* tossire.
council *n* consiglio *m.*
councillor *n* consigliere *m.*
counsel *n* consiglio; avvocato *m.*

counsellor *n* consigliere *m.*
count *vt, vi* contare; * *n* conteggio *m;* conte *m.*
counter *n* banco *m;* * *vt* rispondere.
counteract *vt* neutralizzare.
counterfeit *vt* contraffare; * *adj* contraffatto.
counterpart *n* equivalente *m, f.*
country *n* paese *m;* campagna *f.*
county *n* contea *f.*
coup *n* colpo *m.*
couple *n* coppia *f;* * *vt* associare.
coupon *n* buono *m.*
courage *n* coraggio *m.*
courageous *adj* coraggioso.
courgette *n* zucchino *m.*
courier *n* corriere *m.*
course *n* corso *m;* rotta *f;* portata: — of course naturalmente.
court *n* corte *f.*
courteous *adj* cortese.
courtesy *n* cortesia *f.*
courtroom *n* sala *f* d'udienza.
courtyard *n* cortile *m.*
cousin *n* cugino(a) *m.*
cove *n* baia *f.*
cover *n* copertura; coperchio *m;* riparo *m;* * *vt* coprire; nascondere.
cow *n* mucca *f;* vacca *f.*
coward *n* vigliacco *m.*
cowardice *n* vigliaccheria *f.*
cowardly *adj* vigliacco.
cowboy *n* cowboy *m,* bovaro *m;* (*sl*) pirata *m.*
crab *n* granchio *m.*
crack *n* crepa *f;* * *vt* incrinare; * *vi* incrinarsi.
cradle *n* culla *f.*
craft *n* mestiere *m;* arte *f.*
craftsman *n* artigiano *m.*
crafty *adj* furbo.
cram *vt* infilare; stipare; * *vi* affollarsi.
cranberry *n* mirtillo palustre

m, mirtillo rosso *m*.

crane *n* gru *f*.

crash *vi* precipitare; scontrarsi; * *n* fracasso *m*; incidente *m*.

crate *n* cassa *f*.

crater *n* cratere *m*.

crawl *vi* andare a gattone; camminare carponi; strisciare; procedere lentamente; adulare.

crawler *n* leccapiedi *m* and *f*.

crayfish *n* gambero *m*.

crayon *n* pastello *m*.

craze *n* mania *f*.

crazy *adj* matto; folle.

cream *n* crema *f*, panna *f*.

creamy *adj* cremoso.

crease *n* piega *f*; * *vt* sgualcire.

create *vt* creare.

creation *n* creazione *f*.

creator *n* creatore *m*.

creature *n* creatura *f*.

crèche *n* asilo *m* nido.

credit *n* credito *m*; onore *m*; * *vt* credere; accreditare.

credit card *n* carta *f* di credito.

creed *n* credo *m*.

creek *n* insenatura *f*.

creep *vi* strisciare; andare furtivamente; * *n* tipo viscido *m*, canaglia *m*, mascalzone *m*, leccapiedi *m*.

cremate *vt* cremare.

cremation *n* cremazione *f*.

crescent *n* mezzaluna *f*; via *f*.

cress *n* crescione *m*.

crest *n* cresta *f*.

crew *n* equipaggio *m*.

crib *n* culla *f*, mangiatoia *f*; * *vt* copiare.

cricket *n* grillo *m*; cricket *m*.

crime *n* criminalità *f*; delitto *m*.

criminal *adj*, *n* criminale *m*, *f*.

crimson *adj* cremisi.

cripple *n* zoppo *m*; mutilato *m*; * *vt* lasciare mutilato,

lesionare, mutilare.

crisis *n* crisi *f*.

crisp *adj* croccante; fresco; conciso; * *n* patatina *f*.

criticise *vt* criticare.

crocodile *n* coccodrillo *m*.

crocus *n* croco *m*.

crook *n* bastone *m*; pastorale *m*; (*sl*) ladro *m*.

crop *n* coltivazione *f*; raccolto *m*.

cross *n* croce *f*; incrocio *m*; * *adj* seccato; * *vt* attraversare; sbarrare; incrociare.

crossword *n* cruciverba *m*.

crowd *n* folla *f*; * *vt* affollare.

crown *n* corona *f*; cima *f*; * *vt* incoronare.

crucifix *n* crocefisso *m*.

crucifixion *n* crocifissione *f*.

crucify *vt* crocifiggere.

crude *adj* grezzo; grossolano.

cruel *adj* crudele.

cruelty *n* crudeltà *f*.

crumb *n* briciola *f*.

crush *n* schiacciamento *m*, frantumazione *f*; folla, ressa; cotta, innamoramento *m*; * *vt* schiacciare; * *vi* spiacciarsi; to have a ~ on somebody avere una cotta per qualcuno.

crust *n* crosta *f*.

cry *vi* gridare; piangere; * *vt* gridare; * *n* grido *m*; pianto *m*.

crystal *n* cristallo *m*.

cub *n* cucciolo *m*.

cube *n* cubo *m*.

cubicle *n* cabina *f*.

cucumber *n* cetriolo *m*.

cuddle *n* abbraccio *m*; * *vt* coccolare.

culminate *vi* culminare.

culmination *n* culmine *m*.

cult *n* culto *m*.

cultivate *vt* coltivare.

cultural *adj* culturale.

culture *n* cultura *f*; (agricul-

ture) coltura *f*.
cup *n* tazza *f*.
cupboard *n* armadio *m*; credenza *f*.
curable *adj* guaribile.
curate *n* curato *m*.
cure *n* cura *f*; guarigione *m*; * *vt* guarire; salare; conciare.
curiosity *n* curiosità *f*.
curious *adj* curioso.
curl *n* ricciolo *m*; * *vt* arricciare.
currant *n* uva *f* passa; ribes *m*.
currency *n* moneta *f*; valuta estera *f*.
current *adj* attuale; corrente; * *n* corrente *f*.
currently *adv* attualmente.
curry *n* curry *m*.
curse *vt* maledire, bestemmiare; * *n* maledizione *f*.
curt *adj* brusco.
curtain *n* tenda *f*.
curtsy *n* inchino; * *vi* fare un inchin, inchinarsi a.
curve *vt* curvare; * *vi* curvarsi; * *n* curva *f*.
cushion *n* cuscino *m*; * *vt* attutire.
custard *n* crema pasticcera *f*.
custody *n* custodia *f*, detenzione *f*.
custom *n* costume *m*; consuetudine *f*; abitudine *f*; clientela *f*.
customer *n* cliente *m* or *f*.
customs *npl* dogana *f*.
customs officer *n* doganiere *m*.
cut *vt* tagliare; ridurre; * *n* taglio *m*; incisione *f*, riduzione *f*.
cute *adj* carino.
cutlery *n* posate *fpl*.
cutlet *n* cotoletta *f*.
cuttlefish *n* seppia *f*.
cyanide *n* cianuro *m*.
cycle *n* bicicletta *f*, cielo *m*; * *vi* andare in bicicletta.

cycling *n* ciclismo *m*.
cyclist *n* ciclista *m* or *f*.
cyclone *n* ciclone *m*.
cygnet *n* giovane cigno *m*, cignetto *m*.
cylinder *n* cilindro *m*.
cymbal *n* cembalo *m*.
cynic(al) *adj* cinico; * *n* cinico *m*.
cynicism *n* cinismo *m*.
cypress *n* cipresso *m*.
cyst *n* ciste *f*.

D

dachshund *n* bassotto *m*.
dad(dy) *n* papà *m*, babbo *m*.
daffodil *n* trombone *m*.
dahlia *n* dalia *f*.
daily *adj* quotidiano; giornaliero.
dairy *n* latteria *f*.
daisy *n* margherita *f*, pratolina *f*.
dam *n* diga *f*; * *vt* arginare.
damage *n* danno *m*.
dame *n* gentildonna *f*, dama *f*; vecchia signora *f*.
damp *adj* umido; * *n* umidità *f*; * *vt* inumidire.
dance *n* ballo *m*; danza *f*; * *vt* ballare; * *vi* danzare.
dancer *n* ballerino *m*.
dandelion *n* dente di leone *m*.
dandruff *n* forfora *f*.
danger *n* pericolo *m*.
dangerous *adj* pericoloso.
dare *vt* sfidare; *vi* osare; * *n* sfida *f*.
dark *adj* scuro; buio; * *n* buio *m*; oscurità *f*.
darling *adj* caro; * *n* tesoro *m*.
dart *n* dardo *m*; pince *f*; * *vi* lanciarsi.
data *npl* dati *mpl*.
database *n* database *m*.
date *n* data *f*; appuntamento *m*; dattero *m*; * *vt* datare.

dated *adj* antiquato.
daughter *n* figlia *f*.
daughter-in-law *n* nuora *f*.
dawn *n* alba *f*; * *vi* albeggiare.
day *n* giorno *m*; giornata *f*,
  epoca *f*: — by ~ di giorno:
  ~ by ~ giorno per giorno.
daybreak *n* aurora *f*.
deacon *n* diacono *m*.
dead *adj* morto; intorpidito;
  scarico; * (*sl*) *adv* assolutamente: I'm ~ sure about it ne
  sono assolutamente sicuro.
deaden *vt* attutire.
deadline *n* scadenza *f*.
deaf *adj* sordo.
deal *n* affare *m*; accordo *m*;
  * *vt* dare le carte.
dear *adj* caro.
death *n* morte *f*.
debate *n* dibattito *m*;
  * *vt* dibattere.
debit *n* addebito; * *vt* addebitare.
debt *n* debito *m*.
debtor *n* debitore *m*.
début *n* debutto *m*.
decade *n* decennio *m*.
decadence *n* decadenza *f*.
decadent *adj* decadente.
decaffeinated *adj* decaffeinato.
decanter *n* caraffa *f*.
decay *vi* putrefarsi; deteriorarsi;
  * *n* decomposizione *f*.
deceit *n* inganno *m*.
deceive *vt* ingannare.
December *n* dicembre *m*.
decency *n* decenza *f*.
decent *adj* decente.
decide *vt* decidere.
deciduous *adj* deciduo, caduco.
decimal *adj*, *n* decimale *m*.
decision *n* decisione *f*.
decisive *adj* decisivo.
deckchair *n* sedia *f* a sdraio.
declaration *n* dichiarazione *f*; * to
  make a customs ~ *vt*, *vi* fare
  una dichiarazione in dogana

declare *vt* dichiarare: — not to
  ~ a dividend non dichiarare
  un dividendo.
decline *vt*, *vi* declinare;
  * *n* declino *m*.
décor *n* arredamento *m*.
decorate *vt* decorare.
decrease *vt*, *vi* diminuire;
  * *n* diminuzione *f*.
decree *n* decreto *m*;
  * *vt* decretare.
dedicate *vt* dedicare.
dedication *n* dedizione *f*;
  dedica *f*.
deduce, deduct *vt* dedurre.
deduction *n* deduzione *f*.
deed *n* azione *f*.
deem *vt* giudicare.
deep *adj* profondo.
deepen *vt* approfondire.
deer *n* cervo *m*.
defeat *n* sconfitta *f*;
  * *vt* sconfiggere.
defect *n* difetto *m*;
  * *vi* defezionare.
defection *n* defezione *f*.
defective *adj* difettoso.
defector *n* rifugiato *m*, politico.
defence *n* difesa *f*.
defenceless *adj* indifeso.
defend *vt* difendere.
defensive *adj* difensivo.
defer *vt* rimandare.
defiance *n* sfida *f*.
defiant *adj* ribelle.
deficiency *n* mancanza *f*;
  insufficienza *f*.
deficient *adj* mancante.
deficit *n* deficit *m*.
definable *adj* definibile.
define *vt* definire.
definite *adj* definitivo.
definitely *adv* certamente,
  assolutamente.
defy *vt* sfidare.
degenerate *vi* degenerare;
  * *adj*, *n* degenerato *m*.

degree n grado m; laurea f.
dehydrate vt disidratare.
deign vi degnarsi.
delay vt rimandare;
* vi ritardare; * n ritardo m.
delegate vt delegare;
* n delegato m.
delegation n delegazione f.
delete vt cancellare.
deliberate vt deliberare;
* adj premeditato.
deliberately adv apposta,
deliberatamente.
deliberation n deliberazione f.
delicacy n delicatezza f;
ghiottoneria f.
delicate adj delicato.
delicatessen n salumeria f.
delicious adj delizioso.
delight n delizia f; * vt riempire
di gioia.
delighted adj contentissimo.
deliver vt consegnare.
delta n delta m.
delusion n illusione f.
demand n richiesta f;
* vt esigere.
demanding adj esigente.
demented adj pazzo, demente.
demise n decesso m.
democracy n democrazia f.
democrat n democratico m.
demolish vt demolire.
demolition n demolizione f.
demon n demonio m.
demonstration n
manifestazione f.
demote vt degradare.
denial n rifiuto m; diniego m.
denim n tessuto m jeans.
dense adj denso.
density n densità f.
dentist n dentista m or f.
deny vt negare; smentire.
depart vi partire.
department n reparto m;
sezione f.

departure n partenza f.
depend vi dipendere: ~ on
contare su.
dependable adj affidabile.
dependant n persona f, a carico.
depict vt rappresentare.
deplore vt deplorare.
deploy vt schierare.
deport vt deportare.
deposit vt depositare;
* n deposito m.
depot n deposito m.
depreciation n deprezzamento m.
depress vt deprimere.
depression n depressione f.
deprive vt privare.
depth n profondità f.
deputy n sostituto m.
derive vt derivare da.
descend vt scendere da.
descendant n discendente m, f.
descent n discesa f.
describe vt descrivere.
description n descrizione f.
desecration n profanazione f.
desert n deserto; * adj desertico;
* vt abbandonare.
deserve vt meritare.
design vt progettare;
* n progetto m; disegno m.
designer n disegnatore m.
desirable adj desiderabile.
desire n desiderio m;
* vt desiderare.
desist vi desistere.
desk n scrivania f.
despair n disperazione f;
* vi disperaredi; disperarsi.
desperate adj disperato.
despise vt disprezzare.
despite prep malgrado.
dessert n dessert m.
destination n destinazione f.
destiny n destino m.
destroy vt distruggere.
destruction n distruzione f.
detail n particolare m;

dettaglio *m*; * *vt* dettagliare.
detect *vt* individuare.
detective *n* detective *m*,
  investigatore *m*.
detention *n* detenzione *f*.
deter *vt* dissuadere.
detergent *n* detersivo *m*.
deteriorate *vi* deteriorarsi.
determination *n* determina-
  zione.
determine *vt* determinare.
deterrent *n* deterrente *m*.
detest *vt* detestare.
detestable *adj* detestabile.
detonate *vi* detonare.
detour *n* deviazione *f*.
devaluation *n* svalutazione *f*.
devastate *vt* devastare.
develop *vt* sviluppare.
development *n* sviluppo *m*.
device *n* congegno *m*;
  dispositivo *m*.
devil *n* diavolo *m*.
devilish *adj* diabolico.
devious *adj* subdolo.
devise *vt* escogitare.
devolution *n* decentramento *m*.
devolve *vt* devolvere.
devote *vt* dedicare.
devoted *adj* devoto.
devotion *n* devozione *f*.
diabetes *n* diabete *m*.
diabetic *adj n* diabetico *m*.
diagnose *vt* diagnosticare.
diagnosis *n* diagnosi *f*.
diagonal *adj* diagonale.
diagram *n* diagramma *m*.
dial *n* quadrante *m*.
dialect *n* dialetto *m*.
dialogue *n* dialogo *m*.
dialysis *n* dialisi *f*.
diameter *n* diametro *m*.
diamond *n* diamante *m*.
diaphragm *n* diaframma *m*.
diarrhoea *n* diarrea *f*.
diary *n* diario *m*; agenda *f*.
dick *n* (*sl*) tizio *m*, tipo *m*,

individuo *m*; (*vulg*) cazzo *m*:
~head testa di cazzo:
— clever ~ saputello *m*,
  sapientone *m*.
dictate *vt*, *vi* dettare.
dictator *n* dittatore *m*.
dictionary *n* dizionario *m*.
die *vi* morire.
die (*pl* dice) *n* dado *m*.
diesel *n* gasolio *m*.
diet *n* dieta *f*, alimentazione *f*;
  * *vi* seguire una dieta.
dietary *adj* dietetico.
differ *vi* differire; discordare.
difference *n* differenza *f*.
different *adj* diverso.
difficult *adj* difficile.
difficulty *n* difficoltà *f*.
dig *vi* vangare; scavare.
digest *vi* digerire.
digestion *n* digestione *f*.
dignity *n* dignità *f*.
dilemma *n* dilemma *m*.
diligence *n* diligenza *f*.
diligent *adj* diligente.
dilute *vt* diluire.
dim *adj* fioco; * *vt* abbassare.
dimension *n* dimensione *f*.
diminish *vt* diminuire.
diminished *adj* ridotto.
diminutive *adj* minuto.
dimple *n* fossetta *f*.
dine *vi* pranzare.
dinghy *n* gommone *m*.
dingy *adj* squallido.
dinner *n* cena *f*.
dinosaur *n* dinosauro *m*.
diocese *n* diocesi *f*.
dip *vt* immergere; * *vi* essere
  in pendenza; * *n* nuotatina *f*.
diploma *n* diploma *m*.
diplomacy *n* diplomazia *f*.
diplomat *n* diplomatico *m*.
direct *adj* diretto; * *vt* dirigere.
direction *n* direzione *f*.
directly *adj* direttamente.
director *n* dirigente *m* or *f*.

directory n elenco m.
dirt n sporco m.
disabled adj invalido.
disadvantage n svantaggio m.
disagree vi essere in disaccordo.
disagreement n discordanza f.
disappear vi scomparire.
disappearance n scomparsa f.
disappoint vt deludere.
disappointed adj deluso.
disappointment n delusione f.
disapprove vi disapprovare.
disaster n disastro m.
disc n disco m.
discard vi scartare.
discern vi discernere.
discharge vi scaricare;
  licenziare; assolvere;
  * n scarica f; licenziamento
  m; secrezione f.
disciple n discepolo m.
discipline n disciplina f;
  * vt castigare; punire.
disclose vi rivelare.
disco n discoteca f.
discomfort n disagio m.
disconnect vt staccare.
discord n disaccordo m.
discount n sconto; * vt non
  badare a.
discover vt scoprire.
discovery n scoperta f.
discreet adj discreto.
discriminate vt distinguere;
  fare discriminazione tra.
discuss vt discutere.
discussion n discussione f.
disease n malattia f.
diseased adj malato.
disembark vi sbarcare.
disgrace n vergogna f;
  disonore m; * vt disonorare.
disgraceful adj vergognoso.
disguise vt travestire; mascherare; * n travestimento m.
disgust n disgusto m;
  * vt disgustare.

dish n piatto m; pietanza f;
  * ~ out vt servire.
dishonest adj disonesto.
dishonesty n disonestà f.
disillusion vt disingannare;
  * n disinganno m.
disinfect vt disinfettare.
disinfectant n disinfettante m.
disintegrate vi disintegrarsi.
disk n dischetto m.
dislike n antipatia f; * vt non
  piacere.
dismal adj tetro.
dismantle vt smontare.
dismay n sgomento;
  * vt sgomentare.
dismiss vt congedare; licenziare.
dismissal n licenziamento m;
  congedo m.
disorder n disordine m.
dispatch vt spedire; inviare;
  * n invio m, spedizione f.
dispel vt dissipare.
dispense vt dispensare.
disperse vt disperdere.
display vt esporre; * n mostra f;
  esposizione f.
disposable adj disponibile;
  monouso.
disposal n eliminazione f.
dispose vt disporre.
dispute n disputa f, controversia
  f; * vt contestare; disputarsi.
disrupt vt scombussolare.
dissect vt sezionare.
dissent vi dissentire;
  * n dissenso m.
dissolve vt sciogliere; dissolvere.
distance n distanza f,
  lontananza f; * vt distanziare.
distant adj lontano; distante.
distaste n ripugnanza f.
distil vt distillare.
distinct adj distinto.
distinction n distinzione f.
distinctive adj particolare.
distinguish vt distinguere.

distinguished *adj* eminente; noto.

distort *vt* distorcere.

distract *vt* distrarre.

distraction *n* distrazione *f*.

distraught *adj* stravolto.

distress *n* angoscia *f*, pericolo *m*; * *vt* addolorare.

distribute *vt* distribuire.

district *n* distretto *m*.

distrust *n* diffidenza *f*; * *vt* diffidare.

distrustful *adj* diffidente.

disturb *vt* disturbare.

ditto *adv* idem.

dive *vi* tuffarsi; lanciarsi; * *n* tuffo *m*; bettola *f*.

diver *n* tuffatore *m*.

diverse *adj* svariato.

divide *vt* dividere.

divided *adj* diviso.

divine *adj* divino; * *vt* intuire.

division *n* divisione *f*.

divorce *n* divorzio *m*; * *vi* divorziare.

dizzy *adj* vertiginoso.

do *vt* fare (io faccio, tu fai, lui fa, noi facciamo, voi fate, loro fanno): ~ away with abolire: ~ by trattare: ~ down sparlare di: ~ for fare da, sostituire: ~ in stremare: ~ out pulire a fondo: (*fig*) malmenare, pestare: ~ something to someone (*and*, *archaic* ~ unto) fare qualcosa a qualcuno: ~ up allacciare, abbottonare; (*fig*) ridurre a malpartito: ~ with fare con: ~ without fare senza.

dock *n* (botany) romice *m*; (marine) bacino *m*; darsena *f*; banco degli imputati; * *vt* mozzare; decurtare; * *vi* entrare in bacino.

doctor *n* dottore *m*; medico *m*; * *vt* curare; adulterare.

document *n* documento *m*; * *vt* documentare.

dog *n* cane *m*; * *vt* perseguitare.

dogma *n* dogma *m*.

dogmatic *adj* dogmatico.

doll *n* bambola *f*.

dollar *n* dollaro *m*.

dome *n* cupola *f*.

don *vi* mettersi; * *n* docente *m* universitario.

donate *vt* donare.

donation *n* donazione *f*.

done *adj* fatto; cotto.

donkey *n* asino *m*.

donor *n* donatore *m*.

door *n* porta *f*.

doorbell *n* campanello *m*.

dose *n* dose *f*; * *vt* somministrare; dosare.

dot *n* punto *m*; * *vi* punteggiare.

double *adj* doppio; * *vt* raddoppiare; * *n* sosia *m*.

doubly *adj* doppiamente.

doubt *n* dubbio *m*; * *vt* dubitare di.

doubtful *adj* indeciso.

doubtless *adv* indubbiamente.

dough *n* impasto *m*.

dove *n* colombo *m*.

down *n* piume *fpl*; * *adv* giù; * upside-down *adj* capovolto.

dozen *n* dozzina *f*.

drab *adj* grigio; monotono.

draft *n* abbozzo *m*; tratta *f*; * *vt* abbozzare.

drag *vt* trascinare; * *vi* trascinarsi: ~ about strascicarsi di qua e di là: ~ away, ~ off trascinare via: ~ behind (*sl*) fare da fanalino di coda: ~ down trascinare in basso; ~ out trascinare fuori a viva forza: ~ in trascinare dentro a viva forza: ~ on andare avanti: ~ up tirare su (*also fig*).

dragon *n* drago *m*.

dragonfly *n* libellula *f*.
drain *vt* prosciugare; drenare;
  svuotare; * *n* scarico *m*;
  drenaggio *m*.
drainpipe *n* tubo di scarico *m*.
drama *n* dramma *m*.
drape *vt* drappeggiare.
draper *n* negoziante *m* or *f* di
  stoffe.
drastic *adj* drastico.
draught *n* spiffero *m*; sorsata *f*;
  * on ~ *adj* alla spina.
draughtsman *n* disegnatore *m*
  tecnico.
draw *vt* disegnare; tirare;
  attirare; pareggiare; estrarre;
  * *n* sorteggio *m*; lotteria *f*;
  estrazione *f*; pareggio *m*.
drawer *n* cassetto *m*.
drawing *n* disegno *m*.
dream *n* sogno *m*; * *vt*, *vi*
  sognare.
dress *vt* vestire; condire;
  * *n* vestito *m*, abito *m*;
  abbigliamento *m*.
dresser *n* credenza *f*.
dressing table *n* toilette *f*.
drift *n* deriva *f*; * *vi* andare
  alla deriva.
drill *n* trapano *m*; * *vt* trapanare.
drink *vt*, *vi* bere; * *n* bevanda *f*;
  bibita *f*.
drip *vi* sgocciolare; * *n* goccia *f*,
  (medical) fleboclisi *f*.
drive *vt* spingere; guidare;
  azionare; * *n* giro in macchina
  m; viale *m*; grinta *f*.
driver *n* guidatore *m*; autista
  m or *f*, conducente *m* or *f*.
driving licence *n* patente *m*, di
  guida.
drop *n* goccia *f*; calo *m*; * *vi*
  lasciar cadere; abbandonare;
  piantare; calare.
drought *n* siccità *f*.
drown *vt*, *vi* affogare,
  annegare.

drug *n* medicina *f*; medicinale
  f; droga *f*; * *vt* drogare.
drug addict *n*
  tossicodipendente *m* or *f*.
drum *n* tamburo *m*.
drum *vt* and *vi* tamburellare;
  battere; suonare: ~ in(to)
  inculcare, fare entrare in
  tesa a qualcuno: ~ out of
  radiare, espellere: ~ up
  chiamare a raccolta, cercare.
drunk *adj*, *n* ubriaco *m*.
dry *adj* secco; * *vt* seccare.
dual *adj* doppio; duplice.
duchess *n* duchessa *f*.
duck *n* anatra *f*.
due *adj* pagabile; dovuto;
  atteso.
duel *n* duello *m*.
duct *n* duetto *m*.
duke *n* duca *m*.
dull *adj* ottuso.
dumb *adj* muto.
dump *vt* scaricare;
  * *n* discarica *f*.
dumplings *n* gnocchi *mpl* di
  patate, canederli *mpl*.
dunce *n* somaro *m*.
dune *n* duna *f*.
dungeon *n* segreta *f*, piombi *mpl*.
durable *adj* durevole.
duration *n* durata *f*.
during *prep* durante.
dusk *n* crepuscolo *m*.
dust *n* polvere *f*; * *vt*, *vi*
  spolverare.
dustbin *n* bidone *m*.
duster *n* straccio *m*.
dutiful *adj* deferente;
  rispettoso.
duty *n* dovere *m*; tassa *f*; dazio *m*.
duvet *n* piumone *m*.
dwarf *n* nano *m*.
dwell *vi* dimorare.
dwindle *vi* diminuire;
  affievolirsi.
dye *vt* tingere; * *n* colorante *m*;

tintura f.
dying adj morente; * n morte f.
dyke n diga f; (sl) lesbica f.
dynamic adj dinamico.
dynamite n dinamite f.
dynamo n dinamo f.
dynasty n dinastia f.

E

each adj ogni; ciascuno;
  * pron ognuno; ciascuno;
  * adv ciascuno.
eager adj appassionato.
eagle n aquila f.
ear n orecchio m.
earl n conte m.
early adj primo; precoce;
  prematuro; * adv presto.
earn vt guadagnare.
earring n orecchino m.
earth n terra f; * vt collegare a
  terra.
earthquake n terremoto m.
earthworm n lombrico m.
earwig n forbicina f.
ease n disinvoltura f,
  tranquillità f; * vt facilitare;
  alleviare.
easily adv facilmente.
east n est m; oriente m.
Easter n Pasqua f.
ease vt alleviare, calmare;
  alleggerire: ~ down, ~off
  rallentare; ~ out fare ponti
  d'oro a qualcuno perchè se ne
  vada: ~ up stringersi, fare un
  po' di posto.
easy adj facile.
eat vt mangiare: ~ away
  continuare a mangiare: ~ in
  mangiare a casa: ~ into, ~
  through corrodere, fare un
  buco con I denti in: ~ out
  mangiare fuori: ~ up finire
  tutto, mangiate tutto.

ebony n ebano m.
eccentric adj, n eccentrico m.
echo n eco m or f; * vi echeggiare.
eclectic adj ecelettico.
eclipse n ecclissi f;
  * vt eclissare.
ecology n ecologia f.
economic(al) adj economico.
economics npl economia f.
economy n economia f.
ecstasy n estasi f.
eczema n eczema m.
edge n orlo m; bordo m;
  * vt bordare.
edible adj mangiabile;
  commestibile.
edit vt dirigere; redigere.
edition n edizione f.
editor n direttore m.
educate vt istruire; educare.
educated adj colto.
education n istruzione f;
  educazione f, formazione f.
eel n anguilla f.
effect n effetto m.
effective adj efficace.
efficiency n efficenza f.
effort n sforzo m.
egg n uovo m.
ego n ego m.
egoist n egoista m or f.
egotism n egotismo m.
egotist n egotista m or f.
eight num otto.
eighteen num diciotto.
eighth adj, n ottavo m.
eighty num ottanta.
either pron, adj l'uno o l'altro;
  * adj entrambi; * either ... or
  conj o ... o; * adv neanche.
eject vt espellere.
ejection n espulsione f.
eke vt: — eke out integrare;
  far bastare.
elaborate vt elaborare;
  * adj complicato; ricercato.
elastic adj, n elastico m.

elbow *n* gomito *m*.
elderly *adj* anziano.
eldest *adj* maggiore.
elect *vt* eleggere; decidere;
 * *adj* futuro.
election *n* elezione *f*.
electoral *adj* elettorale.
electrician *n* elettricista *m* or *f*.
electricity *n* elettricità *f*.
electronic *adj* elettronico:
 * ~s *npl* elettronica *f*.
elegance *n* eleganza *f*.
elegant *adj* elegante.
element *n* elemento *m*.
elephant *n* elefante *m*.
elevate *vt* elevare.
elevation *n* elevazione *f*.
elevator *n* montacarichi *m*.
eleven *num* undici.
eleventh *adj*, *n* undicesimo *m*.
eligibility *n* eleggibilità *f*.
eligible *adj* eleggibile.
eliminate *vt* eliminare.
elimination *n* eliminazione *f*.
elm *n* olmo *m*.
eloquence *n* eloquenza *f*.
eloquent *adj* eloquente.
else *adv* altro; altrimenti.
elsewhere *adv* altrove.
embankment *n* argine *m*.
embargo *n* embargo *m*.
embark *vt* imbarcarsi.
embarrass *vt* imbarazzare,
 mettere in imbarazzo.
embassy *n* ambasciata *f*.
embitter *vt* inasprire.
emblem *n* emblema *m*.
embody *vt* inearnare.
embrace *vt* abbracciare;
 * *n* abbraccio *m*.
embroider *vt* ricamare.
embroidery *n* ricamo *m*.
embryo *n* embrione *m*.
emerald *n* smeraldo *m*.
emergency *n* emergenza *f*.
eminent *adj* eminente.
emission *n* emissione *f*.

emit *vt* emettere.
emotion *n* emozione *f*.
emotional *adj* emotivo.
emotive *adj* emotivo;
 commovente.
emperor *n* imperatore *m*.
emphasis *n* accento *m*; enfasi *f*.
emphasise *vt* sottolineare.
emphatic *adj* enfatico.
empire *n* impero *m*.
employ *vt* impiegare; assumere.
employee *n* dipendente *m* or *f*.
employer *n* datore *m* di lavoro.
employment *n* occupazione *f*.
empress *n* imperatrice *f*.
emptiness *n* vuoto *m*.
empty *adj* vuoto; * *vt* vuotare.
emu *n* emù *m*.
enamel *n* smalto; * *vt* smaltare.
enchant *vt* incantare.
enclose *vt* allegare; recintare.
enclosure *n* allegato *m*;
 recinto *m*.
encompass *vt* comprendere.
encore *excl*; *n* bis *m*.
encounter *n* incontro *m*;
 * *vt* incontrare.
encourage *vt* incoraggiare.
encouragement *n*
 incoraggiamento *m*.
encroach *vt* usurpare; invadere.
encrust *vt* incrostare.
encyclopedia *n* enciclopedia *f*.
end *n* fine *f*; estremità *f*;
 * *vi* finire; terminare;
 * *vt* porre fine a.
endive *n* indivia *f*.
endorse *vt* girare; approvare.
endurance *n* resistenza *f*.
endure *vt* sopportare.
enemy *n* nemico *m*.
energy *n* energia *f*.
enforce *vt* applicare; far
 rispettare.
engage *vt* assumere;
 innestare; ingaggiare.
engaged *adj* fidanzato.

engagement n fidanzamento m; impegno m.

engine n motore m; steam ~ locomotiva f.

engineer n ingegnere m.

engineering n ingegneria f.

engrave vt incidere.

engraving n incisione f.

enhance vt valorizzare.

enigma n enigma m.

enjoy vt godere; divertirsi.

enlarge vt ingrandire; ampliare.

enlist vt arruolare.

enlistment n arruolamento m.

enormous adj enorme.

enough adj sufficiente; * adv abbastanza.

enquire vt indagare.

enrol vt iscrivere; immatricolare.

enrolment n iscrizione f, immatricolazione f.

enslave vt rendere schiavo.

enter vt registrare; * vi entrare: ~ in avviare, iniziare: ~ up prendere nota di, registrare: ~ upon cominciare, iniziare.

enterprise n impresa f; iniziativa f.

enterprising adj intraprendente.

entertain vt intrattenere.

entertaining adj divertente.

enthuse vi entusiasmarsi.

enthusiasm n entusiasmo m.

enthusiastic adj appassionato.

entice vt allettare.

entire adj intero.

entitle vt intitolare; dare diritto a.

entity n entità f.

entrance n entrata f, ingresso m, ammissione f; * vt mandare in estasi.

entreat vt implorare.

entrepreneur n imprenditore m.

entry n ingresso m, entrata f;

accesso m; voce f.

envelope n busta f.

enviable adj invidiabile.

envious adj invidioso.

environment n ambiente m.

envoy n inviato m.

envy n invidia f.

epic adj epico; * n epopea f.

epidemic n epidemia f.

Epiphany n Epifania f.

episcopal adj episcopale.

episode n episodio m.

equal adj uguale; * n pari m; * vt uguagliare.

equality n uguaglianza f.

equally adv ugualmente.

equator n equatore m.

equestrian adj equestre.

equilibrium n equilibrio m.

equipment n attrezzatura f.

equity n equità f.

equivalent adj equivalente.

era n era f.

eradicate vt sradicare.

erase vt cancellare.

erect vt erigere; * adj diritto.

erotic adj erotico.

errand n commissione f.

error n errore m.

erupt vi essere in eruzione; * vt eruttare.

eruption n eruzione f.

escalator n scala f mobile.

escape vt sfuggire a; scampare; * vi scappare; evadere; * n fuga f; evasione f.

escort n scorta f; * vt scortare.

especial adj particolare.

essay n saggio m.

essential adj essenziale.

establish vt stabilire; istituire; fondare.

establishment n istituzione f, azienda f.

estimate vt valutare; preventivare; * n preventivo m; valutazione f.

estuary n estuario m.
etching n incisione f,
   acquaforte f.
eternal adj eterno.
eternity n eternità f.
ethics npl etica f.
ethnic adj etnico.
eucalyptus n eucalipto m.
Eucharist n eucarestia f.
evacuate vt evacuare.
evacuation n evacuazione f.
evangelical adj evangelico.
evangelist n evangelista m.
evaporate vi evaporare.
evaporation n evaporazione f.
evasion n evasione f.
evasive adj evasivo.
even adj liscio; regolare; pari;
   * adv perfino; addirittura;
   ancora.
evening n sera f, serata f.
evenly adv uniformemente.
event n avvenimento m.
ever adv sempre; mai.
every adj ogni, tutti; * ~body
   pron ognuno, tutti: ~thing
   tutto; * ~where adv
   dappertutto.
evidence n testimonianza f,
   prove fpl.
evident adj evidente.
evil adj cattivo; malvagio;
   * n male m.
evolution n evoluzione f.
evolve vt elaborare;
   * vi evolversi.
exact adj esatto; * vt esigere.
exactly adj esattamente.
exaggerate vt esagerare.
exaggeration n esagerazione f.
examination n esame m; visita f.
examine vt esaminare;
   visitare.
examiner n esaminatore m.
example n esempio m.
excavate vt scavare.
exceed vt eccedere; superare.

excel vt superare.
excellent adj eccellente.
except prep tranne, eccetto.
exception n eccezione f.
exceptional adj eccezionale.
excess n eccesso m.
exchange vt scambiare;
   * n scambio m.
excite vt eccitare.
exciting adj emozionante.
exclaim vt esclamare.
exclamation n esclamazione f.
exclamation mark n punto
   esclamativo.
exclude vt escludere.
exclusion n esclusione f.
exclusive adj esclusivo.
excursion n gita f, escursione f.
excuse vt scusare; esonerare;
   * n scusa f.
execute vt giustiziare;
   eseguire.
execution n esecuzione f.
executioner n boia m inv,
   carnefice m.
executive adj esecutivo;
   * n dirigente m or f.
exempt adj esente;
   * vt esentare.
exercise n esercizio m;
   * vt esercitare.
exhale vt, vi espirare.
exhaust n gas di scarico m;
   * vt stremare; esaurire.
exhaustion n esaurimento m.
exhibit vt esporre; * n oggetto
   m esposto; reperto m.
exhibition n mostra f.
exhilarate vt rinvigorire.
exile n esilio m; esule m or f;
   * vt esiliare.
exist vi esistere.
existence n esistenza f.
existent adj esistente.
exit n uscita f.
exotic adj esotico.
expand vt espandere.

expansion *n* espansione *f*.
expect *vt* aspettare; pensare; pretendere; esigere.
expel *vt* espellere.
expenditure *n* dispendio *m*.
expense *n* spesa *f*.
expensive *adj* costoso, caro.
experience *n* esperienza *f*; * *vt* sperimentare.
experiment *n* esperimento *m*.
expert *adj*, *n* esperto *m*.
expertise *n* perizia *f*.
expire *vi* scadere; spirare.
expiry *n* scadenza *f*.
explain *vt* spiegare.
explanatory *adj* esplicativo.
explicable *adj* spiegabile.
explode *vi* esplodere.
exploit *vt* sfruttare; * *n* impresa *f*.
explore *vt* esplorare.
explorer *n* esploratore *m*.
explosion *n* esplosione *f*.
explosive *adj*, *n* esplosivo *m*.
export *vt* esportare; * *n* esportazione *f*.
expose *vt* esporre; smascherare.
exposure *n* esposizione *f*.
express *vt* esprimere; * *adj* espresso.
expression *n* espressione *f*.
expressive *adj* espressivo.
extend *vt* tendere; prolungare.
extension *n* prolunga *f*; (numero) interno *m*.
extensive *adj* esteso.
extent *n* estensione *f*, portata *f*.
exterior *adj*, *n* esterno *m*, esteriore *m*.
external *adj* esterno.
extinct *adj* estinto.
extinguisher *n* estintore *m*.
extortion *n* estorsione *f*.
extra *adj* in più; supplementare; maggiore; *adv* extra; eccezionalmente.

extract *vt* estrarre; * *n* spezzone *m*.
extraordinary *adj* straordinario.
extravagant *adj* dispendioso; stravagante.
extreme *adj*, *n* estremo *m*.
extrovert *adj*, *n* estroverso *m*.
eye *n* occhio *m*; * *vt* scrutare.
eyeball *n* bulbo *m* oculare.
eyebrow *n* sopracciglio *m*.
eyelash *n* ciglio *m*.
eyelid *n* palpebra *f*.
eyesight *n* vista *f*.
eyewitness *n* testimone *m* or *f* oculare.

F

fabric *n* stoffa *f*, tessuto *m*.
fabulous *adj* favoloso.
face *n* faccia *f*, viso *m*; (*of animal*) muso *m*, musetto *m*; quadrante *m*; * *vt* affrontare; essere di fronte a.
facet *n* sfaccettatura *f*, aspetto *m*.
fact *n* fatto *m*: — in ~ in realtà.
factor *n* fattore *m*.
factory *n* fabbrica *f*.
faculty *n* facoltà *f*.
fade *vi* appassire; sbiadirsi.
fag *n* sfacchinata *f*, sgobbata *f*; (*sl*) sigaretta *f*, cicca *f*; (*sl*) omosessuale *m*, checca *f*, finocchio *f*: ~ bag moglie di un finocchi *f*: ~ hag amica di finocchi *f*: ~ end mozzicone *m*: at the ~-end of one's holidays alla fine delle vacanze: — brain ~ esaurimento nervoso *m*.
fail *vi* fallire; mancare; * *vt* bocciare.
failure *n* fallimento *m*; insuccesso *m*.
faint *vi* svenire; * *n* svenimento;

* *adj* leggero; fievole; vago.
fair *adj* giusto; imparziale; discreto; chiaro; * *n* fiera *f*.
fairly *adv* in modo imparziale; abbastanza.
fairy *n* fata *f*.
fairy tale *n* fiaba *f*.
faith *n* fede *f*.
faithful *adj* fedele.
fake *n* falso *m*; imitazione *f*; * *adj* fasullo; * *vt* falsificare; * *vi* fingere.
falcon *n* falco *m*.
fall *vi* cadere: ~ about barcollare: ~ among cadere in mano a: ~ apart andare in pezzi: ~ away (of a landscape) digradare; (of rocks) staccarsi: ~ back ritirarsi: ~ back on fare ricorso a: ~ behind rimanere indietro: ~ down gadere giù: ~ for innamorarsi di: ~ in with imbattersi in: ~ into cadere in: ~ off cadere da; essere eliminato da, cadere fuori da: ~ on gettarsi su, assalire: ~ out with litigare, rompere i rapporti con: ~ outside non rientrare, non ricadere: ~ over cadere: ~ overboard cadere in mare: ~ through fallire, andare a monte: ~ to venire alle mani: ~ under cadere sotto: ~ within ricadere, rientrare; * *n* caduta *f*, calo *m*.
fallacy *n* errore *m*.
fallible *adj* fallibile.
fallout *n* pioggia radioattiva *f*.
false *adj* falso.
falsify *vt* falsificare.
falsity *n* falsità *f*, slealtà *f*.
fame *n* fama *f*, celebrità *f*.
famed *adj* famoso.
familiar *adj* conosciuto, familiare.

familiarity *n* familiarità *f*.
family *n* famiglia *f*.
famine *n* carestia *f*.
famish *vi* fare patire la fame a; patire la fame, morire di fame.
famous *adj* famoso.
fan *n* ventaglio *m*; ventilatore *m*; fan *m* or *f*, tifoso *m*; * *vt* fare vento.
fancy *n* voglia *f*, capriccio *m*; * *adj* elaborato.
fang *n* zanna *f*.
far *adv* lontano: — so ~ finora; * *adj* lontano; di gran lunga; estremo.
fare *n* tariffa *f* cibo *m*.
farm *n* fattoria *f*; * *vt* coltivare.
farmer *n* agricoltore *m*.
farming *n* agricoltura *f*.
farmyard *n* aia *f*.
fascism *n* fascismo *m*.
fascist *n* fascista *m* or *f*.
fashion *n* moda *f*, modo *m*; * *vt* modellare.
fast *vi* digiunare; * *adj* veloce, rapido; * *adv* velocemente; saldarnente; * *n* digiuno *m*.
fasten *vi* legare.
fat *adj*, *n* grasso *m*.
fatal *adj* fatale; nefasto.
fatality *n* vittima *f*.
fate *n* destino *m*; sorte *f*.
father *n* padre *m*.
father-in-law *n* suocero *m*.
fault *n* difetto *m*; colpa *f*; faglia *f*; * *vt* criticare.
fauna *n* fauna *f*.
favour *n* favore *m*; * *vt* favorire.
favourite *n* preferito *m*.
fax *n* fax *m*.
fear *vt* temere; * *vi* avere paura di; * *n* paura *f*.
feasible *adj* realizzabile.
feast *n* pranzo *m*; banchetto *m*; festa *f*; * *vi* banchettare.
feat *n* impresa *f*, prodezza *f*.

feather n penna f, piuma f.
feature n caratteristica f;
  * vt dare risalto a.
February n febbraio m.
federal adj federale.
federation n federazione f.
fee n onorario m.
feeble adj debole.
feed vt nutrire, alimentare, dar
  da mangiare a; * vi nutrirsi
  di; * n pappa f; mangiata f;
  mangime m; foraggio m.
feel vt, vi tastare, sentire;
  credere; provare; * n tatto m;
  sensazione f.
feeling n senso m, sensazione f;
  sentimento m; impressione f.
fell vi abbattere.
felt n feltro m.
female adj, n femmina f.
feminine adj femminile.
feminist n femminista m or f.
fence n recinto m; * vt recintare.
fencing n (sport) scherma f;
  recinto m; steccato m.
fennel n finocchio m.
fern n felce f.
ferocious adj feroce.
ferry n traghetto m.
fertile adj fertile.
fertilise vt fecondare; (agriculture) fertilizzare.
festival n festa f, festival m.
festive adj di festa.
fetch vt andare a prendere,
  portare.
feud n faida f.
feudal adj feudale.
feudalism n feudalesimo m.
fever n febbre f.
feverish adj febbrile.
few adj pochi.
fewer adj meno.
fewest adj il minor numero di.
fiancé(e) n fidanzato(a) m(f).
fiasco n fiasco m.
fibber n bugiardo m.

fibre n fibra f.
fiction n narrativa f; finzione f.
fiddle n violino m; imbroglio
  m; * vi giocherellare;
  * vt falsificare.
fidelity n fedeltà f.
fidget n persona irrequieta f;
  * vi agitarsi.
field n campo m.
fierce adj feroce; accanito.
fierceness n ferocia f,
  accanimento m.
fiery adj infocato, focoso,
  ardente.
fifteen num quindici.
fifteenth num quindicesimo.
fifth num quinto.
fifty num cinquanta.
fig n fico m.
fight vt combattere; lottare:
  ~ back reagire: ~ down
  superare, contrastare: ~ off
  respingere: ~ on continuare a
  combattere: ~ out vedersela,
  risolvere una questione
  facendo a pugni: ~ over
  darsele per qualcosa: ~ through
  lottare fino in fondo.
fight n combattmento m;
  lotta f.
fighting n combattimento m.
figure n figura f, cifra f, linea f;
  * vi figurare.
figurehead n (marine) polena
  f, figura rappresentativa f.
filament n filamento m.
file n lima f, cartella f,
  archivio m; fila f; * vt limare;
  archiviare.
fill vt riempire; otturare.
fillet n filetto m; * vt disossare.
film n film m, pellicola f;
  rullino m; strato sottile m;
  * vt filmare.
filter n filtro m; * vt filtrare.
filth n sudiciume f.
filthy adj sudicio.

fin *n* pinna *f*.
final *adj* ultimo, finale;
  * *n* finale *f*.
finalist *n* finalista *m* or *f*.
finance *n* finanza *f*;
  * *vt* finanziare.
financial *adj* finanziario.
financier *n* finanziatore *m*.
find *vt* trovare: ~ out scoprire;
  * *n* scoperta *f*.
fine *adj* fine, sottile, fino;
  ottimo; * *excl* bene; * *n* multa *f*;
  * *vt* multare.
finger *n* dito *m*; * *vt* tastare.
fingernail *n* unghia *f*.
finish *vt* finire; *n* fine *f*,
  traguardo *m*.
finite *adj* finito.
fir *n* abete *m*.
fire *n* fuoco *m*; incendio *m*;
  stufa; * *vt* sparare; licenziare.
fireplace *n* caminetto *m*.
firm *adj* saldo; fermo;
  definitivo; * *n* ditta *f*.
first *adj*, *n* primo *m*;
  * *adv* prima: — at ~ sulle
  prime: ~ly innanzi tutto.
first aid *n* pronto soccorso *m*.
fish *n* pesce *m*; * *vt* pescare.
fisherman *n* pescatore *m*.
fishing *n* pesca *f*.
fist *n* pugno *m*.
fit *n* attacco *m*; accesso *m*;
  * *adj* adatto; in forma;
  * *vt* andare bene a.
fitness *n* idoneità *f*; forma *f*.
five *num* cinque.
fix *vt* fissare; riparare;
  sistemare; * *n* guaio *m*.
flag *n* bandiera *f*; * *vi* stancarsi.
flagpole *n* pennone *m*.
flair *n* disposizione *f* naturale.
flake *n* scaglia *f*; * *vi* scrostarsi.
flame *n* fiamma *f*;
  * *vi* divampare.
flamingo *n* fenicottero *m*.
flap *n* linguetta *f*; ribalta *f*;

agitazione *f*, tumulto *m*;
  * *vt*, *vi* sbattere.
flare *vi* sfolgorare;
  * *n* chiarore *m*.
flash *n* lampo *m*; flash *m*;
  * *vi* lampeggiare.
flask *n* fiaschetta *f*; thermos *m*.
flat *adj* piatto; sgonfio;
  stonato; categorico; bemolle;
  * *n* appartamento *m*; (car
  tyre) gomma a terra *f*.
flatter *vt* lusingare.
flautist *n* flautista *m* or *f*.
flavour *n* gusto *m*; sapore *m*.
flaw *n* difetto *m*.
flea *n* pulce *f*.
flesh *n* carne *f*.
flex *n* filo *m*; * *vt* stirare;
  fletter; contrarre.
flexible *adj* flessibile.
flick *n* colpetto *m*; * *vt* dare un
  colpetto.
flight *n* volo *m*; rampa *f*; fuga *f*.
flint *n* silice *f*.
flip *vi*: ~ through sfogliare;
  * *n* colpetto *m*.
flirt *n* civetta *f*.
flirtation *n* flirt *m*, amoretto *m*.
flog *vt* frustare.
flood *n* inondazione *f*;
  * *vt* inondare; * *vi* straripare.
floor *n* pavimento *m*; piano *m*;
  * *vt* pavimentare;
  sconcertare.
flop *n* fiasco *m*.
floppy *adj* floscio.
flora *n* flora *f*.
flour *n* farina *f*.
flow *vi* fluire; * *n* corrente *f*,
  flusso *m*.
flower *n* fiore *m*; * *vi* fiorire.
flowerbed *n* aiuola *f*.
flowerpot *n* vaso *m* da fiori.
fluency *n* scioltezza *f*.
fluent *adj* scorrevole; corrente.
fluid *adj*, *n* fluido *m*.
flush *vi* arrossire; * *vt* tirare

l'acqua; * *n* sciacquone *m*;
rossore *m*.

flute *n* flauto *m*.

fly *vi* volare; * *n* mosca *f*.

flying saucer *n* disco volante *m*.

foal *n* puledro *m*.

focus *n* fuoco *m*.

foe *n* nemico *m*.

foetus *n* feto *m*.

fog *n* nebbia *f*.

foggy *adj* nebbioso.

foliage *n* fogliame *m*.

folk *n* gente *f*.

folk song *n* canzone popolare *m*.

follow *vt* seguire: ~ after
mettersi al seguito di: ~ on
seguire: ~ out (up) seguire
accuratamente, esaminare a
fondo: ~ through
accompagnare.

font *n* fonte *f* battesimale.

food *n* cibo *m*.

fool *n* sciocco *m*; buffone *m*;
* *vt* ingannare.

foot *n* piede *m*; * *vr* to put
one's ~ down imporsi.

football *n* calcio *m*.

for *prep* per; a favore di; da: —
as ~ me quanto a me: — what
~? perché?; * *conj* poiché.

forbid *vt* proibire.

force *n* forza *f*: ~s le forze *f*
armate; * *vt* forzare.

forceps *n* forcipe *m*.

fore *n* prua *f*; davanti *m*;
* *adj* anteriore.

forearm *n* avambraccio *m*.

forecast *vt* prevedere;
* *n* previsione *f*.

forehead *n* fronte *f*.

foreign *adj* straniero; estero;
estraneo.

foremost *adj* più importante.

forename *n* nome *m*.

forerunner *n* precursore *m*.

foresee *vt* prevedere.

foreseeable *adj* prevedibile.

foresight *n* previdenza *f*.

forest *n* foresta *f*.

forever *adv* eternamente, per
sempre.

forfeit *n* penitenza *f*;
* *vt* perdere.

forge *n* fornace *f*; * *vt* forgiare;
contraffare.

forget *vt* dimenticare.

forgive *vt* perdonare.

forgo *vt* rinunciare a.

fork *n* forchetta *f*;
biforcazione; * *vi* biforcarsi;
* *vt*: ~ out sborsare.

formal *adj* formale.

format *n* formato *m*;
* *vt* formattare.

formation *n* formazione *f*.

former *adj* precedente; * the ~
pron il primo.

formula *n* formula *f*.

fort *n* forte *m*.

fortieth *adj*, *n* quarantesimo *m*.

fortify *vt* fortificare;
rafforzare.

fortnight *n* quindici giorni *mpl*.

fortress *n* fortezza *f*.

forty *adj*, *n* quaranta *m*.

forward *adj* in avanti; precoce;
* ~s *adv* avanti; * *n* attaccante
m; * *vt* inoltrare.

fossil *adj*, *n* fossile *m*.

foul *adj* disgustoso; * *n* fallo *m*;
* *vt* impestare; sporcare.

found *vt* fondare.

foundation *n* fondazione *f*.

foundry *n* fonderia *f*.

fountain *n* fontana *f*.

four *adj*, *n* quattro *m*.

fourfold *adj* quadruplo.

fourteen *adj*, *n* quattordici *m*.

fourteenth *adj*, *n*
quattordicesimo *m*.

fourth *adj*, *n* quarto *m*.

fraction *n* frazione *f*.

fracture *n* frattura *f*.

fragile *adj* fragile.

frame n corporatura f,
montatura f, telaio m;
cornice f.
frame vt formare; costituire;
incorniciare; (sl) incastrare.
franc n franco m.
franchise n concessione f,
franchigia f.
frank adj franco; * vt affrancare.
fraud n truffa f.
fraught adj teso.
fray n zuffa f; * vi consumarsi.
freak n eccentrico m, (sl)
fricchettone; capriccio m;
* adj anormale.
freckle n lentiggine f.
free adj libero; gratuito;
* vt liberare.
freedom n libertà f.
freely adv liberamente.
freeze vt gelare, congelare,
surgelare; * vi gelare,
congelarsi; * n gelata f.
freezer n congelatore m.
freight n nolo m.
frenzied adj forsennato,
frenetico.
frenzy n frenesia f.
frequency n frequenza f.
frequent adj frequente;
* vt frequentare.
fresh adj fresco; sfacciato:
— fresh water acqua dolce;
* adv appena.
freshen vt, vi rinfrescare.
freshly adv appena.
friction n frizione f.
Friday n venerdì m: — Good ~
Venerdì Santo m.
fridge n frigo m.
friend n amico m: — Society of
Friends Quaccheri mpl.
friendship n amicizia f.
frieze n fregio m.
fright n spavento m.
frighten vt spaventare.
frightened adj spaventato,

impaurito.
frightening adj spaventoso.
frightful adj terribile.
frigid adj frigido.
fringe n frangia f.
frisk vt perquisire.
frisky adj vispo.
fritter n frittella f;
* vt sprecare.
frivolity n frivolezza f.
frivolous adj frivolo.
frizzy adj crespo.
frock n vestito m; tonaca f.
frog n rana f.
frolic vi sgambettare.
frolicsome adj giocoso.
from prep da; per.
frond n fronda f.
front n davanti m; fronte m;
lungomare m; * adj davanti.
frontal adj frontale.
front door n porta f d'ingresso.
frontier n frontiera f, confine m.
front page n prima pagina f.
frost n brina f, gelo m.
frostbite n congelamento m.
frostbitten adj congelato.
frosted glass n vetro m
smerigliato.
frosty adj gelido; glaciale.
froth n schiuma f;
* vi schiumare.
frothy adj schiumoso.
frown vi aggrottare le
sopracciglia; * n cipiglio m.
frozen adj congelato, surgelato.
frugal adj frugale.
fruit n frutta f, frutto m.
fruiterer n fruttivendolo m.
fruitful adj fruttifero;
fruttuoso.
fruition n adempimento di m
godimento di m; * come to ~ vi
realizzarsi, maturare,
arrivare a maturazione.
fruit juice n succo m di frutta.
fruitless adj vano.

fruit salad n macedonia f.
fruit tree n albero da frutto m.
frustrate vi frustrare.
frustated adj frustrato.
frustration n frustrazione f.
fry vt friggere.
frying pan n padella f.
fuchsia n fucsia f.
fuck (vulg) vt fottere: ~ about
fare cazzate (vulg), fare lo
stronzo (vulg): ~ off!
vaffanculo! (vulg): — to ~ off
andare a farsi fottere (vulg):
~ up incasinare (vulg): ~ with
fottere (vulg), fregare (vulg).
fuel n combustibile m.
fuel tank n serbatoio del
carburante m.
fugitive adj, n fuggitivo m.
fulcrum n fulcro m.
fulfil vt compiere.
fulfilment n compimento m;
soddisfazione f.
full adj pieno: ~ grown adulto:
~ aged maggiorenne: ~ in the
face in pieno viso: ~ blood
razza pura: ~ board pensione
completa: ~ daylight picno
giorno.
full moon n luna f piena.
fullness n pienezza f,
completezza f; abbondanza f,
ampiezza f: in the ~ of time a
tempo debito, a suo tempo.
full-scale adj su vasta scala.
full-time adj tempo pieno.
fully adv completamente.
fulsome adj insincero.
fumble vi brancolare; andare a
tentoni.
fume n esalazione f; * vi
emettere fumo (o vapore);
essere arrabbiatissimo,
schiumante.
fumigate vi suffumicare.
fun n divertimento m.
function n funzione f.

functional adj funzionale.
fund n fondo m; * vt finanziare.
fundamental adj fondamentale.
funeral n funerale m.
funereal adj funereo.
fun n divertimento m: — for ~
per scherzo, per divertimento:
~ fur pelliccia sintetica: — to
make ~ of prendere in giro:
— he is full of ~ è un tipo
divertente: — I can't see the
~ in it non vedo cosa ci sia da
ridere.
funny adj divertente, comico.
fun fair n luna park m invar.
fungus n muffa f.
funny adj buffo.
fur n pelo m.
fur coat n pelliccia f.
furious adj furioso.
furlong n 201 metri.
furnace n fornace f.
furnish vt arredare; fornire.
furnishings npl mobili mpl.
furniture n mobili mpl.
furore n scalpore m.
furrier n pellicciaio m.
furrow n solco m; * vt solcare.
furry adj peloso.
further adv più avanti; oltre:
~ to con riferimento a;
* adj ulteriore; * vt favorire.
furthermore adv inoltre.
furthest adv, adj più lontano.
furtive adj furtivo.
fury n furia f.
fuse n fusibile m; * vt fondere.
fuse box n scatola f dei fusibili.
fuselage n fusoliera f.
fusion n fusione f.
fuss adj agitazione f, storie fpl.
fussy adj pignolo; schizzinoso.
futile adj futile.
futility n futilità f.
future adj, n futuro m.
fuzz n peluria f, (sl) polizia f.
fuzzy adj crespo; sfocato.

G

gadget n aggeggio m,
  dispositivo m.
gaff n baggianata f,
  sciocchezza f.
gag n bavaglio m; frizzo m, gag
  f; * vt imbavagliare.
gaiety n allegria f.
gain n aumento m; guadagno m;
  * vt ottenere; guadagnare;
  aumentare.
gala n festa f; gala m.
galaxy n galassia f.
gale n bufera f.
gallery n galleria f; tribuna f;
  museo m.
galley n galea f.
gallon n gallone m.
gallop n galoppo m;
  * vi galoppare.
gallows n forca f, capestro m,
  patibolo m; supporto m,
  forcella f: — to send someone
  to the ~ mandare qualcuno
  alla forca: ~ bird avanzo di
  galera m, pendaglio di forca
  m, uomo da capestro:
  ~ humour umorismo macabro
  m: — a ~ look un'aria
  sinistra f, una faccia
  patibolare f: ripe for the ~ da
  forca: ~ tree forca f, patibolo
  f: — to have the ~ in one's
  face avere una faccia
  patibolare.
gamble vt, vi giocare d'azzardo;
  * n azzardo m.
gambler n giocatore m
  d'azzardo.
game n gioco m; partita f;
  selvaggina f.
gammon n prosciutto
  affumicato e molto salato m.
gander n maschio della oca m.
gang n banda f.

gangster n gangster m.
gap n spazio m; vuoto m;
  intervallo m.
gape vi spalancarsi.
garage n autorimessa f,
  garage m; officina f.
garden n giardino m.
gardening n giardinaggio m.
garlic n aglio m.
garment n indumento m.
garnish vt guarnire;
  * n decorazione f.
garter n giarrettiera f.
gas n gas m.
gate n cancello m.
gather vt radunare; raccogliere;
  dedurre.
gauge n calibro m;
  * vt misurare.
gauze n garza f.
gay adj allegro; omosessuale.
gaze vi fissare; * n sguardo m.
gazelle n gazzella f.
gazette n gazzetta f.
gear n cambio m, marcia f;
  attrezzatura f.
gel n gel m.
gelatine n gelatina f.
gem n gemma f.
Gemini n Gemelli mpl.
gender n genere m.
gene n gene m.
general adj generale;
  * in ~ adv generalmente;
  * n generale m.
generate vt generare.
generation n produzione f;
  generazione f.
generator n generatore m.
generic adj generico.
generosity n generosità f.
generous adj generoso.
genetics npl genetica f.
genial adj cordiale.
genitals npl genitali mpl.
genius n genio m.
genteel adj distinto, signorile,

di nobili natali; snob.

gentile *n* gentile *m*, pagano *m*.

gentle *adj* dolce.

gentleman *n* signore *m*; gentiluomo *m*.

gently *adv* dolcemente, gentilmente.

gentry *n* piccola nobiltà *f*.

genuine *adj* genuino.

geography *n* geografia *f*.

geology *n* geologia *f*.

geometry *n* geometria *f*.

geranium *n* geranio *m*.

geriatric *adj* geriatrico.

germ *n* microbo *m*.

gesture *n* gesto *m*.

get *vt* ottenere (io ottengo, tu ottieni, lui [lei] ottiene, noi otteniamo, voi ottenete, loro ottengono); ricevere; prendere; portare; afferrare: ~ afloat rimettere a galla; * *vi* arrivare a; diventare; cominciare a; farsi (io mi faccio, tu ti fai, lui [lei] si fa, noi ci facciamo, voi vi fate, loro si fanno): ~ about, abroad andare in giro: ~ above oneself montarsi la testa: ~ abreast of raggiungere, mettersi alla pari con: ~ across passare dall'altra parte, (*fig*) comunicare: ~ after correre dietro a: ~ ahead riuscire, avere successo: ~ ahead of superare, sorpassare: ~ along andare via, andarsene, tirare avanti, fare progressi, andare d'accordo: ~ anywhere arrivare dappertutto: ~ around riuscire a, farcela: ~ at afferrare: ~ away andar via: ~ back tornare: ~ behind rimanere indietro: ~ between mettersi, intromettersi: ~ by farcela: ~ down venire giù:

~ down to mettersi di buona lena: ~ in entrare: ~ into entrare, penetrare: ~ nowhere non concludere niente: ~ off andare via: ~ on montare, salire: ~ onto montare in, salire su: ~ out andare fuori, scire: ~ out of andare fuori da, uscire da: ~ over superare: ~ round *see* ~ about, around: ~ somewhere arrivare da qualche parte, avere successo: ~ there, through farcela: ~ together incontrarsi, trovarsi: ~ under andare, mettersi, *or* passare sotto: ~ up alzarsi: ~ up to fare ricorso a, ricorrere a.

get-out *n* scusa *f*, cavilo *m*.

ghost *n* fantasma *m*.

giant *n* gigante *m*.

gift *n* dono *m*; regalo *m*.

gifted *adj* dotato.

gigantic *adj* gigantesco.

gin *n* gin *m*.

ginger *n* zenzero *m*; rossiccio *m*.

giraffe *n* giraffa *f*.

girder *n* trave *f*.

girdle *n* busto *m*.

girl *n* ragazza *f*.

girlfriend *n* amica *f*.

giro *n* postagiro *m*.

give *vt*, *vi* dare: ~ away dare via, consegnare, distribuire: ~ back rendere, restituire: ~ forth emettere, annunciare: ~ in cedere, arrendersi: ~ off emettere, emanare: ~ on(to) dare su, guardare, affacciarsi: ~ out venir meno, esaurirsi: ~ over cessare, smettere: ~ round distribuire: ~ up rinunciare.

glacier *n* ghiacciaio *m*.

glad *adj* contento, lieto.

gladiator *n* gladiatore *m*.

glamorous *adj* affascinante; seducente.

glamour *n* fascino *m*.

glance *n* occhiata *f*; * *vi* dare un'occhiata a.

gland *n* ghiandola *f*.

glare *n* bagliore *m*; * *vi* sfolgorare.

glaring *adj* accecante; palese.

glass *n* vetro *m*; bicchiere *m*; calice *m*: — glasses *npl* occhiali *mpl*.

glassware *n* cristalleria *f*.

glaze *n* smalto *m*.

gleam *n* luccichio *m*; * *vi* luccicare.

glean *vt* racimolare.

glimmer *n* barlume *m*; * *vi* baluginare.

glimpse *n* occhiata *f*; * *vt* intravedere.

gloat *vi* gongolare.

global *adj* globale.

globe *n* globo *m*; mappamondo *m*.

gloom *n* buio *m*.

gloomy *adj* cupo; deprimente.

glorification *n* glorificazione *f*.

glorify *vt* glorificare.

glorious *adj* glorioso.

glory *n* gloria *f*.

gloss *n* glossa *f*; lucentezza *f*; * *vt* lucidare; chiosare.

glossary *n* glossario *m*.

glove *n* guanto *m*.

glow *vi* ardere, rosseggiare; * *n* incandescenza *f*.

glue *n* colla *f*; * *vi* incollare.

glutton *n* ghiottone *m*.

gluttony *n* ghiottoneria *f*.

glycerine *n* glicerina *f*.

gnat *n* zanzara *f*.

go *vi* andare (io voado, tu vai, lui [lei] va, noi andiamo, voi andate, loro vanno); andarsene; arrivare: ~ aboard salire a bordo: ~ about andare in giro: ~ across

attraversare: ~ adrift andare alla deriva: ~ after dare la caccia a: ~ against opporsi: ~ aground arenarsi: ~ ahead procedere: ~ ahead of precedere: ~ ahead with andare avanti con, continuare: ~ along andare avanti, procedere: ~ alongside accostare, accostarsi: ~ ashore sbarcare: ~ astray perdersi: ~ away andare via: ~ back ritornare: ~ back on (one's word) non mantenere (la parola): ~ before precedere: ~ behind (one's back) andare dietro (le spalle di qualcuno): ~ by passare via, sfumare: ~ down andare giù, scendere: ~ down to scendere fino a: ~ forth partire: ~ forward andare avanti: ~ in entrare: ~ in for interessarsi di: ~ in with associarsi: ~ into entrare: ~ off andarsene, rinunciare a, (of food) andare a male: ~ on andare avanti: ~ on at dare addosso, stare dietro a, sgridare: ~ on for essere quasi: ~ on with continuare a fare qualcosa: ~ out andare fuori, uscire: ~ out of uscire da: ~ out to andare a: ~ over passare dall'altra parte: ~ overboard cadere in mare: ~ round girare: ~ through penetrare: ~ through with portare avanti: ~ to andare fino a: ~ together andare insieme, fare coppia fissa: ~ under andare sotto, andare in rovina: ~ up salire, passare di grado: ~ up to salire fino a: ~ with andare con, essere insieme a: ~ without astenersi da.

goal *n* goal *m*; scopo *m*.
goat *n* capra *f*.
God *n* Dio *m*.
goddess *n* dea *f*.
godless *adj* empio.
godlike *adj* divino.
goggles *npl* occhiali *mpl*.
gold *n* oro *m*.
golden *adj* d'oro.
golf *n* golf *m*.
gondola *n* gondola *f*.
gondolier *n* gondoliere *m*.
gong *n* gong *m*.
good *adj* buono; * *n* bene *m*.
goodbye *excl* arrivederci,
  addio.
goodness *n* bontà *f*.
goodwill *n* buona volontà *f*;
  (commercial) avviamento *m*.
goose *n* oca *f*.
gooseberry *n* uva spina *f*.
gorgeous *adj* sontuoso,
  splendido.
gorilla *n* gorilla *m*.
gory *adj* sanguinoso.
goshawk *n* astore *m*.
gospel *n* vangelo *m*.
gossip *n* pettegolezzi *mpl*;
  pettegolo *m*; * *vi* chiacchierare.
gothic *adj* gotico.
goulash *n* gulasch *m*.
gourmet *n* buongustaio *m*.
govern *vt* governare.
government *n* governo *m*.
governor *n* governatore *m*.
grab *vt* afferrare.
grace *n* grazia *f*; garbo *m*;
  proroga; * *vt* onorare.
graceful *adj* aggraziato,
  garbato.
grade *n* categoria *f*; voto *m*;
  grado *m*; * *vt* classificare;
  graduare.
gradual *adj* graduale.
graffiti *n* graffiti *mpl*.
graft *n* innesto *m*; duro lavoro
  m; * *vt* innestare.

grammar *n* grammatica *f*.
gramophone *n* grammofono *m*.
granary *n* granaio *m*.
grandfather *n* nonno *m*.
grandmother *n* nonna *f*.
grandparents *npl* nonni *mpl*.
grant *vt* accordare; ammettere;
  * *n* sovvenzione *f*; borsa di
  studio *f*.
granule *n* granello *m*.
grape *n* chicco *m* d'uva.
grapefruit *n* pompelmo *m*.
grapevine *n* vite *f*.
graph *n* grafico *m*.
graphics *npl* grafica *f*.
grasp *vt* afferrare, prendere
  padronanza di; *n* padronanza
  di *f*.
grasping *adj* avido.
grass *n* erba *f*.
grasshopper *n* cavalletta *f*.
grass snake *n* biscia *f*.
grate *n* grata *f*; * *vt* grattare;
  * *vi* cigolare.
grateful *adj* grato.
gratefulness *n* riconoscenza *f*.
gratification *n* soddisfazione *f*.
gratify *vt* soddisfare.
gratitude *n* gratitudine *f*.
gratuitous *adj* gratuito.
gratuity *n* mancia *f*.
grave *n* tomba *f*; * *adj* grave.
gravel *n* ghiaia *f*.
gravestone *n* lapide *f*.
graveyard *n* cimitero *m*.
gravity *n* gravità *f*.
gravy *n* sugo dell' arrosto *m*.
grease *n* grasso *m*, unto *m*;
  * *vt* ungere, lubrificare.
greasy *adj* untuoso, unto.
great *adj* grande; meraviglioso;
  eminente.
greed *n* avidità *f*.
Greek *n* greco *m*.
green *adj, n* verde *m*: ~s *npl*
  verdura *f*.
greengrocer *n* fruttivendolo *m*.

greet *vt* salutare.
greeting *n* saluto *m*.
grenadier *n* granatiere *m*.
grey *adj*, *n* grigio *m*.
grid *n* grata *f*; rete *f*.
grief *n* dolore *m*.
grieve *vi* addolorare.
grill *n* griglia *f*; * *vt* cuocere
   alla griglia.
grim *adj* torvo; macabro.
grimy *adj* sudicio.
grin *n* largo sorriso *m*; * *vi* fare
   un largo sorriso.
grip *n* presa *f*; borsone *m*;
   dolore lancinante;
   * *vt* stringere.
gripping *adj* appassionante.
grit *n* pietrisco *m*.
groan *vi* gemere; * *n* gemito *m*.
grocer *n* negoziante *m* or *f*, di
   alimentari.
groin *n* inguine *m*.
groom *n* paiafreniere *m*,
   stalliere *m*, addetto *m*; sposo
   m; * *vi* governare; aver cura di.
groove *n* solco *m*.
grotto *n* grotta *f*.
ground *n* terra *f*, terreno *m*;
   campo *m*; motivo *m*; ~s *mpl*
   fondi; * *vi* incagliarsi.
group *n* gruppo *m*; complesso *m*;
   * *vt* raggruppare.
grow *vi* crescere; aumentare;
   diventare: ~ up diventare
   grande; * *vi* coltivare;
   aumentare.
growth *n* crescita *f*, tumore *m*.
grub *n* larva *f*; (*sl*) cibo *m*.
grubby *adj* sudicio.
grudge *n* rancore *m*; * *vt*
   invidiare; dare a malincuore.
grudgingly *adv* malvolentieri.
gruelling *adj* estenuante.
gruesome *adj* agghiacciante.
grumpy *adj* scorbutico.
grunt *vi* grugnire; * *n* grugnito *m*.
guarantee *n* garanzia *f*;

* *vt* garantire.
guard *n* guardia *f*; protezione *f*;
   * *vt* fare la guardia a.
guardian *n* tutore *m*.
guerrilla *n* guerrigliero *m*.
guess *vt*, *vi* indovinare;
   supporre; * *n* supposizione *f*.
guest *n* ospite *m* or *f*, invitato *m*.
guidance *n* guida *f*; consigli *mpl*.
guidebook *n* guida *f*.
guilt *n* colpa *f*, colpevolezza *f*.
guilty *adj* colpevole.
guitar *n* chitarra *f*.
gulf *n* golfo *m*; abisso *m*.
gum *n* gengiva *f*; colla *f*;
   * *vt* incollare.
gun *n* fucile *m*, pistola *f*,
   rivoltella *f*.
guru *n* guru *m*.
gush *vi* sgorgare; * *n* ondata *f*.
gust *n* folata *f*, raffica *f*.
gut *n* intestino *m*; budello *m*:
   ~s *npl* budelia *f*; * *vt* sventrare.
gutter *n* grondaia *f*, cunetta *f*.
guzzle *vt* ingozzare; *vi*
   ingozzarsi, darsi ai bagordi.
gym(nasium) *n* palestra *f*.
gymnast *n* ginnasta *m* or *f*.
gymnastic *adj* ginnastico; * ~s
   n ginnastica *f*.
gynaecologist *n* ginecologo *m*.
gypsy *n* zingaro *m*.
gyrate *vi* roteare.

H

habit *n* abitudine *f*; tonaca *f*.
habitat *n* habitat *m*.
habitual *adj* abituale.
haddock *n* eglefino *m*.
hail *n* grandine *f*;
   * *vi* grandinare; * *vt* acclamare.
hailstone *n* chicco *m* di
   grandine.
hair *n* capelli *mpl*; chioma *f*,
   pelo *m*.

hairbrush *n* spazzola per capelli *f*.
haircut *n* taglio dei capelli *m*.
hairdresser *n* parrucchiere *m*.
hairstyle *n* acconciatura *f*.
hake *n* nasello *m*.
half *n* metà *f*; * *adj* metà, mezzo.
halibut *n* ippoglosso *m*.
hall *n* entrata *f*, salone *m*; villa *f*.
hallucination *n* allucinazione *f*.
halt *vt* fermare; * *vi* fermarsi; * *n* fermata *f*; sosta *f*.
halve *vt* dimezzare.
ham *n* prosciutto *m*; radioamatore *m*.
hamlet *n* paesino *m*.
hammer *n* martello *m*; * *vt* martellare.
hammock *n* amaca *f*.
hamper *n* cesto *m*; * *vt* ostacolare.
hamster *n* criceto *m*.
hand *n* mano *f*; * *vt* passare; consegnare.
handbag *n* borsa *f*.
handbrake *n* freno *m* a mano.
handkerchief *n* fazzoletto *m*.
handle *n* manico *m*; * *vt* maneggiare; trattare.
handshake *n* stretta di mano *f*.
handsome *adj* bello; considerevole.
handwriting *n* scrittura *f*.
handy *adj* sottomano; comodo.
handyman *n* tuttofare *m*.
hang *vt* appendere; impiccare; * *vi* pendere.
hanger *n* gruccia *f*.
hangover *n* postumi *mpl* di una sbornia.
hanker *vi* avere molto desiderio di.
haphazard *adj* casuale.
happen *vi* succedere; capitare; accadere.
happily *adv* tranquillamente.
happiness *n* felicità *f*.

happy *adj* contento, felice.
harass *vt* assillare.
harbour *n* porto *m*; * *vt* covare.
hard *adj* duro; rigido; forte; difficile.
hardy *adj* robusto.
hare *n* lepre *f*.
harm *n* male *m*; danno *m*; * *vt* nuocere a; danneggiare.
harmful *adj* nocivo.
harmless *adj* innocuo.
harmonica *n* armonica *f*.
harmonise *vt*, *vi* armonizzare.
harmony *n* armonia *f*.
harp *n* arpa *f*.
harsh *adj* severo.
harvest *n* raccolto *m*; * *vt* fare il raccolto di.
hassock *n* inginocchiatoio *m*.
haste *n* fretta *f*.
hat *n* cappello *m*.
hate *n* odio *m*; * *vt* odiare.
hateful *adj* odioso.
hatred *n* odio *m*.
haughty *adj* superbo.
haul *vt* trascinare; * *n* tragitto *m*; retata *f*.
haulage *n* autotrasporto *m*.
haunt *vt* frequentare; abitare; * *n* covo *m*.
haunted *adj* abitato dai fantasmi, spiritato.
have *vt* avere (io ho, tu hai, lui [lei] ha, noi abbiamo, voi avete, loro hanno) possedere; fare; tenere: ~ about one avere con sè: ~ something against someone avercela con qualcuno: ~ it away with (*vulg*) farsela con, portarsi a letto qualcuno: ~ back avere indietro: ~ down tirare giù: ~ in avere in casa, invitare, farcela: ~ off fare tagliare, (*vulg*) farsela, andare a letto con qualcuno: ~ on indossare, avere prove contro qualcuno:

~ out farsi togliere qualcosa:
~ over invitare, far venire
qualcuno a casa: ~ up alzare,
tirare su qualcosa: — to ~ an
affair with someone avere
una relazione amorosa con
qualcuno.
haven *n* rifugio *m*.
hawk *n* falco *m*; * *vt* vendere
per strada.
hay *n* fieno *m*.
haystack *n* pagliaio *m*.
hazard *n* rischio *m*; * *vt* rischiare.
haze *n* foschia *f*.
hazelnut *n* nocciola *f*.
hazy *adj* sfocato.
he *pron* egli, lui.
head *n* testa *f*; capo *m*;
* *vt* essere in testa a.
headache *n* mal di testa *f*;
grattacapo *m*.
headmaster *n* preside *m*,
direttore *m*.
heal *vt* guarire.
health *n* salute *f*.
healthy *adj* sano.
heap *n* mucchio *m*;
* *vt* ammucchiare.
bear *vt*, *vi* sentire.
hearing *n* udito *m*.
hearse *n* carro *m* funebre.
heart *n* cuore *m*: ~ attack
attacco cardiaco *m*: ~ and
soul con tutta l'anima: — the
~ of the matter il nocciolo della
faccenda: ~throb battito
cardiaco, (*fig*) passione
d'amore.
hearth *n* focolare *m*.
heartless *adj* spietato.
heat *n* calore *m*; * *vt* scaldare.
heater *n* stufa *f*.
heathen *n* pagano *m*.
heating *n* riscaldamento *m*.
heave *vt* sollevare; anelare a;
vi tracinarsi; alzarsi; ansare;
* *n* sforzo *m*.

heaven *n* cielo *m*, paradiso *m*.
heavily *adv* pesantemente.
heavy *adj* pesante; intenso-,
opprimente.
Hebrew *adj* ebreo, ebraico; * *n*
ebreo.
hectic *adj* agitato, febbrile,
frenetico.
hedge *n* siepe *f*; * *vi* premunirsi;
tergiversare.
hedgehog *n* riccio *m*.
heed *vt* badare a; * *n* attenzione *f*.
heedless *adj* non curante.
heel *n* calcagno *m*; tacco *m*.
hefty *adj* pesante.
height *n* altezza *f*; (of persons)
statura *f* (*also fig*).
heighten *vt* alzare; aumentare;
* *vi* aumentare.
heir, heiress *n* erede *m* or *f*.
heirloom *n* ricordo *m* di
famiglia.
helicopter *n* elicottero *m*.
hell *n* inferno *m*.
helmet *n* elmo *m*, casco *m*.
hello *excl* ciao! *or* pronto?
help *vt* aiutare; assistere;
soccorrere; * *n* aiuto *m*;
aiutante *m* or *f*; soccorso *m*;
assistenza *f*.
helper *n* assistente *m* or *f*.
hem *n* orlo *m*.
hemisphere *n* emisfero *m*.
hen *n* gallina *f*.
hepatitis *n* epatite *f*.
her *pron* la, lei.
herb *n* erba aromatica *f*.
herbaceous *adj* erbaceo.
here *adv* qui, qua.
heresy *n* eresia *f*.
heretic *adj*, *n* eretico *m*.
heritage *n* eredità *f*,
patrimonio *m*.
hermit *n* eremita *m*.
hernia *n* ernia *f*.
hero *n* eroe *m*.
heroin *n* eroina *f*.

heroine *n* eroina *f*.
heroism *adj* eroismo.
herring *n* aringa *f*.
hers *poss pron* suo, di lei.
herself *pron* se stessa, lei
  stessa.
hesitant *adj* esitante.
hesitate *vi* esitare.
hesitation *n* esitazione.
heterosexual *adj*, *n*
  eterosessuale *m* or *f*.
hexagon *n* esagono *m*.
hexagonal *adj* esagonale.
hibernate *vi* cadere in letargo.
hiccup *n* singhiozzo *m*;
  * *vi* avere il singhiozzo.
hidden *adj* nascosto.
hide *vt* nascondere; * *n* cuoio *m*.
hideous *adj* orribile.
hierarchy *n* gerarchia *f*.
hi-fi *n* stereo *m*; * *adj* hi-fi.
high *adj* alto.
hijack *n* dirottamento *m*;
  * *vt* dirottare.
hike *n* escursione a piedi *f*.
hilarious *adj* spassoso.
hill *n* collina *f*, colle *m*.
hilly *adj* collinoso.
him *pron* lo, lui.
himself *pron* lui stesso.
hind *adj* posteriore; * *n* cerva *f*.
hinge *n* cardine *m*, cerniera *f*.
hint *n* allusione *f*; * *vt* alludere.
hip *n* anca *f*.
hippopotamus *n* ippopotamo *m*.
hire *vt* noleggiare;
  * *n* noleggio *m*.
his *poss pron* suo, di lui.
hiss *vt* sibilare; * *n* sibilo *m*.
historian *n* storico *m*.
historic(al) *adj* storico.
history *n* storia *f*.
hit *vt* colpire; picchiare;
  sbattere; raggiungere;
  * *n* colpo *m*; successo *m*.
hitch-hike *vi* fare l'autostop.
hive *n* alveare *m*.

hearse *adj* rauco.
hoax *n* scherzo *m*; * *vt* ingannare.
hobby *n* hobby *m*, passatempo *m*.
hockey *n* hockey *m*.
hoe *n* zappa *f*; * *vt* zappare.
hog *n* porco *m*; * *vt* accaparrarsi.
hold *vt* tenere (io tengo, tu
  tieni, lui [lei] tiene, noi
  teniamo, voi tenete, loro
  tengono); mantenere;
  trattenere; avere: ~ something against someone
  imputare qualcuno a
  qualcosa: ~ back trattenere,
  tenere a bada: ~ by attenersi
  a, rispettare: ~ down tenere
  giù, tenere fermo: ~ forth
  pontificare, sprologuiare su
  qualcosa: ~ in trattenere:
  ~ on restare attaccato,
  aspettare: ~ on to tenere *or*
  tenersi stretto a: ~ out tener
  duro, resistere: ~ out on
  nascondere un segreto: ~
  over tenere in serbo: ~ to (by)
  restare fedele, mantenere,
  confermare: ~ together stare
  (rimanere) insieme: ~ under
  tenere sotto (sottomesso),
  opprimere: ~ up tenere su,
  sostenere: ~ up on rimandare,
  rinviare: ~ with essere
  d'accordo con; approvare.
hold *n* presa *f*; stiva *f*.
hole *n* buca *f*, buco *m*, falla *f*;
  tana *f*; * *vt* bucare.
holiday *n* vacanza *f*.
hollow *adj* cavo; falso;
  * *n* cavità; * *vt* scavare.
holly *n* agrifoglio *m*.
hollyhock *n* malvone *m*.
holocaust *n* olocausto *m*.
holy *adj* santo, religioso.
home *n* casa *f*; patria *f*;
  habitat *m*; istituto *m*.
homely *adj* semplice,
  familiare.

homeopath *adj, n* omeopatico*m*.
homeopathy *n* omeopatia*f*.
homesickness *n* nostalgia (di casa)*f*.
homesick *n* nostalgico, che ha nostalgia di.
homicide *n* omicidio*m*.
homosexual *adj, n* omosessuale *m* or *f*.
honest *adj* onesto.
honey *n* miele*m*.
honeymoon *n* luna *f* di miele.
honorary *adj* onorario.
honour *n* onore *m*; * *vt* onorare.
hoof *n* zoccolo *m*.
hook *n* gancio *m*; * *vt* agganciare.
hooked *adj* (nose) aquilino; fanatico.
hooker *n* puttana*f*.
hooligan *n* teppista *m* or *f*.
hop *n* saltello *m*; (botany) luppolo; * *vi* saltellare.
hope *n* speranza *f*; * *vi* sperare.
hopeful *adj* fiducioso.
hopeless *adj* impossibile; incorreggibile; disperato.
horizon *n* orizzonte *m*.
horn *n* corno *m*; clacson *m*.
horoscope *n* oroscopo*m*.
horrible *adj* orribile.
horrific *adj* spaventoso.
horror *n* orrore *m*.
horse *n* cavallo *m*.
horseradish *n* rafano*m*.
hosepipe *n* tubo di gomma*f*.
hospital *n* ospedale*m*.
hospitality *n* ospitalità*f*.
host *n* ospite *m*; presentatore *m*; moltitudine*f*; (religious) ostia*f*.
hostage *n* ostaggio*m*.
hostel *n* ostello *m*.
hostile *adj* ostile.
hot *adj* caldo; piccante; focoso.
hotel *n* albergo *m*.

hound *n* segugio*m*; * *vt* perseguitare.
hour *n* ora *f*.
hourly *adv* ogni ora.
house *n* casa *f*; * *vt* sistemare, alloggiare.
housewife *n* casalinga*f*.
hover *vi* librarsi.
how *adv* come.
however *adv* comunque, tuttavia.
howl *vi* ululare; urlare; piangere; * *n* ululato *m*.
hub *n* mozzo *m*; (*fig*) fulcro *m*.
hubcap *n* coprimozzo*m*.
hue *n* tinta *f*.
hug *vt* abbracciare; * *n* abbraccio*m*.
huge *adj* enorme.
hull *n* scafo *m*.
human *adj* umano; * *n* essere *m*, umano.
humane *adj* umanitario.
humanitarian *adj* umanitario.
humanity *n* umanità*f*.
humanly *adv* umanamente.
humble *adj* umile; * *vt* umiliare.
humbly *adv* umilmente.
humid *adj* umido.
humidity *n* umidità*f*.
humiliate *vt* umiliare.
humiliation *n* umiliazione*f*.
humility *n* umiltà *f*.
humorist *n* umorista *m* or *f*.
humorous *adj* spiritoso.
humour *n* umorismo *m*; umore *m*; * *vt* accontentare.
hunch *n* gobba*f*; pezzo *m*; tozzo *m*; impressione*f*; intuizione*f*.
hunchback gobbo*m*; * ~ed *adj* gobbo.
hundred *adj, n* cento *m*.
hundredth *adj, n* centesimo *m*.
hunger *n* fame*f*.
hunger strike *n* sciopero *m*

della fame.
hungrily *adv* avidamente.
hungry *adj* affamato:
— be ~ aver fame.
hunt *vi* cacciare; cercare;
  * *n* caccia *f*; ricerca *f*.
hunter *n* cacciatore *m*.
hunting *n* caccia *f*.
hurdle *n* ostacolo *m*.
hurricane *n* uragano *m*.
hurried *adj* frettoloso.
hurry *vi* affrettarsi, fare in
  fretta; * *n* fretta *f*.
hurt *vt* ferire; danneggiare; far
  male; * *n* ferita *f*, lesione *f*.
hurtful *adj* ingiurioso.
husband *n* marito *m*.
hush *n* silenzio *m*; * *vt* quietare.
hut *n* baracca *f*.
hutch *n* gabbia *f*.
hyacinth *n* giacinto *m*.
hybrid *adj*, *n* ibrido *m*.
hydrangea *n* ortensia *f*.
hydro-electric *adj*
  idroelettrico.
hydrofoil *n* aliscafo *m*.
hydrogen *n* idrogeno *m*.
hyena *n* iena *f*.
hygiene *n* igiene *f*.
hygienic *adj* igienico.
hymn *n* inno *m*.
hypermarket *n* ipermercato *m*.
hyphen *n* trattino *m*.
hypnosis *n* ipnosi *f*.
hypnotic *adj* ipnotico.
hypnotism *n* ipnotismo *m*.
hypochondria *n* ipocondria *f*.
hypochondriac *n* ipocondriaco *m*.
hypocrisy *n* ipocrisia *f*.
hypocrite *n* ipocrita *m* or *f*.
hypodermic *adj* ipodermico.
hypothesis *n* ipotesi *f*.
hypothetical *adj* ipotetico.
hysteria *n* isterismo *m*.
hysterical *adj* isterico.

I

I *pron* io.
ice *n* ghiaccio *m*; gelato *m*.
iceberg *n* iceberg *m*.
ice cream *n* gelato *m*.
icing *n* glassa *f*.
icon *n* icona *f*.
icy *adj* ghiacciato, gelido.
idea *n* idea *f*.
ideal *adj*, *n* ideale *m*.
identical *adj* identico.
identification *n*
  identificazione *f*.
identify *vt* identificare.
identity *n* identità *f*.
ideology *n* ideologia *f*.
idiosyncrasy *n* peculiarità *f*.
idiot *n* idiota *m* or *f*.
idiotic *adj* stupido.
idle *adj* pigro; inattivo;
  infondato.
idol *n* idolo *m*.
if *conj* se, qualora.
ignite *vt* accendere.
ignition *n* iniezione *f*,
  accensione *f*.
ignoble *adj* ignobile.
ignorance *n* ignoranza *f*.
ignorant *adj* ignorante.
ignore *vt* ignorare; fingere di
  non vedere.
ill *adj* malato; indisposto;
  cattivo.
illegal *adj* illegale.
illegality *n* illegalità *f*.
illegible *adj* illeggibile.
illegitimate *adj* illegittimo.
illiterate *adj*, *n* analfabeta
  m or *f*.
illness *n* malattia *f*.
illogical *adj* illogico.
illuminate *vt* illuminare.
illusion *n* illusione *f*.
illustrate *vt* illustrare.
illustration *n* illustrazione *f*.

illustrative *adj* illustrativo.
illustrious *adj* illustre.
image *n* immagine *f*.
imagination *n* immaginazione *f*.
imagine *vt* immaginare.
imbalance *n* squilibrio *m*.
imitate *vt* imitare.
imitation *n* imitazione *f*.
immaculate *adj* impeccabile.
immaterial *adj* irrilevante.
immature *adj* immaturo.
immediate *adj* immediato.
immense *adj* immenso.
immerse *vt* immergere.
immigrant *n* immigrato *m*.
immigration *n* immigrazione *f*.
imminent *adj* imminente.
immobile *adj* immobile.
immodest *adj* impudico.
immoral *adj* immorale.
immortal *adj* immortale.
immune *adj* immune.
immunity *n* immunità *f*.
immunise *vt* immunizzare.
impartial *adj* imparziale.
impartiality *n* imparzialità *f*.
impatience *n* impazienza *f*.
impatient *adj* impaziente.
impeccable *adj* impeccabile.
impediment *n* impedimento *m*.
impending *adj* incombente.
imperceptible *adj*
  impercettibile.
imperfect *adj* difettoso;
  imperfetto.
imperfection *n* imperfezione *f*.
imperial *adj* imperiale.
impermeable *adj* impermeabile.
impersonal *adj* impersonale.
impertinence *n* impertinenza *f*.
impetus *n* spinta *f*.
implant *vt* innestare.
implement *n* utensile *m*,
  mezzo *m*, strumento *m*;
  * *vt* attuare.
implication *n* implicazione *f*.
imply *vt* implicare.

impolite *adj* scortese.
import *vt* importare;
  * *n* importazione *f*.
importance *n* importanza *f*.
important *adj* importante.
importation *n* importazione *f*.
importer *n* importatore *m*.
impose *vt* imporre.
impossible *adj* impossibile.
impostor *n* impostore *m*.
imprecise *adj* impreciso.
impregnable *adj* inattaccabile.
impregnate *vt* impregnare.
impress *vt* colpire, fare
  impressione a.
impression *n* impressione *f*.
impressive *adj* imponente, che
  colpisce.
imprison *vt* imprigionare.
imprisonment *n* reclusione *f*.
improbable *adj* improbabile.
improper *adj* scorretto.
improve *vt*, *vi* migliorare.
improvement *n*
  miglioramento *m*.
improvise *vt*, *vi* improvvisare.
impulse *n* impulso *m*.
impulsive *adj* impulsivo.
impurity *n* impurità *f*.
in *prep* in; a.
inability *n* inabilità *f*.
inaccurate *adj* inesatto.
inaction *n* inazione *f*.
inactive *adj* inattivo.
inadequate *adj* inadeguato.
inaugural *adj* inaugurale.
inauguration *n* inaugurazione *f*.
incalculable *adj* incalcolabile.
incapable *adj* incapace.
incapacitate *vt* rendere
  incapace.
incapacity *n* incapacità *f*.
incendiary *adj* incendiario.
incense *n* incenso *m*;
  * *vt* rendere furibondo.
incentive *n* incentivo *m*.
inception *n* principio *m*.

incest *n* incesto *m*.

inch *n* pollice *m*.

incidence *n* incidenza *f*.

incident *n* avvenimento *m*;
episodio *m*.

incidental *adj* secondario;
fortuito.

incinerator *n* inceneritore *m*.

inclination *n* tendenza *f*;
inclinazione *f*; voglia *f*.

incline *vi* tendere a;
* *n* pendenza *f*.

include *vt* includere.

including *adj* incluso.

inclusion *n* inclusione.

inclusive *adj* incluso.

incognito *adj* in incognito.

income *n* reddito *m*.

incomparable *adj*
incomparabile.

incompetence *n* incompetenza *f*.

incomplete *adj* incompleto.

incomprehensible *adj*
incomprensibile.

inconceivable *adj*
inimmaginabile.

inconclusive *adj* inconcludente.

incongruous *adj* incongruo.

inconsequential *adj*
insignificante.

inconsiderate *adj* irriguardoso.

inconsistency *n* incoerenza *f*.

inconsistent *adj*
contraddittorio.

inconsolable *adj* inconsolabile.

inconspicuous *adj* poco
appariscente.

incontinence *n* incontinenza *f*.

incontinent *adj* incontinente.

inconvenience *n* scomodità *f*;
* *vt* incomodare.

incorporate *vt* incorporare.

incorrect *adj* scorretto.

increase *vt*, *vi* aumentare;
* *n* aumento *m*.

incredible *adj* incredibile.

increment *n* incremento *m*.

incriminate *vt* incriminare.

incubator *n* incubatrice *f*.

incur *vt* contrarre.

indebted *adj* obbligato.

indecency *n* indecenza *f*.

indecent *adj* indecente.

indecision *n* indecisione *f*.

indecisive *adj* indeciso.

indeed *adv* infatti.

indefinite *adj* indefinito.

indemnity *n* indennizzo *m*.

indent *vt* rientrare dal margine.

independence *n* indipendenza *f*.

independent *adj* indipendente.

index *n* indice *m*.

indicate *vt* indicare;
* *vi* mettere la freccia.

indication *n* indicazione.

indifference *n* indifferenza *f*.

indigestion *n* indigestione *f*.

indignant *adj* indignato.

indirect *adj* indiretto.

indiscreet *adj* indiscreto.

indiscretion *n* indiscrezione.

indiscriminate *adj*
indiscriminato.

individual *adj* individuale;
* *n* individuo *m*.

individuality *n* individualità *f*.

indoors *adv* all'interno.

induction *n* induzione *f*.

indulge *vt* accontentare;
viziare.

indulgence *n* indulgenza *f*.

indulgent *adj* indulgente.

industrial *adj* industriale.

industry *n* industria *f*.

inedible *adj* immangiabile.

inefficient *adj* inefficiente.

inequality *n* ineguaglianza *f*.

inert *adj* inerte.

inertia *n* inerzia.

inescapable *adj* inevitabile.

inevitable *adj* inevitabile.

inexpensive *adj* economico.

inexplicable *adj* inspiegabile.

infamous *adj* infame.

infamy n infamia f.
infancy n infanzia f.
infant n bambino m.
infantry n fanteria f.
infatuated adj infatuato.
infatuation n infatuazione f.
infect vt infettare.
infection n infezione f.
infectious adj infettivo.
infer vt dedurre.
inference n deduzione f.
inferior adj inferiore.
inferiority n inferiorita f.
infernal adj infernale.
infest vt infestare.
infidel adj, n infedele m.
infinite adj infinito.
infinitive n infinito m.
infinity n infinità f.
infirm adj infermo.
inflate vt gonfiare.
inflation n inflazione f.
inflexible adj inflessibile.
inflict vt infliggere.
influence n influenza f;
  * vt influenzare.
influential adj influente.
influenza n influenza f.
inform vt informare.
informal adj informale.
information n informazioni fpl.
infrequent adj infrequente.
infuriate vt rendere furioso.
infusion n infusione f.
ingenuity adj ingegnosità f.
ingratitude n ingratitudine f.
ingredient n ingrediente m.
inhabit vt abitare.
inhabitant n abitante m or f.
inhale vt inalare.
inherit vt creditare.
inheritance n eredità f.
inhibit vt inibire.
inhuman adj inumano.
inimical adj ostile.
inimitable adj inimitabile.
initial adj, n iniziale f.

initially adv all'inizio.
initiate vt iniziare.
initiation n iniziazione f.
initiative n iniziativa f.
inject vt iniettare.
injection n iniezione f.
injure vt ferire.
injury n ferita f.
injustice n ingiustizia f.
ink n inchiostro m.
inlay vt intarsiare.
inlet n insenatura f.
inn n locanda f.
innocence n innocenza f.
innocent adj innocente.
innovate vt fare innovazioni.
inoculate vt inoculare.
inoculation n inoculazione f.
inoffensive adj inoffensivo.
inpatient n ricoverato m.
input n alimentazione f; input m.
inquest n inchiesta f.
inquire vt indagare; informarsi.
inquiry n domanda f; inchiesta f.
inquisition n inquisizione f.
inquisitive adj curioso.
insane adj pazzo, folle.
insanity n follia f; inferinità f;
  mentale.
insatiable adj insaziabile.
inscribe vt incidere.
inscription n iscrizione f;
  dedica f.
insect n insetto m.
insecticide n insetticida m.
insecure adj malsicuro.
insecurity n insicurezza f.
insensitive adj insensibile.
inseparable adj inseparabile.
insert vt inserire; * n inserto m.
insertion n inserzione f.
inside n interno m; * adv, prep
  dentro.
inside-out adv alla rovescia.
insignificant adj insignificante.
insincere adj insincero.
insincerity n insincerità f.

insist *vt*, *vi* insistere.
insistence *n* insistenza *f*.
insistent *adj* insistente.
insoluble *adj* insolubile.
insolvency *n* insolvenza *f*.
insolvent *adj* insolvente.
insomnia *n* insonnia *f*.
inspect *vt* controllare.
inspection *n* controllo *m*;
  ispezione *f*.
instability *n* instabilità *f*.
instal *vt* installare.
installation *n* installazione *f*.
instalment *n* rata *f*, puntata *f*.
instance *n* esempio *m*.
instant *adj* immediato;
  solubile; * *n* istante *m*.
instantaneous *adj* istantaneo.
instead *adv* invece.
instinct *n* istinto *m*.
institution *n* istituzione *f*.
instruct *vt* istruire.
instruction *n* istruzione *f*.
instructive *adj* istruttivo.
instrument *n* strumento *m*.
insufficient *adj* insufficiente.
insulate *vt* isolare.
insulation *n* isolamento *m*.
insulin *n* insulina *f*.
insult *vt* insultare; * *n* insulto *m*.
insurance *n* assicurazione *f*.
insure *vt* assicurare.
insurer *n* assicuratore *m*.
intact *adj* intatto.
intake *n* immissione *f*.
integral *adj* integrante.
integrate *vt* integrare.
integration *n* integrazione *f*.
intellect *n* intelletto *m*.
intellectual *adj*, *n* intellettuale
  m or *f*.
intelligence *n* intelligenza *f*.
intelligent *adj* intelligente.
intend *vt* avere intenzione di,
  intendere; destinare
  qualcosa a.
intense *adj* intenso.

intensive *adj* intensivo.
intent *adj* assorto, intento;
  * *n* intenzione *f*, intento *m*.
intention *n* intenzione *f*.
intentional *adj* intenzionale.
inter *vt* seppellire, sotterrare,
  interrare, inumare.
interaction *n* interazione *f*.
intercept *vt* intercettare.
interest *vt* interessare;
  * *n* interesse *m*.
interfere *vi* interferire;
  intromettersi.
interior *adj*, *n* interno *m*.
intermediary *n* intermediario *m*.
intermediate *adj* intermedio.
interment *n* sepoltura *m*,
  interramento *m*,
  seppellimento *m*.
intermission *n* interruzione *f*.
internal *adj* interno.
international *adj*
  internazionale.
interpret *vt* interpretare.
interpretation *n*
  interpretazione *f*.
interpreter *n* interprete *m* or *f*.
interrelated *adj* correlato.
interrogate *vt* interrogare.
interrogation *n*
  interrogatorio *m*.
interrogative *adj* interrogativo.
interrupt *vt*, *vi* interrompere.
interruption *n* interruzione *f*.
interval *n* intervallo *m*.
intervene *vi* sopraggiungere;
  intervenire.
intervention *n* intervento *m*.
interview *n* colloquio *m*,
  intervista *f*.
interviewer *n* intervistatore *m*.
intestine *n* intestino *m*.
intimacy *n* intimità *f*.
intimate *adj* intimo; * *vt* fare
  capire.
intimidate *vt* intimidire.
into *prep* in, dentro.

intolerant *adj* intollerante.
intoxicate *vt* intossicare.
intoxicating *adj* intossicante,
  inebriante.
intoxication *n* intossicazione *f*.
intravenous *adj* endovenoso.
intrepid *adj* intrepido.
intricate *adj* intricato.
intrigue *n* intrigo *m*; tresca *f*;
  * *vt* incuriosire.
introduce *vt* introdurre;
  presentare.
introduction *n* introduzione *f*;
  presentazione *f*.
introductory *adj* introduttivo.
intrude *vi* intromettersi.
intruder *n* intruso *m*.
intrusion *n* intrusione *f*.
intuition *n* intuito *m*.
invade *vt* invadere.
invader *n* invasore *m*.
invalid *adj* invalido; nullo;
  * *n* invalido *m*.
invaluable *adj* inestimabile.
invasion *n* invasione *f*.
invent *vt* inventare.
invention *n* invenzione *f*.
inventive *adj* inventivo.
inventor *n* inventore *m*.
inventory *n* inventario *m*.
invest *vt* investire.
investigate *vt* indagare.
investigation *n* indagine *f*.
investigator *n* investigatore *m*.
investment *n* investimento *m*.
invincible *adj* invincibile.
invisible *adj* invisibile.
invitation *n* invito *m*.
invite *vt* invitate; sollecitare.
invoice *n* fattura *f*;
  * *vt* fatturare.
involve *vt* coinvolgere.
inward *adj* interiore.
iodine *n* iodio *m*.
iris *n* iride *f*; (botany) iris *f*.
iron *n* ferro *m*; * *vt*, *vi* stirare.
ironic *adj* ironico.

irony *n* ironia *f*.
irrational *adj* irragionevole.
irregular *adj* irregolare.
irrelevant *adj* non pertinente.
irresistible *adj* irresistibile.
irresponsible *adj* irresponsabile.
irrigate *vt* irrigare.
irritable *adj* irritabile.
irritate *vt* irritare.
irritating *adj* irritante.
irritation *n* irritazione *f*.
Islam *n* Islam *m*.
island *n* isola *f*.
isle *n* isola *f*.
isolate *vt* isolare.
issue *n* questione *f*; emissione *f*;
  rilascio *m*; numero *m*; prole *f*;
  * *vt* rilasciare; pubblicare;
  emettere.
it *neuter pron* esso: — to catch
  ~ prenderle, buscarle,
  prendersi una sgridata: — to
  lord ~ fare da padrone: — to
  make ~ riuscire, farcela:
  — to have done ~ averla fatta
  grossa: — to face ~ out
  affrontare qualcosa (le
  conseguenze di qualcosa) con
  coraggio: — to keep at ~ non
  mollare: — to run for ~
  correre per farcela: — that's
  ~! Basta così! — So ~ appears! Sembra proprio di sì!
  — How's ~ going? Come va?
itch *n* prurito *m*; * *vi* prudere.
item *n* voce *f*, articolo *m*.
itinerary *n* itinerario *m*.
its *poss pron* suo.
itself *pron* si, se stesso, sè.
ivy *n* edera *f*.

J

jackal *n* sciacallo *m*.
jackdaw *n* taccola *f*.
jacket *n* giacca *f*.

jade *n* giada *f*.
jaguar *n* giaguaro *m*.
jail *n* carcere *m*, prigione *f*.
jailer *n* carceriere *m*.
jam *n* marmellata *f*; ingorgo *m*; pasticcio *m*; * *vt* bloccare; ficcare; * *vi* incepparsi.
janitor *n* portinaio *m*; bidello *m*.
January *n* gennaio *m*.
jar *vi* stonare, dissonare; dare ai nervi; *n* barattolo *m*.
jasmine *n* gelsomino *m*.
jaundice *n* itterizia *f*.
javelin *n* giavellotto *m*.
jaw *n* mascella *f*.
jay *n* ghiandaia *f*.
jazz *n* jazz *m*.
jealousy *n* gelosia *f*.
jeans *npl* jeans *mpl*.
jelly *n* gelatina *f*.
jelly-fish *n* medusa *f*.
jeopardise *vt* mettere in pericolo.
jersey *n* maglia *f*.
jester *n* buffone *m*.
Jesuit *n* gesuita *f*.
Jesus *n* Gesù *m*.
jet *n* (mineral) giaietto *m*; getto *m*; jet *m*.
jetty *n* molo *m*.
Jew *n* ebreo *m*.
jewel *n* gioiello *m*.
jewellery *n* gioielli *mpl*.
jib *n* (marine) braccio *m*.
jig *n* giga *f*.
jigsaw *n* puzzle *m*.
job *n* lavoro *m*; compito *m*; impiego *m*.
jockey *n* fantino *m*.
jogging *n* jogging *m*.
join *vt* unire, collegare; * *vi* unirsi a; confluire: ~ in something prendere parte a qualcosa: ~ on collegare, unire: ~ up collegare: ~ up into something unirsi a formare qualcosa.

joint *n* articolazione *f*, pezzo *m* di carne; spinello *m*; * *adj* comune.
joke *n* battuta *f*; barzelletta *f*; scherzo *m*; * *vi* scherzare.
joker *n* burlone *m*; (at cards) jolly *m*.
journal *n* periodico *m*.
journey *n* viaggio *m*.
jovial *adj* gioviale.
joy *n* gioia *f*.
jubilee *n* giubileo *m*.
judge *n* giudice *m*; * *vt* giudicare.
judgment *n* giudizio *m*.
judo *n* judo *m*.
jug *n* brocca *f*.
juice *n* succo *m*.
juke-box *n* juke-box *m*.
July *n* luglio *m*.
jump *vt, vi* saltare; * *n* salto *m*.
jumper *n* saltatore *m*; maglione *m*.
jumpy *adj* nervoso.
junction *n* incrocio *m*.
June *n* giugno *m*.
jungle *n* giungla *f*.
juniper *n* (botany) ginepro *m*.
junk *n* giunca *f*; cianfrusaglie *fpl*: ~ food robaccia *f*.
jury *n* giuria *f*.
just *adj* giusto; * *adv* proprio; appena; soltanto: ~ as altrettanto: ~ now attualmente.
justice *n* giustizia *f*.
justify *vt* giustificare.
juvenile *adj* giovanile; minorile; * *n* minorenne *m* or *f*.

K

kaleidoscope *n* caleidoscopio *m*.
kangaroo *n* canguro *m*.
karate *n* karatè *m*.
keen *adj* entusiasta; tagliente; acuto.

keep *vt* tenere (io tengo, tu tieni, lui [lei] tiene, noi teniamo, voi tenete, loro tengono); mantenere; trattenere; osservare:
~ abreast of tenere testa a qualcosa:
~ after stare dietro a qualcosa:
~ at continuare a fare qualcosa:
~ away stare, tenersi lontano da:
~ back trattenere:
~ back from stare alla larga da:
~ behind restare indietro:
~ by tenere a portata di mano:
~ down tenere basso, a freno:
~ from celare (nascondere) qualcosa a qualcuno:
~ handy tenere qualcosa a portata di mano:
~ in lasciare stare:
~ in with rimanere in buoni rapporti con qualcuno:
~ indoors tenere (stare) in casa:
~ off stare lontano:
~ on tenere addosso, tenersi:
~ out tenere fuori *or* alla larga:
~ out of tenere fuori da:
~ to attenersi a:
~ together tenere insieme:
~ under tenere sotto:
~ up tenere su, sostenere:
~ up to rimanere alla pari con:
~ within stare dentro, non superare.
keep *n* vitto e alloggio *m*; torrione *m*.
keepsake *n* ricordo *m*.
ketchup *n* ketchup *m*.
kettle *n* bollitore *m*.
key *n* chiave *f*; (music) tasto *m*.
key-ring *n* portachiavi *m*.
kick *vt* dare un calcio: ~ about essere ancora vivo: ~ against ribellarsi contro, opporsi: ~ at fare l'atto di dare un calcio: ~ away spostare a calci: ~ back restituire un

calcio: ~ back at colpire a propria volta, reagire contro: ~ down buttare qualcosa a terra con un calcio: ~ in fare entrare qualcosa con un calcio: ~ off respingere a calci: ~ on mettersi in moto: ~ out cacciare a calci: ~ over rovesciare qualcosa a calci: ~ up alzare con i piedi.
kick *n* calcio *m*.
kid *n* capretto *m*; ragazzino *m*; * *vt* scherzare.
kidnap *vt* rapire.
kidney *n* rene *m*; (cookery) rognone *m*.
kill *vt* uccidere, ammazzare.
killer *n* assassino *m*.
kilo *n* chilo *m*.
kilogramme *n* chilogrammo *m*, chilo *m*.
kilometre *n* chilometro *m*.
kind *adj* gentile; * *n* genere *m*.
kindergarten *n* asilo infantile *m*.
kindness *n* gentilezza *f*.
king *n* re *m*.
kingdom *n* regno *m*.
kiosk *n* chiosco *m*.
kiss *n* bacio *m*; * *vt* baciare.
kit *n* equipaggiamento *m*.
kitchen *n* cucina *f*.
kite *n* aquilone *m*.
kitten *n* gattino *m*.
knapsack *n* zaino *m*.
knead *vt* impastare.
knee *n* ginocchio *m*.
kneel *vi* inginocchiarsi.
knickers *npl* mutande *fpl*.
knife *n* coltello *m*.
knight *n* cavaliere *m*; (at chess) cavallo *m*.
knit *vt* lavorare a maglia; aggrottare: ~ one's brow aggrottare le sopracciglia.
knock *vt*, *vi* bussare; colpire: ~ down demolire; * *n* colpo *m*.

knocker *n* battente *m*.
knot *n* nodo *m*; * *vt* annodare.
know *vt*, *vi* sapere (io so, tu sai, lui [lei] sa, noi sappiamo, voi sapete, loro sanno); conoscere; riconoscere:
~ about essere al corrente di:
~ apart distinguere:
~ backwards conoscere alla perfezione: ~ for conoscere da: ~ of essere al corrente di.
know-all *n* sapientone *m*.
knowledge *n* conoscenza *f*; sapere *m*.
knowledgeable *adj* informato.
knuckle *n* nocca *f*.

L

label *n* etichetta *f*.
laboratory *n* laboratorio *m*.
labour *n* lavoro *m*; mano d'opera *f*; * *adj* (political) laburista: — be in ~ avere le doglie; * *vt* faticare.
lace *n* pizzo *m*; laccio *m*; * *vt* allacciare.
lack *vt*, *vi* mancare; * *n* mancanza *f*.
lad *n* ragazzo *m*.
ladder *n* scala *f*; * *vt* smagliare.
lady *n* signora *f*.
ladybird *n* coccinella *f*.
lager *n* birra bionda *f*.
lagoon *n* laguna *f*.
lake *n* lago *m*.
lamb *n* agnello *m*.
lame *adj* zoppo.
laminated *adj* laminato.
lamp *n* lampada *f*.
lampshade *n* paralume *m*.
land *n* terra *f*, terreno *m*; paese *m*; * *vt* atterrare; sbarcare.
landing *n* pianerottolo *m*; atterraggio *m*; sbarco *m*.

landlord *n* proprietario *m*.
landmark *n* punto *m* di riferimento.
landscape *n* paesaggio *m*.
lane *n* stradina *f*.
language *n* linguaggio *m*, lingua *f*.
lantern *n* lanterna *f*.
lap *n* grembo *m*; giro *m*; * *vt* lambire; * *vt* (*sl*) slappare, slapparsi.
lapel *n* risvolto *m*.
lapse *n* svista *f*; intervallo *m*; * *vi* scadere; sgarrare.
larch *n* larice *m*.
larder *n* dispensa *f*.
large *adj* grande: — at ~ in libertà; * ~ly *adv* in gran parte.
lark *n* allodola *f*, scherzo *m*.
larva *n* larva *f*.
laryngitis *n* laringite *f*.
larynx *n* laringe *f*.
laser *n* laser *m*.
lash *n* ciglio *m*; frustata *f*; * *vt* frustare; legare.
lasso *n* lasso *m*.
last *adj* ultimo; scorso; * at ~ *adv* finalmente: ~ ly in fine; * *vi* durare.
latch *n* chiavistello *m*.
late *adj* in ritardo, tardi; defunto; * ~ly *adv* ultimamente.
lateral *adj* laterale.
latitude *n* latitudine *f*.
latter *adj* ultimo: * ~ ly *adv* negli ultimi tempi.
lattice *n* reticolato *m*.
laugh *vi* ridere; * *n* risata *f*.
laughter *n* risata *f*.
launch *vt* varare; * *n* varo *m*; motolancia *f*.
laundrette *n* lavanderia *f* (automatica).
laundry *n* lavanderia *f*, biancheria *f*.
laurel *n* alloro *m*.

lava *n* lava *f*.
lavatory *n* gabinetto *m*.
lavender *n* lavanda *f*.
lavish *adj* sontuoso;
 * *vt* colmare di.
law *n* legge *f*.
law court *n* tribunale *m*.
lawn *n* prato *m*.
lawnmower *n* tagliaerba *m*.
lawyer *n* avvocato *m*.
laxative *n* lassativo *m*.
lay *vt* porre; posare; stendere;
 apparecchiare; * *adj* laico.
layer *n* strato *m*.
laze *vi* oziare.
laziness *n* pigrizia *f*.
lazy *adj* pigro.
lead *n* piombo *m*; indizio *m*;
 ruolo *m* principale;
 guinzaglio *m*; filo *m*.
lead *vt* condurre, guidare;
 * *vi* andare avanti: ~ astray
 sviare, mettere fuori strada:
 ~ away portare via: ~ back
 ricondurre, riportare: ~ in
 introdurre, fare entrare:
 ~ nowhere non portare da
 nessuna parte, non dare
 alcun risultato: ~ off
 condurre fuori: ~ on guidare,
 fare strada: ~ out fare uscire:
 ~ up condurre, giudare: ~ up
 to condurre, portare a.
leader *n* capo *m*; leader *m*;
 guida *f*.
leadership *n* direzione *f*.
leading *adj* in testa;
 preminente: ~ question *n*
 domanda *f* tendenziosa.
leaf *n* (botany) foglia *f*, foglio *m*.
leaflet *n* volantino *m*.
league *n* lega *f*, campionato *m*.
leak *n* perdita *f*; * *vt* perdere;
 divulgare; * *vi* perdere.
lean *vi* pendere; appoggiarsi;
 * *vt* appoggiare; * *adj* snello,
 magro.

leap *vi* saltare; balzare;
 * *n* salto *m*.
leap year *n* anno *m*; bisestile.
learn *vi* imparare.
lease *n* contratto *m* di affitto;
 * *vt* affittare.
leasehold *n* proprietà *f* in
 affitto.
least *adj*, *n* minimo *m*;
 * *adv* meno: — at ~ almeno:
 — not in the ~ niente affatto.
leather *n* pelle *f*, cuoio *m*.
leave *n* autorizzazione *f*,
 permesso *m*; licenza *f*;
 * *vt* lasciare; restare;
 * *vi* partire.
lecture *n* conferenza *f*;
 * *vi* tenere una conferenza.
ledge *n* sporgenza *f*; cengia *f*.
leech *n* sanguisuga *f*.
leek *n* (botany) porro *m*.
left *adj* sinistro; * ~ handed
 adj mancino: — on the ~ a
 sinistra.
leftish *adj* di sinistra.
leg *n* gamba *f*; coscia *f*; tappa *f*.
legacy *n* eredità *f*.
legal *adj* legale;
 * ~ ly *adv* legalmente.
legality *n* legalità *f*.
legend *n* leggenda *f*.
legendary *adj* leggendario.
legible *adj* leggibile.
legion *n* legione *f*.
legislate *vt* legiferare.
legislation *n* legislazione *f*.
legitimate *adj* legittimo;
 * *vt* legittimare.
leisure *n* svago *m*, tempo *m*
 libero: * ~ ly *adj* tranquillo.
lemon *n* limone *m*.
lemonade *n* limonata *f*.
lend *vt* prestare.
length *n* lunghezza *f*; durata:
 — at ~ esaurientemente.
lenient *adj* indulgente.
lens *n* lente *f*; obiettivo *m*.

Lent *n* quaresima *f*.
lentil *n* lenticchia *f*.
leopard *n* leopardo *m*.
leotard *n* body *m*.
leper *n* lebbroso *m*.
leprosy *n* lebbra *f*.
lesbian *adj* lesbico; * *n* lesbica *f*.
less *adj, pron* meno; * *adv* meno;
  * *prep* meno.
lesser *adj* minore.
lesson *n* lezione *f*.
let *vt* lasciare; affittare: ~ by,
  past far passare: ~ down
  allungare, calare, fare
  scendere: ~ in lasciare
  entrare: ~ in for costringere
  a fare: ~ in on far entrare,
  mettere dentro: ~ in
  ammettere a: ~ off scaricare:
  ~ on far salire: ~ through far
  passare: ~ up (on) diminuire.
lethal *adj* letale.
letter *n* lettera *f*.
lettuce *n* lattuga *f*.
leukaemia *n* leucemia *f*.
level *adj* piano, piatto, alla pari;
  * *n* livello *m*; * *vt* livellare,
  spianare.
lever *n* leva *f*.
liability *n* responsabilità *f*.
liable *adj* responsabile;
  soggetto; * *adv* probabile.
liar *n* bugiardo *m*.
liberal *adj* liberale.
liberate *vt* liberare.
liberation *n* liberazione *f*.
liberty *n* libertà *f*.
libido *n* libido *f*.
Libra *n* Bilancia *f*.
library *n* biblioteca *f*.
libretto *n* libretto *m*.
licence *n* autorizzazione *f*,
  canone *m*; patente *f*.
lick *vt* leccare; * *n* leccata *f*.
lid *n* coperchio *m*.
lie *n* menzogna *f*; * *vi* mentire;
  sdraiarsi.

lieutenant *n* tenente *m*.
life *n* vita *f*.
lifeboat *n* lancia di
  salvataggio *f*.
lifelike *adj* realistico.
lift *vt* sollevare; revocare;
  * *n* ascensore *m*; montacarichi
  mpl; passaggio *m*.
ligament *n* legamento *m*.
light *n* luce *f*; * *adj* chiaro;
  leggero; * *vt* accendere;
  illuminare.
lighthouse *n* faro *m*.
lightning *n* fulmine *m*.
like *adj* simile; * *prep* come;
  * *vt* piacere: —I ~ coffee mi
  piace il caffè: —he ~s
  chocolates gli piacciono i
  cioccolatini: —which do you
  ~ best? quale preferisci?
likely *adj* probabile.
lilac *n* lilla *m*; (botany) lillà *m*.
lily *n* giglio *m*: ~ of the valley
  mughetto *m*.
limb *n* arto *m*.
lime *n* calce *f*; tiglio *m*; laim *f*,
  limetta *f*.
limit *n* limite *m*; * *vt* limitare.
limp *vi* zoppicare;
  * *n* zoppicamento *m*;
  * *adj* floscio, molle.
line *n* linea *f*; tratto *m*; ruga *f*;
  lenza *f*; fila *f*; riga *f*;
  * *vt* foderare.
linen *n* lino *m*.
liner *n* transatlantico *m*.
linesman *n* guardalinee *m*.
lingerie *n* biancheria intima *f*.
linguist *n* linguista *m* or *f*.
linguistics *n* linguistica *f*.
link *n* legame *m*; anello *m*;
  * *vt* collegare.
linseed *n*: ~ oil olio *m* di lino.
lint *n* garza *f*.
lintel *n* architrave *f*.
lion *n* leone *m*.
lioness *n* leonessa *f*.

lip n labbro m.
liqueur n liquore m.
liquid adj, n liquido m.
liquor n bevande alcoliche fpl.
list n lista f, elenco m;
  * vt elencare.
listen vt ascoltare.
literature n letteratura f.
litre n litro m.
litter n rifiuti mpl; (zoological)
  cucciolata f.
little adj piccolo; * pron poco;
  * ~ by ~ adv gradualmente;
  * n poco m.
live vi vivere, abitare: ~ above
  abitare, stare sopra a: ~ again
  rivivere: ~ apart vivere
  separato da qualcuno, vivere
  per conto proprio: ~ by
  vivere presso: ~ down fare or
  farsi perdonare con il tempo:
  ~ high (well) vivere bene: ~ in
  essere a tutto servizio: ~ off
  vivere or cibarsi di qualcosa,
  vivere alle spese di qualcuno:
  ~ on continuare a vivere:
  ~ out of vivere fuori (lontano) da:
  ~ over vivere di, rivivere:
  ~ through sopravvivere:
  ~ together vivere insieme con:
  ~ it up darsi alla bella vita:
  ~ with someone vivere con
  qualcuno: ~ within vivere
  dentro; * adj vivente: — a ~ bomb
  una bomba inesplosa; * adv
  dal vivo; * ~ly adj vivace.
liver n fegato m.
livid adj furibondo; livido.
living adj vivente, vita.
living room n soggiorno m.
lizard n lucertola f.
load vt caricare; * n carico m.
loaded adj carico.
loaf n pane m: — meat ~
  polpettone m.
loafer n bighellone m.
loan n prestito m; * vt prestare.

lobster n aragosta f.
local adj locale.
locate vt localizzare, collocare.
location n posizione f.
lock n serratura f; chiusa f;
  sterzo m; (of hair) ciocca f;
  * vt chiudere a chiave:
  ~ away chiudere qualcosa in
  cassaforte: ~ into ingranare
  con: ~ on agganciare: ~ onto
  localizzare: ~ out chiudere
  fuori: ~ together incastrare
  insieme: ~ up mettere or
  tenere sotto chiave.
locker n armadietto m.
locket n medaglione m.
locomotive n locomotiva f.
locust n locusta f.
loft n soffitta f.
log n tronco m.
logbook n (marine) giornale di
  bordo m; libretto di
  circolazione m.
logic n logica f.
logical adj logico.
loll vi ciondolare.
loneliness n solitudine f.
lonely adj solitario.
long adj lungo; * vi desiderare.
longitude n longitudine f.
look vt guardare; vi guardare;
  sembrare; assomigliare:
  ~ after seguire, badare a:
  ~ ahead guardare avanti,
  pensare al futuro: ~ aside
  distogliere lo sguardo: ~ at
  guardare: ~ back guardare
  indietro: ~ beyond guardare
  oltre: ~ down abbassare lo
  sguardo: ~ down on
  disapprovare, disprezzare:
  ~ for cercare: ~ forward to
  attendere con ansia, non
  vedere l'ora: ~ in guardare
  dentro: ~ into esaminare a
  fondo: ~ on stare a guardare:
  ~ onto guardare su: ~ out

fare attenzione a: ~ out for
cercara qualcosa, stare
attenti a qualcosa: ~ over
guardare oltre esaminare
attentamente: ~ round
guardarsi intorno: ~ round
for cercare: ~ through
guardare attraverso:
~ to(wards) guardare verso:
~ up alzare gli occhi: ~ up to
ammirare; * n occhiata f,
aria f, aspetto m.
looking glass n specchio m.
loop n cappio m.
loose adj allentato; sciolto;
staccato; dissoluto.
lord n signore m.
lorry n camion m.
lose vt, vi perdere.
loss n perdita f: — to be at a ~
non saper come fare.
lost property office n ufficio
oggetti smarriti m.
lot n destino m, sorte f;
partita f; lotto m; molto m.
lotion n lozione f.
lottery n lotteria f.
loud adj forte.
loudspeaker n altoparlante m.
lounge n soggiorno m, sala
d'attesa f.
love n amore m: — to fall in ~
innamorarsi di; vt amare,
voler bene a.
lover n amante m or f.
low adj basso; scadente;
malfamato; * n depressione f;
* vi muggire.
lower adj inferiore; * vt calare;
ridurre.
loyal adj leale.
lozenge n pastiglia f; (geometry) losanga f.
lubricant n lubrificante m.
lubricate vt lubrificare.
luck n fortuna f.
lucky adj fortunato.

luggage n bagagli mpl.
lukewarm adj tiepido.
lump n zolletta f, grumo m;
nodulo m.
lunacy n pazzia f.
lunatic adj, n matto m, pazzo m.
lunch, luncheon n pranzo m,
(seconda) colazione f.
lung n polmone m.
lurk vi girare furtivamente.
luscious adj appetitoso.
lust n libidine f; * vi desiderare.
lustful adj libidinoso.
lusty adj vigoroso.
luxurious adj lussuoso.
luxury n lusso m.
lynx n lince f.
lyrics npl parole fpl.

M

macaroni n maccheroni mpl.
mace n mazza f.
machination n macchinazione f.
machine n macchina f.
machinery n macchinari mpl.
mackerel n sgombro m.
mackintosh n impermeabile m.
mad adj pazzo.
madam n signora f.
madness n follia f.
magazine n rivista f;
caricatore m.
magic n inagia f; * adj magico.
magician n mago m.
magistrate n magistrato m.
magnet n calamita f.
magnetism n magnetismo.
magnificent adj magnifico.
magnify vt ingrandire.
magnifying glass n lente
d'ingrandimento f.
magnitude n vastità f.
magpie n gazza f.
maid n cameriera f.
mail n posta f; * vt spedire (per

posta).
main *adj* principale;
  * *n* conduttura principale *f.*
mainly *adv* principalmente.
maintain *vt* mantenere;
  ritenere.
maize *n* granturco *m.*
majesty *n* maestà *f.*
major *adj* maggiore;
  * *n* (military) maggiore *m.*
majority *n* maggioranza *f.*
make *vt* fare; fabbricare:
  ~ after inseguire: ~ at assalire:
  ~ away with svignarsela:
  ~ for dirigersi: ~ into fare
  diventare: ~ of fare qualcosa
  con: ~ on guadagnarci: ~ out
  compilare: ~ over cedere: ~ up
  recuperare: ~ up for
  compensare, rimediare a:
  ~ up on recuperare su: ~ up to
  fare in modo che: ~ with fare
  qualcosa con; * *n* marca *f.*
malaise *n* malessere *m.*
malaria *n* malaria *f.*
male *adj* maschile;
  * *n* maschio *m.*
malfunction *n* cattivo
  funzionamento *m.*
malice *n* malizia *f.*
malicious *adj* cattivo.
malignant *adj* maligno.
mall *n* viale *m.*
mallet *n* mazzuolo *m.*
mallow *n* (botany) malva *f.*
malnutrition *n* denutrizione *f.*
malt *n* malto *m.*
mammal *n* mammifero *m.*
mammoth *n* mammut *m;*
  * *adj* colossale.
man *n* uomo *m;* * *vt* fornire di
  uomini.
manage *vt* gestire.
manager *n* gestore *m,* manager
  m.
mane *n* criniera *f.*
mango *n* mango *m.*

manhood *n* virilità *f.*
mania *n* mania *f.*
maniac *n* maniaco *m.*
manicure *n* manicure *f.*
mankind *n* umanità *f.*
manliness *n* virilità *f.*
manly *adj* virile.
man-made *adj* artificiale.
manner *n* maniera *f;*
  * ~s *npl* educazione *f.*
manoeuvre *n* manovra *f;*
  * *vt, vi* manovrare.
mansion *n* palazzo *m.*
manual *adj, n* manuale *m.*
manufacture *n* fabbricazione *f;*
  * *vt* fabbricare.
manufacturer *n* fabbricante *m.*
many *adj* molti, tanti;
  — ~ a time più volte:
  — how ~? quanti?
  — as ~ as tanti quanti.
map *n* carta *f,* pianta *f;*
  * *vt* tracciare una mappa.
maple *n* acero *m.*
marathon *n* maratona *f.*
marble *n* marmo *m;* bilia *f;*
  * *adj* di marmo.
March *n* marzo *m.*
march *n* marcia *f;* * *vi* marciare.
mare *n* giumenta *f.*
margarine *n* margarina *f.*
margin *n* margine *m.*
marigold *n* calendola *f.*
marina *n* marina *f.*
marine *adj* marino; * *n* marina *f.*
marjoram *n* maggiorana *f.*
mark *n* segno *m;* voto *m;*
  marco *m;* * *vt* macchiare;
  segnare; correggere.
market *n* mercato *m.*
marmalade *n* marmellata
  d'arance *f.*
marquee *n* grande tenda *f.*
marriage *n* matrimonio *m.*
married *adj* sposato, coniugato.
marrow *n* midollo *m;* (botany)
  zucca *f.*

marry *vt* sposare; *vi* sposarsi.
marshal *m* maresciallo *m*;
  * *vt* schierare.
marsupial *adj, n* marsupiale *m*.
martial *adj* marziale:
  ~ law stato d'assedio; legge
  marziale.
martyr *n* martire *m*.
marvel *n* meraviglia *f*;
  * *vi* stupirsi.
marvellous *adj* meraviglioso.
mascot *n* portafortuna *m*.
masculine *adj, n* maschile *m*.
mask *n* maschera *f*;
  * *vt* inascherare.
masochist *n* masochista *m* or *f*.
masonry *n* muratura *f*;
  massoneria *f*.
masquerade *n* mascherata *f*.
mass *n* messa *f*, massa *f*;
  * *vt* adunare; * *vi* adunarsi,
  ammassarsi.
massacre *n* massacro *m*;
  * *vt* massacrare.
massage *n* massaggio *m*;
  * *vt* massaggiare.
masseur *n* massaggiatore *m*.
masseuse *n* massaggiatrice *f*.
massive *adj* massiccio.
mast *n* albero *m*.
master *n* padrone *m*;
  insegnante *m*; * *vt* dominare;
  (*fig*) impadronirsi.
mat *n* tappetino *m*, zerbino *m*.
match *n* fiammifero *m*;
  partita *f*; incontro *m*; pari *m*
  or *f*, uguale *m* or *f*;
  * *vt* eguagliare; * *vi* intonarsi;
  corrispondere.
mate *n* compagno *m*;
  * *vt* accoppiare;
  * *vi* accoppiarsi.
material *adj* materiale;
  * *n* stoffa *f*, tessuto *m*;
  materiale *m*.
maternal *adj* materno.
mathematical *adj* matematico.

mathematics *npl* matematica *f*.
maths *npl* matematica *f*.
matt *adj* opaco.
matted *adj* infeltrito.
matter *n* materia *f*, faccenda *f*:
  — what is the ~? che cosa c'è?
  — a ~ of fact per la verità ;
  * *vi* importare.
mattress *n* materasso *m*.
mature *adj* maturo;
  * *vi* maturarsi.
mauve *adj* malva.
maximum *adj, n* massimo *m*.
May *n* maggio *m*: — ~ Day il
  primo maggio *m*: m~day
  S.O.S. *m*.
maybe *adv* forse, può darsi.
mayonnaise *n* maionese *f*.
mayor *n* sindaco *m*.
maze *n* labirinto *m*.
me *pron* mi, me, a me.
meadow *n* prato *m*.
meal *n* pasto *m*.
mean *adj* avaro; meschino;
  medio; * *n* mezzo *m*;
  ~s *npl* mezzi *mpl*: — in the
  meantime, meanwhile nel
  frattempo; * *vt* significare;
  intendere.
measles *n* morbillo *m*.
measure *n* misura *f*, provvedi-
  mento *m*; * *vt* misurare.
meat *n* carne *f*.
mechanic *n* meccanico *m*.
mechanism *n* meccanismo *m*.
medal *n* medaglia *f*.
media *npl* media *mpl*.
mediate *vi* mediare.
medical *adj* medico; * *n* visita
  f medica.
medicine *n* medicina *f*.
medieval *adj* medievale.
mediocre *adj* mediocre.
meditate *vt, vi* meditare.
meditation *n* meditazione *f*.
Mediterranean *adj* mediterraneo; * *n* Mediterraneo *m*.

medium *n* mezzo; * *adj* medio.
meet *vt* incontrare; soddisfare:
— they met with an accident
hanno avuto un incidente.
meeting *n* incontro *m*;
riunione *f*; raduno *m*.
melody *n* melodia *f*.
melon *n* melone *m*.
melt *vt* fondere, sciogliere.
member *n* membro *m*; socio *m*.
memento *n* ricordo *m*.
memo *n* promemoria *m*.
memoir *n* saggio monografico *m*.
memorable *adj* memorabile.
memorandum *n* memorandum
m.
memorial *n* monumento *m*;
* *adj* commemorativo.
memorise *vt* imparare a
memoria.
memory *n* memoria *f*, ricordo *m*.
mend *vt* aggiustare,
accomodare.
mending *n* rammendo *m*.
meningitis *n* meningite *f*.
menopause *n* menopausa *f*.
menstruation *n* mestruazione *f*.
mental *adj* mentale.
mentality *n* mentalità *f*.
mentally *adv* mentalmente.
mention *n* menzione *f*;
* *vt* accennare a.
mentor *n* mentore *m*, guida *f*.
menu *n* menu *m*.
merchant *n* commerciante *m* or *f*.
mercury *n* mercurio *m*.
mercy *n* misericordia *f*.
mere *adj* puro;
* ~ly *adv* semplicemente.
merit *n* merito *m*; * *vt* meritare.
mermaid *n* sirena *f*.
merry *adj* allegro; brillo.
mesh *n* maglia *f*.
mesmerise *vt* ipnotizzare.
mess *n* disordine *m*, pasticcio *m*,
caos *m*; * ~ up *vt* scompigliare.
message *n* messaggio *m*.

messenger *n* messaggero *m*.
metal *n* metallo *m*.
metamorphosis *n*
metamorfosi *f*.
metaphor *n* metafora *f*.
mete (out) *vi* ripartire.
meteor *n* meteora *f*.
meteorite *n* meteorite *m*.
meteorological *adj*
meteorologico.
meter *n* contattore *m*.
method *n* metodo *m*.
metric *adj* metrico.
metropolis *n* metropoli *f*.
metropolitan *adj*
metropolitano.
mew *n* miagolio *m*;
* *vi* miagolare.
microbe *n* microbo *m*.
microchip *n* chip *m*.
microphone *n* microfono *m*.
microscope *n* microscopio *m*.
microwave *n* microonda *f*.
mid *adj* meta.
middle *adj* centrale; * *n* mezzo
m, centro *m*.
midge *n* moscerino *m*.
midget *n* nano *m*.
midnight *n* mezzanotte *f*.
midway *adv* a metà strada.
midwife *n* ostetrica *f*.
midwinter *n* pieno inverno *m*.
might *n* forza *f*.
mighty *adj* possente.
migraine *n* emicrania *f*.
migrate *vi* migrare.
mild *adj* mite.
mile *n* miglio *m*.
military *adj* militare;
* *n* esercito *m*.
milk *n* latte *m*.
milkshake *n* frappé *m*.
milky *adj* latteo: * M~ Way *n*
Via Lattea *f*.
mill *n* mulino *m*; fabbrica *f*;
* *vt* macinare.
milligramme *n* milligrammo *m*.

millilitre *n* millilitro *m*.
millimetre *n* millimetro *m*.
million *n* milione *m*.
millionaire *n* milionario *m*.
millionth *adj*, *n* milionesimo *m*.
millipede *n* millepiedi *m*.
millstone *n* macina *f*.
mime *n* mimo *m*; * *vt*, *vi* mimare.
mimic *n* imitatore; * *vt* imitare.
mince *vt* tritare; * *n* carne
  macinata *f*.
mind *n* mente *f*; * *vt* badare a;
  * *vi* preoccuparsi.
minded *adj*: — open-~ di
  mente aperta.
mine *pron* mio; * *n* miniera *f*,
  mina *f*; * *vt* estrarre, minare.
miner *n* minatore *m*.
mineral *adj*, *n* minerale *m*.
minimal *adj* minimo.
minimise *vt* minimizzare.
minimum *n* minima *f*.
mining *n* estrazione *f*
  mineraria.
minister *n* ministro *m*;
  * *vi* assistere.
ministry *n* ministero *m*.
mink *n* visone *m*.
minor *adj* minore;
  * *n* minorenne *m* or *f*.
minority *n* minoranza *f*.
mint *n* menta; zecca *f*;
  * *vt* coniare.
minus *adv* meno.
minute *n* minuto *m*; ~s *npl*
  verbale *m*.
minute *adj* minuscolo.
miracle *n* miracolo *m*.
mirage *n* miraggio *m*.
mirror *n* specchio *m*;
  * *vt* riflettere.
misbehave *vi* comportarsi male.
miscalculate *vt* calcolare male.
miscarry *vi* abortire.
miscellaneous *adj* vario.
mischief *n* birichinata *f*;
  cattiveria *f*.

misconception *n* idea *f*;
  sbagliata.
miscreant *adj* scellerato.
misdemeanour *n* trasgressione *f*.
misdirect *vt* indirizzare male.
miser *n* avaro *m*.
miserable *adj* infelice.
misery *n* tristezza *f*, miseria *f*.
misfortune *n* disgrazia *f*.
misinterpret *vt* interpretare
  male.
mislay *vt* smarrire.
mislead *vt* trarre in inganno.
misogynist *n* misogino *m*.
misplace *vt* smarrire.
Miss *n* signorina *f*.
miss *vt* perdere; mancare;
  evitare; * *n* colpo mancato *m*.
missile *n* missile *m*.
mission *n* missione *f*.
missionary *n* missionario *m*.
mist *n* foschia *f*.
mistake *vt* sbagliare;
  * *vi* sbagliarsi; * *n* errore *m*,
  sbaglio *m*.
Mister *n* signore *m*.
mistreat *vt* maltrattare.
mistress *n* amante *f*; padrona *f*.
misty *adj* brumoso.
misunderstand *vt* fraintendere.
misunderstanding *n*
  malinteso *m*.
misuse *vt* abusare di; * *n* abuso *m*.
mix *vt* mescolare;
  * *n* mescolanza *f*.
mixer *n* frullatore *m*; betoniera *f*.
mixture *n* mistura *f*; miscela *f*.
moan *n* gemito *m*; * *vi* gemere.
mobile *adj* mobile.
mode *n* modo *m*.
model *n* modello *m*; indossatore
  m; * *vt* modellare; indossare;
  * *vi* posare.
moderate *adj*, *n* moderato *m*;
  * *vi* attenuarsi.
moderation *n* moderazione *f*.
modern *adj* moderno.

modest *adj* modesto.
modesty *n* modestia *f*.
modify *vt* modificare.
module *n* modulo *m*.
moist *adj* umido.
moisture *n* umidità *f*.
molar *n* molare *m*.
mole *n* neo *m*; talpa *f*.
molest *vt* molestare.
moment *n* momento *m*.
momentous *adj* importante.
monarch *n* monarca *m*.
monastery *n* monastero *m*.
Monday *n* lunedì *m*.
money *n* denaro *m*, soldi *mpl*.
mongrel *n* bastardo *m*.
monk *n* monaco *m*.
monkey *n* scimmia *f*.
monopoly *n* monopolio *m*.
monster *n* mostro *m*;
  * *adj* gigantesco.
monstrous *adj* colossale;
  mostruoso.
month *n* mese *m*.
monthly *adj* mensile.
monument *n* monumento *m*.
moo *vi* muggire; * *n* muggito *m*.
mood *n* (grammar) modo *m*;
  umore *m*.
moon *n* luna *f*.
mop *n* scopa di filacce *f*;
  * *vt* lavare, pulire, asciugare
  con lo staccio.
moped *n* ciclomotore *m*.
moral *adj* morale;
  * ~s *npl* principi morali *mpl*.
morale *n* morale *m*.
morality *n* moralità *f*.
morbid *adj* morboso.
more *adj* più, ancora, altro:
  — once ~ un'altra volta;
  * *adv* ~ and ~ sempre di più.
morgue *n* orbitorio *m*; (*fig*)
  mortorio *m*.
morning *n* mattina *f*:
  — good ~ buon giorno.
morphine *n* morfina *f*.

Morse code *n* alfabeto *m* Morse.
mortal *adj*, *n* mortale *m*.
mortgage *n* ipoteca *f*;
  * *vt* ipotecare.
mortuary *n* obitorio *m*.
mosaic *n* mosaico *m*.
mosque *n* moschea *f*.
mosquito *n* zanzara *f*.
most *adj* più; * *pron* quasi
  tutto.
mother *n* madre *f*.
mother-in-law *n* suocera *f*.
motif *n* motivo *m*.
motion *n* moto *m*, movimento
  m; cenno *m*.
motive *n* motivo *m*.
motor *n* motore *m*.
motorbike *n* moto *f*.
motorcycle *n* motocicletta *f*.
motorist *n* automobilista *m* or *f*.
motorway *n* autostrada *f*.
motto *n* motto *m*.
mound *n* mucchio *m*.
mountain *n* montagna *f*.
mountainous *adj* montagnoso.
mourn *vt*, *vi* piangere.
mouse *n* topo *m*.
moustache *n* baffi *mpl*.
mouth *n* bocca *f*.
mouthful *n* boccone *m*.
moveable *adj* movibile.
move *vt* spostare, muovere;
  commuovere; * *vi* traslocare:
  ~ about (round) muoversi:
  ~ ahead procedere: ~ along
  muoversi, spostarsi: ~ away
  andarsene, cambiar casa;
  andare indietro, riandare ad
  abitare: ~ down spostarsi in
  giù, scendere: ~ downwards
  diminuire, calare: ~ for
  richiedere: ~ forward fare
  progressi, avanzare; entrare,
  andare a stare in una nuova
  casa: ~ in on andare a stare
  da, sfruttare l'ospitalità di:
  ~ off (out) muoversi, partire:

~ over spostarsi, lasciare il posto: ~ on andare avanti, spostarsi, circolare: ~ upwards aumentare, salire, crescere; * n mossa f, movimento m, trasloco m.
movement n movimento m.
movie n film m.
mow vt falciare.
Mrs n signora f.
much adj, pron, adv molto.
mud n fango m.
muddle n confusione f.
muddy adj fangoso.
mug n tazzone m; boccale m; * vt aggredire.
mugger n rapinatore m.
multiple adj, n multiplo m.
multiplication n moltiplicazione f.
multiplication table tavola pitagorica f.
multiply vt moltiplicare.
mummy n mummia f; mamma f.
mumps npl orecchioni mpl.
municipality n comune m.
mural n pittura f, murale; * adj murale.
murder n omicidio m, assassinio m; * vt assassinare.
murderer n assassino m.
muscle n muscolo m.
museum n museo m.
mushroom n fungo m; * vi svilupparsi rapidamente, esplodere.
music n musica f.
mussel n cozza f.
must vb dovere; * n necessità f.
mustard n senape f.
mutate vt, vi cambiare, mutare.
mute adj muto.
my pron mio.
myself pron io stesso, me stesso.
mysterious adj misterioso.

mystery n mistero m.
mystique n fascino m.
myth n mito m.
mythology n mitologia f.

N

nail n unghia f; chiodo m; * vt inchiodare.
naive adj ingenuo.
naked adj nudo.
name n nome m; * vt chiamare; nominare; stabilire.
namely adv cioè.
nanny n bambinaia f.
napkin n tovagliolo m.
narcissus n (botany) narciso m.
narrate vt narrare.
narrative adj narrativo; * n narrazione f.
narrow adj stretto; * vt restringere; * vi stringersi.
nasal adj nasale.
nasturtium n nasturzio m.
nasty adj cattivo, sgradevole, maligno.
nation n nazione f.
nationalist adj, n nazionalista m or f.
nationality n nazionalità f.
nationwide adj a livello nazionale.
native adj natale; indigeno; * n nativo m; indigeno m.
Nativity n Natività f.
natural adj naturale.
naturalist n naturalista m or f.
nature n natura f.
naughty adj disubbidiente; birichino: — a ~ trick uno scherzo spinto.
nausea n nausea f.
nautical adj nautico.
navel n ombelico m.
navy n marina f.
Nazi adj, n nazista m or f.

near *prep, adj, adv* vicino:
— the ~ way la via diretta:
— a ~ miss un colpo [un
incontro] per poco mancato:
~ money (economics) quasi
moneta: — a ~ monopoly
(economics) un monopolio
imperfetto: — a ~ race una
corsa combattuta: — a ~
translation una traduzione
letterale: — to give a ~ guess
indovinare o quasi: — in the
~ distance in secondo piano:
— it was a ~ escape ce
l'abbiamo fatta per un pelo:
~ sighted miope; * *vi*
avvicinarsi a; * ~ly *adv* quasi.
neat *adj* ordinato.
necessarily *adv* necessaria-
mente.
necessary *adj* necessario.
neck *n* collo *m*.
necklace *n* collana *f*.
nectar *n* nettare *m*.
need *n* bisogno *m*; * *vi* aver
bisogno di.
needle *n* ago *m*;
* *vt* punzecchiare.
needy *adj* bisognoso.
negative *adj* negativo;
* *n* (grammar) negazione *f*,
(photography) negativa *f*.
neglect *vt* trascurare.
negligence *n* negligenza *f*.
negotiate *vt* trattare; superare.
neighbour *n* vicino *m*.
neither *adv, pron, adj* né;
* *conj* nemmeno, neanche,
neppure.
neon *n* neon *m*.
nephew *n* nipote *m*.
nerve *n* nervo *m*.
nest *n* nido *m*; * *vi* nidificare.
net *n* rete *f*; * *adj* netto.
netball *n* specie di pallacanestro.
nettle *n* ortica *f*.
neuter *adj* (grammar) neutro;

* *vt* castrare.
never *adv* mai: ~ mind non fa
niente.
nevertheless *adv* ciò nonostante.
new *adj* nuovo.
news *npl* notizie *fpl*; notiziario
m, telegiornale *m*; giornale
radio *m*.
newsagent *n* giornalaio *m*.
New Year *n* Anno Nuovo *m*:
— ~'s Day capodanno; ~'s Eve
la Notte di San Silvestro.
newt *n* tritone *m*.
next *adj* prossimo, successivo;
* *adv* dopo; * *n* prossimo *m*;
* *prep* accanto a.
nibble *vi* rosicchiare.
nice *adj* simpatico, piacevole,
gentile, bello.
nick *n* taglietto *m*;
* *vt* (*sl*) fregare: — in the ~ of
time appena in tempo.
nicotine *n* nicotina *f*.
niece *n* nipote *m* or *f*.
night *n* notte *f*: — by ~ di
notte: — good ~ buona notte.
nightingale *n* usignolo *m*.
nightmare *n* incubo *m*.
nil *n* nulla *m*, zero *m*.
nimble *adj* agile.
nine *adj, n* nove *m*.
nineteen *adj, n* diciannove *m*.
nineteenth *adj, n*
diciannovesimo *m*.
ninetieth *adj, n* novantesimo *m*.
ninth *adj, n* nono *m*.
nipple *n* capezzolo *m*.
nitrogen *n* azoto *m*.
no *adv* no; * *adj* nessuno.
nobility *n* nobiltà *f*.
noble *adj, n* nobile *m*.
nobody *n* nullità *f*;
* *pron* nessuno.
noise *n* rumore *m*, fracasso *m*.
nomad *n* nomade *m* or *f*.
none *pron* nessuno, niente.
nonentity *n* nullità *f*.

nonetheless *adv* nondimeno.
nonsense *n* sciocchezze *fpl*.
noodles *npl* tagliatelle *fpl*.
nook *n* angolino *m*.
noon *n* mezzogiorno *m*.
noose *n* cappio *m*.
nor *conj* né.
normal *adj* normale.
north *n* nord *m*, settentrione *m*;
 * *adj* nord.
North America *n* America del
 Nord *f*.
north-east *n* nordest *m*.
northerly *adj* del nord; verso
 nord.
northern *adj* settentrionale,
 del nord.
north pole *n* polo nord *m*.
northwards *adv* verso nord.
north-west *n* nordovest *m*.
nose *n* naso *m*.
nostalgia *n* nostalgia *f*.
nostril *n* narice *f*.
not *adv* non.
notable *adj* notevole.
notably *adv* notevolmente.
notary *n* notaio *m*.
notation *n* notazione *f*.
notch *n* tacca *f*; * *vt* intaccare.
note *n* nota *f*, biglietto *m*;
 * *vt* notare.
notebook *n* taccuino *m*.
noted *adj* famoso.
nothing *n* niente; * *adv* per
 niente: — think ~ of it!
 s'immagini!
notice *n* avviso *m*; preavviso *m*;
 recensione *f*; * *vt* accorgersi di.
notify *vt* notificare.
notion *n* idea *f*, nozione *f*.
notorious *adj* famigerato.
notwithstanding *conj* benché;
 * *adv* ciononostante;
 * *prep* nonostante.
nougat *n* torrone *m*.
nought *n* zero *m*.
noun *n* sostantivo *m*.

nourish *vt* nutrire.
nourishment *n* nutrimento *m*.
novel *n* romanzo;
 * *adj* originale.
novelist *n* romanziere *m*.
novelty *n* novità *f*.
November *n* novembre *m*.
novice *n* novizio *m*.
now *adv* adesso, ora;
 * *conj* adesso che, ora che:
 ~ and then ogni tanto.
nowhere *adv* in nessun posto.
nuclear *adj* nucleare.
nucleus *adj* nucleo.
nude *adj*, *n* nudo *m*.
nudist *adj*, *n* nudista *m* or *f*.
nuisance *n* seccatura *f*.
numb *adj* intorpidito;
 * *vt* intorpidire.
number *n* numero *m*;
 * *vt* numerare; contare.
nun *n* suora *f*.
nurse *n* infermiere *m*.
nursery *n* camera *f* dei
 bambini; vivaio *m*.
nursery school *n* asilo *m*
 infantile.
nurture *vt* nutrire.
nut *n* noce *f* (walnut), mandorla
 f (almond), nocciola (hazelnut) *f*; (mechanical) dado; (*sl*)
 matto *m*; *adj* (*sl*) svitato.
nutmeg *n* noce moscata *f*.
nutritious *adj* nutriente.
nylon *n* nailon *m*.

O

oak *n* quercia *f*.
oasis *n* oasi *f*.
oath *n* giuramento *m*.
obedience *n* ubbidienza *f*.
obedient *adj* ubbidiente.
obese *adj* obeso.
obey *vt* ubbidire.
obituary *n* necrologio *m*.

object *n* oggetto *m*;
* *vt* obiettare.
objective *n* obiettivo *m*.
obligatory *adj* obbligatorio.
oblivion *n* oblio *m*.
oblivious *adj* ignaro.
oblong *adj* oblungo;
* *n* rettangolo *m*.
obscene *adj* osceno.
obscure *adj* oscuro;
* *vt* oscurare.
observation *n* osservazione *f*.
obsess *vt* ossessionare.
obsolete *adj* obsoleto.
obstacle *n* ostacolo *m*.
obstruct *vt* ostruire.
obstruction *n* ostruzione *f*.
obtain *vt* ottenere.
obtainable *adj* ottenibile.
obvious *adj* ovvio.
occasion *n* occasione *f*;
* *vt* causare.
occupant, occupier *n*
inquilino *m*, titolare *m*.
occur *vi* accadere.
ocean *n* oceano *m*.
ochre *n* ocra *f*.
octagon *n* ottagono *m*.
October *n* ottobre *m*.
octopus *n* piovra *f*.
odd *adj* strano; dispari;
scompagnato.
odour *n* odore *m*.
oesophagus *n* esofago *m*.
of *prep* di.
off *adv* distante; * *adj* spento;
andato a male; * *prep* da.
offence *n* infrazione *f*, offesa *f*.
offend *vt* offendere.
offensive *adj* offensivo.
offer *n* offerta *f*; * *vt* offrire.
ottice *n* ufficio *m*.
officer *n* ufficiale *m*.
official *adj* ufficiale;
* *n* funzionario *m*.
often *adv* spesso, di frequente.
oil *n* olio *m*; petrolio *m*;

* *vt* oliare.
oil painting *n* quadro *m* a olio.
oil well *n* pozzo *m* petrolifero.
ointment *n* unguento *m*.
OK, okay *excl* OK, va bene;
* *vt* approvare.
old *adj* vecchio, anziano;
precedente.
oleander *n* oleandro *m*.
olive *n* oliva *f*: ~ tree *n* ulivo *m*.
omelette *n* frittata *f*.
omen *n* auspicio *m*.
omit *vt* omettere.
on *prep* su, a, sopra;
* *adj* acceso.
once *adv* una volta:
— at ~ subito: — all at ~
improvvisamente: ~ more
ancora una volta.
one *adj* uno, unico, stesso;
* *n* uno *m*.
oneself *pron* se stesso.
onion *n* cipolla *f*.
only *adj* solo; * *adv* solo,
solamente.
onset *n* inizio *m*.
onwards *adj* in avanti.
opal *n* opale *f*.
opaque *adj* opaco.
open *adj* aperto.
open *vt* aprire: ~ down (finance)
aprire in ribasso: ~ into dare
accesso a, aprirsi su: on dare
su: ~ out aprire, spiegare:
~ up aprire.
opening *n* apertura *f*,
inaugurazione *f*, breccia *f*.
opera *n* opera *f*.
operation *n* operazione *f*,
intervento *m*.
opinion *n* opinione *f*, parere *m*.
opium *n* oppio *m*.
opponent *n* avversario *m*.
opportunity *n* occasione *f*.
oppose *vt* opporsi a.
opposite *adv* di fronte;
* *n* contrario *m*.

oppression *n* oppressione *f*.
opt *vi* optare.
optician *n* ottico *m*.
optimist *n* ottimista *m* or *f*.
optional *adj* facoltativo.
or *conj* o.
oral *adj*, *n* orale *m*; * ~ly *adv* oralmente.
orange *n* arancia *f*: ~ tree *n* arancio *m*; (colour, also *adj*) arancio *m*.
orangeade *n* aranciata *f*.
orchard *n* frutteto *m*.
orchestra *n* orchestra *f*.
orchid *n* orchidea *f*.
order *n* ordine *m*, comando *m*, ordinazione *f*; * *vt*, *vi* ordinare.
ordinary *adj* abituale, comune; ordinario.
ore *n* minerale *m* grezzo.
oregano *n* origano *m*.
organ *n* organo *m*.
organic(al) *adj* organico.
organism *n* organismo *m*.
organise *vt* organizzare.
orgasm *n* orgasmo *m*.
oriental *adj* orientale.
origin *n* origine *f*.
original *adj*, *n* originale *m*.
ornament *n* ornamento *m*; * *vt* ornare.
orphan *adj*, *n* orfano *m*.
orthodox *adj* ortodosso.
osprey *n* falco pescatore *m*.
osteopathy *n* osteopatia *f*.
other *adj*, *pron* altro; * ~ than *adv* diversamente.
otter *n* lontra *f*.
ouch! *excl* ahi!
ought *vb aux* dovere.
ounce *n* oncia *f*.
our *adj* nostro.
ourselves *pron* noi stessi.
out *adv* fuori; * *prep* fuori, per, da, senza.
outback *n* entroterra *m*.
outcast *n* emarginato *m*.

outing *n* escursione *f*.
outlaw *n* fuorilegge *m*; * *vt* bandire.
outlay *n* spesa *f*.
outlet *n* scarico *m*; punto *m* vendita.
outline *n* contorno *m*; * *vt* riassumere.
outlook *n* veduta *f*.
outrage *n* oltraggio *m*, offesa *f*, indignazione *f*, sdegno *m*; * *vt* offendre, oltraggiare.
outrageous *adj* scandaloso.
outset *n* inizio *m*.
outshine *vt* eclissare; * *vi* eclissarsi.
outside *n* esterno *m*; * *adj* esterno; * *adv* fuori; * *prep* fuori di.
outskirts *npl* periferia *f*.
outspoken *adj* franco.
outward *adj* esterno; apparente.
ovary *n* ovaia *f*.
oven *n* forno *m*.
over *prep* su, sopra; * *adj* finito: ~ again da capo: ~ and ~ mille volte.
overall *adj* generale; * ~s *npl* tuta *f*.
overboard *adv* fuori bordo.
overcharge *vt* far pagare troppo.
overcoat *n* soprabito *m*.
overestimate *vt* sopravvalutare.
overjoyed *adj* felicissimo.
overleaf *adv* a tergo.
overseas *adv* all'estero; * *adj* estero.
oversee *vt* sorvegliare.
overseer *n* sorvegliante *m*.
overshadow *vt* eclissare.
overtake *vt* superare.
owe *vt* dovere: — to ~ dovere, essere debitore di: — I ~ him much gli devo molto;

186

* *vi* essere indebitato:
— to ~ for dovere pagare:
— to ~ someone a grudge
serbar rancore a qualcuno:
— to ~ someone ill will avere
malanimo verso qualcuno:
— to ~ no thanks to anybody
non dovere ringraziare
nessuno: — to ~ someone
essere in debito di un favore
con qualcuno: — I ~ you
pagherò; * ~ing *adj* da pagare;
* ~ing to *prep* a causa di.
own *adj* proprio; * *vt* possedere.
owl *n* civetta *f*, gufo *m*.
owner *n* proprietario *m*.
ownership *n* proprietà *f*.
ox *n* bue *m*: ~en *npl* buoi *mpl*.
oxidise *vt* ossidare.
oxygen *n* ossigeno *m*.
oyster *n* ostrica *f*.
ozone *n* ozono *m*.

P

pace *n* passo *m*; * *vi* camminare
su e giù.
pacemaker *n* pace-maker *m*.
pacific *adj* pacifico;
* *n* pacifico *m*.
pack *n* pacco *m*; branco *m*;
* *vt* imballare; stipare di;
* *vi* fare le valigie.
package *n* pacchetto *m*;
* *vt* confezionare.
packet *n* pacchetto *m*.
pact *n* patto *m*.
pad *n* cuscinetto *m*;
blocchetto *m*; rampa di
lancio *f*; (*sl*) casa *f* imbottire.
paddle *vi* sguazzare; * *n* pala *f*.
paddock *n* recinto *m*.
padlock *n* lucchetto *m*.
pagan *adj*, *n* pagano *m*.
page *n* paggio *m*; pagina *f*.
pail *n* secchio *m*.

pain *n* dolore *m*; * *vt* addolorare.
paint *n* tinta; vernice;
* *vt* dipingere; verniciare.
painter *n* pittore *m*,
imbianchino *m*.
painting *n* quadro *m*; pittura *f*.
pair *n* paio *m*, copia *f*.
palate *n* palato *m*.
pale *adj* pallido.
palette *n* tavolozza *f*.
palm *n* palma *f*.
Palm Sunday *n* Domenica
delle Palme.
pamphlet *n* opuscolo *m*.
pari *n* pentola *f*.
pancake *n* frittata *f*.
pancreas *n* pancreas *m*.
panda *n* panda *m*.
pane *n* vetro *m*.
panel *n* pannello *m*; giuria *f*.
panic *adj*, *n* panico *m*.
pansy *n* (botany) pensée *f*.
panties *npl* mutandine *fpl*.
pantihose *n* collant *m*.
pants *npl* mutande *fpl*.
papacy *n* papato *m*.
paper *n* carta *f*, relazione *f*,
giornale *m*: ~s *pl* documenti
mpl; * *vt* tappezzare.
paprika *n* paprica *f*.
parachute *n* paracadute *m*.
parade *n* sfilata *f*, parata *f*.
paradise *n* paradiso *m*.
paragraph *n* paragrafo *m*.
parallel *adj* parallelo;
* *n* parallela *f*.
paralysis *n* paralisi *f*.
paralyse *vt* paralizzare.
parasite *n* parassita *m*.
parasol *n* parasole *m*.
parcel *n* pacco *m*;
* *vt* impacchettare.
parchment *n* pergamena *f*.
pardon *n* perdono *m*;
* *vt* perdonare.
parent *n* genitore *m* or *f*.
parentage *n* natali *mpl*.

park n parco m; * vt, vi
   parcheggiare.
parliament n parlamento m.
Parmesan n parmigiano m.
parrot n pappagallo m.
parsley n prezzemolo m.
parsnip n pastinaca f.
part n parte f; * vt separare;
   * vi lasciarsi: ~ with disfarsi di.
partial adj parziale.
participant n partecipante m, f.
participle n participio m.
particle n particella f.
particular adj particolare;
   scrupoloso, preciso, pignolo;
   * n particolare m dettaglio m.
partition n parete f divisoria.
partner n partner m or f,
   socio m.
partnership n associazione f.
partridge n pernice f.
party n partito m; festa f.
pass vt, vi passare: — come to
   ~ succedere, accadere: ~ along
   passare oltre, andare avanti:
   ~ a remark fare
   un'osservazione:
   ~ as passare per; ~ away
   cessare, finire, andare via:
   ~ back restituire:
   ~ between accadere:
   ~ criticism on someone
   (something) criticare
   qualcuno (qualcosa):
   ~ down passare, spostarsi:
   ~ for passare per:
   ~ forward passare avanti:
   ~ in far passare:
   ~ into entrare in:
   ~ off finire:
   ~ on passare oltre, tirare avanti:
   ~ one's oath impegnarsi con
giuramento:
   ~ out svenire:
   ~ over tralasciare:
   ~ round far circolare:
   ~ the ball passare la palla:

~ the buck fare a scaricabarile:
~ the buck to someone
scaricare la responsabilità
sulle spalle di qualcuno:
~ through essere di passaggio:
~ through customs passare la
dogana:
~ water fare acqua, orinare:
~ wind fare un peto:
~ under passare sotto:
~ up passare; * n passo m;
lascia passare m; sufficienza
f: — make a ~ at fare delle
avances a.
passage n passaggio m.
passenger n passeggero m.
passion n passione f.
passion flower n passiflora f,
fior di passione m.
Passover n Pasqua ebraica f.
passport n passaporto m.
password n parola d'ordine f.
past adj passato; * n passato m;
   * prep davanti; oltre; passato.
pasta n pasta f.
pat vi dare dei colpetti
leggeri; * n colpetto m.
patent adj palese; brevettato;
   * n brevetto m; * vt brevettare.
paternal adj paterno.
path n sentiero m.
pathetic adj patetico.
patience n pazienza f.
patient adj, n paziente m.
patio n terrazza f.
patriotic adj patriottico.
patriotism n patriottismo m.
patrol n pattuglia f;
   * vt perlustrare.
pattern n disegno m, modello m.
pause n pausa f; * vi fare una
pausa.
pave vt lastricare.
pavement n marciapiede m.
paw n zampa f; * vt scalpitare,
dare una zampata.
pay vt, vi pagare: ~ back

restituire: ~ down pagare per
intero: ~ for pagare per:
~ in versara: ~ into versare
in: ~ off saldare, estinguere:
~ out sborsare, ripagare:
~ over liquidare: ~ up pagare
in toto, saldare.
pay n paga f, stipendio m.
pea n pisello m.
peace n pace f.
peach n pesca f: ~ tree pesco m.
peacock n pavone m.
peal n scampanio m.
peanut n arachide f.
pear n pera f: ~ tree pero m.
pearl n perla f.
pebble n ciottolo m.
peculiar adj strano.
pedal n pedale m; * vi pedalare.
pedant n pedante m or f.
pedantic adj pedante.
peddle vt vendere al minuto;
  spacciare; fare il venditore
  ambulante.
pedestal n piedistallo m.
pedestrian n pedone m;
  * adj mediocre.
peel vt sbucciare; * vi spellarsi;
  * n buccia f.
pelican n pellicano m.
pelvis n bacino m.
pen n penna f, recinto m;
  * vt scrivere; rinchiudere.
pencil n matita f, lapis m.
pendant n pendaglio m.
penetrate vt, vi penetrare.
penguin n pinguino m.
penicillin n penicillina f.
peninsula n penisola f.
penis n pene m.
penny n penny m.
pension n pensione f.
Pentecost n Pentecoste f.
peony n peonia f.
people n gente f, popolo m,
  persone fpl; * vt popolare.
pepper (spice) pepe m; (vegeta-

ble) peperone m; * vt pepare.
peppermint n menta peperita f.
perceive vt percepire.
percentage n percentuale f.
perch n pesce persico m;
  pertica f; posatoio m;
  * vi appollaiarsi.
percolator n caffettiera a
  filtro f.
perfect adj perfetto;
  * vt perfezionare.
perfection n perfezione f.
perform vt svolgere;
  rappresentare; eseguire;
  * vi esibirsi.
performance n rappresen-
  tazione f, interpretazione f;
  rendimento m.
performer n artista m or f.
perfume n profumo m;
  * vt profumare.
perhaps adv forse.
peril n pericolo m.
perimeter n perimetro m.
period n periodo m; ora f,
  punto m, mestruazioni fpl.
periphery n periferia f.
perish vi perire.
perishable adj deperibile.
peritonitis n peritonite f.
perk n vantaggio m.
perm n permanente f.
permanent adj permanente.
permission n permesso m.
permit vt, vi permettere;
  * n autorizzazione f.
perpetual adj perpetuo.
perplex vt lasciare perplesso.
persecute vt perseguitare.
persecution n persecuzione f.
persevere vi perseverare.
persist vi persistere.
persistence n perseveranza f.
persistent adj persistente.
person n persona f.
personal adj personale.
personality n personalità f.

perspiration *n* traspirazione *f*.
perspire *vi* traspirare.
persuade *vt* persuadere.
pessimist *n* pessimista *m* or *f*.
pet *n* animale da compagnia
  m, animale d'affezione *m*;
  beniamino *m*; * *vt* accarezzare,
  coccolare, viziare.
petal *n* petalo *m*.
petrol *n* benzina *f*.
petroleum *n* petrolio *m*.
petty *adj* insignificante.
pewter *n* peltro *m*.
phantom *adj*, *n* fantasma *m*.
Pharaoh *n* faraone *m*.
pharmacist *n* farmacista *m* or *f*.
pharmacy *n* farmacia *f*.
phase *n* fase *f*.
philosopher *n* filosofo *m*.
philosophy *n* filosofia *f*.
phlegm *n* flemma *f*.
phobia *n* fobia *f*.
phone *n* telefono *m*;
  * *vt* telefonare.
phoney *adj* falso.
photocopier *n* fotocopiatrice *f*.
photograph *n* fotografia *f*;
  * *vt* fotografare.
photographer *n* fotografo *m*.
phrase *n* frase *f*; * *vt* esprimere.
phrase book *n* frasario *m*.
physical *adj* fisico.
physics *n* fisica *f*.
piano *n* pianoforte *m*.
pick *n* piccone *m*; picca *f*;
  scelta *f*.
pick *vt* scegliere; cogliere:
  ~ apart fare a pezzi: ~ at
  piluccare: ~ off levare,
  staccare: ~ on scegliere,
  selezionare; dare addosso,
  prendersela: ~ out togliere,
  cavare: ~ over passare al
  vaglio: ~ up raccogliere.
picket *n* picchetto *m*; * *vt*, *vi*
  picchettare.
pickle *n* salamoia *f*;

~s sottaceti *mpl*; * *vt* mettere
  sottaceto; guaio *m*, pasticcio *m*.
picnic *n* picnic *m*.
picture *n* quadro *m*; fotografia
  f, disegno *m*; * *vt* immaginare.
picturesque *adj* pittoresco.
pie *n* torta *f*, pasticcio *m*.
piece *n* pezzo *m*.
pier *n* pontile *m*.
pierce *vt* forare.
piercing *adj* lacerante.
pig *n* maiale *m*, porco *m*; (*vulg*)
  stronzo *m*.
pigeon *n* piccione *m*.
pilchard *n* sardina *f*.
pile *n* mucchio *m*; pila *f*:
  ~s emorroidi *fpl*; * *vt* impilare;
  ammucchiare.
pilgrim *n* pellegrino *m*.
pilgrimage *n* pellegrinaggio *m*.
pill *n* pillola *f*.
pilot *n* pilota *m* or *f*;
  * *vt* pilotare.
pimp *n* lenone.
pimple *n* foruncolo *m*.
pin *n* spillo *m*: ~s and needles
  n formicolio *m*; * *vt* attaccare
  con uno spillo.
pinch *vt* pizzicare; (*sl*) fregare;
  * *n* pizzicotto *m*; pizzico *m*.
pine (botany) *n* pino *m*;
  * *vi* languire.
pineapple *n* ananas *m*.
pink *n* rosa *m*.
pint *n* pinta *f*.
pioneer *n* pioniere *m*.
pipe *n* tubo *m*; pipa *f*:
  ~s *mpl* cornamusa *m*.
piping *n* tubature *fpl*.
pirate *n* pirata *m*.
Pisces *n* Pesci *mpl*.
piss *vi* (*vulg*) pisciare.
pistol *n* pistola *f*.
pit *n* buca *f*.
pitch *n* pece *f*, campo *m*;
  intonazione *f*; * *vt* lanciare;
  piantare.

pity n compassione f, peccato m; * vt compatire.

pivot n perno m.

pixie n folletto m.

pizza n pizza f.

place n luogo m, posto m; * vt posare, mettere; situare; piazzare.

plague n peste f; * vt tormentare.

plaice n passera f.

plain adj evidente; semplice; in tinta unita; * n pianura f.

plan n piano m; * vt pianificare; organizzare.

plane n (botany) platano m; pialla f; aeroplano m; * adj plano; * vt piallare; * vi planare.

planet n planeta m.

planetarium n planetario m.

plank n tavola f.

planning n planificazione f.

plant n pianta f, impianto m; stabilimento m; * vt piantare.

plantation n piantagione f.

plaque n placca f.

plaster n intonaco m; gesso m; cerotto m; * vt intonacare.

plastic adj plastico; * n plastica.

plastic surgery n chirurgia f plastica.

plate n piatto m; targa f, piastra f; vt placcare.

platform n plattaforma f, binario m.

platinum n platino m.

platonic adj platonico.

platoon n plotone m.

platter n piatto da portata m.

play n gioco m; commedia f.

play vt giocare; suonare; interpretare; * vi giocare; suonare: ~ about spassarsela: ~ along tenere sulla corda, fingere di essere d'accordo: ~ at giocare a: ~ back

riascoltare: ~ down minimizzare: ~ in giocare in: ~ off giocare lo spareggio: ~ on continuare a giocare: ~ out giocare all'aperto: ~ over giocare di nuovo: ~ through giocare (recitare) una commedia fino in fondo: ~ up mettere in evidenza: ~ up to fare da spalla.

player n giocatore m; suonatore m.

plea n supplica f.

pleasant adj piacevole.

please vi piacere; * vt accontentare; * excl per piacere.

pleat n piega; * vt pieghettare.

plenty n abbondanza f.

plot n appezzamento m; complotto m; trama f; * vt tracciare; * vi complottare.

plough n aratro m; * vt, vi arare.

plug n tappo m; spina f; * vt tappare.

plughole n scarico m.

plum n prugna f, susina f: ~ tree prugno m, susino m.

pluperfect n piuccheperfetto m.

plural adj, n plurale m.

plus n vantaggio m; più m; * prep più; * adj positivo.

plutonium n plutonio m.

ply vt maneggiare; esercitare; incalzare; * vi fare la spola tra; * n strato m; velo m.

pneumonia n polmonite.

poach vi cacciare di frodo; * vt cuocere in bianco.

pocket n tasca f; * vt intascare.

pod n baccello m.

podgy adj grassottello.

podium n podio m.

poem n poesia f.

poet n poeta m.

poetry n poesia f.

point n punto m; virgola f,

punta f, scopo m: ~ of view
punto m di vista; * vt puntare;
indicare: ~ at additare:
~ down indicare in basso:
~ out indicare: ~ to(wards)
segnare a dito: ~ up mettere
in evidenza.
poise n portamento m.
poison n veleno m;
* vt avvelenare.
polar adj polare.
pole n palo m; asta f, polo m.
police n polizia f;
* vt presidiare.
polish vt lucidare; lustrare;
* n lùcido m, cera f, lucidata f,
raffinatezza f.
polite adj educato.
politician n politico m.
politics npl politica f.
poll n votazione f, sondaggio m.
pollution n inquinamento m.
pomegranate n melagrana f.
pomp n fasto m.
pompous adj pomposo.
pond n laghetto m.
pony n pony m.
ponytail n coda di cavallo f.
poof n (sl) finocchio m.
pool n pozza f, piscina f, cassa
comune f; riserva f, biliardo m;
* vt mettere insieme.
poor adj povero; misero;
* the ~ n i poveri mpl.
poorly adj indisposto.
pop n schiocco m; bevanda
gassata f; * adj pop; * vt fare
scoppiare.
Pope n Papa m.
poplar n pioppo m.
poppy n papavero m.
populace n popolo m.
popular adj popolare;
benvoluto.
popularity n popolarità f.
populate vt popolare.
population n popolazione f.

porcelain n porcellana f.
porch n veranda f.
porcupine n porcospino m.
pork n maiale m.
porpoise n focena f, delfino m.
porridge n farinata d'avena f,
porridge m.
port n porto m, (marine)
babordo m.
portion n porzione f.
portrait n ritratto m.
portray vt ritrarre.
pose n posa f; * vi posarsi;
* vt posare, porre.
position n posizione f,
impiego m; * vt sistemare.
positive adj positivo.
possess vt possedere.
possession n possesso m.
possibility n possibilità f.
possible adj possibile.
post n palo m; posta f, posto m;
* vt spedire per posta;
affiggere.
postage n affrancatura f.
poster n manifesto m, poster m.
posterior n deretano m,
posteriore m.
posterity n posterità f.
posthumous adj postumo.
postman n postino m.
post-mortem n autopsia f.
postpone vt rimandare.
postulate vt postulare.
posture n portamento m.
pot n pentola f, vasetto m;
erba f; * vt invasare.
potassium n potassio m.
potato n patata f.
potted adj conservato (in vaso);
condensato.
pottery n ceramica f.
poultry n pollame m.
pounce n balzo m; * vt balzare.
pound n libbra (= 0.45 kg) f,
(lira) f sterlina; canile mpl
municipale; deposito m auto;

* *vt* picchiare, pestare.
pour *vt* versare.
poverty *n* miseria *f*, povertà *f*.
powder *n* polvere *f*; * *vt* ridurre
 in polvere; * *vi* incipriarsi.
power *n* forza *f*, potenza *f*,
 capacità *f*, potere *m*;
 * *vt* azionare.
powerful *adj* potente; possente.
pragmatic *adj* pragmatico.
praise *n* elogio *m*; * *vt* lodare.
prawn *n* gambero *m*.
pray *vt* pregare.
prayer *n* preghiera *f*.
preach *vt*, *vi* predicare.
preacher *n* predicatore *m*.
precaution *n* precauzione *f*.
precede *vt* precedere.
precious *adj* prezioso.
precise *adj* preciso.
predator *n* predatore *m*.
predecessor *n* predecessore *m*.
predict *vt* predire.
predictable *adj* prevedibile.
prediction *n* predizione *f*.
preface *n* prefazione *f*.
prefer *vt* preferire.
prefix *n* prefisso *m*.
pregnancy *n* gravidanza *f*.
pregnant *adj* in cinta, gravida.
preparation *n* preparazione *f*.
preparatory *adj* preparatorio.
prepare *vt* preparare.
preposition *n* preposizione *f*.
prerequisite *n* presupposto
 necessario *m*.
prescribe *vt* prescrivere.
prescription *n* ricetta *f*.
presence *n* presenza *f*.
present *n* presente *m*;
 * *adj* presente; attuale;
 * *vt* presentare.
presentable *adj* presentabile.
presentation *n* presentazione *f*.
presenter *n* presentatore *m*.
preservation *n* conservazione *f*.
preservative *n* conservante *m*.

presidency *n* presidenza *f*.
president *n* presidente *m*.
press *vt*, *vi* premere; stirare:
 ~ ahead andare avanti:
 ~ down schiacciare, abbassare;
 * *vi* ~ forward spingersi
 innanzi; * *vt* spingere avanti:
 ~ hard incalzare: ~ in
 sopraggiungere: ~ into
 comprimere: ~ on andare
 avanti: ~ out fare uscire a
 forza: ~ round stringersi
 attorno a qualcuno: ~ up
 sollevare con forza.
press *n* pressa *f*, torchio *m*;
 stampa *f*.
pressure *n* pressione *f*.
prestige *n* prestigio *m*.
presume *vt* supporre.
presumption *n* presunzione *f*.
presuppose *vt* presupporre.
pretend *vi* fingere.
preterite *n* passato *m*.
pretty *adj* grazioso;
 * *adv* piuttosto.
prevent *vt* prevenire.
prevention *n* prevenzione *f*.
preventive *adj* preventivo.
preview *n* anteprima *f*.
previous *adj* precedente.
prey *n* preda *f*.
price *n* prezzo *m*.
priceless *adj* di valore
 inestimabile.
price list *n* listino *m* prezzi.
prick *vi* bucare; pungere;
 * *n* puntura *f*, (*vulg*) cazzo *m*.
prickle *n* spina *f*.
pride *n* orgoglio *m*; branco *m*.
priest *n* prete *m*.
priestess *n* sacerdotessa *f*.
prime *n* apice *m*;
 * *adj* principale; * *vi* preparare.
Prime Minister *n* Primo
 Ministro *m*.
primrose *n* (botany) primula *f*.
prince *n* principe *m*.

princess n principessa f.
principality n principato m.
principle n principio m.
print vt stampare;
   * n impronta f, stampato m;
   stampa f: — out of ~ fuori
   stampa.
printer n tipografo m;
   stampante f.
prior adj precedente;
   * n priore m.
priority n priorità f.
priory n prioria f.
prise vt apprezzare; aprire
   facendo leva; fare leva su.
prism n prisma m.
prison n prigione f.
prisoner n prigioniero m.
pristine adj perfetto;
   incorrotto; immacolato.
privacy n privacy f.
private adj privato;
   confidenziale; * n soldato
   semplice m.
private detective n detective
   privato m.
privet n ligustro m.
privilege n privilegio m.
prize n premio m; * vt valutare.
prizewinner n premiato m.
probability n probabilità f.
probable adj probabile.
probation n periodo di prova m;
   libertà vigilata f.
probe n sonda f; * vt sondare.
problem n problema m.
procedure n procedura f.
proceed vi procedere;
   * proceeds npl ricavato m.
proceedings n provvedimenti
   mpl.
process n processo m,
   procedimento m; * vi trattare.
procession n processione f.
proclaim vi proclamare.
proclamation n proclama m.
procure vt procurare.

procurement n
   approvvigionamento m.
prodigal adj prodigo.
prodigy n prodigio m.
produce vt produrre;
   * n prodotto m.
producer n produttore m;
   regista m or f.
product n prodotto m.
production n produzione f.
productive adj produttivo.
productivity n produttività f.
profess vt professare.
profession n professione f.
professional adj professionale;
   * n professionista m or f.
professor n professore m.
proficiency n competenza f.
profile n profilo m.
profit n profitto m;
   * vi approfittare.
profitability n redditività f.
profitable adj redditizio.
profiteer vt speculare;
   * n speculatore m.
profusion n profusione f.
programme n programma m.
programmer n
   programmatore m.
progress n progresso m;
   * vi procedere.
progression n progressione f.
prohibit vt proibire; vietate.
prohibition n proibizione f.
project vt proiettare;
   * n progetto m.
projection n proiezione f.
projector n proiettore m.
proletarian adj, n proletario m.
proletariat n proletariato m.
prolific adj prolifico.
prologue n prologo m.
prolong vt prolungare.
promenade n passeggiata f.
prominence n prominenza f.
prominent adj prominente.
promise n promessa f;

* *vt* promettere.
promising *adj* promettente.
promontory *n* promontorio *m*.
promote *vt* promuovere.
promoter *n* promotore *m*.
promotion *n* promozione *f*.
prompt *adj* tempestivo;
 * *vt* suggerire.
prompter *n* suggeritore *m*.
prone *adj* a faccia in giù;
 soggetto a.
prong *n* rebbio *m*; dente *m*;
 punta *f*.
pronoun *n* pronome *m*.
pronounce *vt* pronunciare.
pronounced *adj* netto.
pronunciation *n* pronuncia *f*.
proof *n* prova *f*, bozza *f*.
prop *vt* appoggiare;
 * *n* sostegno *m*.
propaganda *n* propaganda *f*.
propel *vt* spingere.
propeller *n* elica *f*.
proper *adj* appropriato;
 giusto; decente.
property *n* proprietà *f*.
prophecy *n* profezia *f*.
prophesy *vt* profetizzare.
prophet *n* profeta *m*.
prophetic *adj* profetico.
proportion *n* proporzione *f*.
proportional *adj* proporzionale.
proportionate *adj*
 proporzionato.
proposal *n* proposta *f*.
propose *vt* proporre;
 * *vi* dichiararsi, fare una
 proposta di matrimonio.
proposition *n* proposizione *f*.
proprietor *n* proprietario *m*.
propriety *n* decoro *m*.
propulsion *n* propulsione *f*.
prosaic *adj* prosaico.
prose *n* prosa *f*.
prosecute *vt* proseguire;
 * *vi* ricorrere in giudizio.
prosecution *n* azione

giudiziaria *f*.
prosecutor *n* procuratore *m*.
prospect *n* prospettiva *f*;
 * *vt* esplorare.
prospective *adj* futuro.
prospector *n* cercatore d'oro *m*;
 prospettore *m*.
prospectus *n* prospetto *m*.
prosper *vi* prosperare.
prosperity *n* prosperità *f*.
prosperous *adj* prospero.
prostitute *n* prostituta *f*.
prostitution *n* prostituzione *f*.
protagonist *n* protagonista
 m or *f*.
protect *vt* proteggere.
protection *n* protezione *f*.
protective *adj* protettivo.
protector *n* protettore *m*.
protein *n* proteina *f*.
protest *vt*, *vi* protestare;
 * *n* protesta *f*.
Protestant *n* protestante *m*.
protester *n* contestatore *m*.
protocol *n* protocollo *m*.
prototype *n* prototipo *m*.
protracted *adj* protratto.
protrude *vi* sporgere.
proud *adj* orgoglioso.
prove *vt* dimostrare, provare;
 * *vi* rivelarsi.
proverb *n* proverbio *m*.
proverbial *adj* proverbiale.
provide *vt* fornire.
provided *conj*: ~ that a patto che.
providence *n* provvidenza *f*.
province *n* provincia *f*.
provincial *adj* provinciale.
provision *n* fornitura *f*.
provisional *adj* provvisorio.
provocation *n* provocazione *f*.
provocative *adj* provocatorio.
provoke *vi* provocare.
prow *n* (marine) prua *f*.
prowess *n* prodezza *f*.
prowl *vi* aggirarsi.
prowler *n* chi si aggira

furtivamente *m* or *f*.
proxy *n* procura *f*.
prudence *n* prudenza *f*.
prudent *adj* prudente.
prudish *adj* puritano.
prune *vt* potare; * *n* prugna.
psalm *n* salmo *m*.
pseudonym *n* pseudonimo *m*.
psyche *n* psiche *f*.
psychiatric *adj* psichiatrico.
psychiatrist *n* psichiatra *m* or *f*.
psychiatry *n* psichiatria *f*.
psychic *adj* psichico.
psychoanalysis *n* psicanalisi *f*.
psychoanalyst *n* psicanalista
  m or *f*.
psychological *adj* psicologico.
psychologist *n* psicologo *m*.
psychology *n* psicologia *f*.
psychopath *n* psicopatico *m*.
psychosomatic *adj*
  psicosomatico.
pub *n* pub *m*.
pubes *n* pube *m*.
puberty *n* pubertà *f*.
pubic *adj* pubico.
public *adj*, *n* pubblico *m*.
public address system *n*
  impianto di amplificazione *m*.
publican *n* gestore di un pub *m*.
publication *n* pubblicazione *f*.
publicity *n* pubblicità *f*.
publicise *vt* reclamizzare.
publish *vt* pubblicare.
publisher *n* editore *m*.
publishing house *n* casa
  editrice *f*.
pucker *vt* increspare.
pudding *n* dolce *m*; budino *m*;
  dessert *m*.
puddle *n* pozzanghera *f*.
puerile *adj* puerile.
puff *n* soffio *m*; * *vi* ansimare,
  soffiare.
puff pastry *n* pasta *f*, sfoglia.
puffin *n* pulcinella di mare *f*.
puffy *adj* gonfio.

puke *vt*, *vi* vomitare.
pull *vi* tirare.
pulley *n* puleggia *f*.
pullover *n* pullover *m*.
pulp *n* pasta (di legno) *f*, polpa *f*.
pulpit *n* pulpito *m*.
pulsate *vi* pulsare.
pulse *n* polso *m*.
pulverise *vt* polverizzare.
puma *n* puma *m*.
pumice *n* pomice *f*.
pummel *vi* prendere a pugni.
pump *n* pompa *f*; * *vt* pompare.
pumpkin *n* zucca *f*.
pun *n* gioco *m* di parole.
punch *n* pugno *m*; perforatrice
  f, punzonatrice *f*; * *vt* dare un
  pugno; forare.
punctual *adj* puntuale.
punctuate *vt* punteggiare.
punctuation *n* punteggiatura *f*.
pundit *n* esperto *m*.
pungent *adj* pungente.
punish *vt* punire.
punishment *n* punizione *f*.
punk *n* punk *m*.
punt *n* barchino *m*.
puny *adj* gracile; striminzito;
  (*fig*) meschino.
pup *n* cucciolo *m*.
pupil *n* allievo *m*; pupilla *f*.
puppet *n* burattino *m*.
puppy *n* cucciolo *m*, cagnolino *m*.
purchase *vt* acquistare;
  * *n* acquisto *m*; presa *f*.
purchaser *n* acquirente *m* or *f*.
pure *adj* puro.
purée *n* purè *m*.
purge *n* purga *f*; * *vt* purgare.
purification *n* depurazione *f*.
purify *vt* depurare.
purist *n* purista *m* or *f*.
puritan *adj*, *n* puritano *m*.
purity *n* purezza *f*.
purl *n* rovescio *m*.
purple *adj*, *n* viola *m*.
purport *vt* voler sembrare;

* *n* significato *m*.
purpose *n* scopo *m*; * on ~ *adv* apposta.
purposeful *adj* risoluto.
purr *vi* fare le fusa.
purse *n* borsellino *m*; portamonete *m*.
purser *n* commissario *m* di bordo.
pursue *vt* inseguire; proseguire.
pursuit *n* inseguimento *m*; attività *f*.
purveyor *n* fornitore *m*.
pus *n* pus *m*.
push *vt* spingere; * *n* spinta.
pusher *n* spiacciatore *m*.
pussy *n* micio *m*.
put *vt* mettere, posare; esprimere: ~ about invertire la rotta: ~ across mettere di traverso: ~ aside (by) mettere da parte: ~ away mettere via: ~ back tirare indietro: ~ before mettere davanti: ~ behind tenere indietro, gettarsi dietro alle spalle: ~ down posare: ~ forth produrre, fare, pubblicare: ~ forward mettere avanti: ~ in mettere dentro, inserire: ~ in for chiedere, fare domanda: ~ into mettere, investire: ~ off rinviare: ~ on mettere su, indossare: ~ onto mettere in contatto con: ~ out mettere fuori: ~ over far passare: ~ over on darla da bere: ~ through portare a compimento, realizzare: ~ together mettere insieme: ~ under fare perdere i sensi: ~ up alzare: ~ up to indurre: ~ up with sopportare: ~ upon recare disturbo.
putrid *adj* putrido.
putt *n* putting *m*.

putty *n* stucco *m*.
puzzle *n* rompicapo *m*, rebus *m*, puzzle *m*.
puzzling *adj* sconcertante.
pylon *n* pilone *m*.
pyramid *n* piramide *f*.
pyromaniac *n* piromane *m* or *f*.
python *n* pitone *m*.

Q

quack *vi* fare qua qua; * *n* qua qua *m*; ciarlatano *m*, impostore *m*.
quadrangle *n* quadrangolo *m*; cortile *m*.
quadrant *n* quadrante *m*.
quadrilateral *adj* quadrilatero.
quadruple *adj* quadruplo.
quail *n* quaglia *f*.
quaint *adj* pittoresco; singolare.
quake *vi* tremare.
Quaker *n* quacchero *m*.
qualification *n* qualificazione *f*; riserva *f*; condizione *f*.
qualified *adj* qualificato.
qualify *vt* qualificare.
quality *n* qualità *f*.
quantitative *adj* quantitativo.
quantity *n* quantità *f*.
quarrel *n* lite *f*, litigio *m*; * *vi* litigare.
quarry *n* cava *f*; selvaggina *f*; * *vt* estrarre, cavare (fuori).
quarter *n* quarto *m*: ~ of an hour quarto d'ora; quartiere *m*; * *vt* dividere in quattro.
quartet *n* (music) quartetto *m*.
quartz *n* (mineral) quarzo *m*.
quay *n* molo *m*.
queen *n* regina *f*.
queer *adj* strano; (*vulg*) finocchio *m*.
query *n* domanda *f*; * *vt* contestare.

quest *n* ricerca *f*.

question *n* domanda *f*,
 questione *f*; * *vt* interrogare.

questionable *adj* discutibile.

question mark *n* punto *m*
 interrogativo.

questionnaire *n* questionario *m*.

queue *n* coda *f*.

quick *adj* veloce.

quicken *vt* affrettare.

quid *n* (*sl*) sterlina *f*.

quiet *adj* silenzioso, tranquillo.

quietness *n* tranquillità *f*,
 silenzio *m*.

quieten *vt* placare.

quill *n* (feather) penna *f*.

quilt *n* trapunta *f*.

quince *n* cotogna *f*, (tree)
 cotogno *m*.

quintet *n* (music) quintetto *m*.

quit *vt* lasciare; smettere:
 — to ~ someone (something)
 lasciare qualcuno (qualcosa):
 ~ doing something smettere
 di fare qualcosa:
 ~ a debt pagare un debito:
 ~ town levare le tende:
 — notice to ~ disdetta,
 escomio, licenziamento;
 * *vi* dimettersi.

quite *adv* proprio, piuttosto.

quiver *vi* tremare; * *n* faretra *f*.

quiz *n* quiz *m*; * *vt* interrogare.

quizzical *adj* canzonatorio;
 interrogativo.

quorum *n* quorum *m*.

quota *n* quota *f*.

quotation *n* citazione *f*,
 preventivo *m*.

quote *vt* citare; indicare.

R

rabbi *n* rabbino *m*.

rabbit *n* coniglio *m*.

rabies *n* rabbia *f*.

raccoon *n* procione *m*.

race *n* corsa *f*, razza *f*;
 * *vt* gareggiare contro;
 * *vi* correre.

racial *adj* razziale.

racing *n* corsa *f*.

racism *n* razzismo *m*.

radar *n* radar *m*.

radial *adj* radiale.

radiation *n* radiazione *f*.

radiator *n* radiatore *m*;
 termosifone *m*.

radical *adj*, *n* radicale *m*.

radio *n* radio *f*.

radioactive *adj* radioattivo.

radioactivity *n* radioattività *f*.

radiographer *n* radiologo *m*.

radish *n* ravanello *m*.

raffle *n* riffa; * *vt* mettere in
 palio.

raft *n* zattera *f*.

rag *n* straccio *m*, cencio *m*.

rage *n* collera *f*, furia *f*;
 * *vi* infuriarsi.

raid *n* irruzione *f*, rapina *f*;
 * *vt* fare irruzione in;
 saccheggiare.

rail *n* sbarra *f*; corrimano *m*;
 rotaia *f*; * ~ against *vi* inveire.

railway *n* ferrovia *f*.

rain *n* pioggia *f*; * *vi* piovere.

rainbow *n* arcobaleno *m*.

raincoat *n* impermeabile *m*.

raise *vt* sollevare; erigere;
 alzare; * *n* aumento *m*.

raisin *n* uvetta *f*.

rally *n* raduno *m*; rally *m*;
 * *vi* radunare; riunire.

ram *n* montone *m*, ariete;
 * *vt* speronare; ficcare.

ramp *n* rampa *f*.

random *adj* a caso.

range *n* portata *f*, autonomia
 f, gamma *f*, catena *f*;
 * *vi* variare, estendersi.

ranger *n*: — forest ~ guardia
 forestale *f*.

rank *adj* puzzolente, rancido;
  * *n* grado; posteggio *m*;
  * *vt* ritenere.
rape *n* stupro *m*; * *vt*
  violentare, stuprare.
rapid *adj* rapido; * ~s *npl*
  rapida *f*.
rapist *n* violentatore *m*,
  stupratore *m*.
rare *adj* raro; al sangue.
rarity *n* rarità *f*.
rash *adj* avventato; * *n* sfogo,
  orticaria *f*; eruzione cutanea
  f: — to have a rash avere
  un'eruzione cutanea.
raspberry *n* lampone *m*:
  ~ cane lampone *m*.
rat *n* ratto *m*.
rat *vt* cacciare topi: ~ on
  someone fare la spia, tradire:
  ~ on one's debts non pagare i
  debiti.
rate *n* tasso *m*; tariffa *f*;
  * *vt* valutare.
rather *adv* piuttosto.
ratio *n* rapporto *m*.
ration *n* razione *f*; * *vt* razionare.
rattle *vt* innervosire;
  acciottolare; * *vi* sferragliare;
  blaterare; * *n* rumore secco
  m; acciottolio *m*; raganella *f*;
  rantolo *m*; sonaglio *m*.
rattlesnake *n* crotalo *m*,
  serpente a sonagli *m*.
raven *n* corvo *m*.
raw *adj* crudo, greggio; gelido.
ray *n* raggio *m*; razza *f*.
razor *n* rasoio *m*.
reach *vt* raggiungere;
  * *vi* estendersi; * *n* portata *f*,
  tratto *m*.
reaction *n* reazione *f*.
read *vt* leggere; * *vi* studiare.
reader *n* lettore *m*; antologia *f*.
readily *adv* prontamente.
readjust *vt* regolare;
  * *vi* riadattarsi.

ready *adj* pronto.
reappear *vi* ricomparire.
rear *n* parte *f* posteriore;
  * *adj* posteriore; * *vt* allevare;
  * *vi* impennarsi.
reason *n* ragione *f*, motivo *m*;
  * *vi* ragionare.
rebel *adj*, *n* ribelle *m* or *f*;
  * *vi* ribellarsi.
rebellion *n* ribellione *f*.
recede *vi* ritirarsi.
receipt *n* ricevuta *f*.
receive *vt* ricevere.
recent *adj* recente.
reception *n* ricevimento *m*;
  reception *f*, accettazione *f*.
recession *n* recessione *f*.
recipe *n* ricetta *f*.
recline *vi* sdraiarsi;
  * *vt* reclinare.
recognition *n* riconoscimento *m*.
recognise *vt* riconoscere.
recoil *vi* indietreggiare.
recollect *vt* rammentare.
recollection *n* ricordo *m*.
recommend *vt* raccomandare;
  consigliare.
record *vt* annotare; registrare;
  * *n* registro *m*; precedenti
  penali *mpl*; record *m*; disco *m*;
  ~s annali *mpl*; archivi *mpl*.
recover *vt* ricuperare;
  ricoprire; * *vi* riprendersi.
recovery *n* ricupero *m*; ripresa *f*.
recreation *n* ricreazione *f*.
recruit *vt* reclutare;
  * *n* recluta *f*.
recruitment *n* reclutamento *m*.
rectangle *n* rettangolo *m*.
rectum *n* retto *m*.
recuperate *vi* ristabilirsi.
red *adj*, *n* rosso *m*.
redeem *vt* redimere.
Redeemer *n* Redentore *m*.
reduce *vt* ridurre;
  * *vi* diminuire.
reduction *n* riduzione *f*.

redundancy n ridondanza f,
licenziamento m.
redundant adj ridondante;
licenziato.
refectory n refettorio m.
refer vi riferirsi a; consultare;
* vt rimandare.
referee n arbitro m.
reference n riferimento m.
referendum n referendum m.
refill n ricambio; * vt riempire.
refine vt raffinare.
refinery n raffineria f.
reflect vt, vi riflettere;
* vt rispecchiare.
reflection n riflessione f,
riflesso m.
reflex adj, n riflesso m.
reform vt riformare;
* n riforma f.
Reformation n Riforma f.
refreshment n ristoro m.
refrigerate vt refrigerare.
refrigerator n frigorifero m.
refuge n riparo m, rifugio m.
refugee n profugo m.
refusal n rifiuto m.
refuse vt rifiutare; * n rifiuti
mpl.
regal adj regale.
regard vt considerare;
riguardare; * n riguardo m.
regarding prep riguardo a.
régime n regime m.
region n regione f.
regional adj regionale.
register n registro m;
* vt registrare; immatricolare;
* vi iscriversi.
registered letter n
raccomandata f.
registrar n ufficiale di stato
civile m.
registration n registrazione f.
registry office n anagrafe f.
regress vi regredire.
regret n rimpianto m;

rammarico m; * vt rimpiangere;
dispiacersi di.
regrettable adj deplorevole.
regular adj regolare; fedele.
regularity n regolarità f.
regulate vt regolare.
regulation n regolamento m.
regulator n regolatore m.
rehabilitate vt riabilitare.
rehabilitation n
riabilitazione f.
rehearse vt provare.
reign n regno m; * vi regnare.
reincarnation n
reincarnazione f.
reinforce vt rinforzare.
reject vt scartare; * n scarto m.
rejection n rigetto m.
rejoice vi rallegrarsi.
relapse vi ricadere;
* n ricaduta f.
relate vt collegare; raccontare.
relation n relazione f,
rapporto m; parente m or f.
relationship n nesso m;
relazione f, legami mpl di
parentela.
relax vt rilassare.
relaxation n relax m.
relay n ricambio m; relé m;
* vt ritrasmettere; passare.
release vt rilasciare; mollare;
emettere; * n rilascio m;
emissione f; uscita f.
relevance n pertinenza f.
relevant adj pertinente.
reliable adj affidabile.
reliance n dipendenza.
relic n reliquia f.
relief n sollievo m; rilievo m.
relieve vt alleviare.
religion n religione f.
religious adj religioso.
relish n gusto m; condimento m;
* vt gustare.
reluctance n riluttanza f.
rely vi contare su.

remain *vi* rimanere.
remains *npl* resti *mpl*; avanzi *mpl*.
remark *n* osservazione *f*;
* *vt* osservare.
remarkable *adj* notevole.
remedial *adj* correttivo.
remedy *n* rimedio *m*;
* *vt* rimediare.
remember *vt* ricordare.
remind *n* ricordare.
remote *adj* remoto; vago.
remunerate *vt* rimunerare.
remuneration *n*
rimunerazione *f*.
Renaissance *n* Rinascimento *m*.
renal *adj* renale.
rendezvous *n* appuntamento *m*;
* *vi* ritrovarsi.
renew *vt* rinnovare.
renewal *n* rinnovo *m*.
renounce *vt* rinunciare.
renovate *vt* rinnovare.
renovation *n* restauro *m*.
renown *n* rinomanza *f*.
renowned *adj* rinomato.
rent *n* affitto *m*, pigione *m*;
* *vt* affittare.
rental *n* nolo *m*.
repair *vt* aggiustare, riparare;
* *n* riparazione *f*.
repeat *vt* ripetere; * *n* replica *f*.
repeatedly *adv* ripetutamente.
replace *vt* rimpiazzare;
sostituire.
replacement *n* sostituto *m*.
replete *adj* sazio.
replica *n* replica *f*.
reply *n* risposta *f*; * *vt*, *vi*
rispondere.
report *vt* riportare;
denunciare; * *n* rapporto *m*;
pagella *f*; reportage *m*.
reporter *n* cronista *m* or *f*.
representative *adj*
rappresentativo;
* *n* rappresentante *m*.
reproduce *vt* riprodurre.

reproduction *n* riproduzione *f*.
reptile *n* rettile *m*.
republic *n* repubblica *f*.
republican *n* repubblicano *m*.
repulse *vt* respingere.
repulsive *adj* ripugnante.
reputation *n* reputazione *f*.
request *n* richiesta *f*;
* *vt* richiedere.
require *vt* richiedere.
requirement *n* esigenza *f*.
rescue *vt* salvare;
* *n* salvataggio *m*.
research *vi* fare ricerca;
* *n* ricerca *f*.
resemblance *n* somiglianza *f*.
resemble *vt* somigliare.
resent *vt* risentirsi per.
reservation *n* prenotazione *f*,
riserva *f*.
reserve *vt* prenotare; riservare;
* *n* riserva *f*, riservo *m*.
reservoir *n* bacino *m* idrico.
reside *vi* risiedere.
residence *n* residenza *f*.
resign *vi* dimettersi.
resignation *n* dimissioni *fpl*.
resist *vt*, *vi* resistere.
resistance *n* resistenza *f*.
resolve *vt* decidere; risolvere;
* *n* risolutezza *f*.
resort *vi* fare ricorso a;
* *n* ricorso *m*; località *f* di
villeggiatura.
resound *vi* risonare.
resource *n* risorsa *f*.
respect *n* rispetto *m*: — in
some ~s sotto certi aspetti;
* *vt* rispettare.
respectability *n* rispettabilità *f*.
respectable *adj* rispettabile.
respond *vt*, *vi* rispondere.
respondent *n* (law) convenuto *m*.
response *n* risposta *f*.
responsibility *n* responsabilità *f*.
responsible *adj* responsabile.
rest *n* riposo *m*; pausa *f*;

appoggio m; resto m;
* vt riposare; * vi riposarsi;
poggiare.
restaurant n ristorante m.
restoration n restauro m:
— the R~ la Restaurazione f.
restore vt restaurare;
restituire.
restrict vt limitare.
restriction n restrizione f.
restrictive adj restrittivo.
result vi avere come risultato;
* n risultato m.
resume vt, vi riprendere.
resuscitate vt risuscitare.
retail vt vendere al dettaglio;
. * adj al dettaglio.
retailer n dettagliante m or f,
venditore al dettaglio.
retain vt tenere; conservare.
retina n retina f.
retire vt mandare in pensione;
* vi ritirarsi, andare in
pensione.
retort vt, vi ribattere;
* n risposta f, storta f.
retreat n rifugio m;
* vi ritirarsi.
retrieve vt recuperare;
richiamare.
return vt restituire;
* vi tornare; * n ritorno m;
resa f, guadagno m: ~ ticket
andata e ritorno.
reunion n riunione f.
reveal vt rivelare.
revelation n rivelazione f.
revenge vt vendicare;
* n vendetta f.
revenue n reddito m.
Reverend n reverendo m.
reverse vt invertire; * vi fare
marcia indietro; * n opposto
m; rovescio m; retromarcia f;
* adj inverso; marcia indietro.
review vt fare una revisione
di; recensire; * n revisione f,

rivista f.
revise vt ripassare; rivedere.
revision n ripasso m; revisione f.
revival n risveglio m;
ripristino m.
revive vt rianimare.
revolution n rivoluzione f.
revolutionary adj, n
rivoluzionario m.
revolve vt, vi girare.
revolver n rivoltella f.
reward vt premiare;
* n ricompensa f.
rheumatism n reumatismo m.
rhinoceros n rinoceronte m.
rhododendron n rododendro m.
rhubarb n rabarbaro m.
rhyme n rima f; * vi fare rima
con.
rib n costola f.
ribbon n nastro m.
rice n riso m.
rich adj ricco.
rid vt sbarazzare.
ride vi cavalcare: ~ a horse
andare a cavallo: ~ a bike
andare in bicicletta: ~ across
attraversare [a cavallo or in
bicicletta]: ~ away (off)
andarsene: ~ back ritornare:
~ down travolgere: ~ on
proseguire: ~ out superare:
~ over something passare
sopra: ~ over someone (fig)
bistrattare: ~ up arrivare;
* n cavalcata f, giro m:
— to take a ~ fare un giro.
ridicule n ridicolo m;
* vt mettere in ridicolo.
ridiculous adj ridicolo.
rifle vt svaligiare; * vi frugare;
* n fucile m; carabina f.
rift n spaccatura f.
right adj giusto, retto, adatto;
destro; diritto; corretto;
* adv completamente; bene;
giustamente; * n diritto m;

destra *f*; * *vt* raddrizzare;
correggere: — to be ~ avere
ragione.
righteous *adj* virtuoso.
rigid *adj* rigido.
rim *n* orlo *m*.
rind *n* buccia *f*, cotenna *f*.
ring *n* anello *m*; cerchio *m*; ring
m; squillo *m*; scampanellata *f*;
* *vt* accerchiare; * *vt* suonare;
* *vi* telefonare; risuonare:
~ around fare un giro di
telefonate: ~ back
ritelefonare: ~ in telefonare:
~ off riattaccare: ~ out
risuonare, squillare: ~ up
someone telefonare a.
rinse *vt* sciacquare;
* *n* sciacquatura *f*.
rip *vt* strappare; lacerare,
strappare: — to let ~ scatenarsi:
~ across stracciare: ~ apart
spaccare in due: ~ away
strappare via: ~ down
strappare, tirar giù: ~ into
azzannare, assalire con
violenza: ~ off strappare via,
squarciare; (*fig*) derubare;
(*sl*) fregare: ~ out, ~ up fare a
pezzi: * *n* strappo *m*.
ripe *adj* maturo, stagionato.
ripen *vt*, *vi* maturare.
rise *vi* alzarsi; sorgere;
lievitare; aumentare: ~ above
alzarsi su, sopra: ~ from
alzarsi da, provenire da: ~ up
alzarsi in piedi; * *n* ascesa *f*,
aumento *m*; salita *f*; the sun~
il sorgere del sole *m*, l'alba *f*.
risk *n* rischio *m*; * *vt* rischiare.
rite *n* rito *m*.
ritual *adj*, *n* rituale *m*.
rival *adj*, *n* rivale *m*;
* *vt* rivaleggiare.
road *n* strada *f*, via *f*.
road sign *n* cartello *m* stradale.
roadworks *npl* lavori *mpl*

stradali.
roam *vi* gironzolare.
roar *vi* ruggire; * *n* ruggito *m*.
roaring *adj* strepitoso.
roast *vt* arrostire; torrefare;
* *n* arrosto *m*.
roast beef *n* rosbif *m*.
rob *vt* derubare.
robber *n* rapinatore *m*.
robbery *n* rapina *f*.
robe *n* tunica *f* accappatoio *m*.
robin pettirosso *m*.
robot *n* robot *m*.
robust *adj* robusto.
rock *n* roccia *f*; (music) rock *m*;
* *vt* cullare; * *vi* dondolare;
oscillare.
rocket *n* razzo *m*.
rocky *adj* roccioso; vacillante.
rod *n* bacchetta *f*, bastone *m*.
rodent *n* roditore *m*.
roe *n* uova di pese *mpl*.
rogue *n* mascalzone *m*.
role *n* ruolo *m*.
roll *vt*, *vi* rotolare: ~ about,
~ around (*sl*) sbellicarsi dalle
risa; * *n* rotolo *m*; rullino *m*;
panino *m*; lista *f*.
roller *n* rullo *m*; rotella *f*,
bigodino *m*.
roller skate *n* pattino a
rotelle *m*.
rolling pin *n* matterello *m*.
Roman Catholic *adj*, *n*
cattolico *m*.
romance *n* storia *f* romantica.
romantic *adj* romantico.
romp *vi* giocare
chiassosamente; * *n* gioco *m*
chiassoso.
roof *n* tetto *m*; * *vt* mettere il
tetto.
rook *n* corvo *m*; (chess) torre *f*.
room *n* stanza *f*, spazio *m*;
posto *m*.
roomy *adj* spazioso.
rooster *n* gallo *m*.

root *n* radice *f*; * *vt* far radicare;
 * *vi* attecchire: ~ out sradicare.
rope *n* fune *f*, corda *f*;
 * *vt* legare.
rosary *n* rosario *m*.
rose *n* rosa *f*, rosone *m* di
 stucco; (of watering can)
 cipolla *f*.
rosebed *n* rosaio *m*.
rosebud *n* bocciolo *m* di rosa.
rosemary *n* rosmarino *m*.
rosy *adj* roseo.
rot *vi* marcire; * *n* marciume *m*.
rotate *vi* rotare.
rotten *adj* marcio; schifoso.
rotund *adj* grassoccio.
rough *adj* ruvido, rozzo; rauco;
 approssimativo; burrascoso.
roughen *vt* irruvidire.
roughly *adv* brutalmente;
 grossolamamente.
roughness *n* ruvidità *f*.
roulette *n* roulette *f*.
round *adj* rotondo; * *n* cerchio
 m; giro *m*; round *m*;
 * *prep* intorno a;
 * *vt* arrotondare.
roundabout *adj* indiretto;
 * *n* giostra *f*, rotatoria *f*.
roundup *n* retata *f*.
rouse *vt* svegliare; scuotere.
route *n* itinerario *m*, percorso
 m; rotta *f*.
routine *n* routine *f*;
 * *adj* comune, abituale.
row *n* fila *f*; (*sl*) baccano *m*, lite
 f; * *vt* remare; * *vi* (*sl*) litigare.
rowdy *adj* turbolento.
royal *adj* reale.
royalty *n* reali *mpl*; royalty *m*,
 diritto d'autore *mpl*.
rub *vt* strofinare: ~ along
 tirare avanti: ~ away
 continuare a strofinare:
 ~ down consumare: ~ in(to)
 far penetrare strofinando:
 ~ off cancellare: ~ out

togliere una macchia
 strofinando: ~ through
 cavarsela alla meno peggio:
 ~ up lucidare, pulire: ~ up
 against (important people)
 venire in contatto con
 (persone importanti):
 ~ elbows with someone
 essere a contatto si gomito
 con qualcuno.
rub *n* strofinamento *m*.
rubber *n* gomma *f*, cauccid *m*.
rubbish *n* spazzatura *f*,
 immondizie *fpl*.
rubble *n* macerie *fpl*.
ruby *adj*, *n* rubino *m*.
rucksack *n* zaino *m*.
rudder *n* timone *m*.
rudeness *n* maleducazione *f*.
rudiment *n* rudimento *m*.
rug *n* tappeto *m*; plaid *m*.
rugby *n* rugby *m*.
rugged *adj* accidentato;
 frastagliato; marcato.
ruin *n* rudere *m*, rovina *f*;
 * *vt* rovinare.
rule *n* regola *f*, regolamento *m*;
 * *vt* governare; decretare;
 * *vi* regnare.
ruler *n* sovrano *m*; righello *m*.
rum *n* rum *m*; * *adj* strambo.
rumble *vi* brontolare;
 * *vt* scoprire; * *n* rombo *m*.
rumour *n* voce *f*, diceria *f*.
run *vt* correre; dirigere;
 gestire; organizzare;
 * *vi* correre; funzionare;
 scorrere: ~ about, ~ around
 andare in giro: ~ across
 incontrare per caso: ~ after
 correre dietro: ~ against
 gareggiare con: ~ downstairs
 correre dabbasso: ~along (*sl*)
 andarsene: ~ ashore
 approdare: ~ at correre verso:
 ~ away fuggire: ~ away with
 sfuggire al controllo di:

~ back tornare: ~ before correre davanti, fuggire: ~ down correre giù, travolgere, indebolire: ~ hard correre a più non posso: ~ high gonfiarsi: ~ in correre dentro, rodare: ~ into entrare di corsa, urtare, (*fig*) tentare l'impossibile: ~ low scarseggiare: ~ off andarsene: ~ up(on) correre senza sosta: ~ out correre fuori: ~ out at ammontare a: ~ out of correre fuori da; rimanere senza: ~ out on (*fam*) abbandonare: ~ over traboccare, travolgere: — to ~ round to the shop fare un salto al negozio: ~ through scorrere, infilzare: ~ to correre da: ~ together correre insieme, attaccarsi: ~ up correre su: ~ up against andare a sbattere contro: ~ upstairs correre di sopra: ~ with correre con, frequentare; * *n* corsa *f*, giro *m*; tragitto *m*; serie *f*, recinto *m*; smagliatura *f*; a ~away un fuggitivo *m* or *f*.

rung *n* piolo *m*; traversa *f*.

running *adj* corrente; * *n* gestione *f*.

runny *adj* sciolto.

runway *n* pista *f*.

rupture *n* rottura *f*; * *vi* rompere.

rural *adj* rurale.

rush *n* giunco *m*; ressa *f*, premura *f*, fretta *f*: — to be in a ~ avere fretta; * *vt* fare fretta a; * *vi* precipitarsi: ~ at avventarsi contro: ~ back tornare indietro in tutta fretta: ~ down precipitarsi giù: ~ for precipitarsi per prendere: ~ in precipitarsi dentro;

entrare precipitosamente: ~ someone into spingere qualcuno a fare in fretta: ~ off andarsene in tutta fretta, mandare via: ~ out uscire in fretta, pubblicare in fretta: ~ past sfrecciare accanto: ~ through sfrecciare attraverso, far passare in fretta e in furia: ~ up salire in fretta.

rusk *n* fetta biscottata *f*.

rust *n* ruggine *f*; * *vt, vi* arrugginire.

rustic *adj* rustico; * *n* contadino *m*.

rustle *vi* frusciare; * *n* fruscio *m*.

rusty *adj* rugginoso.

ruthless *adj* spietato.

rye *n* segale *f*.

S

Sabbath *n* giorno festivo *m*; (Christian) domenica *f*.

sabotage *n* sabotaggio *m*; * *vt* sabotare.

saccharine *n* saccarina *f*.

sack *n* sacco *m*; saccheggio *m*; * *vt* licenziare; saccheggiare.

sacred *adj* sacro.

sacrifice *n* sacrificio *m*; * *vt* sacrificare.

sad *adj* triste; deplorevole.

sadism *n* sadismo *m*.

sadist *n* sadico *m*.

sadness *n* tristezza *f*.

safe *adj* salvo; sicuro: ~ and sound sano e salvo; * *n* cassaforte *f*.

safeguard *n* salvaguardia *f*; * *vt* salvaguardare.

safety *n* sicurezza *f*.

sage *n* (botany) salvia *f*, saggio *m*.

Sagittarius *n* Sagittario *m*.

sail *n* vela *f*, pala *f*;
* *vt* condurre; * *vi* salpare,
navigare.
sailor *n* marinaio *m*.
saint *n* santa *f*.
salad *n* insalata *f*.
salami *n* salame *m*.
salary *n* stipendio *m*.
sale *n* vendita *f*, svendita *f*.
saliva *n* saliva *f*.
salmon *n* salmone *m*.
salmon trout *n* trota
salmonata *f*.
saloon *n* salone *m*; saloon *m*.
salt *n* sale *m*; * *vt* salare.
salvage *vt* ricuperare;
* *n* salvataggio *m*.
same *adj*, *pron* stesso.
sample *n* campione *m*;
* *vt* assaggiare.
sanctuary *n* santuario *m*.
sand *n* sabbia *f*;
* *vt* cartavetrare; cospargere
di sabbia.
sandal *n* sandalo *m*.
sandwich *n* tramezzino *m*,
sandwich *m*.
sane *adj* sano di mente.
sanity *n* sanità mentale *f*.
sapphire *n* zaffiro *m*.
sarcasm *n* sarcasmo *m*.
sardine *n* sardina *f*.
Satan *n* Satana *m*.
satellite *n* satellite *m*.
satin *n* raso *m*.
satisfaction *n* soddisfazione *f*.
satisfy *vt* soddisfare.
Saturday *n* sabato *m*.
sauce *n* salsa *f*.
saucepan *n* pentola *f*.
sausage *n* salsiccia *f*, salame *m*.
savage *adj*, *n* selvaggio *m*;
* *vt* sbranare.
save *vt* salvare; risparmiare;
parare; * *n* parata *f*;
* *prep* salvo.
saving *n* risparmio *m*;

* ~s *n* risparmi *mpl*.
Saviour *n* Salvatore *m*.
savoury *adj* salato; *n* piatto *m*
salato.
saw *n* sega *f*; * *vt* segare.
saxophone *n* sassofono *m*.
say *vt*, *vi* dire (io dico, tu dici,
lui [lei] dice, noi diciamo, voi
dite, lore dicono): ~ about
fare osservazioni su: ~ after
ripetere: ~ against
biasimare: ~ for difendere:
~ of dire di: ~ on (*sl*)
continuare a dire: ~ out dire
chiaro e tondo: ~ over
ripetere; raccomandare a.
saying *n* detto *m*.
scab *n* crosta *f*; (veterinary)
scabbia *f*.
scale *n* scaglia *f*, squama *f*,
scala *f*; * *vi* squamarsi.
scales *n* bilancia *f*.
scallop *n* (zoology) pettine *m*;
dentellatura *f*; smerlo *m*;
(cookery) capasanta *f*.
scalp *n* cuoio capelluto *m*;
scalpo *m*; * *vt* scotennare.
scalpel *n* bisturi *m*.
scampi *npl* gamberoni *mpl*.
scandal *n* scandalo *m*.
scar *n* cicatrice *f*; * *vt* sfregiare;
* *vi* cicatrizzarsi.
scare *vt* spaventare;
impaurire; * *n* spavento *m*.
scarf *n* sciarpa *f*, foulard *m*.
scarlet *adj*, *n* scarlatto *m*.
scene *n* scena *f*, luogo *m*.
scenery *n* paesaggio *m*.
scenic *adj* pittoresco.
scent *n* profumo *m*; pista *f*;
* *vt* profumare; fiutare.
sceptic *n* scettico *m*.
sceptical *adj* scettico.
scepticism *n* scetticismo *m*.
schedule *n* programma *m*;
orario *m*; tabella *f*.
scheme *n* piano *m*; * *vt* tramare.

schizophrenia *n* schizofrenia *f*.
scholar *n* studioso *m*.
school *n* scuola *f*, facoltà *f*,
  banco *m*; * *vt* addestrare.
schoolteacher *n* maestro *m*,
  insegnante *m* or *f*.
science *n* scienza *f*.
scientist *n* scienziato *m*.
scooter *n* monopattino *m*;
  motoretta *f*, vespa *f*.
scope *n* possibilità *fpl*, ambito
  m, capacità *f*.
scorch *vt* bruciacchiare;
  * *n* bruciacchiatura *f*.
score *n* punteggio *m*; motivo
  m; scalfittura *f*; (music)
  partitura *f*; * *vt* segnare;
  incidere; (music) orchestrare.
Scorpio *n* Scorpione *m*.
scorpion *n* scorpione *m*.
scramble *vi* inerpicarsi;
  * *vt* (cookery) strapazzare;
  ingarbugliare; *n* parapiglia
  m, gara di motocross *f*.
scrap *n* pezzetto *m*; briciolo *m*;
  ferraglia *f*, baruffa *f*;
  * *vt* demolire.
scrape *vt* raschiare: ~ along,
  ~ by (*sl*) tirare avanti:
  ~ away grattare via: ~ down
  scrostare: ~ in(to) essere
  ammesso per il rotto della
  cuffia: ~ off scrostare: ~ out
  pulire raschiando: ~ through
  passare a stento: ~ up cavare,
  togliere raschiando.
scratch *vt* graffiare; grattare;
  cancellare.
scratch *n* graffio *m*.
scrawl *vt* scribacchiare;
  * *n* grafia illeggibile *f*.
scream *vt*, *vi* urlare; * *n* urlo *m*,
  strillo *m*.
screen *n* paravento *m*; schermo
  m; * *vt* nascondere;
  proiettare; (*fig*) vagliare.
screw *n* vite *f*, elica *f*, (*sl*)

secondino *m*; * *vt* avvitare;
spiegazzare; (*vulg*) scopare,
chiavare; (to cheat, *vulg*)
fregare: ~ around
bighellonare:~ down avvitare:
~ off svitare: ~ on avvitare:
~ together avvitare insieme:
~ up avvitare; (*fig*, *sl*)
mettere a disagio, confondere.
script *n* copione *m*, scrittura *f*.
Scripture *n* Sacre Scritture *fpl*.
scrotum *n* scroto *m*.
scull *vt* remare.
scullery *n* retrocucina *m*.
sculpt *vt*, *vi* scolpire.
sculptor *n* scultore *m*.
sculpture *n* scultura *f*.
scythe *n* falce *f*; * *vt* falciare.
sea *n* mare *m*.
seal *n* foca *f*, sigillo *m*;
  * *vt* sigillare.
sealing wax *n* ceralacca *f*.
seam *n* cucitura *f*, vena *f*.
seaman *n* marinaio *m*.
seamstress *n* sarta *f*.
search *vt* perquisire;
  perlustrare; * *vi* cercare;
  * *n* ricerca *f*, perquisizione *f*.
season *n* stagione *f*;
  * *vt* stagionare; condire.
seat *n* sedia *f*, posto *m*; sedile
  m; sellino *m*; seggio *m*; sede *f*;
  * *vt* far sedere.
seclusion *n* isolamento *m*.
second *adj* secondo;
  * *n* secondo *m*; * *vt* appoggiare;
  distaccare.
secondary *adj* secondario.
secrecy *n* segretezza *f*.
secret *adj*, *n* segreto *m*.
secretary *n* segretario *m*.
section *n* sezione *f*, tratto *m*.
secure *adj* sicuro;
  * *vt* assicurare; garantire.
security *n* sicurezza *f*.
seduce *vt* sedurre.
seducer *n* seduttore *m*.

seduction *n* seduzione *f*.
see *vt* vedere; capire;
accompagnare: ~ about
provvedere a: ~ across fare
attraversare, accompagnare:
~ after pensare a: ~ ahead
vedere avanti: ~ around
guardarsi intorno: ~ back,
~ home riaccompagnare a
casa: ~ beyond vedere oltre:
~ in vedere dentro, fare
entrere: ~ into esaminare:
~ off salutare alla partenza:
~ out vederci: ~ over vedere
al di soprea di: ~ through
vedere attraverso, (*fig*) vederci
chiaro: ~ to provvedere a;
* *n* sede vescovile *f*; the Holy
S~ la Santa Sede.
seed *n* seme *m*; * *vt* seminare.
seek *vt* cercare.
seem *vi* sembrare, parere.
see-through *adj* trasparente.
segment *n* segmento *m*;
spicchio *m*.
segregation *n* segregazione *f*.
seize *vt* afferrare; cogliere.
seldom *adj* raramente.
select *vt* selezionare, scegliere;
* *adj* scelto; esclusivo.
selection *n* scelta *f*, selezione.
self *n* io *m*, se *m* stesso.
selfish *adj* egoista.
selfless *adj* altruista.
sell *vt* vendere; to be sold for
£5 a yard si vende a cinque
sterline la iarda: ~ off
svendere: ~ on convincere:
~ out esaurire: ~ up svendere.
seller *n* venditore *m*.
sellotape *n* scotch *m*, nastro
adesivo *m*.
semantics *npl* semantica *f*.
semblance *n* apparenza *f*.
semen *n* sperma *m*.
semicircle *n* semicerchio *m*.
semicolon *n* punto e virgola *m*.

semifinal *n* semifinale *f*.
seminar *n* seminario *m*.
semi-precious *adj* semiprezioso.
semolina *n* semolino *m*.
senate *n* senato *m*.
senator *n* senatore *m*.
send *vt* mandare, inviare;
spedire: ~ across mandare:
~ after mandare a cercare:
~ ahead mandare avanti:
~ along (*sl*) mandare:
~ around mandare in giro:
~ away mandare via:
~ back restituire:
~ for mandare a chiamare:
~ forth mandare, spedire:
~ in mandare dentro:
~ off inviare per posta:
~ on mandare avanti:
~ out mandare fuori:
~ over mandare, spedire:
~ round far circolare:
~ down (*sl*) mettere sotto,
sconfiggere: ~ up mandare
su, far salire.
senile *adj* senile.
senior *adj* maggiore,
superiore.
sensation *n* sensazione *f*,
scalpore *m*.
sense *n* senso *m*; ragione *f*,
senno *m*; * *vt* intuire,
avvertire.
sensibility *n* suscettibilità *f*.
sensible *adj* assennato;
pratico.
sensitive *adj* sensibile.
sensual *adj* sensuale.
sensuality *n* sensualità *f*.
sensuous *adj* voluttuoso.
sentence *n* frase *f*, sentenza *f*;
* *vt* condannare.
sentiment *n* sentimento *m*.
separate *vt* separare;
* *adj* separato: * ~ly *adv*
separatamente.
September *n* settembre *m*.

septic *adj* settico.
sequel *n* seguito *m*.
sequin *n* lustrino *m*.
serenade *n* serenata *f*; * *vt* fare
  la serenata a.
sergeant *n* sergente *m*.
serial *n* programma a puntate
  m: ~ killer pluriomicida *m* or *f*.
series *n* serie *f*.
serious *adj* serio; grave.
sermon *n* sermone *m*.
serpent *n* serpente *m*.
serpentine *n* serpentina *f*.
serrated *adj* seghettato.
scrum *n* siero *m*.
servant *n* domestico *m*.
serve *vt*, *vi* servire: * *vt* ~ a
  warrant notificare: ~ out
  mettere in tavola: ~ round
  servire ingiro: ~ under
  someone essere agli ordini di
  qualcuno: ~ up something
  servire una pietanza:
  — to ~ someone with pork
  servire a qualcuno del maiale.
service *n* servizio *m*; funzione *f*,
  revisione *f*; * *vt* revisionare.
serviette *n* tovagliolo *m*.
session *n* seduta *f*, anno *m*.
set *vi* porre; regolare; stabilire;
  assegnare; * *vi* tramontare,
  saldarsi; indurirsi; * *n* serie *f*,
  raccolta *f*, batteria *f*, set *m*,
  apparecchio *m*; * *adj* fisso;
  obbligatorio; stabilito;
  deciso.
settle *vi* sistemare; definire;
  saldare; appianare;
  colonizzare; * *vi* depositarsi;
  insediarsi; concordare.
settlement *n* regolamento *m*;
  accordo *m*; insediamento *m*.
settler *n* colono *m*.
seven *n* sette.
seventeen *n* diciasette.
seventeenth *adj*
  diciassettesimo.

seventh *adj* settimo.
seventieth *adj* settantesimo.
seventy *n* settanta.
sever *vi* tagliare, troncare.
several *adj* parecchi.
severe *adj* severo.
sew *vt*, *vi* cucire.
sewage *n* acque di fogna *fpl*.
sewer *n* fogna *f*.
sewing machine *n* macchina
  da cucire *f*.
sex *n* sesso *m*; rapporti
  sessuali *mpl*.
sexual *adj* sessuale.
sexuality *n* sessualità *f*.
sexy *adj* sexy.
shade *n* ombra *f*, paralume *m*;
  tonalità *f*; * *vt* riparare.
shadow *n* ombra *f*; * *vt* pedinare.
shady *adj* ombroso.
shake *vt* scuotere; * *vi* tremare:
  ~ hands dare la mano;
  * *n* scossa *f*.
shallow *adj* poco profondo.
shame *n* vergogna *f*, peccato *m*;
  * *vt* disonorare; far
  vergognare.
shame-faced *adj* vergognoso.
shameful *adj* vergognoso.
shameless *adj* spudorato.
shammy *n* pelle *f* di camoscio.
shampoo *n* shampoo *m*.
shamrock *n* trifoglio *m*.
shank *n* stinco *m*; gambo *m*.
shanty *n* canzone marinaresca
  f; baracca *f*.
shanty town *n* bidonville *f*.
shape *vt* formare; * *n* forma *f*.
share *n* parte *f*; azione *f*;
  * *vt* dividere; condividere.
shark *n* squalo *m*, pesce cane *m*.
sharp *adj* affilato, aguzzo.
shatter *vt* frantumare.
shave *vt* radere; * *vi* radersi.
shaver *n* rasoio *m* elettrico.
she *pron* ella, lei.
sheep *n* pecora *f*.

sheet *n* lenzuolo *m*; foglio *m*.

sheik *n* sceicco *m*.

shelf *n* ripiano *m*.

shell *n* conchiglia *f*, guscio *m*; struttura *f*; * *vt* sgranare; bombardare.

shellfish *n* crostaceo *m*.

shelter *n* riparo *m*; rifugio *m*; * *vt* riparare.

sheriff *n* sceriffo *m*.

sherry *n* sherry *m*.

shine *vt* lustrare; *vi* brillare: ~ on, out etc splendere: ~ through trasparire: ~ up to someone cercare di ingraziarsi qualcuno adulandolo; * *n* lucentezza *f*.

ship *n* nave *f*; * *vt* imbarcare; spedire.

shirt *n* camicia *f*.

shit *n* (*vulg*) merda *f*.

shiver *n* brivido *m*; * *vi* rabbrividire.

shock *n* scossa *f*; * *vt* scandalizzare; * *vi* scandalizzarsi.

shoe *n* scarpa *f*: — horseshoe ferro di cavallo; * *vt* ferrare.

shoot *vt* sparare; fucilare; lanciare; (film) girare; * *vt* sparare; * *n* germoglio *m*; partita *f* di caccia.

shop *n* negozio *m*; officina *f*; * *vt* fare la spesa; tradire.

shore *n* sponda *f*.

short *adj* basso; corto; breve: ~ly *adv* tra poco.

shorthand *n* stenografia *f*.

shorts *npl* calzoncini *mpl*.

short-sightedness *n* miopia *f*.

shot *n* sparo *m*; tiratore *m*; iniezione *f*, foto *f*.

shotgun *n* fucile da caccia *f*.

shoulder *n* spalla *f*; * *vt* accollarsi.

shout *vt*, *vi* gridare; * *n* grido *m*.

shovel *n* pala *f*; * *vt* spalare.

show *vt* mostrare; esporre; presentare; segnare; * *vt* vedersi; * *n* manifestazione *f*, esposizione *f*, spettacolo *m*; fiera *f*, figura *f*.

shower *n* acquazzone *m*; doccia *f*; * *vt* coprire; * *vi* fare la doccia.

shrimp *n* gamberetto *m*.

shrine *n* santuario *m*.

shrink *vi* restringersi.

shroud *n* sudario *m*; * *vt* avvolgere.

Shrove Tuesday *n* martedì grasso *m*.

shrub *n* cespuglio *m*.

shut *vt* chiudere; *vi* chiudersi: ~ away rinchiudere: ~ down (to) chiudere bene: ~ someone in chiudere dentro qualcuno: ~ off interrompere: ~ someone out chiudere fuori qualcuno: ~ up chiudere bene; (*fig*, *sl*) far tacere: ~ up! sta zitto!

shutter *n* persiana *f*, saracinesca *f*, otturatore *m*.

shy *adj* timido.

shyness *n* timidezza *f*.

sick *adj* malato; macabro; * *vi*: — to be ~ vomitare.

sickness *n* malattia *f*.

side *n* fianco *m*, lato *m*; faccia *f*, ciglio *m*; parte *f*, squadra *f*; * *adj* laterale; * *vi* parteggiare per.

sideboard *n* credenza *f*.

siege *n* assedio *m*.

sieve *n* setaccio *m*; * *vt* setacciare.

sigh *vi* sospirare; * *n* sospiro *m*.

sight *n* vista *f*, spettacolo *m*; mirino *m*; ~s attrazioni turistiche *fpl*.

sightseeing *n* turismo *m*.

sign *n* segno *m*; gesto *m*; indizio *m*; segnale *m*.

sign *vt*, *vi* firmare: ~ away,

~ over alienare, cedere, trasferire per iscritto: ~ off licenziarsi: ~ on sottoscrivere, firmare la disoccupazione: ~ out registrarsi alla partenza, firmare una ricevuta: ~ to fare cenno a qualcuno: ~ up impegnarsi per iscritto, iscriversi.

signal *n* segnale *m*; * *vt*, *vi* segnalare.

signature *n* firma *f*; (music) segnatura *f*.

significant *adj* significativo.

signify *vt* significare.

signpost *n* indicazione *f* stradale.

silence *n* silenzio *m*; * *vt* fare tacere.

silent *adj* silenzioso.

silk *n* seta *f*.

silly *adj* sciocco.

silver *n* argento *m*; argenteria *f*.

similar *adj* simile.

similarity *n* somiglianza *f*.

simple *adj* semplice; ingenuo.

simply *adv* semplicemente.

sin *n* peccato *m*; * *vi* peccare.

since *adv* da allora; * *prep* da; * *conj* siccome.

sincere *adj* sincero: * yours ~ly *adv* distinti saluti.

sincerity *n* sincerità *f*.

sing *vt*, *vi* cantare.

singer *n* cantante *m* or *f*.

single *adj* solo, unico, celibe, nubile; * *n* singolo *m*; di andata.

sinister *adj* sinistro.

sink *vi* cedere; abbassarsi; sommergersi; tramontare; * *vt* affondare; scavare: ~ below tramontare dietro: ~ back lasciarsi cadere all'indietro: ~ down cadere giù: ~ to cadere a: ~ low abbassarsi: ~ under

afflosciarsi; * *n* lavello *m*, acquaio *m*.

sinner *n* peccatore *m*.

sinus *n* seno *m*.

sip *vt* sorseggiare; * *n* sorso *m*.

sir *n* signore *m*.

siren *n* sirena *f*.

sister *n* sorella *f*, suora *f*.

sister-in-law *n* cognata *f*.

sit *vi* sedersi; riunirsi: ~ about, ~ around bigellonare: ~ back rilassarsi: ~ down accomodarsi: ~ down on opporsi a, bocciare: ~ down to accomodarsi a: ~ down under (*sl*) sopportare, mandar giù: ~ for concorrere per; fare da baby-sitter a qualcuno: ~in for rimpiazzare: ~ on sedere su: ~ out sedere all'aperto: ~ over starsene seduto a: ~ under (*sl*) studiare con (un insegnante): ~ up sedere diritto: ~ with someone stare seduto con qualcuno; * ~-in *n* raduno di protesta *m*.

site *n* ubicazione *f*; * *vt* collocare.

sitting room *n* salotto *m*.

situation *n* posizione *f*, situazione *f*.

six *num* sei.

sixteen *num* sedici.

sixteenth *num* sedicesimo.

sixth *num* sesto.

sixtieth *num* sessantesimo.

sixty *num* sessanta.

size *n* dimensioni *fpl*; taglia *f*, misura *f*, numero *m*.

skeleton *n* scheletro *m*.

skill *n* capacità *f*, abilità *f*, tecnica *f*.

skilled *adj* abile, specializzato.

skilful *adj* abile.

skim *vt* schiumare; scremare.

skimmed milk *n* latte

scremato m.

skin n pelle f, buccia f, pellicola f; * vt spellare; sbucciare.

skin diving n immersione con autorespiratore.

skinned adj scuoiato, spennato; senza soldi, (sl) al verde.

skirt n gonna f; * vt aggirare.

sky n cielo m.

skyscraper n grattacielo m.

slab n lastra f.

slander vi calunniare; * n calunnia f.

slang n slang m, gergo m.

slap n schiaffo m, ceffone m; * adv in pieno; * vt dare uno schiaffo.

slat n stecca f.

slaughter n macellazione f, massacro m; strage f; * vt macellare; massacrare; trucidare.

slave n schiavo m; * vi sgobbare.

sleek adj lucente, liscio.

sleep vi dormire; * n sonno m.

sleeve n manica f.

slender adj snello; scarso.

slenderness n snellezza f.

slice n fetta f, paletta f; * vt affettare.

slight adj minuto; * n affronto m; * vt snobbare.

slightly adv leggermente.

slim adj esile; insufficiente.

sling n fionda f, fascia f; * vt scagliare.

slink vi svignarsela.

slip vi scivolare; sfuggire; sbagliarsi: ~ along scivolare via: ~ away andar via alla chetichella: ~ back slittare indietro: ~ by, ~ past scivolare accanto; ~ down scivolare a terra: ~ in infilarsi: ~ into infilarsi

dentro: ~ off scivolare: ~ on affilarsi: ~ out scivolare, cadere: ~ out of sfilarsi, togliersi: ~ over scivolare su: ~ through passare inosservato: ~ up scivolare; * n smottamento m; scivolata f, sbaglio m; sottoveste f, federa f, foglietto m.

slipper n pantofola f.

slipway n scalo m.

slope n versante m, pendio m; * vi essere inclinato.

slow adj lento: * ~ly adv piano; * vt, vi rallentare.

slug n lurnaca f.

sly adj astuto; scaltro.

smack n schiaffo m; schiocco m; * vi sculacciare, schiaffeggiare.

small adj piccolo.

smallpox n vaiolo m.

smart adj elegante, chic; sveglio; svelto; * vi bruciare.

smash vi rompere; frantumare; * n fracasso m; scontro m; successone m.

smashing adj meraviglioso.

smear n traccia f, (medical) striscio m; * vt spalmare; sporcare; diffamare.

smell n olfatto m, fiuto m; odore m; profumo m; puzzo m; * vt sentire odore di; * vi sapere; puzzare.

smile vi sorridere; * n sorriso m.

smog n smog m.

smoke vi fumare; affumicare; * vt and vi fumare; * n fumo m.

smoker n fumatore m.

smooth adj liscio; omogeneo; * vt lisciare, spianare.

snack n spuntino m.

snail n chiocciola f.

snake n serpente m.

snap vt rompere; schioccare; fotografare: ~ at cercare di

mordere: ~ back scattare
indietro; ~ into it (sl)
scattare, darci sotto: ~ down
sbattere giù, chiudere di
botto: ~ off spezzare: ~ on
chiudere di scatto: ~ out ·
gridare: ~ out of (sl) liberarsi
di: ~ up (sl) portare via.
snap n schiocco; rubamazzo;
* adj improvviso.
snatch vt strappare; afferrare;
cogliere; * n furto m,
rapimento m; pezzo m.
sneeze vi starnutire;
* n starnuto m.
sniff vt annusare; sniffare.
sniper n franco tiratore m.
snob n snob m or f.
snooty adj altezzoso.
snooze n sonnellino m;
* vt sonnecchiare.
snore vi russare.
snow n neve f; * vi nevicare.
snuff n tabacco m da fiuto.
so adv così, in questo modo;
* conj affinché.
soak vt inzuppare; mettere a
mollo.
soap n sapone m; * vt insaponare.
soar vi librarsi.
sob vi singhiozzare; n
singhiozzo m.
sober adj sobrio.
soccer n calcio m.
sociable adj socievole.
socialism n socialismo m.
socialist n socialista m or f.
society n società f, compagnia f.
sock n calzino m, calzettone
m; pugno m; * vt picchiare.
sofa n sofà m, divano m.
soft adj morbido, soffice;
dolce; indulgente; * ~ly adv
silenziosamente.
soil vt sporcare; infangare;
* n terreno m.
solar adj solare.

solarium n solarium m.
soldier n soldato m.
solicitor n avvocato m.
solid adj, n solido m.
solitude n solitudine f.
solo n (music) a solo.
solution n soluzione f.
solve vt risolvere.
sombre adj tetro.
some adj di, qualche, alcuno,
certo; * pron alcuni, certi;
* adv circa.
somebody pron qualcuno.
somehow adv in qualche modo.
something pron qualcosa.
sometimes adv qualche volta.
somewhat adv piuttosto,
alquanto.
somewhere adv in qualche
parte; circa.
son n figlio m.
song n canzone f, canto m.
sonic adj sonico.
son-in-law n genero m.
soon adv presto: — as ~ as
possible appena possibile.
sooner adv prima; piuttosto.
soot n fuliggine f.
soothe vt calmare.
soothing adj calmante;
rassicurante.
sophisticated adj sofisticato,
raffinato.
sophistication n complessità f.
sore n piaga f; * adj indolenzito;
doloroso.
sorrel n (botany) acetosa f.
sorrow n dolore m.
sorry adj dispiacente; pietoso;
* vi dispiacersi; * excl scusa,
scusi.
sort n gènere m, tipo m, specie
f; * vt classificare; smistare;
risolvere.
soul n anima f.
sound adj sano; valido;
profondo; * n suono m, rumore

m; volume *m*; (geography)
stretto *m*; * *vt* suonare;
sondare; * *vi* suonare.
soup *n* minestra *f*, zuppa *f*.
south *n* sud *m*, meridione *m*;
* *adj* sud, meridionale.
southerly, southern *adj* del sud.
souvenir *n* souvenir *m*, ricordo
m.
sovereign *adj*, *n* sovrano *m*.
sovereignty *n* sovranità *f*.
soviet *adj* sovietico.
sow *vi* seminare.
sowing *n* semina *f*.
soya *n* soia *f*.
spa *n* stazione *f* termale.
space *n* spazio *m*; * *vt* distanziare.
spacecraft *n* veicolo *m* spaziale.
spaceman, ~woman *n*
astronauta *m* or *f*,
cosmonauta *m* or *f*.
spacious *adj* spazioso.
spade *n* vanga *f*, paletta *f*:
~s picche.
spaghetti *n* spaghetti *mpl*.
spank *vt* sculacciare.
spanner *n* chiave *f* fissa.
spare *vt* risparmiare; prestare;
* *adj* di riserva; in più;
asciutto; * *n* pezzo *m* di
ricambio: ~ time tempo
libero: ~ wheel ruota di
scorta.
spark *n* scintilla *f*;
* *vi* provocare.
sparkling *adj* frizzante.
sparrow *n* passero *m*.
spastic *adj*, *n* spastico *m*.
spatula *n* spatola *f*.
speak *vt* dire; parlare;
* *vi* parlare.
special *adj* speciale;
particolare.
speciality *n* specialità *f*.
species *n* specie *f*.
specific *adj* specifico.
spectacle *n* spettacolo *m*.

spectacles *npl* occhiali *mpl*.
speech *n* parola *f*, parlata *f*,
linguaggio *m*; discorso *m*.
speechless *adj* senza parola.
speed *n* velocità *f*, rapidità *f*,
marcia *f*; * *vi* procedere
velocemente; andare a
velocità eccessiva.
spell *n* incantesimo *m*; periodo
m; * *vt* descrivere lettera per
lettera.
spend *vt* spendere; trascorrere.
spent *adj* usato; esaurito.
sperm *n* sperma *m*.
sperm whale *n* capodoglio *m*.
sphere *n* sfera *f*.
sphinx *n* sfinge *f*.
spice *n* droga *f*, spezie *fpl*;
* *vi* drogare.
spider *n* ragno *m*.
spider-web *n* ragnatela *f*.
spill *vt* rovesciare, versare.
spin *vt*, *vi* filare: ~ along
sfrecciare: ~ off scappare,
sfilarsi: ~ out allungare,
ruotare; girare; * *n* giro *m*;
effetto *m*; giretto *m*.
spinach *n* spinaci *mpl*.
spin-drier *n* centrifuga *f*.
spine *n* spina dorsale *f*.
spinster *n* zitella *f*.
spirit *n* spirito *m*; coraggio *m*:
~s liquori *mpl*.
spiritualist *n* spiritista *m* or *f*.
spirituality *n* spiritualità *f*.
spit *n* spiedo *m*; sputo *m*;
* *vt*, *vi* sputare.
spite *n* dispetto *m*; * in ~ of
conj nonostante, malgrado;
* *vt* fare dispetto a.
spittle *n* sputo *m*.
splash *vt*, *vi* schizzare.
splash *n* tonfo *m*; spruzzo *m*.
splendid *adj* splendido.
splinter *n* scheggia *f*;
* *vi* scheggiarsi.
split *n* fessura *f*, spacco *m*;

scissione *f.*
split *vt* spaccare; dividere;
* *vi* spaccarsi, dividersi:
~ away, ~ off staccarsi,
distaccarsi: ~ on (*sl*) fare la
spia a, tradire: ~ up spaccare,
separarsi.
spoil *vt* rovinare;
* *vi* guastarsi; * *n* bottino *m.*
sponge *n* spugna *f*, pan di
Spagna; * *vt* lavare con una
spugna; scroccare.
spoon *n* cucchiaio *m.*
sport *n* sport *m*; divertimento
m; persona *f* di spirito.
spot *n* macchia *f*, puntino *m*;
pois *m*; foruncolo *m*; posto *m*;
* *vt* macchiare; notare.
sprain *n* slogatura *f*;
* *vt* slogarsi.
sprat *n* spratto *m.*
spread *vt* spiegare; spalmare;
cospargere; propagare;
* *n* propagazione *f*, apertura
f, banchetto *m.*
spring *vi* saltare; sorgere; *n*
sorgente *f*, primavera *f*, salto
m; molla *f.*
sprout *n* germoglio *m*;
cavolino (di Bruxel) *m*;
* *vi* germogliare.
spruce *n* abete; * *adj* azzimato.
spry *adj* arzillo.
spur *n* sperone *m*, sprone *m*;
* *vt* spronare.
spurn *vt* rispingere.
spy *n* spia *f*; * *vt* scorgere;
* *vt* spiare.
spying *n* spionaggio *m.*
square *adj* quadrato; onesto;
* *n* quadrato *m*; quadro;
piazza *f*; (*sl*) matusa *m*;
* *vt* squadrare; quadrare.
squarely *adv* direttamente.
squash *n* concentrato *m* di
frutta; calca *f*, squash *m*;
* *vt* schiacciare.

squeeze *vt* premere; strizzare,
spremere; * *n* stretta *f*,
strizzata *f.*
squib *n* petardo *m.*
squid *n* calamaro *m.*
squint *vi* essere strabico;
* *n* strabismo *m.*
squirrel *n* scoiattolo *m.*
stab *vt* pugnalare;
* *n* coltellata *f*, fitta *f.*
stability *n* stabilità *f.*
stable *n* stalla *f*; scuderia *f*;
~s maneggio *m*; * *adj* stabile.
staff *n* personale *m*; bastone *m*;
pentagramma *m.*
stag *n* cervo *m.*
stage *n* palco *m*; stadio *m*;
tappa *f.*
stain *vt* macchiare; tingere;
* *n* macchia *f*, colorante *m.*
stainless *adj* inossidabile.
stair *n* scalino: ~s *npl* scale *fpl.*
staircase *n* scala *f.*
stake *n* palo *m*; puntata *f*;
* *vt* (*fig*) rivendicare.
stale *adj* stantio; raffermo.
stalemate *n* stallo *m.*
stalk *vt* inseguire; * *n* gambo
m, torsolo *m.*
stall *n* stalla *f*, bancarella *f*,
stand *m*; ~s platea *f*;
* *vi* andare in stallo; bloccarsi.
stallion *n* stallone *m.*
stamina *n* resistenza *f.*
stammer *vt, vi* balbettare;
* *n* balbuzie *f.*
stamp *vt* pestare; affrancare;
timbrare; * *n* francobollo *m*;
timbro *m.*
stand *vt* mettere; reggere a;
sopportare; offrire; * *vi* stare
in piedi; trovarsi; riposare;
presentarsi: ~ aside farsi da
parte: ~ at rimanere in piedi:
~ back tirarsi indietro:
~ behind stare indietro:
~ by stare vicino: ~ (*fig*)

tenere fede a: ~ clear of stare alla larga da: ~ down ritirarsi: ~ fast tener duro: ~ for alzarsi in piedi: ~ in supplire: ~ in for sostituire: ~ in with andare d'accordo con: ~ off stare alla larga da: ~ out sporgere: ~ out against prendere posizione contro: — my eyes stood out on stalks mi uscivano gli occhi dalla testa: ~ over essere rinviato: ~ up alzarsi in piedi: ~ up against prendere posizione contro: ~ up for essere favorevole a: ~ up to resistere a: ~ with stare con, stare accanto a; * *n* posizione *f*, stand *m*; leggío *m*: — to make a ~ fare resistenza, opporsi fermamente.

standard *n* insegna *f*, stendardo *m*; * *adj* standard, classico.

staple *n* graffetta *f*, prodotto *m* principale; * *adj* base.

stapler *n* cucitrice *f*.

star *n* stella *f*, asterisco *m*; divo *m*.

stare *vt* fissare; * *n* sguardo *m* fisso.

starfish *n* stella *f* di mare.

stark *adj* austero.

starling *n* storno *m*.

starry *adj* stellato.

start *vt* cominciare; iniziare, avviare; * *vi* partire; trasalire: ~ again ricominciare: ~ back saltare indietro, ripartire: ~ for partire per: ~ in on in cominciare a: ~ off balzare via: ~ on cominciare a: ~ out balzare fuori: ~ up balzare su: ~ with cominciare con.

start *n* sobbalzo *m*; inizio *m*; vantaggio *m*.

starvation *n* inedia *f*.

starve *vt* far morire di fame;

* *vi* morire di fame.

starving *adj* affamato.

state *n* stato *m*; condizione *f*, agitazione *f*; * *vt* affermare; indicare.

station *n* stazione *f*; * *vt* stanziare; piazzare.

stationary *adj* fermo, stazionario.

statistics *npl* statistica *f*.

statue *n* statua *f*.

stay *n* soggiorno *m*, degenza *f*, sospensione dell'esecuzione *f*; * *vi* rimanere, restare, stare; alloggiare; * *vt* sospendere, fermare.

steady *adj* fermo, saldo; costante; fisso; * *vt* tenere fermo; calmare.

steak *n* bistecca *f*.

steal *vt* rubare.

steam *n* vapore *m*; * *vt* cuocere a vapore; * *vi* fumare.

steel *n* acciaio *m*.

steep *adj* ripido; * *vt* immergere; impregnare.

stem *n* stelo *m*; * *vt* arrestare.

step *n* passo *m*; misura *f*; gradino *m*; * *vi* fare un passo.

stepbrother *n* fratellastro *m*.

stepdaughter *n* figliastra *f*.

stepfather *n* patrigno *m*.

stepmother *n* matrigna *f*.

stepsister *n* sorellastra *f*.

stepson *n* figliastro *m*.

stereo *n* stereo *m*, stereofonia *f*.

sterile *adj* sterile.

sterilise *vt* sterilizzare.

sterling *n* sterlina *f*; * *adj* genuino.

stew *vt* stufare; * *n* stufato *m*.

stick *n* bastone *m*, bastoncino *m*; asticella *f*; * *vt* incollare; conficcare; *vi* appiccicarsi; bloccarsi; incepparsi; attenersi a: ~ about rimanere vicino: ~ at stare accanto:

~ by essere fedele a: ~ down incollare: ~ fast restare bloccato: ~ in infilare dentro: ~ in with fare comunella con, andare a stare con: ~ indoors restare inchiodato a casa: ~ on incollare, (*fig*) tener duro: ~ out sporgere: ~ out for cercare di ottenere: ~ to attaccarsi, appiccicarsi: ~ together incollare, incollarsi, rimanere insieme: ~ up attaccare, affiggere: ~ up for prendere le parti di qualcuno: ~ with (*fig*) attenersi a, incollare: ~ within restare dentro, restere nell'ambito.

stigma *n* stigma *m*.

stigmatise *vt* stigmatizzare.

stiletto *m* stiletto *m*.

still *adj* fermo, immobile; non gassato; * *n* alambicco; * *adv* ancora.

still life *n* natura morta *f*.

stimulate *vt* stimolare.

stimulation *n* stimolazione *f*.

stimulus *n* stimolo *m*.

sting *vt* pungere; pizzicare; * *vi* bruciare; * *n* pungiglione *m*, puntura *f*.

stint *n* dovere *m*.

stipulate *vt* stabilire.

stipulation *n* stipulazione *f*.

stir *vt* mescolare; agitare; risvegliare; * *vi* muoversi; * *n* scalpore *m*.

stitch *vt* cucire; * *n* punto *m*; maglia *f*, fitta *f*.

stoat *n* ermellino *m*.

stock *n* provvista *f*, stock *m*; bestiame *m*; brodo *m*; stirpe *f*; * *vt* tenere; rifornire.

stocks *npl* titoli *mpl*; * *adj* solito.

stock exchange *n* borsa *f*, valori.

stocking *n* calza *f*.

stomach *n* stomaco *m*, ventre *f*; * *vt* sopportare.

stone *n* pietra *f*; * *vt* lapidare: * **stony** *adj* sassos; ~~deaf sordo come una campana.

stool *n* sgabello *m*.

stoop *vi* chinarsi, abbassarsi.

stop *vt* arrestare, fermare; impedire; sniettere; bloccare; * *vi* cessare, fermarsi; * *n* arresto *m*, pausa *f*, sosta *f*, fermata *f*, punto.

stopover *n* breve sosta *f*.

store *n* provvista *f*, deposito *m*; grande magazzino *m*; * *vt* accumulare; immagazzinare.

stork *n* cicogna *f*.

storm *n* tempesta *f*, temporale *m*; * *vt* prendere d'assalto; * *vi* infuriare.

story *n* storia *f*, trama *f*, racconto *m*; articolo *m*.

stove *n* stufa *f*.

straight *adj* diritto; liscio; onesto; semplice; eterosessuale; * *adv* diritto; direttamente.

strain *vt* tendere, tirare; slogare; affaticare; passare; * *n* tensione *f*; pressione *f*; sforzo *m*; (medical) strappo *m*; (biology) razza *f*.

strange *adj* sconosciuto; strano.

stranger *n* sconosciuto *m*, forestiero *m*.

strangle *vt* strangolare, strozzare.

strap *n* cinturino *m*; spallina *f*, tracollo *m*; * *vt* legare, fasciare.

strategy *n* strategia *f*.

stratum *n* strato *m*.

straw *n* paglia *f*, cannuccia *f*.

strawberry *n* fragola *f*.
stray *vi* smarrirsi;
 * *adj* randagio.
streak *n* striscia *f*, vena *f*;
 * *vt* striare; rigare.
stream *n* ruscello *m*; (*fig*) fiume;
 * *vt* grondare; * *vi* scorrere.
street *n* strada *f*.
strength *n* forza *f*; resistenza *f*;
 gradazione *f* alcolica.
stress *n* sforzo *m*, stress *m*,
 tensione *f*; enfasi *f*;
 * *vt* mettere in rilievo.
stretch *vt* tendere, stendere;
 far bastare; * *vi* stiracchiarsi;
 esagerare; * *n* elasticità *f*,
 distesa *f*; tratto *m*.
stretcher *n* barella *f*.
strict *adj* severo, rigido;
 stretto: ~ly speaking a rigor
 di termini.
strike *vt* colpire; sbattere
 contro; accendere; scoprire;
 * *vi* scioperare; rintoccare:
 ~ at tentare di colpire:
 ~ back replicare, rispondere:
 ~ down abbattere: ~ home
 andare a segno: ~ into
 intervenire, interporsi,
 immischiarsi in: ~ off
 mozzare: ~ (up)on battere:
 ~ over ribattere: ~ through
 cancellare *or* fendere,
 tagliare; * *n* sciopero *m*;
 scoperta *f*, attacco *m*.
striking *adj* impressionante,
 sorprendente, che fa colpo.
string *n* spago *m*; filo *m*, corda
 f; * *vt* infilare; incordare.
stringy *adj* fibroso.
strip *vt* spogliare; sverniciare;
 smontare; * *vi* spogliarsi;
 * *n* striscia *f*, divisa *f*.
stripe *n* riga *f*.
stripper *n* spogliarellista *m* or *f*.
strive *vi* sforzarsi.
stroke; * *n* colpo *m*; carezza *f*

rintocco *m*; * *vt* accarezzare.
stroll *n* passeggiatina *f*;
 * *vi* gironzolare.
strong *adj* forte; resistente;
 concentrato.
strongbox *n* cassaforte *f*.
structure *n* struttura *f*;
 * *vt* strutturare.
struggle *vt*, *vi* lottare;
 * *n* lotta *f*.
strum *vt* (music) strimpellare.
stub *n* mozzicone *m*; matrice.
stubble *n* stoppia *f*; barba *f*
 corta.
stud *n* chiodo *m*; stallone *m*.
student *n* studente *m*.
studio *n* studio *m*.
study *n* studio *m*; * *vt*, *vi*
 studiare.
stuff *n* roba *f*; * *vt* riempire;
 imbottire; farcire.
stumble *vi* inciampare.
stump *n* troncone *m*;
 * *vt* sconcertare.
stun *vt* tramortire.
stunning *adj* splendido.
stuntman *n* controfigura *f*,
 stuntman *m*.
stupid *adj* stupido.
sturgeon *n* storione *m*.
style *n* stile *m*; classe *f*.
stylish *adj* elegante.
stylus *n* puntina *f*.
subconscious *adj* subcosciente;
 * *n* subconscio *m*.
subcontract *vt* subappaltare.
subdue *vt* sottomettere;
 dominare.
subdued *adj* pacato, tenue.
subject *adj* assoggettato;
 soggetto a; * *n* suddito *m*;
 soggetto *m*; argomento *m*;
 materia *f*; * *vt* sottoporre.
subjection *n* sottomissione *f*.
subjective *adj* soggettivo.
subjunctive *adj*, *n*
 congiuntivo *m*.

sublet *vt*, *vi* subaffittare.
sublime *adj* sublime.
subliminal *adj* subliminale.
submarine *n* sommergibile *m*.
submerge *vi* sommergere.
submission *n* sottomissione *f*.
submit *vi* presentare;
  * *vi* cedere a.
subnormal *adj* subnormale.
subordinate *adj* subalterno;
  (grammar) subordinato;
  * *n* subalterno *m*; subordinato
  m; * *vt* subordinare.
subordination *n*
  subordinazione *f*.
subpoena *n* citazione *f*;
  * *vt* citare ingiudizio.
subscribe *vi* abbonarsi;
  approvare.
subside *vi* abbassarsi;
  decrescere; avvallarsi.
subsidence *adj* avvallamento.
subsidiary *n* sussidiario *m*;
  complementare.
subsidise *vt* sovvenzionare.
subsidy *n* sovvenzione *f*.
substance *n* sostanza *f*.
substantial *adj* sostanzioso;
  sostanziale; notevole.
substantiate *vi* comprovare.
substantive *adj*, *n* sostantivo *m*.
substitute *vt*, *vi* sostituire;
  * *n* sostituto *m*.
substitution *n* sostituzione *f*.
subterfuge *n* sotterfugio *m*.
subterranean *adj* sotterraneo.
subtitle *n* sottotitolo *m*.
subtle *adj* sottile.
subtlety *n* sottigliezza *f*.
subtly *adj* sottilmente.
subtract *vi* sottrarre.
subtraction *n* sottrazione *f*.
suburb *n* sobborgo *m*.
suburban *adj* suburbano.
suburbia *n* periferia *f*.
subversion *n* sovversione *f*.
subversive *adj*, *n* sovversivo *m*.

subway *n* sottopassaggio *m*.
succeed *vi* riuscire;
  * *vt* succedere.
succeeding *adj* successivo;
  futuro.
success *n* successo *m*; riuscita *f*.
successful *adj* riuscito;
  affermato.
succession *n* serie *f*;
  successione *f*.
succulent *adj* succulento;
  * *n* pianta *f* grassa.
succumb *vi* soccombere.
such *adj* tale: ~ as come;
  * *adv* talmente, così.
suck *vt*, *vi* succhiare.
suction *n* aspirazione *f*.
sudden *adj* improvviso.
sue *vt* citare; * *vi* intentare
  causa.
suède *n* pelle *f* scamosciata.
suffer *vi* soffrire; tollerare;
  * *vi* soffrire.
suffering *n* sofferenza *f*.
suffice *vi* bastare.
sufficient *adj* sufficiente.
suffocate *vt*, *vi* soffocare.
suffocation *n* soffocazione *f*.
suffrage *n* suffragio *m*.
sugar *n* zucchero *m*;
  * *vt* zuccherare.
sugar beet *n* barbabietola da
  zucchero *f*.
sugar cane *n* canna da
  zucchero *f*.
suggest *vt* suggerire.
suggestion *n* suggerimento *m*;
  punta *f*.
suggestive *adj* spinto.
suicidal *adj* suicida.
suicide *n* suicidio *m*; suicida
  m or *f*.
suit *n* completo *m*; tailleur *m*;
  causa *f*, colore *m*;
  * *vt* adattare; andare bene a;
  contentare.
suitcase *n* valigia *f*.

suite *n* suite *f*; appartamento *m*.
suitor *n* corteggiatore *m*.
sulk *vi* tenere il broncio.
sulphate *adj* solfato.
sulphide *n* solfuro *m*.
sulphur *n* zolfo *m*.
sulphuric *adj* solforico.
sultan *n* sultano *m*.
sultana *n* uva *f* sultanina.
sultry *adj* afoso; passionale.
sum *n* somma *f*: ~ up riassumere.
summary *n* riassunto *m*.
summer *n* estate *f*.
summerhouse *n* padiglione *m*.
summit *n* cima *f*, vetta *f*;
  vertice *m*.
summon *vt* convocare.
sumptuous *adj* sontuoso.
sun *n* sole *m*.
sunbathe *vi* prendere il sole.
sunburn *n* scottatura *f*.
Sunday *n* domenica *f*.
sundial *n* meridiana *f*.
sundry *adj* diversi.
sunflower *n* girasole *m*.
sunglasses *npl* occhiali da sole
  mpl.
sunlight *n* luce del sole *f*.
sunny *adj* assolato, soleggiato;
  radioso.
sunrise *n* alba *f*.
sunset *n* tramonto *m*.
sunshade *n* parasole *m*.
sunstroke *n* insolazione *f*.
super *adj* (*sl*) fantastico.
superb *adj* superbo.
superficial *adj* superficiale.
superhuman *adj* sovrumano.
superior *adj*, *n* superiore *m* or *f*.
superiority *n* superiorità *f*.
superlative *adj*, *n* superlativo *m*.
supermarket *n* supermercato *m*.
supernatural *adj*, *n*
  soprannaturale *m*.
supersede *vt* soppiantare.
superstition *n* superstizione *f*.
supervise *vt* sorvegliare.

supper *n* cena *f*.
supplant *vt* soppiantare.
supple *adj* flessibile.
supplement *n* supplemento *m*;
  * *vt* integrare.
supplication *n* supplica *f*.
supplier *n* fornitore *m*.
supply *vt* fornire; * *n* fornitura *f*.
support *vt* sostenere;
  mantenere; appoggiare;
  * *n* sostegno *m*.
supporter *n* sostenitore *m*;
  tifoso *m*.
suppose *vt* supporre.
supposition *n* supposizione.
suppress *vt* reprimere;
  sopprimere.
suppression *n* repressione *f*.
supremacy *n* supremazia *f*.
supreme *adj* supremo; sommo.
surcharge *n* sovrapprezzo *m*.
sure *adj* sicuro, certo:
  — make ~ of assicursi di;
  * ~ly *adv* sicuramente,
  certamente.
surf *n* (marine) cavalloni *mpl*.
surface *n* superficie *f*;
  * *vt* asfaltare; * *vi* risalire in
  superficie.
surfboard *n* surf *m*.
surge *n* ondata *f*; * *vi* riversarsi.
surgeon *n* chirurgo *m*.
surgery *n* chirurgia *f*,
  ambulatorio *m*.
surgical *adj* chirurgico.
surly *adj* burbero.
surmise *vt* congetturare;
  * *n* congettura *f*.
surmount *vt* sormontare.
surname *n* cognome *m*.
surpass *vt* superare.
surplus *n* surplus *m*; * *adj* di
  sovrappiù.
surprise *vt* sorprendere;
  * *n* sorpresa *f*.
surprising *adj* sorprendente.
surrealism *n* surrealismo *m*.

surrealistic *adj* surreale.
surrender *vi* rinunciare a;
 * *vi* arrendersi; * *n* resa *f*.
surrogate *adj*, *n* surrogato *m*.
surround *vt* circondare;
 * *n* borgo *m*.
survey *vt* guardare;
 esaminare; * *n* indagine *f*,
 perizia *f*, rilevamento *m*.
survive *vt*, *vi* sopravvivere.
susceptibility *n* suscettibilità *f*.
susceptible *adj* predisposto.
suspect *vt* sospettare;
 * *adj* sospetto; * *n* persona
 sospetta *f*.
suspend *vt* sospendere.
suspense *n* suspense *m*;
 incertezza *f*.
suspension *n* sospensione *f*.
suspicion *n* sospetto *m*.
suspicious *adj* sospettoso.
sustain *vt* sostenere; subire.
sustenance *n* nutrimento *m*.
suture *n* sutura *f*.
swallow *n* deglutizione *f*; (bird)
 rondine *f*; * *vt*, *vi* inghiottire.
swamp *n* palude *f*; * *vt* inondare.
swan *n* cigno *m*.
swap *vi* scambiare;
 * *n* scambio *m*.
swarm *n* sciame *m*; * *vi* sciamare.
swathe *vt* avvolgere.
sway *vi* ondeggiare; oscillare;
 * *vt* influenzare;
 * *n* ondeggiamento *m*;
 influenza *f*.
swear *vt*, *vi* giurare,
 bestemmiare: ~ at imprecare,
 bestemmiare: ~ by giurare
 su: ~ for promettere,
 assicurare, garantire: ~ in
 far giurare: ~ off giurare di
 smettere di: ~ to giurare di.
swearword *n* parolaccia *f*.
sweat *n* sudore *m*; * *vt*, *vi* sudare.
sweater *n* maglione *m*.
sweatshirt *n* felpa *f*.

sweep *vt*, *vi* scopare; spazzare;
 * *n* scopata *f*, spazzacamino
 m; ampio gesto *m*.
sweet *adj* dolce, carino;
 * *n* caramella *f*, dolce *m*.
sweetbreads *npl* animelle *fpl*.
sweeten *vt* zuccherare,
 addolcire.
sweetener *n* dolcificante *m*.
sweetheart *n* tesoro *m*.
sweetness *n* dolcezza *f*.
swell *vi* gonfiarsi; * *n* mare
 lungo *m*; * *adj* eccellente,
 ottimo.
swelling *n* gonfiore *m*.
sweltering *adj* soffocante.
swerve *n* sterzata *f*; * *vi* sterzare.
swift *adv* rapido; *n* rondone *m*.
swiftness *n* rapidità *f*.
swill *vt* risciacquare;
 tracannare; * *n* brodaglia *f*.
swim *vt*, *vi* nuotare;
 * *n* nuotata *f*.
swimming *n* nuoto *m*.
swimming pool *n* piscina *f*.
swimsuit *n* costume da bagno *m*.
swindle *vt* truffare; * *n* truffa *f*.
swindler *n* imbroglione *m*.
swine *n* suino, porco, maiale;
 (*vulg*) stronzo.
swing *vt* dondolare; brandire;
 influenzare; * *vi* dondolare;
 penzolare; * *n* oscillazione *f*,
 altalena *f*, ritmo *m*; swing *m*.
switch *n* interruttore *m*;
 mutamento *m*; * *vt* cambiare;
 invertire: ~ off spegnere:
 ~ on accendere.
swoon *vi* svenire;
 * *n* svenimento *m*.
swoop *vi* scendere in picchiata;
 fare una incursione;
 * *n* picchiata *f*, incursione *f*.
sword *n* spada *f*.
swordfish *n* pesce *f* spada.
sycamore *n* sicomoro *m*.
symbol *n* simbolo *m*.

symbolic *adj* simbolico.
symmetry *n* simmetria *f*.
sympathy *n* comprensione *f*.
symphony *n* sinfonia *f*.
synagogue *n* sinagoga *f*.
syndicate *n* sindacato *m*.
syndrome *n* sindrome *f*.
synod *n* sinodo *m*.
synonym *n* sinonimo *m*.
synonymous *adj* sinonimo di.
synopsis *n* sinossi *f*.
syntax *n* sintassi *f*.
synthesis *n* sintesi *f*.
syphilis *n* sifilide *f*.
syringe *n* siringa *f*;
  * *vt* siringare.
system *n* sistema *m*.
systematic *adj* sistematico.

T

tabby *n* gatto soriano *m*, gatto
  tigrato *m*.
table *n* tavolo *m*; tavola *f*,
  tabella *f*.
table d'hôte pasto a prezzo
  fisso *m*; * *vt* presentare.
tablecloth *n* tovaglia *f*.
tablespoon *n* cucchiaio da
  portata *m*.
tablet *n* compressa *f*, pastiglia *f*.
taboo *n* tabù *m*.
tacit *adj* tacito.
tack *n* bulletta *f*, (marine)
  bordo *m*; (sewing) punto *m*
  d'imbastitura; * *vt* fissare
  con chiodi; imbastire;
  * *vi* bordeggiare.
tackle *n* paranco *m*;
  attrezzatura *f*; * *vt* affrontare.
tact *n* tatto *m*.
tactical *adj* tattico.
tactless *adj* indelicato.
tadpole *n* girino *m*.
taffeta *n* taffettà *m*.
tag *n* etichetta *f*.

tail *n* coda *f*; * *vt* pedinare.
tailor *n* sarto *m*;
  * *vt* confezionare.
taint *vt* infangare; * *n* macchia *f*.
take *vt* prendere; portare;
  accettare; contenere;
  sopportare; *vi* attecchire:
  ~ aback cogliere di sorpresa:
  ~ aboard prendere a bordo:
  ~ about accompagnare:
  ~ across fare attraversare:
  ~ after inseguire *or* prendere
  da: ~ against prendersela
  con: ~ along portare con sè:
  ~ amiss aversela a male:
  ~ apart prendere in disparte
  or fare a pezzi: ~ ashore
  sbarcare: ~ away portare via,
  togliere: ~ back riprendere:
  ~ before portare davanti a,
  presentare: ~ below
  accompagnare (di sotto):
  ~ down calare dall'alto,
  portare giù: ~ from prendere
  da: ~ home accompagnare a
  casa: ~ ill prendere male
  qualcosa: ~ in portare
  dentro: ~ off togliere,
  decollare: ~ on prendere a
  bordo: ~ out tirare fuori:
  ~ out on fare ricadere su:
  ~ over, round portare (in
  giro), accompagnare:
  ~ someone under one's wing
  prendere qualcuno sotto le
  proprie ali: ~ through
  portere oltre, portare a
  compimento: ~ to portare a:
  ~ unawares prendere alla
  sprovvista: ~ up alzare,
  sollevare: ~ up on prendere in
  parola: ~ up something with
  someone sollevare una
  questione con qualcuno.
talc, talcum powder *n* talco *m*.
talent *n* talento *m*.
talk *vt*, *vi* parlare: ~ about

222

parlare di: ~ at parlare a
qualcuno con sussiego:
~ away continuare a parlare:
~ back replicare: ~ down
ridurre al silenzio or parlare
con sussiego: ~ into
convincere: ~ of parlare di:
~ on continuare a parlare:
~ out of dissuadere:
~ over discutere a fondo:
~ round girare intorno or
convincere: ~ through
trattare in modo esauriente:
~ to parlare a: ~ up alzare la
voce, parlare più forte: ~ with
parlare con.

talk n conversazione f,
conferenza f.

tall adj alto.

tame adj addomesticato;
* vt addomesticare; domare.

tamper vt manomettere.

tampon n tampone m.

tan vi abbronzarsi;
* n abbronzatura f.

tangerine n mandarino m.

tangle vt aggrovigliare;
* n groviglio m.

tank n serbatoio m; cisterna f,
carro armato m.

tanker n autocisterna f, nave
cisterna f.

tantrum n collera f.

tap vt intercettare; sfruttare;
* vi bussare; * n rubinetto m;
colpetto m.

tape n nastro m; fettuccia f;
* vt registrare.

tape recorder n registratore m.

tapestry n arazzo m.

tar n catrame m.

tarantula n tarantola f.

target n bersaglio m;
obiettivo m.

tariff n tariffa f.

tarragon n (botany)
dragoncello m.

tart adj aspro; * n crostata f;
(sl) signora di facili costumi
f, puttana f.

taste n gusto m; sapore m;
* vt assaggiare; assaporare.

Taurus n Toro m.

tavern n taverna f.

tax n tassa f; imposta f;
* vt tassare; gravare.

taxi n taxi m; * vi rullare,
andare in taxi.

tea n tè m.

teach vt, vi insegnare.

teacher n insegnante m or f,
maestro m; professore m.

teaching n insegnamento m.

team n squadra f, équipe f.

teamwork n lavoro di gruppo
or di squadra or d'équipe m.

teapot n teiera f.

tear vt strappare; * n strappo m.

tear n lacrima f.

tease vt stuzzicare; * n burlone m.

teaspoon n cucchiaino m.

teat n tettarella f.

technical adj tecnico.

technique n tecnica f.

technology n tecnologia f.

teddy (bear) n orsacchiotto m.

teenage adj adolescenziale.

teenager n adolescente m or f,
teenager m or f.

teeth npl denti mpl.

telecommunications npl
telecomunicazioni fpl.

telegram n telegramma m.

telephone n telefono m.

telescope n telescopio m.

televise vt trasmettere per
televisione.

television set n televisore m.

telex n telex m.

tell vr dire; raccontare;
indicare; distinguere;
* vi parlare; sapere: ~ about
dire di, raccontare: ~ against
andare a discapito: ~ apart

distinguere: ~ of dire, parlare di: ~ off (*sl*) sgridare: ~ on farsi sentire, fare la spia: re~ raccontare di nuovo.

temper *vt* moderare; * *n* indole *f*, temperamento *m*; collera *f*.

temperament *n* temperamento *m*.

temperature *n* temperatura *f*.

temple *n* tempio *m*; (anatomy) tempia *f*.

temporarily *adv* temporaneamente.

temporary *adj* provvisorio.

tempt *vt* tentare.

temptation *n* tentazione *f*.

ten *adj*, *n* dieci *m*.

tenacity *n* tenacia *f*.

tenancy *n* contratto *m* d'affitto.

tenant *n* inquilino *m*.

tendency *n* tendenza *f*.

tender *adj* tenero, sensibile; * *n* tender *m*; offerta *f*; * *vt* presentare; offrire.

tenement *n* casamento *m*.

tennis *n* tennis *m*.

tennis court *n* campo da tennis *m*.

tennis racket *n* racchetta da tennis *f*.

tense *n* (grammar) tempo *m*; * *adj* teso; * *vt* tendere.

tension *n* tensione *f*.

tent *n* tenda *f*.

tenth *adj*, *n* decimo *m*.

terminal *adj* incurabile; * *n* terminale *m*; capolinea *m*.

terminate *vt*, *vi* terminare.

terrace *n* terrazza *f*.

terrible *adj* terribile.

terrier *n* terrier *m*.

terrific *adj* stupendo; enorme.

terrify *vt* terrificare.

terror *n* terrore *m*; peste *f*.

terrorism *n* terrorismo *m*.

test *n* prova *f* collaudo *m*;

esame *m*; * *vt* controllare; collaudare; sperimentare.

testicle *n* testicolo *m*.

tetanus *n* tetano *m*.

text *n* testo *m*.

textbook *n* libro *m* di testo.

textile *adj* tessile: * ~s *npl* tessuti *mpl*.

texture *n* consistenza *f*.

than *conj* che; di.

thank *vt* ringraziare.

thankful *adj* grato, riconoscente.

that *adj* quel; * *pron* ciò; * *dem pron* così; * *rel pron* che; * *conj* che: — so ~ affinché.

the *def art* il, lo, là, i, gli, le.

theatre *n* teatro *m*.

theft *n* furto *m*.

their *poss adj* loro.

them *pron* gli; loro.

theme *n* tema *m*.

themselves *pron* si; se stessi.

then *adv* allora; poi: — now and ~ ogni tanto.

theory *n* teoria *f*.

therapy *n* terapia *f*.

there *adv* la, lì.

thermal *adj* termale.

thermometer *n* termometro *m*.

these *dem adj*, *dem pron* questi.

they *pers pron* essi.

thick *adj* grosso; spesso; ottuso.

thief *n* ladro *m*.

thigh *n* coscia *f*.

thin *adj* sottile; magro; * *vt* diradarsi.

thing *n* cosa *f*: ~s *npl* roba *f*.

think *vt* pensare; credere: ~ again ripensarci: ~ ahead guardare avanti: ~ aloud pensare a voce alta: ~ back ripensare, tornare con la memoria: ~ of ripensare a, ricordare: ~ out riflettere bene su: ~ over riconsiderare:

~ up escogitare.
thinker *n* pensatore *m*.
thinking *adj* ragionevole;
  * *n* pensiero *m*.
third *adj, n* terzo *m*.
thirst *n* sete *f*.
thirsty *adj* assetato.
thirteen *num* tredici.
thirteenth *num* tredicesimo.
thirtieth *num* trentesimo.
thirty *num* trenta.
this *dem adj, dem pron* questo.
thorn *n* spina *f*.
thorough *adj* minuzioso;
  approfondito.
those *dem adj* quel; * *dem pron*
  quelli.
though *conj* benché;
  * *adv* tuttavia.
thought *n* pensiero *m*.
thoughtful *adj* pensieroso;
  gentile.
thoughtless *adj* sconsiderato.
thousand *adj, n* mille *m*.
thousandth *adj, n* millesimo *m*.
thrash *vt* percuotere.
thread *n* filo *m*; * *vt* infilare.
threat *n* minaccia *f*.
three *num* tre.
thrill *vt* entusiasmare;
  * *vi* fremere; * *n* brivido;
  fremito *m*.
thriller *n* thriller *m*.
thrive *vi* prosperare.
thriving *adj* fiorente.
throat *n* gola *f*.
throne *n* trono *m*.
through *prep* attraverso; per;
  * *adj* finito; di passaggio.
throughout *prep* in tutto;
  * *adv* dappertutto.
throw *n* lancio *m*.
throw *vt* lanciare; gettare:
  ~ about gettare qua e là:
  ~ across gettare su: ~ around
  gettare attorno a: ~ aside
  gettare da una parte: ~ away

gettare via: ~ back buttare
indietro: ~ down buttare giù:
  ~ in(to) buttare dentro: ~ off
gettare via: ~ on aggiungere:
  ~ out buttare fuori: ~ over
rilanciare: ~ overboard
gettare a mare: ~ together
raccogliere alla svelta: ~ up
lanciate in aria *or* vomitare.
thrush *n* tordo *m*; (medical)
  candida.
thug *n* teppista *m* or *f*.
thumb *n* pollice *m*.
thunder *n* tuono *m*; * *vi* tonare.
Thursday *n* giovedì *m*.
thyme *n* (botany) timo *m*.
tick *n* tic tac *m*; segno *m*;
  zecca *f*; * *vi* spuntare;
  ticchettare.
ticket *n* biglietto *m*.
tickle *vt* fare il solletico a.
tidal *adj* (marine) di marca.
tide *n* marea *f*, ondata *f*.
tidy *adj* ordinato; * *vt* mettere
  in ordine.
tie *vt* legare; allacciare;
  pareggiare: ~ back raccogliere:
  ~ down assicurare: ~ in
  collegarsi: ~ on attaccare
  con lo spago: ~ up legare,
  fasciare * *n* cravatta *f*,
  pareggio *m*.
tiger *n* tigre *f*.
tight *adj* stretto; sbronzo.
tile *n* tegola *f*, mattonella *f*;
  * *vt* piastrellare.
till *vt* coltivare; incassare;
  * *n* cassa *f*; * *prep* fino a.
time *n* tempo *m*; momento *m*;
  periodo *m*; ora *f*, era *f*, volta *f*;
  * *vt* programmare;
  cronometrare.
timetable *n* orario *m*.
timid *adj* timido.
tin *n* stagno *m*; lattina *f*;
  * *vt* inscatolare.
tinfoil *n* carta stagnola *f*.

tin opener *n* apriscatole *m*.

tiny *adj* minuscolo.

tip *n* punta *f*, mancia *f*,
suggerimento *m*; * *vt* dare la
mancia a; pronosticare;
rovesciare; * *vi* rovesciarsi.

tire *vt* stancare.

tissue *n* velina *f*, fazzolettino di
carta *m*; (anatomy) tessuto *m*.

tit *n* cincia *f*.

title *n* titolo *m*.

to *prep* a; secondo; per; da.

toad *n* rospo *m*.

toadstool *n* fungo velenoso *m*.

toast *vt* tostare; brindare; * *n*
pane tostato *m*; brindisi *m*.

tobacco *n* tabacco *m*.

tobacconist *n* tabaccaio *m*.

today *adv*, *n* oggi *m*.

toe *n* dito del piede *m*.

together *adv* insieme.

toilet *n* gabinetto *m*, toilette *f*.

toilet paper *n* carta igienica *f*.

toiletries *npl* articoli da
toilette *m*.

token *n* buono *m*; segno *m*;
* *adj* simbolico.

toll *n* pedaggio *m*.

tomato *n* pomodoro *m*.

tomb *n* tomba *f*.

tomorrow *adv*, *n* domani *m*.

ton *n* tonnellata *f*.

tone tono *m*; * *vi* intonarsi:
~ down attenuare.

tongue *n* lingua *f*.

tonic *n* (medical) ricostituente
m; acqua tonica *f*.

tonight *adv* stasera.

tonsil *n* tonsilia *f*.

tonsillitis *n* tonsillite *f*.

too *adv* troppo, anche.

tool *n* arnese *m*, attrezzo *m*,
strumento *m*.

tooth *n* dente *m*.

toothache *n* mal *m* di denti.

toothbrush *n* spazzolino *m* da
denti.

toothpaste *n* dentifricio *m*.

top *n* cima *f*, superficie *f*,
tappo *m*; trottola *f*;
— big ~ tendone *m*;
* *adj* ultimo; migliore;
* *vt* sormontare; superare.

topaz *n* topazio *m*.

topic *n* argomento *m*.

topography *n* topografia *f*.

torch *n* torcia *f* (*sl*) pila *f*.

torment *vi* tormentare;
* *n* tormento *m*.

tornado *n* tornado *m*.

torso *n* torso *m*.

tortoise *n* tartaruga *f*.

torture *n* tortura *f*;
* *vt* torturare.

total *adj* totale: * ~ly *adv*
conipietamente; * *n* totale *m*;
* *vt* ammontare.

totalitarian *adj* totalitario.

touch *vt* toccare;
commuovere; uguagliare:
~ at fare scalo, approdare:
~ on toccare, sfiorare: ~ up
ritoccare.

touch *n* tatto *m*; tocco *m*;
pizzico *m*; contatto *m*.

tough *adj* resistente; faticoso.

tour *n* giro *m*; tournée *f*, visita *f*;
* *vt* fare un giro.

tourism *n* turismo *m*.

tourist *n* turista *m* or *f*.

tourist office *n* ufficio del
turismo *m*.

toward(s) *prep* verso.

towel *n* asciugamano *m*.

tower *n* torre *f*.

town *n* città *f*.

tow rope *n* cavo per rimorchio *m*.

toxic *adj* tossico.

toxin *n* tossina *f*.

toy *n* giocattolo *m*;
* ~ with *vi* giocherellare.

toy boy *n* gigolo *m*.

trachea *n* trachea *f*.

track *n* orma *f*, sentiero *m*;

pista *f*, binario *m*; * *vt* essere
sulle tracce di.
tractor *n* trattore *m*.
trade *n* commercio *m*;
industria *f*, mestiere *f*;
* *vt* barattare;
* *vi* commerciare.
tradition *n* tradizione *f*.
traditional *adj* tradizionale.
traffic *n* traffico *m*;
* *vi* trafficare.
traffic lights *npl* semaforo *m*.
tragedy *n* tragedia *f*.
tragic *adj* tragico:
* ~ally *adv* tragicamente.
train *vt* addestrare; alienare;
* *vi* fare tirocinio; * *n* treno *m*;
codazzo *m*; serie *f*.
traitor *n* traditore *m*.
tram *n* tram *m*.
tramp *n* vagabondo *m*;
* *vi* camminare pesantemente.
tranquil *adj* tranquillo.
tranquilliser *n* tranquillante *m*.
transatlantic *adj*
transatlantico.
transfer *vt* trasferire;
* *n* trasferimento *m*.
transform *vt* trasformare.
transformation *n*
trasformazione *f*.
transfusion *n* trasfusione *f*.
translate *vt*, *vi* tradurre.
translation *n* traduzione *f*.
translator *n* traduttore *m*.
transparent *adj* trasparente.
transport *vt* trasportare;
* *n* trasporto *m*.
transportation *n* trasporto *m*.
transvestite *n* travestito *m*.
trap *n* trappola *f*, calesse *m*;
* *vt* intrappolare.
trauma *n* trauma *m*.
traumatic *adj* traumatizzante.
travel *vi* viaggiare: ~ back
tornare indietro: ~ by (on)
viaggiare per mezzo di:

~ over viaggiare per.
travel *n* viaggio *m*.
tray *n* vassoio *m*.
treasure *n* tesoro *m*;
* *vt* stimare.
treasurer *n* tesoriere *m*.
treat *vt* trattare; considerare;
offrire; curare; * *n* sorpresina *f*.
treatment *n* trattamento *m*.
treaty *n* trattato *m*.
treble *adj* triplo; alto;
* *vt* triplicare.
tree *n* albero *m*.
trellis *n* graticcio *m*.
tremble *vi* tremare;
* *n* tremito *m*.
tremor *n* scossa *f*.
trial *n* processo *m*; prova *f*.
triangle *n* triangolo *m*.
triangular *adj* triangolare.
tribal *adj* tribale.
tribe *n* tribù *f*.
trick *n* scherzo *m*; trucco *m*;
inganno *m*; * *vt* ingannare.
trickery *n* astuzia *f*.
tricky *adj* difficile.
trifle *n* sciocchezza *f*, zuppa *f*
inglese; * *vi* prendere alla
leggera.
trim *adj* snello; * *n* spuntata *f*;
* *vt* spuntare.
Trinity *n* Trinità *f*.
trio *n* trio *m*.
trip *vi* inciampare; * *n* viaggio
m; gita *f*, trip *m*.
tripe *n* trippa *f*.
triple *adj* triplo.
triumph *n* trionfo *m*.
troop *n* squadrone *m*: ~s *npl*
truppe *fpl*.
trophy *n* trofeo *m*.
tropical *adj* tropicale.
trot *n* trotto *m*; * *vi* trottare.
trouble *vt* preoccupare;
disturbare; * *n* problemi *mpl*;
guai *mpl*.
trough *n* mangiatoia *f*, cavo *m*.

trousers *npl* pantaloni *mpl*.
trout *n* trota *f*.
trowel *n* cazzuola *f*.
truck *n* camion *m*.
true *adj* vero; sincero; fedele.
trumpet *n* tromba *f*.
trunk *n* tronco *m*; proboscide *f*, baule *m*.
trust *n* fiducia *f*, (commercial) trust *m*; * *vt* fidarsi.
truth *n* verità *f*.
try *vt* provare; cercare; verificare; processare; * *vi* provare: ~ again riprovare: ~ on provare, misurare: ~ out mettere alla prova; * *n* tentativo *m*.
tsar *n* zar *m*.
T-shirt *n* maglietta *f*.
tuberculosis *n* tubercolosi *f*.
Tuesday *n* martedì *m*.
tuition *n* lezioni *fpl*.
tulip *n* tulipano *m*.
tumbler *n* bicchiere *m*.
tummy *n* pancia *f*.
tumour *n* tumore *m*.
tuna *n* tonno *m*.
tune *n* melodia *f*; * *vt*, *vt* accordare.
tunic *n* tunica *f*.
turkey *n* tacchino *m*.
turmoil *n* confusione *f*.
turn *vt* girare; voltare; trasformare; * *vi* girarsi; virare; alzare: ~ about girarsi: ~ adrift mandare alla deriva: ~ again girare: ~ against rivoltarsi contro: ~ around girarsi, voltarsi: ~ aside girare la testa: ~ away andare via, scostarsi: ~ back tornare indietro: ~ down abbassare, calare: ~ from allontanarsi: ~ in piegare in dentro: ~ inside out rivoltare: ~ into trasformare in:

~ off chiudere: ~ on aprire: ~ out spegnere: ~ over girarsi: ~ to girarsi verso, rivolrersi a: ~ under piegare in giù, rincalzare: ~ up voltare in sù, arricciare: ~ upside down rivoltare, capovolgere; * *n* giro *m*; curva *f*, crisi *f*, turno *m*.
turquoise *adj*, *n* turchese *m*.
turtle *n* tartaruga *f* acquatica.
tutor *n* insegnante *m* privato.
twelfth *n*, *adj* dodicesimo *m*.
twelve *n* dodici *m*.
twentieth *n*, *adj* ventesimo *m*.
twenty *n* venti *m*.
twice *adv* due volte.
twin *adj*, *n* gemello *m*.
twine *vi* attorcigliarsi; * *n* cordicella *f*.
twist *vt* attorcigliare; * *vi* slogarsi; attorcigliarsi; * *n* piega *f*, sviluppo *m*; twist *m*.
two *adj*, *n* due *m*.
tycoon *n* magnate *m*, tycoon *m*.
type *n* tipo *m*; carattere *m*; * *vt* battere a macchina.
typhoid *n* tifoidea *f*.
typhoon *n* tifone *m*.
typhus *n* tifo *m*.
typical *adj* tipico.
tyranny *n* tirannia *f*.
tyrant *n* tiranno *m*.
tyre *n* gomma *f*.

U

udder *n* mammella *f*.
ugh *excl* puah!
ugliness *n* bruttezza *f*.
ugly *adj* brutto.
ulcer *n* ulcera *f*.
ultramarine *adj*, *n* oltremarino *m*.
umbrella *n* ombrello *m*.
umpire *n* arbitro *m*.

unable *adj* incapace.
unaccountable *adj* inesplicabile.
unaccustomed *adj* non abituato.
unacknowleged *adj* senza risposta.
unacquainted *adj* non al corrente; ignorante di.
unadorned *adj* disadorno.
unadulterated *adj* puro.
unaffected *adj* naturale.
unaided *adj* senza aiuto.
unalterable *adj* inalterabile.
unaltered *adj* inalterato.
unambitious *adj* poco ambizioso.
unanimity *n* unanimità *f*.
unanimous *adj* unanime.
unanswerable *adj* irrefutabile.
unapproachable *adj* inavvicinabile.
unarmed *adj* disarmato.
unashamed *adj* sfrontato.
unassuming *adj* modesto.
unattached *adj* staccato; libero.
unattainable *adj* irraggiungibile.
unattended *adj* incustodito.
unauthorised *adj* non autorizzato.
unavailable *adj* non disponibile.
unavoidable *adj* inevitabile.
unaware *adj* ignaro.
unbalanced *adj* squilibrato.
unbearable *adj* insopportabile.
unbecoming *adj* indecoroso, sconveniente.
unbelievable *adj* incredibile.
unbiased *adj* imparziale.
unblemished *adj* senza macchia.
unblock *vt* sbloccare.
unborn *adj* non ancora nato.
unbounded *adj* sconfinato.
unbreakable *adj* infrangibile.
unbroken *adj* intatto; ininterrotto; insuperato.

unbutton *vt* sbottonare.
uncalled-for *adj* fuori luogo.
uncertain *adj* incerto.
uncertainty *n* incertezza *f*.
unchallenged *adj* incontestato.
unchanged *adj* invariato.
uncharitable *adj* severo.
unchecked *adj* incontrollato.
unchristian *adj* poco cristiano.
uncle *n* zio *m*.
uncombed *adj* spettinato.
uncomfortable *adj* scomodo.
uncomfortably *adv* in modo disagevole.
uncommon *adj* insolito.
uncompromising *adj* assoluto.
unconcerned *adj* tranquillo.
unconditional *adj* incondizionato.
unconfirmed *adj* non confermato.
unconnected *adj* sconnesso.
unconscious *adj* privo di sensi; inconscio; * *n* inconscio *m*.
unconstrained *adj* disinvolto.
uncontrollable *adj* incontrollabile.
unconventional *adj* non convenzionale.
unconvincing *adj* non convincente.
uncooked *adj* crudo.
uncorrected *adj* non riveduto.
uncover *vt* scoprire.
uncultivated *adj* incolto.
uncut *adj* non tagliato.
undamaged *adj* intatto.
undaunted *adj* imperterrito.
undecided *adj* indeciso.
undefined *adj* indefinito.
undeniable *adj* innegabile.
under *prep* sotto; secondo; * *adv* sotto.
undercarriage *n* carello *m* d'atterraggio.
undercharge *vt* far pagare di meno.

undercoat *n* prima mano *f*.
undercover *adj* clandestino.
undercurrent *n* vena nascosta *f*.
undercut *vt* vendere a minor
prezzo di.
underdeveloped *adj*
sottosviluppato.
underestimate *vt* sottovalutare.
underexposed *adj* sottoesposto.
underfed *adj* denutrito.
undergo *vt* subire.
undergraduate *n* studente
universitario *m*.
underground *n* (railway)
metropolitana *f*; controcul-
tura *f*; * *adj* sotterraneo.
undergrowth *n* sottobosco *m*.
underhand *adj* equivoco.
underline *vt* sottolineare.
undermine *vt* minare.
underneath *prep*, *adv* sotto.
undernourished *adj* denutrito.
underpaid *adj* mal pagato.
underpants *npl* slip *m*.
underpass *n* sottopassaggio *m*.
underplay *vt* minimizzare.
underprivileged *adj*
svantaggiato.
underrate *vt* sottovalutare.
under-secretary *n*
sottosegretario *m*.
underside *n* parte *f* di sotto.
undersigned *adj*, *n*
sottoscritto *m*.
understand *vt* capire; credere;
* *vi* capire.
understandable *adj*
comprensibile.
understanding *n*
comprensione *f*, intesa *f*;
* *adj* comprensivo.
understate *vt* sminuire.
understatement *n*
dichiarazione attenuata *or*
troppo modesta *f*.
understudy *n* doppio *m*.
undertake *vt* assumersi.

undertaker *n* impresario di
pompe funebri *m* (*sl*) becchino *n*.
undertaking *n* impresa *f*,
assicurazione *f*.
undervalue *vt* sottovalutare.
underwater *adj* subacqueo;
sottomarino.
underwear *n* biancheria *f*,
intima.
underweight *adj* sottopeso.
underwrite *vt* sottoscrivere.
undeserved *adj* immeritato.
undeserving *adj* indegno.
undesirable *adj* sgradevole.
undetermined *adj*
indeterminato.
undiminished *adj* non diminuito.
undisciplined *adj*
indisciplinato.
undisguised *adj* palese.
undismayed *adj* imperterrito.
undisputed *adj* incontrastato.
undisturbed *adj* imperturbato.
undivided *adj* completo.
undo *vt* disfare; slacciare.
undoubted *adj* indubbio.
undress *vt* spogliare;
* *vi* spogliarsi.
undue *adj* esagerato.
undying *adj* imperituro.
unearth *vt* dissotterrare.
unearthly *adj* innaturale.
uneasy *adj* inquieto; precario.
uneducated *adj* incolto.
unemotional *adj* impassibile.
unemployed *adj*, *n*
disoccupato *m*.
unemployment *n*
disoccupazione *f*.
unending *adj* interminabile.
unendurable *adj* insopportabile.
unenviable *adj* poco
invidiabile.
unequal *adj* disuguale.
unequalled *adj* insuperato.
unequivocal *adj*
inequivocabile.

uneven *adj* ineguale;
  accidentato.
unexpected *adj* inatteso.
unexplained *adj* inspiegato.
unexplored *adj* inesplorato.
unfailing *adj* immancabile.
unfair *adj* ingiusto.
unfaithful *adj* infedele.
unfaltering *adj* risoluto.
unfamiliar *adj* sconosciuto.
unfashionable *adj* fuori moda.
unfasten *vt* slacciare.
unfavourable *adj* sfavorevole.
unfeeling *adj* insensibile.
unfinished *adj* incompiuto.
unfit *adj* inadatto.
unflagging *adj* instancabile.
unfold *vt* spiegare;
  * *vi* schiudersi.
unforeseeable *adj*
  imprevedibile.
unforeseen *adj* imprevisto.
unforgettable *adj*
  indimenticabile.
unforgiveable *adj*
  imperdonabile.
unfortunate *adj* sfortunato.
unfounded *adj* infondato.
unfriendly *adj* ostile.
unfruitful *adj* infruttuoso.
unfurnished *adj* non
  ammobiliato.
ungainly *adj* goffo.
ungovernable *adj*
  ingovernabile.
ungrateful *adj* ingrato.
unhappily *adv*
  sfortunatamente.
unhappiness *n* infelicità *f*.
unhappy *adj* infelice.
unharmed *adj* illeso.
unhealthy *adj* malsano;
  malaticcio.
unheeding *adj* disattento.
unhinge *vt* scardinare.
unhook *vt* sganciare.
unhoped-for *adj* insperato.

unhurt *adj* sano e salvo.
unhygienic *adj* insalubre.
unicorn *n* unicorno *m*.
unification *n* unificazione *f*.
uniform *adj* uniforme;
  * *n* divisa *f*.
uniformity *n* uniformità *f*.
unify *vt* unire; unificare.
unilateral *adj* unilaterale.
unimaginable *adj*
  inimmaginabile.
unimpaired *adj* intatto.
unimpeachable *adj*
  irreprensibile.
unimportant *adj* trascurabile.
uninformed *adj* non al corrente.
uninhabitable *adj* inabitabile.
uninhabited *adj* disabitato.
uninjured *adj* incolume.
unintelligible *adj*
  inintelligibile.
unintentional *adj* involontario.
uninterested *adj* indifferente.
uninterrupted *adj*
  ininterrotto.
uninvited *adj* non invitato.
union *n* unione *f*, sindacato *m*.
unionist *n* sindacalista *m*.
unionise *vt* sindacalizzare.
unique *adj* unico: * ~ly *adv*
  eccezionalmente.
unison *n* unisono *m*.
unit *n* unità *f*; reparto *m*.
unite *vt* unire; unificare.
united *adj* unito.
unity *n* unità *f*, unione *f*.
universal *adj* universale.
universe *n* universo *m*.
university *n* università *f*.
unjust *adj* ingiusto.
unjustified *adj* ingiustificato.
unkempt *adj* scarmigliato.
unkind *adj* scortese; crudele.
unknowingly *adv*
  inconsapevolmente.
unknown *adj* sconosciuto,
  ignoto.

unlawful *adj* illecito.
unleash *vt* liberare.
unless *conj* a meno che.
unlicensed *adj* senza licenza.
unlike *adj* dissimile.
unlikely *adj* improbabile;
 inverosimile.
unlikelihood *n* improbabilità *f*.
unlimited *adj* illimitato.
unlined *adj* sfoderato.
unload *vt, vi* scaricare.
unlock *vt* aprire.
unluckily *adv* purtroppo.
unlucky *adj* sfortunato;
 disgraziato.
unmanageable *adj* intrattabile;
 poco maneggevole.
unmarried *adj* scapolo (*man*);
 nubile (*woman*).
unmask *vt* smascherare.
unmentionable *adj*
 innominabile.
unmerited *adj* immeritato.
unmistakable *adj*
 inconfondibile.
unmotivated *adj* immotivato.
unmoved *adj* indifferente.
unnamed *adj* anonimo.
unnatural *adj* innaturale.
unnecessary *adj* non
 necessario.
unneighbourly *adj* non da
 buon vicino.
unnoticed *adj* inosservato.
unobserved *adj* inosservato.
unobtainable *adj* introvabile.
unobtrusive *adj* discreto.
unoccupied *adj* libero; vuoto.
unoffending *adj* inoffensivo.
unofficial *adj* ufficioso.
unorganised *adj* disorganizzato.
unorthodox *adj* eterodosso.
unpack *vt* disfare.
unpaid *adj* non retribuito.
unpalatable *adj* immangiabile.
unparalleled *adj* senza pari.
unpleasant *adj* spiacevole.

unpleasantness *n*
 sgradevolezza *f*.
unpolished *adj* non lucidato.
unpopular *adj* impopolare.
unpractised *adj* inesercitato.
unprecedented *adj* senza
 precedenti.
unpredictable *adj*
 imprevedibile.
unprejudiced *adj* obiettivo.
unprepared *adj* impreparato.
unproductive *adj*
 improduttivo.
unprofitable *adj* non redditizio.
unpronounceable *adj*
 impronunciabile.
unprotected *adj* indifeso.
unpublished *adj* inedito.
unpunished *adj* impunito.
unqualified *adj* non
 qualificato; incondizionato.
unquestionable *adj*
 indiscutibile.
unquestioned *adj* indiscusso.
unravel *vt* dipanare.
unreadable *adj* illeggibile.
unreal *adj* irreale.
unrealistic *adj* illusorio.
unreasonable *adj* irrazionale;
 irragionevole.
unrecognisable *adj*
 irriconoscibile.
unrefined *adj* greggio.
unrelated *adj* senza nesso; non
 imparentato.
unrelenting *adj* implacabile.
unreliable *adj* non attendibile.
unrepeatable *adj* irripetibile.
unrepentant *adj* impenitente.
unreserved *adj* incondizionato.
unripe *adj* acerbo.
unsafe *adj* pericoloso.
unsatisfactory *adj* poco
 soddisfacente; insufficiente.
unsatisfying *adj*
 insoddisfacente.
unsavoury *adj* poco

raccomandabile.
unscathed *adj* indenne.
unscrew *vt* svitare.
unseenily *adj* indecoroso.
unseen *adj* inosservato.
unsettle *vt* scombussolare.
unsettled *adj* instabile.
unshaken *adj* non scosso.
unsightly *adj* non bello a
  vedersi.
unskilful *adj* inesperto.
unskilled *adj* non specializzato.
unsociable *adj* poco socievole.
unsound *adj* cagionevole.
unspeakable *adj* indicibile.
unstable *adj* instabile.
unsteady *adj* vacillante.
unsuccessful *adj* non riuscito.
unsuitable *adj* inadatto;
  inopportuno.
unsure *adj* incerto.
unsympathetic *adj* non
  comprensivo.
untamed *adj* indomato.
untangle *vt* sbrogliare.
untenable *adj* insostenibile.
unthinkable *adj* impensabile.
unthinking *adj* irriguardoso.
untidy *adj* disordinato.
until *prep* fino a; * *conj* finché.
untimely *adj* prematuro.
untiring *adj* infaticabile.
untold *adj* mai rivelato.
untouchable *n* intoccabile *m*
  or *f*, paria *m*.
untried *adj* intentato;
  inesperto; non processato.
untrue *adj* falso.
untrustworthy *adj* infido,
  indegno di fiducia.
unused *adj* inutilizzato.
unusual *adj* insolito.
unvaried *adj* monotono.
unwavering *adj* incrollabile.
unwelcome *adj* sgradito.
unwell *adj* indisposto.
unwieldy *adj* poco

maneggevole.
unwilling *adj* riluttante:
  * ~ly *adv* malvolentieri.
unwind *vt* srotolare;
  * *vi* distendersi.
unwise *adj* avventato.
unwitting *adj* involontario.
unworkable *adj* inattuabile.
unwrap *vt* scartare.
unwritten *adj* tacito.
up *adv* su.
upbringing *n* educazione *f*.
update *vt* aggiornare.
upheaval *n* sconvolgimento *m*.
uphill *adj* in salita; faticoso.
upholstery *n* tappezzeria *f*.
upkeep *n* manutenzione *f*.
uplift *vt* sollevare.
upper *adj* superiore;
  * *n* tomaia *f*.
upper-class *adj* dell'alta
  borghesia.
upright *adj* ritto; retto;
  * *adv* diritto; * *n* montante *m*.
uprising *n* insurrezione *f*.
uproar *n* trambusto *m*.
upset *vt* rovesciare; turbare;
  scombussolare; * *n* contrattempo *m*; * *adj* turbato;
  scombussolato; offeso.
upshot *n* risultato *m*.
upside-down *adv* sottosopra;
  * *adj* capovolto.
upstairs *adv* di sopra;
  * *n* piano di sopra *m*.
upstanding *adj* aitante.
upstart *n* parvenu *m*.
uptight *adj* teso.
up-to-date *adj* aggiornato;
  attuale.
upturn *n* ripresa *f*.
upward *adj* verso l'alto;
  * ~s *adv* verso l'alto; in su.
uranium *n* uranio *m*.
urban *adj* urbano.
urbane *adj* civile.
urchin *n* monello *m*.

urge *vi* insistere: ~ on
  spronare; * *n* impulso *m*.
urgency *n* urgenza *f*.
urgent *adj* urgente; pressante.
urinal *n* vespasiano *m*.
urinate *vi* orinare.
urine *n* orina *f*.
urn *n* urna *f*.
us *pron* noi; ci.
usable *adj* utilizzabile.
usage *n* usanza *f*, uso *m*.
use *n* uso *m*; impiego *m*;
  * *vt* usare; adoperare.
used *adj* usato.
useful *adj* utile.
useless *adj* inutile.
uselessness *n* inutilità *f*.
usher *n* usciere *m*.
usherette *n* maschera *f*.
usual *adj* solito: * ~ly *adv* di
  solito.
utensil *n* utensile *m*.
uterus *n* utero *m*.
utility *n* utilità *f*.
utilise *vi* utilizzare.
utmost *n* massimo *m*; estremo
  m; * *adj* totale.
utter *vi* pronunciare.
utterly *adv* completamente.

V

vacancy *n* vuoto *m*; stanza *f*
  libera.
vacant *adj* libero; vacuo.
vacate *vi* lasciare.
vacation *n* vacanza *f*.
vaccinate *vt* vaccinare.
vaccination *n* vaccinazione *f*.
vaccine *n* vaccino *m*.
vacuum *n* vuoto *m*.
vacuum flask *n* termos *m*.
vagina *n* vagina *f*.
vague *adj* vago.
vain *adj* vano; vanitoso.
valid *adj* valido.

validity *n* validità *f*.
valley *n* valle *f*.
valour *n* coraggio *m*.
valuable *adj* prezioso: * ~es
  npl preziosi *mpl*.
valuation *n* valutazione *f*,
  stima *f*.
value *n* valore *m*; * *vt* valutare.
vampire *n* vampiro *m*.
van *n* furgone *m*.
vandalism *n* vandalismo *m*.
vanilla *n* vaniglia *f*.
vanish *vi* svanire.
vanity *n* vanità *f*.
vapour *n* vapore *m*.
variable *adj* variabile.
variation *n* variazione *f*.
varicose vein *n* vena *f* varicosa.
varied *adj* vario.
variety *n* varietà *f*.
varnish *n* vernice *f*,
  trasparente.
vary *vt*, *vi* variare.
vase *n* vaso *m*.
vasectomy *n* vasectomia *f*.
vaseline *n* vaselina *f*.
vast *adj* vasto.
VAT *n* IVA (Imposta sul
  Valore Aggiunto) *f*.
vat *n* tino *m*.
vault *n* volta *f*; * *vt* saltare con
  un balzo.
veal *n* vitello *m*.
veer *vi* virare.
vegetable *n* ortaggio *m*; ~s *npl*
  verdure *fpl*.
vegetable garden *n* orto *m*.
vegetarian *adj*, *n* vegetariano *m*.
vegetate *vi* vegetare.
vehicle *n* veicolo *m*.
vein *n* vena *f*.
velocity *n* velocità *f*.
velvet *n* velluto *m*.
vendor *n* venditore *m*.
veneer *n* impiallacciatura *f*.
venerate *vt* venerare.
vengeance *n* vendetta *f*.

venom *n* veleno *m*.
venomous *adj* velenoso.
ventilator *n* ventilatore *m*.
venture *n* impresa *f*;
   * *vt* rischiare.
venue *n* luogo d'incontro *m*.
verandah *n* veranda *f*.
verb *n* verbo *m*.
verbal *adj* verbale.
verdict *n* verdetto *m*.
verge *n* bordo *m*; orlo *m*.
verify *vt* verificare.
vermin *n* animali nocivi *mpl*.
vermouth *n* vermut *m*.
versatile *adj* versatile.
verse *n* verso *m*; poesia *f*.
version *n* versione *f*.
versus *prep* contro.
vertebra *n* vertebra *f*.
vertebrate *adj*, *n* vertebrato *m*.
vertical *adj*, *n* verticale *f*.
vertigo *n* vertigine *f*.
very *adj* stesso; solo;
   * *adv* molto.
vessel *n* vascello *m*; recipiente *m*.
vest *n* canottiera *f*.
vet *vt* esaminare;
   * *n* veterinario *m*.
veteran *n* veterano *m*.
veterinary *adj* veterinario.
veterinary surgeon *n*
   veterinario *m*.
veto *n* veto *m*; * *vt* porre il veto.
via *prep* attraverso; via.
viaduct *n* viadotto *m*.
vibrant *adj* vibrante.
vibrate *vi* vibrare.
vibration *n* vibrazione *f*.
vicar *n* pastore *m*.
vice *n* vizio *m*; morsa *f*.
vice-versa *adv* viceversa.
vicinity *n* vicinanze *fpl*.
vicious *adj* maligno.
victim *n* vittima *f*.
victory *n* vittoria *f*.
video *n* video *m*.
view *n* vista *f*, veduta *f*, punta

f di vista; * *vt* guardare;
   vedere.
vigil *n* veglia *f*.
vigilance *n* vigilanza *f*.
vigilant *adj* vigile.
vigour *n* vigore *m*.
vile *adj* detestabile.
villa *n* villa *f*.
village *n* paese *m*.
villain *n* mascalzone *m*.
vine *n* vite *f*.
vinegar *n* aceto *m*.
vineyard *n* vigneto *m*, vigna *f*.
viola *n* (music) viola *f*.
violate *vt* violare.
violation *n* violazione *f*.
violence *n* violenza *f*.
violent *adj* violento.
violet *n* (botany) viola *f*,
   violetto *m*.
violin *n* violino *m*.
viper *n* vipera *f*.
virgin *adj*, *n* vergine *f*.
Virgo *n* Vergine *f*.
virile *adj* virile.
virtual *adj* effettivo:
   * ~ly *adv* praticamente.
virtue *n* virtù *f*.
virus *n* virus *m*.
visa *n* visto *m*.
visibility *n* visibilita *f*.
visible *adj* visibile.
vision *n* vista *f*, visione *f*.
visit *vt* visitare; * *n* visita *f*.
vista *n* vista *f*.
visual *adj* visivo.
visual aid *n* sussidi *mpl* visivi.
vital *adj* vitale; fattale.
vitamin *n* vitamina *f*.
vivacious *adj* vivace.
vivisection *n* vivisezione *f*.
vocabulary *n* vocabolario *m*.
vocal *adj* vocale.
vociferous *adj* rumoroso.
vodka *n* vodka *f*.
vogue *n* moda *f*.
voice *n* voce *f*; * *vt* esprimere.

volcanic *adj* vulcanico.
volcano *n* vulcano *m*.
volleyball *n* pallavolo *f*.
volt *n* volt *m*.
voltage *n* voltaggio *m*.
volume *n* volume *m*.
voluntary *adj* volontario.
vomit *vt, vi* vomitare;
  * *n* vomito *m*.
vote *n* votazione *f*, voto *m*.
vote *vt, vi* votare: ~ against
  votare contro: ~ down
  resoingere, bocciare: ~ in
  eleggere: — to ~ a party into
  power mandare un partito al
  potere: ~ someone onto
  eleggere qualcuno a: ~ out
  destituire, bocciare con una
  votazione: ~ through
  approvare con una votazione:
  — to ~ with someone else
  votare come qualcun altro:
  — to ~ with one's feet
  disertare le urne.
voucher *n* buono *m*.
vow *n* voto *m*; * *vi* giurare.
vowel *n* vocale *f*.
voyage *n* viaggio per mare *m*.
vulgar *adj* volgare.
vulnerable *adj* vulnerabile.
vulture *n* avvoltoio *m*.

W

wad *n* batuffolo *m*; tampone *m*.
waffle *vi* ciarlare; * *n* cialda *f*.
wag *vi* scodinzolare;
  * *vt* dimenare.
wage *vi* intraprendere:
  * ~s *npl* stipendio *m*.
wagon *n* carro *m*; vagone *m*.
waist *n* vita *f*.
waistline *n* vita *f*.
wait *vi, vi* aspettare;
  * *vi* aspettare; servire;
  * *n* attesa *f*.

waiter *n* cameriere *m*.
waive *vi* rinunciare a.
wake *vi* svegliarsi;
  * *vt* svegliare; * *n* (marine)
  scia *f*, veglia *f*.
walk *vt* percorrere;
  * *vi* camminare; passeggiare:
  ~ about gironzolare: ~ abroad
  camminare all'aperto:
  ~ away andare via:
  ~ away with andarsene con:
  ~ back tornare a piedi:
  ~ down scendere:
  ~ in(to) entrare a piedi:
  ~ off andarsene: ~ on
  continuare a camminare:
  ~ out uscire: ~ out on
  piantare in asso, lasciare,
  abbandonare: ~ over andare a
  piedi: ~ round to andare a
  trovare qualcuno: ~ through
  camminare attraverso: ~ up
  salire a piedi: ~ with someone
  accompagnare qualcuno a
  piedi.
walk *n* passeggiata *f*,
  andatura *f*.
wall *n* muro *m*; parete *f*.
wallet *n* portafoglio *m*.
wallflower *n* (botany)
  violacciocca *f*.
wallpaper *n* carta *f* da pareti.
walnut *n* noce *f*, (tree) noce *m*.
waltz *n* valzer *m*.
wander *vi* gironzolare;
  * *vt* girovagare per.
wane *vi* calare, declinare.
wanker *n* uomo *m* insulso;
  masturbatore *m*, (*vulg*)
  segaiolo.
want *vt* volere (io voglio, tu
  vuoi; lui [lei] vuole, noi
  vogliamo, voi volete, loro
  vogliono), desiderare;
  * *vi* mancare: ~ back volere
  indietro: ~ for volere per,
  esserci bisogno di: ~ in volere

236

entrare: ~ off volere
scendere: ~ out volere uscire,
volersi ritirare: ~ up volersi
alzare; * n mancanza f,
miseria f, bisogno m.
war n guerra f.
ward n corsia f.
wardrobe n guardaroba m.
warily adj cautamente.
wariness n cautela f.
warm adj caldo; sentito;
* vt scaldare; * vi: ~ up
scaldarsi.
warmth n calore m.
warn vt avvertire.
warning n avvertimento m.
warrant n mandato m;
giustificazione f.
warrior n guerriero m.
wart n porro m.
wash vt lavare; * vi lambire;
trascinare; lavarsi;
* n lavata f.
washbasin n lavabo m.
washing machine n lavatrice.
wasp n vespa f.
waste vt sprecare; perdere;
* n spreco m; perdita f;
* adj di scarto.
watch n orologio m;
sorveglianza f, guardia f;
* vt, vi guardare.
water n acqua f; * vt innaffiare.
watercolour n acquerello m.
waterfall n cascata f.
waterlily n ninfea f.
watermelon n anguria f,
cocomero m.
watt n watt m.
wave n onda f, ondata f, cenno
m; * vt sventolare; salutare
con un cenno della mano;
* vi gesticolare.
wax n cera f; * vt dare la cera a,
incerare.
way n strada f, direzione f,
modo m; abitudine f; * to give

~ vt dare la precedenza.
we pron noi.
weak adj debole.
weaken vt indebolire;
allentare; * vi indebolirsi.
wealth n ricchezza f.
wealthy adj ricco.
weapon n arma f.
wear vt portare; indossare;
consumare; * n uso m;
logoramento m; usura f,
abbigliamento m.
weather n tempo m;
* vt superare.
weave vt, vi tessere;
intrecciare; * n trama f.
weaving n tessitura f.
web n tela f, ragnatela f.
wed vt sposare.
wedding n matrimonio m;
nozze fpl.
wedding ring n fede f.
wedge n zeppa f, cuneo m.
Wednesday n mercoledì m.
week n settimana f:
— a ~ today oggi a otto.
weekday n giorno feriale m.
weekend n weekend m; fine
settimana m.
weekly adj, n settimanale m.
weeping willow n salice m
piangente.
weigh vt, vi pesare.
weight n peso m.
weighty adj importante.
welcome adj gradito,
benvenuto; * n accoglienza f,
benvenuto m; * vt accogliere.
welfare n bene m; benessere m.
well n pozzo m; * vi sgorgare;
* adj, adv bene: — as ~ anche.
west adj ovest, occidentale;
* n ovest m; * adv verso ovest.
westerly adj di ponente.
western adj occidentale;
* n (film) western m.
wet adj bagnato; umido;

piovoso; * *n* umidità *f*;
* *vt* bagnare.
whale *n* balena *f*.
what *pron* cosa; * *adj* che,
quale.
whatever *pron* qualsiasi cosa.
wheat *n* grano *m*, frumento *m*.
wheel *n* ruota *f*; * *vi* roteare.
wheelchair *n* sedia a rotelle *f*.
when *adv, conj* quando.
whenever *adv* in qualsiasi
momento.
where *adv, conj* dove.
whereabouts *adv* dove.
whereas *conj* mentre.
whereby *adv* per cui.
wherever *conj* dovunque.
whet *vt* affilare, arrotare;
stimolare.
whether *conj* se.
which *adj, pron* quale;
* *rel pron* che.
while *n* tempo *m*; * *conj* mentre.
whim *n* capriccio *m*.
whimper *vi* piagnucolare;
* *n* piagnucolio *m*.
whine *vi* guaire; * *n* guaito *m*.
whinny *vi* nitrire.
whip *n* frusta *f*; * *vi* frustare.
whisky *n* whisky *m*.
whisper *vt, vi* bisbigliare;
* *n* bisbiglio *m*.
whistle *vi* fischiare;
* *vt* fischiettare; * *n* fischio *m*.
Whitsun *n* Pentecoste *f*.
white *adj, n* bianco *m*.
who *pron* chi; * *rel pron* che.
whoever *pron* chiunque.
whole *adj* intero; tutto;
completo; * *n* tutto *m*.
whom *pron* chi; * *rel, dir, obj*
che.
whooping cough *n* pertosse *f*.
whore *n* puttana *f*.
whose *pron* di chi; * *rel pron* il
cui.
why *adv, conj* perché.

wicked *adj* cattivo, malvagio,
perfido.
wicker *n* vinùne *m*; * *adj* di
vimine.
wide *adj* largo: *~ly *adv* molto.
widow *n* vedova *f*.
widower *n* vedovo *m*.
width *n* larghezza *f*.
wife *n* moglie *f*.
wig *n* parrucca *f*.
wiggle *vi* ancheggiare.
wild *adj* selvatico; selvaggio;
furibondo.
wilful *adj* ostinato.
will *n* volontà *f*, testamento *m*;
* *vt* volere; pregare;
* *vi* volere.
willing *adj* volenteroso;
disposto.
willow *n* salice *m*.
wilt *vi* appassire.
win *vt* vincere; conquistare;
* *vi* vincere; * *n* vittoria *f*.
wind *n* vento *m*; flatulenza *f*,
fiato *m*.
wind *vt* avvolgere; caricare.
winding *adj* serpeggiante.
windmill *n* mulino *m* a vento.
window *n* finestra *f*, vetrina *f*,
finestrino *m*.
windpipe *n* trachea *f*.
wine *n* vino *m*.
wing *n* ala *f*.
wink *vi* ammiccare;
* *n* strizzatina *f*.
winner *n* vincitore *m*.
winter *n* inverno *m*;
* *adj* invernale.
wipe *vt* pulire; * *n* passata *f*.
wire *n* filo *m*.
wisdom *n* saggezza *f*.
wise *adj* saggio.
wish *vt* volere; desiderare;
augurare; * *n* desiderio *m*;
augurio *m*.
wishbone *n* forcella *f*.
wishful *adj* desideroso.

wit n intelligenza f, arguzia f.
witch n strega f.
with prep con.
withhold vt trattenere.
within prep dentro;
* adv all'interno.
without prep senza.
witness n testimone m;
* vt autenticare;
* vi testimoniare.
witness box n banco m dei
testimoni.
wizard n mago m.
wolf n lupo m, * vt divorare.
woman n donna f.
womanly adj femminile.
womb n utero m; grembo m.
wood n legno m; bosco m.
woodcutter n tagliaboschi m.
woodpecker n picchio m.
wool n lana f.
word n parola f; notizia f;
* vt formulare.
word-blind adj dislessico.
word-processor n word
processor m.
work vt azionare;
* vi lavorare; funzionare;
* n lavoro m; opera f.
works npl meccanismo m;
fabbrica f.
world n mondo m;
* adj mondiale.
worldly adj mondano.
worry vt preoccupare;
importunare;
* vi preoccuparsi;
* n preoccupazione f.
worse adj peggiore;
* adv peggio; * n peggio m.
worship n adorazione f:
— your ~ Vostro Onore;
* vt adorare.
worst adj peggiore;
* adv peggio; * n peggio m.
worth n valore m.
worthless adj inutile.

worthwhile adj valido.
worthy adj lodevole.
wound n ferita f; * vt ferire.
wreath n ghirlanda f.
wreck n naufragio m; relitto m;
* vt distruggere.
wrinkle n ruga f;
* vt stropicciare.
wrist n polso m.
wristwatch n orologio m, da
polso.
write vt, vi scrivere: ~ about,
~ of, ~ up scrivere su: ~ away
(on) scrivere di continuo:
~ back rispondere: ~ down
prendere nota: ~ home
scrivere a casa: ~ in(to)
inserire, includere: ~ off
cancellare: ~ out scrivere per
esteso: ~ to scrivere a.
writer n autore m; scrittore m.
writing desk n scrivania f.
wrong n torto m; male m;
* adj sbagliato; ingiusto m;
* vt fare torto a.
wrongly adv erroneamente.

X

Xmas n Natale m.
X-ray n radiografia f.
xylophone n xilofono m.

Y

yacht n yacht m.
yachting n velismo m.
Yankee n yankee m.
yard n yard f, cortile m;
cantiere m.
yardstick n criterio m.
yarn n filato m; racconto m.
yawn vi sbadigliare;
* n sbadiglio m.
yawning n spalancato.

yeah *adv* sì.
year *n* anno *m*; annata *f*.
yearbook *n* annuario *m*.
yearling *n* yearling *m*.
yearly *adj* annuale.
yearn *vt* bramare.
yearning *n* desiderio *m*
  intenso; * *adj* bramoso.
yeast *n* lievito *m*.
yell *vt, vi* urlare; * *n* urlo *m*.
yellow *adj, n* giallo *m*.
yen *n* yen *m*.
yes *adv, n* sì *m*.
yesterday *adv* ieri.
yet *conj* ma; tuttavia;
  * *adv* già; ancora.
yew *n* tasso *m*.
yield *vt* fruttare; cedere;
  * *vi* cedere; * *n* resa *f*.
yoga *n* yoga *m*.
yoghurt *n* yogurt *m*.
yoke *n* giogo *m*; sprone *m*.
you *pron* tu, lei, voi, loro.
young *adj* giovane; * *n* prole *f*;
  * ~er *adj* minore.
youngster *n* giovane *m*.
your(s) *pron* tuo, suo, vostro,
  loro: ~ sincerely distinti
  saluti.
yourself *pron* ti, si, vi, si.
youth *n* gioventù *f*, giovane *m*.
youthful *adj* giovanile.
yuppie *n* yuppy *m* or *f*.

zodiac *n* zodiaco *m*.
zone *n* zona *f*.
zoo *n* zoo *m*.
zoological *adj* zoologico.
zoologist *n* zoologo *m*.
zoology *n* zoologia *f*.
zoom *vi* zumare; sfrecciare
  via; * *n* zoom *m*.

Z

zeal *n* zelo *m*.
zealous *adj* zelante.
zebra *n* zebra *f*.
zenith *n* zenit *m*.
zero *n* zero *m*.
zest *n* entusiasmo *m*; buccia *f*.
zigzag *n* zigzag *m*.
zinc *n* zinco *m*.
zip *n* cerniera *f*, zip *m*.
zither *n* cetra *f*.